Light in the Dark

Light in the Dark

A History of Filmmaking in Iceland

BJÖRN NORÐFJÖRÐ

OXFORD
UNIVERSITY PRESS

Oxford University Press is a department of the University of Oxford.
It furthers the University's objective of excellence in research, scholarship,
and education by publishing worldwide. Oxford is a registered trade mark of
Oxford University Press in the UK and certain other countries.

Published in the United States of America by Oxford University Press
198 Madison Avenue, New York, NY 10016, United States of America.

© Oxford University Press 2025

All rights reserved. No part of this publication may be reproduced, stored in a retrieval system, transmitted, used for text and data mining, or used for training artificial intelligence, in any form or by any means, without the prior permission in writing of Oxford University Press, or as expressly permitted by law, by license or under terms agreed with the appropriate reprographics rights organization. Inquiries concerning reproduction outside the scope of the above should be sent to the Rights Department, Oxford University Press, at the address above.

You must not circulate this work in any other form
and you must impose this same condition on any acquirer

Library of Congress Control Number: 2024048836

ISBN 978-0-19-776214-1

DOI: 10.1093/oso/9780197762141.001.0001

Printed by Marquis Book Printing, Canada

Contents

Preface	vii
Introduction	1
1. Overview I, 1901–1979	7
2. Iceland in Living Pictures	13
3. Adapting a Literary Nation to Film	29
4. A Cinema of Fire and Ice	49
5. Overview II, 1980–1999	71
6. The Countryside versus the City	76
7. The Transnational Imperative	88
8. Adaptation as Transnationalization	109
9. Overview III, 2000–2020	124
10. Crime Fiction, Film, and Television	131
11. Hollywood Does Iceland	156
12. Icelandic Women's Cinema	176
13. Animals and Nature	197
Epilogue	213
Notes	231
Bibliography	251
Index	259

Preface

This work has been in the making for a very long time. It started life as a dissertation completed toward the end of 2005, and looking back I wonder why I did not turn it into a book earlier. It may have something to do with the fact that only a couple of weeks after gradation I was busy with all kinds of courses and departmental organization in my new position as Director of the Film Studies program at the University of Iceland. Perhaps I was also excited to turn to something else after focusing so solely on Icelandic cinema while writing my dissertation. Nonetheless, I continued to devote most of my research and writing in the following years to Icelandic cinema, keeping up with its evolving form. New and exciting filmmakers emerged, one after another, garnering success abroad while noteworthy changes were also taking place at the home front. It was difficult to pinpoint an ending as Icelandic cinema kept taking unexpected turns. As one should not spoil film endings, I will say no more on the topic for now, but the patient reader will find it in the Epilogue.

The current book draws on many of my prior publications on Icelandic cinema, while I also have added a lot of new material. Some of its early chapters stem at least in part from the dissertation I defended at the University of Iowa where I spent the first five years of the new century. It was a wonderful place to study film, with colleagues from so many different backgrounds united in their enthusiasm and love for cinema. They fostered an environment that has not only contributed to this book directly and indirectly but also left me with treasured memories to last a lifetime and then another. I have lost touch with too many but I think of them often. Jay Beck, Ofer Eliaz, David Ellsworth, Abe Geil, Mike Meneghetti, Claudia Pummer, Rufo Quintavalle, and Gerald Sim were among those to leave a lasting mark for sure. My dissertation committee was led by the ever-reliable Rick Altman and also included Corey Creekmur, Guðni Elísson, Kathleen Newman, and John Durham Peters. Many thanks to all of them for their solid support and inspiration, along with the many other excellent faculty members I had the opportunity to work with, including Nataša Ďurovičová, Rosalind Galt, Lauren Rabinovitz, and Garett Stewart.

My ruminations on small national cinemas were first published in the chapter "Iceland" by Edinburgh University Press, which also published "Hollywood Does Iceland: Authenticity, Genericity and the Picturesque," the basis for chapter eleven, and "Crime Up North" that provided material for a section in the chapter "Crime Fiction, Film, and Television." The latter is the longest chapter of the book, and as such also includes material from "'A Typical Icelandic Murder?' The 'Criminal' Adaptation of *Jar City*" and "The Transnational Remake: Crossing Borders with *Contraband*," both published by the *Journal of Scandinavian Cinema*, as well as a section from "The Emergence of a Tradition in Icelandic Cinema: From *Children of Nature* to *Volcano*," published by Wiley-Blackwell, not to mention plenty of new material. The second and third chapters are little changed from their original publication under their respective lengthier titles, "Iceland in Living Pictures: A Meeting Place of Cinema and Nation" in *Studia Humanistyczne* and "Adapting a Literary Nation to Film: National Identity, Neoromanticism and the Anxiety of Influence" in *Scandinavian Canadian Studies*.[1] Many thanks to all these publishers for permitting me to reuse this extensive material herein. Furthermore, all this work was much improved by its many splendid editors, Tommy Gustafsson, Mette Hjort, Pietari Kääpä, Ursula Lindquist, Scott MacKenzie, Anders Marklund, Duncan Petrie, Anna Westerstahl Stenport, and John Tucker, in addition to numerous unnamed peer reviewers, all of whom are due thanks. Chapter thirteen began as a presentation, "Birds, Horses, Fishes and Sheep: Icelandic Cinema Returns to the Fold," delivered at the Society for Cinema and Media Studies conference in Toronto in 2018, but is much altered. The remaining chapters are altogether new. This book also draws upon interviews with film directors, producers, scriptwriters, and commissioners, conducted over a span of almost two decades. In that way, Ottó Geir Borg, Ágúst Guðmundsson, Hrafn Gunnlaugsson, Guðný Halldórsdóttir, Dagur Kári, Skúli Fr. Malmquist, Hilmar Oddson, Hafsteinn Gunnar Sigurðsson, Þórir Snær Sigurjónsson, Einar Hansen Tómasson, Ísold Uggadóttir, Halldór Þorgeirsson, and Snorri Þórisson have all offered unique insights into the workings of Icelandic cinema. I thank them for sharing their time and valuable experiences with me.

For the long duration of this project I have received various kinds of funding and assistance. My superiors at the University of Iceland, Ástráður Eysteinsson and Guðni Elísson, were always extremely supportive and understanding of my research interests and obligations, and my sabbaticals were indeed crucial for this as well other research projects. My colleagues in the Department of Icelandic and Comparative Cultural Studies came from so many different disciplines that there was always something new to discuss over a cup of coffee, and I was lucky enough that my office faced our little coffee room in the good old Main-building (*Aðalbygging*) of the University. It was in 2014 that I made the switch to St. Olaf College in Minnesota and joined the faculty in the English department, where I have gained not only new colleagues but also many good friends. The College has also provided me with financial support for this project in terms of materials and travel costs, including the concluding research visit to Iceland in the summer of 2023. As often in the past, one of my destinations was the Icelandic Film Museum, an institution crucial to anyone with a serious interest in the history of Icelandic cinema. From my very first visit two decades ago, Gunnþóra Halldórsdóttir has been a crucial supporter of my work. After Gunnar Tómas Kristófersson joined the Museum, his assistance has been invaluable as well, and he has been my go-to person when trying to navigate the murky waters of early Icelandic cinema. I want to thank him in particular for his careful reading of chapters one through four and helpful suggestions for improvement. Ester Bíbí Ásgeirsdóttir and Museum director Þóra Ingólfsdóttir also helped gather and prepare all the Icelandic images found in the book. As regards contemporary films, the Icelandic Film Centre has through the years provided me with access to the latest ones. Last but far from least, the American-Scandinavian Foundation provided the most financial support, and its generous fellowship grant allowed me to take a semester off from my teaching in Fall 2020 and devote myself fully to the book. Finally, at Oxford University Press, senior editor Norman Hirschy welcomed this project with open arms and directed it into the secure hands of project editor Rachel Ruisard who has been the perfect guide throughout. And in her careful reading of the manuscript, copyeditor Dorothy Bauhoff caught numerous mistakes both small and large.

While many people have contributed to this project at one point or another, Linda Mokdad has been by my side the two long decades that it has taken to reach its current form. In addition to reading chapters at various stages of completion and helping to bring them to their current form, she has watched with me so many of the key films analyzed here and engaged in the most fruitful of discussions about them. She has been incredibly encouraging of this project throughout the years, and I doubt I would have completed it without her. And before Linda there were my parents, Jóhanna

Guðbjörnsdóttir and Wilhelm Norðfjörð, who have always had my back and supported me on this journey that began as I left my home in Reykjavík and headed to Iowa City to study film—not the most typical career for an Icelander, nota bene. To them I dedicate this book.

Björn Norðfjörð

Introduction

As an isolated country in the North Atlantic, Iceland is a geographical and geological anomaly. It sits on top of the Mid-Atlantic Ridge, which separates the North American and Eurasian Plates and is the source of its unique geology. Today we consider it part and parcel of Europe, but for long it was marginal to the continent and a place of whimsy and exoticism rather than the grounded world of the mainland. But even now it does not appear fully European; Iceland is either squeezed into the top left corner of maps of Europe or left out entirely. The title character of *Noi the Albino* (Dagur Kári, 2003, *Nói albínói*) likens it to spit, a fleck on the world map. Alternately, Iceland is regularly made the center of the world—singled out for its isolated location, or made visible as a link between Europe and North America, and situated in the middle of world maps. The nation's oscillation between obscurity and transparency is mirrored in the volatile history of Icelandic cinema itself, in its fluctuation between darkness and visibility.

Each and every national cinema has its own unique and distinguishable qualities, but the specificity hinted at here moves beyond such conventional differences. This is not an argument on behalf of exoticism or exceptionalism, as this book makes exceedingly clear. Rather, it is an attempt to draw attention to considerable differences informing Icelandic national cinema that are not accounted for in the broader literature on the topic. Furthermore, my own approach deviates from the familiar path of national cinema studies, instead privileging world cinema and the transnational turn in film studies. Despite Iceland's geographical isolation, this work prioritizes the country's international currency and its place in the world cinema system.[1]

Throughout its history Icelandic cinema has been shaped by contradictory local and global forces. It arises within an international context during the silent era, moves toward and reaches its national apogee in the 1980s before gradually returning to a global emphasis. The major turning points of this history are described in detail with arguments that characterize the tendencies of each decade from the 1980s onward. The eighties were local in tenor, the nineties were informed by the transnational norms of art cinema, the aughts welcomed popular genre cinema à la Hollywood, and finally the teens were greatly impacted by runaway productions, as Iceland became a popular destination for Hollywood blockbusters. The complex relations between the local, national, transnational, and global dimensions of Icelandic cinema, therefore, are crucial to charting its emergence and development.

National Cinemas and Scale

For long the question of scale was largely neglected in national cinema studies, considering that attempts at theorizing the concept of national cinema were rooted in studies of larger national cinemas.[2] As a result, some of the field's most influential work did not accommodate or accurately apply to smaller cinemas. For example, in his study of British cinema, Andrew Higson lists five distinct economic policies that national cinemas can adopt in response to Hollywood's domination: (1) distribution and exhibition of Hollywood films; (2) direct competition with Hollywood; (3) low-budget film production directed at the home market, or production of art cinema for international consumption; (4) protective measures in the form of quotas and incentives for national production; and, finally, (5) international cooperation.[3] For most small national cinemas such policies are simply not available options. In the case of Iceland, national film production could never amount to more than a fraction of the exhibition market, always making Hollywood or other foreign films the central film source. The small domestic market simply lacks the financial resources needed to compete with Hollywood. Usually, films must both appeal to the international art cinema circuit and target the home market because of the latter's small size. Without state funding few small national cinemas would be able to operate (making the debate on the feasibility of state involvement mostly irrelevant), while quotas on foreign films are almost out of the question considering the low levels of domestic productivity. And lastly, there is no choice but to seek out international funding. In summary, small national cinemas do not have the economic infrastructure needed to enact Higson's second policy, and therefore need to combine policies three (both options), four, and five, in order to exist. In other words, these policies are only available as options to populous and wealthy nation-states, leaving the smaller ones with little choice in such matters.[4] Similarly, there is little room for small national cinemas among the seven varieties of national cinemas outlined by Stephen Crofts. These categories implicitly belong to large nation cinemas, as smaller ones can neither afford to ignore nor imitate Hollywood, let alone support their own totalitarian cinema. Regional and ethnic variations are economically implausible, and although not necessarily defined by size, Third Cinema applies to little of today's cinema. Small national cinemas (and many medium-sized ones)—and thus most national cinemas—are forced to combine in one form or another what Crofts refers to as "European-model art cinema" and "Third World and European Commercial Cinemas."[5]

An awareness of the specificity of small national cinemas must also take into account the range of films produced by countries classified under the category. In fact, the term "small national cinemas" as a designation has been applied to everything from countries producing the occasional feature film to industries producing dozens of films annually. For example, out of the 102 countries listed in UNESCO's survey of its member states' film production during the years 1988–1999, the great majority are classified as small, or producing less than twenty films annually. However, it would seem important to distinguish between the economic infrastructure and consistent film production of countries such as Denmark and Australia (classified as small in the survey, although they have now surpassed the twenty-films criterion) and the occasional forays of local filmmakers from countries with largely absent infrastructures and production limited to single digits (fifty-four, or the majority of the countries listed).[6] We might account for these considerable differences by referring to the latter as extra-small cinemas. Furthermore, cinemas can be small in a variety of ways; Iceland, a country of only 350,000 inhabitants, produces more films annually than many countries with much larger populations. In 2010, for instance, Iceland produced nineteen feature films, surpassing Bulgaria, Chile, and Tunisia, and making it the 48th largest national cinema by this measure.[7] The size of a national cinema depends not only on its respective population/audience, but also on its economic situation, its state's cultural policy (assuming there is one) and language, among other factors.[8] It is only because of Iceland's relative wealth, the state's generous cultural policy, and conversely, the lack of such wealth and/or policy in other countries, that Iceland produces more films than countries with much larger populations. Nonetheless, population is a crucial factor, as it delimits the possible expansion of the cinema in question. While many other countries can make the transition from extra-small to medium size, Iceland's small national audience simply prevents this as a possibility. Unlike with some other small national cinemas, including those of its Nordic neighbors, even a very successful film cannot recuperate its costs at the local box office. Thus Iceland seems destined to remain an extra-small cinema, struggling to develop an industry by carefully balancing local and global elements. This is a study of that balancing act.

The National and the Transnational

Icelandic national cinema encompasses neither all films produced in Iceland nor all films made by Icelanders. Two crucial distinctions need to be made. First, in a debate with Andrew Higson regarding British cinema, John Hill emphasizes the significance of distinguishing between "*cinema in Britain* and British *national cinema*."[9] Along these lines, many films shot in Iceland, like Hollywood runaway productions, may be an important part of its film industry while not belonging to Icelandic national cinema proper. The former is an industrial and economic category, while the latter is first and foremost a cultural one. The two categories often overlap but not always. Second, a few sporadically made films do not constitute a national cinema on their own. As Duncan Petrie writes in relation to Scottish cinema but with wider implications: "The necessary conditions for a sustainable national cinema require more than the existence of a handful of films. What is needed are certain structures and institutions that can provide the resources to enable films to be produced on a relatively consistent and regular basis. Without this, there can be no national cinema, only isolated film-makers."[10] For these reasons, the origins of Icelandic national cinema can be traced to the early 1980s, even if the history of Icelandic film production goes back much further and is broader in scope.

A film belonging to Icelandic national cinema typically displays a specific quality of Icelandic identity and culture that is excluded from Hollywood productions filmed in Iceland.[11] This national inscription was especially evident in the early years of the national cinema proper, but it was later altered in its encounter with emerging international financial arrangements and aesthetic influences, first from the European art film and, subsequently, from Hollywood-style genre production. Crucially, this transnational shift does not imply an erasure but rather a transformation of the national. While the concept of the transnational often emphasizes the combination of two or more nations, as when they come together and make a film, I also use it to describe how one nation addresses or presents itself to other nations.

Put differently, the film's national inscription is directed outward as much as inward.

Overview

The book is divided into three parts, each covering a particular historical period: the first, everything up to 1979; the second, the last two decades of the twentieth century; and, finally, the third, the first two decades of the twenty-first century. The historical parameters of these parts are not always strictly enforced, as in the case of certain filmmaking trends or directors, whose careers cannot be fully accommodated by one or the other. The three parts are followed by an Epilogue assessing Icelandic cinema today.

Each part commences with an overview chapter that aims for a balanced synopsis of that period, followed by three to four more chapters that analyze specific topics, trends, styles, filmmakers, modes, genres, literary adaptations, and so on. Following the first overview chapter, "Iceland in Living Pictures" (chapter two) looks closely at many of the earliest films made in Iceland while raising theoretical questions about the relationship between the nation and filmic images. Chapter three, "Adapting a Literary Nation to Film," is a study of the earliest narrative films shot in Iceland. As Scandinavian adaptations based on Icelandic literature, these films are fascinating examples of proto-transnationalism in Icelandic cinema. Throughout its history and especially during the mid-twentieth century, Icelandic documentary filmmakers have captured and depicted the island's nature. The fourth chapter, "A Cinema of Fire and Ice," examines numerous documentaries about volcanic eruptions and considers their role in the global imagery of Iceland.

After the opening chapter of the second part, I direct attention in chapter six, "The Countryside versus the City," to the fraught relationship between the capital Reykjavík and the countryside in the decidedly local cinema of the 1980s. Chapter seven, "The Transnational Imperative," subsequently explains how that local cinema was transformed into one with a much greater international outlook. In particular, it focuses on the oeuvre of director Friðrik Þór Friðriksson and the production trends he helped to establish during the 1990s. Chapter eight, "Adaptation as Transnationalization," considers the role of adaptations during this transition. It proposes that many literary texts go through a process I refer to as transnationalization when adapted to film.

Like the other two parts, the last part begins with an overview chapter, before moving on to "Crime Fiction, Film, and Television" (chapter ten) about the unexpected but remarkable local popularity of the crime genre that marks the shift toward Hollywood-style cinema during the first decade of the twenty-first century. The chapter foregrounds the work of director Baltasar Kormákur. The next chapter, "Hollywood Does Iceland," obliquely explores Iceland by focusing on Hollywood runaway productions filmed in the country, while also considering the global image of Iceland more broadly. Chapter twelve, "Icelandic Women's Cinema," surveys the role that women have played in Icelandic cinema, addressing how a new generation of directors have not only challenged conventional views of gender but also ushered in themes centering on cultural and racial diversity. Finally, chapter thirteen, "Animals and Nature," takes up a topic introduced in previous chapters, but argues that the representation of nature in contemporary Icelandic cinema radically departs from earlier iterations. The three parts are followed by an Epilogue surveying the production trends of contemporary Icelandic cinema, drawing upon examples from the 2020s.

The book's organization opens itself to readers looking for a historical overview of Icelandic cinema as well as those interested in more detailed analysis pertaining to specific topics. I expect that many readers will be looking for both, and that this format will strike a helpful balance. It is my hope that this work will not only fill some of the gaps in Icelandic film history but also cast light on others that might be addressed in the future.

1
Overview I, 1901–1979

At the turn of the twentieth century, Icelanders numbered fewer than one hundred thousand inhabitants and lived mostly on farms and in fishing villages around the island's coast. Iceland remained a Danish colony, as it had been for centuries. There was no possibility of developing an infrastructure for exhibiting and making films at this time—let alone anything akin to a film industry. But following in the wake of magic lantern shows and other visual entertainment, cinema began making inroads on this isolated island in the midst of the North Atlantic in the early 1900s.

It was in September 1901 that the Dutchman Franz Anton Nöggerath journeyed from Hull in England to shoot the first films in Iceland for the Warwick Trading company. He traveled to well-known sites in the southwest part of the country and filmed *Geysir*, the country's most famous geyser, erupt, but was disappointed by the lack of volcanic activity in Mount *Hekla*. Judging by their titles, many of the films seem to have been shot in trollers near the Icelandic coast.[1] Nöggerath's films have not survived, so we can only speculate about how these first films represented the country, but we do know that many local entrepreneurs hoped they would attract visitors to the island. Thus, even before films were exhibited in Iceland, they were already expected to invigorate tourism, and this impetus continues to serve as one of the primary arguments for state support of filmmaking in the country to this day.

It was not until two years later that the first film exhibition took place in the country. Following upon their success in Scandinavia, Swede David Fernander and Norwegian Rasmus Hallseth took their traveling exhibition to Iceland, where they were met with tremendous excitement, repeatedly adding performances to meet demand. The program was varied in nature and included everything from actualities to Georges Méliès's *A Trip to the Moon* (1902, *Le Voyage dans la Lune*). Fernander and Hallseth likely sold their film equipment before leaving the island, as written sources confirm that exhibitions continued in the hands of locals later in 1903 (if with mixed results).[2] The following year, the first films shot by Icelanders were projected as well, but none of them have survived. The oldest extant film shot in Iceland, *Firemen Practice in Reykjavík* (*Slökkviliðsæfing í Reykjavík*), was filmed by Dane Alfred Lind in 1906, who had traveled to the country that year having been hired to establish a permanent film theater. He in turn hired fellow Dane Peter Petersen, who subsequently ran the theater and did so with great success.[3] Lind, on the other hand, left the following year and these early local filmmaking efforts came to an end, but Petersen stayed on and purchased the theater in 1913 and it remained popular far into the twentieth century.

It was not until 1919 that filmmaking re-emerged, and with quite some vigor, as numerous films, displaying Reykjavík or fishing villages around the country, bear witness to. Although many of these were shot by the Dane Petersen, the films are quintessentially Icelandic, shot in Iceland with a local audience in mind. The same cannot be said of three contemporaneous silent feature films, even though they were based on Icelandic literature, two were shot in Iceland, and one even was directed by an Icelander. The first and best known of these is Victor Sjöström's classic *The Outlaw and His Wife* (1917, *Berg-Ejvind och hans hustru*), which was based on a popular play by Jóhann Sigurjónsson, but was shot in Northern Sweden with Sjöström in the role of the outlaw. It was succeeded by the *Story of the Borg Family* (Gunnar Summerfeldt, 1920, *Saga Borgarættarinnar*), an adaptation of Gunnar Gunnarsson's sprawling epic novel about an Icelandic family. Although shot in Iceland, it was a Danish production intended for the Danish market. The third film, *Hadda Padda* (1924), was the first feature directed by an Icelander. Based on the director Guðmundur Kamban's own play, the film, however, was a Danish production with interiors shot in Denmark and exteriors shot in Iceland. All three features offer clear cases of proto-transnationalism in filmmaking in Iceland.

The first full-length local film, a documentary of sorts, however, was shot by the Icelandic photographer Loftur Guðmundsson, who was to become a major figure in Icelandic cinema for the next three decades. For *Iceland in Living Pictures* (1925, *Ísland í lifandi myndum*) Guðmundsson traveled all over Iceland to gather material of locals at work and play, and in doing so paved the way for what would soon be called Iceland-films (*Íslandsmyndir*), which as the name suggests, made the country and its people their primary topic. It would remain by far the most popular "genre" until World War II, made by Icelanders and visiting filmmakers alike.

The 1930s saw the arrival of two other pioneering documentary filmmakers, Vigfús Sigurgeirsson and Kjartan Ó. Bjarnason, whose careers were to span well into the 1960s. According to Gunnar Tómas Kristófersson, their emergence and considerable filmmaking activity are best explained by what he refers to as the "institutionalization" of Icelandic filmmaking in the 1930s.[4] To be clear, the state did not establish any direct source of film funding, but various state or state-related institutions, especially the National Fishing Agency and later the State Travel Office, began financing films for marketing or other related purposes. In fact, it was the National Fishing Agency that financed Sigurgeirsson's lengthy stay in Germany to learn the craft of filmmaking. Sigurgeirsson's career was shaped by such official commitments, and with the establishment of the Republic in 1944 he become the official photographer (and by implication, filmmaker) of the president.

In addition to government and business institutions, various regional, cultural, social and sports organizations became interested in both film production and exhibition during this period. For Bjarnason in particular, these activities went hand in hand as he frequently exhibited his own films (in Iceland and abroad, especially Denmark). This dual role as producer and exhibitor allowed him to devote himself fully to a film career beginning in 1945—the first Icelander to do so. It is also the reason that his films are difficult to assess today. As silent pictures, they relied on live narration which he provided during exhibition. He also regularly excised and repurposed footage from earlier films, rendering them nonexistent because there were no additional copies.[5] Much of what remains of his most celebrated and widely seen film, *Days of Sunshine in Iceland* (1950, *Island i Sommersol*), a ninety-minute-long documentary, takes the form of the twenty-five-minute-long *This Is Iceland* (1960), compiled for the Foreign Ministry to support tourism.

While the Second World War mostly put an end to filmmakers' visits from the continent (Germans had figured prominently before), it drew some from the other side of the Atlantic. Most notably, Samuel Kadorian filmed extensively in Iceland during the American occupation (the United States took over from the British soon after entering the conflict). A surge of filmmaking followed Iceland's full independence in 1944 and the end of the war, including a new Iceland-film by Guðmundsson that was shot in color. Of the newcomers that emerged during the 1940s, Óskar Gíslason was to become the most important one. His two-part *Reykjavík of Our Days* (1947/1948, *Reykjavík vorra daga*) and *The Great Latrabjarg Sea-Rescue* (1949,

Björgunarafrekið við Látrabjarg) attest to new aspirations and topics in the country's filmmaking. But the key event for documentary film production during the 1940s was arguably neither the war nor the founding of the Republic, but rather a major eruption in the legendary volcano *Hekla*, which was filmed by both Sigurgeirsson and Bjarnason. More noteworthy, though, was a film made about it by another newcomer, Ósvaldur Knudsen, who would become the country's major film chronicler of volcanic eruptions. Meanwhile, the early documentary work of Magnús Jóhannsson focused on the many glaciers of the highlands.[6]

Although documentary filmmaking continued unabated, Guðmundsson and Gíslason turned to narrative feature filmmaking halfway through the century. Guðmundsson had actually directed *The Adventures of Jon and Gvendur* (*Ævintýri Jóns og Gvendar*), a Chaplin-inspired short (of which a small part survives) all the way back in 1923. But in 1948 he directed the first Icelandic narrative feature, *Between Mountain and Shore* (*Milli fjalls og fjöru*), which was soon followed by Gíslason's debut feature, *Last Farm in the Valley* (1950, *Síðasti bærinn í dalnum*). These films and the directors' subsequent features were generally popular among the local population despite production limitations. It is also worth noting that *Covetousness* (1952, *Ágirnd*), the first narrative short directed by a woman filmmaker in Iceland, Svala Hannesdóttir, was made in this period.[7] This surge of productivity in narrative filmmaking came to an end halfway through the fifties. The photographers Guðmundsson and Gíslason were pioneers in the fullest sense of the word and made their films without any organized financial or industrial support—at a time when Icelanders numbered only 140,000 and were more widely dispersed around the island than today. Although many new film theaters were built during this era, especially in Reykjavík, in the long run they could not sustain Icelandic cinema on their own.

Aware of these limitations, the group that established Edda-film in 1949 sought professional partners abroad to assist in the adaptation of Icelandic literature. To a certain extent, their aspirations materialized with Arne Mattson's *Salka Valka* (1954), the first adaptation of a novel by Halldór Laxness, winner of the Nobel Prize in Literature the following year. Although exteriors were shot in Iceland, by Sven Nykvist nota bene, it was in every other sense a Swedish film production. Another literary adaptation, *The Girl Gogo* (1962, *79 af stöðinni*), on the other hand, was a successful Icelandic production, despite being directed by Dane Erik Balling. Nonetheless, Edda-film would not go on to make another film, although it assisted in the production of the Danish film *The Red Mantle* (Gabriel Axel, 1967, *Den røde knappe*). The company's demise is likely related to the establishment of the Icelandic state television channel RÚV in 1966, which became the home to Icelandic cinema broadly defined until the Icelandic Film Fund was established in 1978. Although locally produced fiction material constituted only a small fraction of its output and the rare television play was typically more indebted to theater than cinema—especially early on—many of the leading figures of Icelandic cinema that came on the scene in the early 1980s gained their first experiences working for RÚV.

No Icelandic director made a narrative feature film during the extended period from 1955 to 1976, but in the sixties a couple of ambitious filmmakers, Þorgeir Þorgeirson and Reynir Oddsson, returned to Iceland having studied the craft in Europe. Both tried to build their film careers in the "institutionalized" system that had emerged during the 1930s by making films for various firms and institutions, but the process did not go as smoothly as it had with past generations. In *Flying to Greenland* (1966, *Grænlandsflug*), made for the airline *Flugfélag Íslands*, cinematographer and director Þorgeirson seems far more interested in the local Inuit children and the spectacular environment than the airline's role in connecting Greenland to Iceland and Denmark. His next film, *To Build* (1967, *Að byggja*), made for the municipal *Kópavogur* to mark its anniversary, has little to say about its history or community and instead playfully intercuts construction workers with children building timber huts. With its montage-style editing and jazzy music, it has much in common with Þorgeirson's most celebrated film, *Man and Factory* (1967, *Maður og verksmiðja*), an experimental documentary that uses dramatic factory footage to foreground the alienation of workers. Clearly, Þorgeirson's aesthetics and worldview did not conform to the marketing and commercial ambitions of these projects. After *Rowing* (1972, *Róður*), another such failed partnering, Þorgeirson mostly gave up filming. It had become clear that institutions could not be expected to provide the platform needed for filmmakers to express their artistic vision. A different platform was needed.

Similarly, Oddsson spent much of the early sixties on such institutional undertakings before releasing *The Occupation* (1967, *Hernámsárin*), one of the most ambitious documentary projects of Icelandic film history. A decade later, he became the first Icelandic director to make a narrative feature since Gíslason directed *A New Life* back in 1954. The success of his surreal bourgeois crime drama *Murder Story* (1977, *Morðsaga*) indicated that there was still a strong desire for a national cinema despite the introduction of a national theater and television. The following year the Icelandic Film Fund was established, marking the single most important event in the history of Icelandic cinema. Its impact will be the focus of part II of this volume.

The following three chapters take a closer look at the pioneers of Icelandic cinema. Chapter two begins by examining the oldest extant films before exploring the work of Guðmundsson and Gíslason. It also addresses the few narrative features that bridge the gap between their films and the establishment of the Film Fund—especially *The Girl Gogo* as a national allegory par excellence. Chapter three considers the strong relationship between Icelandic national identity and language and literature, and how these ties have informed filmmaking in the country. To illustrate such connections, I will highlight Scandinavian adaptations of Icelandic literature during the silent period and the anxiety of influence in adapting the literary canon (the medieval sagas and Laxness). Finally, I take a closer look at nature and volcano documentaries in chapter four, to consider how the innovative style of Knudsen's volcano films is very much shaped by the specific "nature" of their subject matter. The result is a film form that straddles documentary and experimental cinema.

2
Iceland in Living Pictures

In this chapter we travel all the way back to the very beginning of cinema in Iceland when a few pioneers set out to shoot the first films, long before anything resembling a film industry had been established. In today's emphasis on world cinema, these films risk being forgotten altogether given their insignificance to a global audience. This chapter therefore serves as a reminder of a particular type of local filmmaking that is arguably disappearing in Iceland, as many other places.

We will begin by looking at films of a documentary nature, tracing a thread from the oldest extant film to the so-called Iceland-films (*Íslandsmyndir*) of the interwar era, and concluding with the changes that followed in the aftermath of World War II and the founding of the Republic in 1944. After that we will turn our attention to the first locally made narrative features and trace their history all the way to the instigation of the Icelandic Film Fund in 1978, which laid the ground for Icelandic cinema's modern phase.

Iceland-Films and the Aura of the Past

A fire-carriage is being pulled along a bumpy street, but the children that have gathered are more interested in the camera documenting their excitement and curiosity than the carriage itself (see Figure 2.1). The Reykjavík one can glimpse here is a small town that has little in common with the city we know today. The location might be a mystery if it had not been for the film's eponymous title, *Firemen Practice in Reykjavík* (Alfred Lind, 1906, *Slökkviliðsæfing í Reykjavík*). These scratched black-and-white images give us a glimpse of a distant past.

As an encounter between a particular place and the medium of film, *Firemen Practice* is typical of the earliest actualities and their celebration of the apparatus's recording capability. Cinema has caught a glimpse of "life" in the Reykjavík of 1906. The film's representation of the town to a population now accustomed to seeing foreign metropolises and exotic locations on the

14   LIGHT IN THE DARK

Figure 2.1 In the oldest extant Icelandic film, *Firemen Practice in Reykjavík*, the young passersby are much more interested in the novel film camera than the film's actual subject. Source: The National Film Archive of Iceland/ Kvikmyndasafn Íslands.

screen held the fascination of local audiences who flocked to the Reykjavík Biograph-Theater to view it. For Icelanders today, this little film offers the oldest "living pictures" (*lifandi myndir*)—as the locals referred to them in the early twentieth century—of the past.

Firemen Practice was not the first Icelandic film made, but it is the oldest extant one. If it was followed up with further filmmaking activities, those efforts have not survived. Still the more likely scenario is that local filmmaking took a long hiatus, returning only in 1919 with Dane Peter Petersen taking the lead. Despite assisting Alfred Lind in the making of *Firemen Practice*, he was best known in Reykjavík for his key role in theater exhibition and was fondly nicknamed Bíópetersen (or "Movie-Peter") by the locals. In the early 1920s he was joined by others from all over the country who made films documenting everyday life. One cannot but wonder whether the establishing of a sovereign state in 1918 helped foster this unparalleled film activity.[1]

Petersen's extant films are mostly limited to representations of Reykjavík and the neighboring area, which already look strikingly different in 1919 than they did in 1906. Lacking the organized voice of modern documentaries, these panoramas (Petersen systematically pans from right to left) revel in the camera as a recording apparatus. He often placed the camera on higher ground, for example when offering a pleasing overview of the city or vista of the houses located by *Tjörnin*, the downtown pond. His camera frequently lingers on landmarks, including the parliament, the cathedral, the Women's School, and the Danish Embassy. In addition to these panoramas, Petersen filmed events of interest, screening these movies at his own theater.

Outside of Reykjavík, other filmmakers approached their hometowns in an equally panoramic manner. Martinus Simson's portrait of the fishing village *Ísafjörður* in the summer of 1923 includes not only views from inside the village, but also shots filmed from a long distance. Capturing the entirety of the village and its surrounding mountain scenery, his frames evoke postcard imagery. Sveinn Guðnason's film *Eskifjörður* (1924) provides another portrayal of a typical fishing village. Livelier than Petersen's work, the film is more invested in capturing the daily life of villagers than featuring scenery. Differences aside and in the vein of Lind's *Firemen Practice*, most films from this period use the camera to record people and their everyday environment.

The unique capability of the photographic image to establish a direct link with the object reproduced may help explain why these early films have a particular historical resonance.[2] The children seen in *Firemen Practice* did run after the camera in this manner in late 1906, in a little town called Reykjavík so different from the city it is today. Even this very short film gives some indication of what "life" was like in Reykjavík in the early twentieth century, with a much fuller picture appearing with the help of films made in the late teens and early twenties. While not substituting for traditional historiography, this aspect of the past is one that can only be mediated by cinema. The authenticity of these images is also enhanced by the circulation of the films themselves; their wear and tear—scratches, water damage, missing scenes, or speed irregularities—function as markers of an original historical record. While Walter Benjamin famously argued that the aura of an artwork withers in the age of mechanical reproduction, these rare documents might now be understood as imbued with an aura of their own.[3] Watching these films today may not give us the aura of art, but certainly they evoke an aura of the past. The primary value of early Icelandic cinema is thus found in giving a vibrant appearance of the past—the feeling and sense of days long gone.

The events and places depicted may have little relevance outside the island when compared to important historical events of the early twentieth century, but for domestic viewers, then and now, these local films constitute the visual history of the nation, along with paintings and photographs.

The archive of everyday life culminates in Loftur Guðmundsson's *Iceland in Living Pictures* (*Ísland í lifandi myndum*), the first locally made feature-length film. Shot in 1924, its premiere in early 1925 was a huge success. Described by film historian Erlendur Sveinsson as "an ode to land and nation," it bore all the hallmarks of Guðmundsson's oeuvre.[4] If the "Iceland" in the title suggests as much, the "Living Pictures" part indicates the particular capability of cinema in capturing land and nation. Unlike the earlier shorts, Guðmundsson's film moves beyond specific regions to feature the entirety of Iceland. Proceeding from a concise title-card introduction to the nation's history and culture, the film begins with high-angle and atmospheric panorama shots of Reykjavík. The following intertitles boast: "Reykjavík has more beautiful and grandiose views than most other capitals. And Reykjavík could easily be called, particularly in summer, the city of the beautiful sunsets." While these intertitles characterize the lofty written components of the film, which reach their heights with quotations of patriotic poetry, the images themselves are more restrained. Guðmundsson is satisfied with recording external reality, shying away from manipulating the images through editing, excessive framing, or elaborate camera movement. It is not clear whether this approach is the result of limited professional experience or a carefully considered aesthetic choice. Regardless, the effect is one of restraint and respect for the pro-filmic world.[5] Following Reykjavík, the film successively introduces large villages such as *Ísafjörður*, *Vestmannaeyjar*, and *Siglufjörður*, providing detailed accounts of both fishing and farming. It is not until about an hour into the film that an automobile is first seen, rather suggestive of modernity's belated arrival to Iceland. Ranging from close-ups to long shots, the camera frequently lingers on the inhabitants themselves, along with domestic animals.

While *Iceland in Living Pictures* does not reflect the flourishes of contemporaneous film aesthetics, its dynamism emerges from what Siegfried Kracauer has described as an approach that prioritizes unstaged reality. He defined film's five inherent affinities as the unstaged, the fortuitous, endlessness, the indeterminate, and finally, the "flow of life" (all are common to film and photography except the last category).[6] Kracauer gets at these affinities by alluding to D. W. Griffith's claim about cinema's ability to capture "the beauty of moving wind in the trees."[7] If Guðmundsson shares little with the masters of world cinema Kracauer references in *Theory of Film*, his images are nonetheless strikingly cinematic: waves crashing against the shore, fishermen at work out at sea in high winds, cliffs being climbed for eggs, horses ridden across heavy streams, and colts, puppies, and kittens playing in a field. A familiar scene that makes its way into Guðmundsson's film as well as others is the short but hectic haddock season. Fish heaved up from boats at harbor, carried in wheelbarrows to cutting tables, thrown into barrels, stacked up to great heights, and shipped out to sea again—all happening at a frantic pace—make for a notably cinematic subject (see Figure 2.2). Another recognizable scene in early Icelandic films is the valley *Laugar* where women in Reykjavík washed laundry. As steam rises up from hot pools and mist floats around the women, the scene atmospherically captures the unstaged, the fortuitous, endlessness, the indeterminate, and ultimately the "flow of life" (see Figure 2.3).

Iceland in Living Pictures distinguishes itself from earlier films not only by its extensive running time, but also as the first Icelandic film to be distributed internationally. The film clearly addresses a local audience; however, Guðmundsson turned his eye to the foreign market after the realization that his film would not break even, even with the film's local box-office success and meager belated support from the state. Eventually exhibition rights were sold to Germany, Austria, England, France, Czechoslovakia, Finland, and Denmark, and at least one print survives with German intertitles.[8]

As soon as film projection was introduced in Iceland, calls were made for local productions to take advantage of the medium to increase tourism, and to counter what were perceived as inaccurate, and often unflattering, portrayals in foreign films.[9] If we chalk up the images that *Iceland in Living Pictures* first disseminates outside the country to financial necessity, soon after locals would strategically seize on images of Iceland for marketing purposes abroad, a practice that would peak in the 1930s. The same decade also saw a considerable increase in foreign productions, especially German and Danish, which hoped to capture the people's character and the country's geology. Regardless of approach or whether they were made by locals or foreigners, these films were simply referred to as Iceland-films (*Íslandsmyndir*), a nomenclature that foregrounds that land as the subject itself.[10] Remarkably, this intertwining of cinema and nation, rather than being limited to a national undertaking, was a transnational affair that prefigures much of today's Icelandic cinema.

Figures 2.2 and 2.3 Loftur Guðmundsson's *Iceland in Living Pictures* captures the unstaged reality that Siegfried Kracauer considered essential to the film medium. A case in point is the lively herring season, where everything happens at a hectic pace as men transfer the fish from boats to women who cut and salt it before placing it into barrels (2.2). Another scene shows steam engulfing a group of women as they wash their laundry (2.3). Source: The National Film Archive of Iceland/Kvikmyndasafn Íslands.

In agitating for state-funding for his own Iceland-film, celebrated playwright and novelist Guðmundur Kamban described in considerable detail the harm inflicted on the country's image by foreign filmmakers, singling out the 1932 short "Iceland: The Land of the Vikings," part of James A. FitzPatrick's MGM *Traveltalks* series. FitzPatrick repeatedly suggests that Iceland—the "grim land of the Vikings"—and Icelanders have changed little over the course of millennia. He describes the country as "cold and barren," "bleak and dreary," and outright "weird." To counter such representations, Kamban called for local productions "that present our country and nation as we ourselves wish, supervised and guaranteed by the state."[11] Having garnered funding from the National Fishing Agency, which intended to use the film to market Icelandic fish products abroad, Kamban began production in 1935, securing the services of German filmmaker Paul Burkert as cinematographer. Irony is not lost on the fact that Burkert's German films about Iceland adhered to the norms of the *kulturfilm* genre, which typically exoticized foreign cultures, by romantically presenting the people and their awe-inspiring natural surroundings as unspoiled by modernity.[12] The film he made with Kamban for the Fishing Agency included many such elements, but they were intercut with modern city scenes and industrial footage, which resulted in a contradictory and incoherent montage. The Agency was not impressed with the result and the film was shelved.

After a lull during World War II, the latter part of the 1940s saw a significant increase in film activity. Sveinsson attributes this rise in production to the founding of the Republic in 1944, and the need to represent and articulate the nation visually.[13] Gunnar Tómas Kristófersson instead credits the optimisim that followed the end of the war and "much greater opportunities in accessing funding, equipment and other material needed for filmmaking."[14] Both explanations seem plausible, but what is indisputable is that the Icelandic documentary that came into prominence halfway through the 1940s had a new outlook. When not foreign productions altogether, the national presentation in the Iceland-films had been made with at least one eye on foreign audiences. The new documentaries, on the other hand, shared little with the *kulturfilm* and only rarely expressed a nationalist longing for the past, engaging instead with contemporary sensibility and current events.[15]

A variety of filmmakers also filmed the 1947 eruption of the volcano *Hekla*, including Ósvaldur Knudsen, who would become a prolific director of documentaries in future decades (see chapter four). The key figure of the late 1940s was, however, Óskar Gíslason, who directed *Reykjavík of Our Days* (*Reykjavík okkar daga*), a considerable contemporary portrait of the capital that premiered in two parts in 1947 and 1948. In many ways it did for the capital what Guðmundsson's *Iceland in Living Pictures* had done for the country at large. Rather than being a traditional documentary, *Reykjavík of Our Days* recalls the city symphony film. Gíslason may not reach the heights of Dziga Vertov or Walter Ruttmann, but his film features rhythmic editing and an overall dynamic style. An invaluable account of the city and its growth, *Reykjavík of Our Days* documents dramatic changes around work and leisure, providing shots from on the ground, in the sky, and underwater. The following year Gíslason directed what is perhaps Iceland's best-known documentary, *The Great Latrabjarg Sea-Rescue* (*Björgunarafrekið við Látrabjarg*). The film combines re-enactments of a famous rescue of English seamen stranded at the treacherous sheer-cliffs of *Látrabjarg* in awful weather conditions with on-location footage of a different sea-rescue that Gíslason remarkably stumbled upon while shooting the re-enactments. The film was not only extremely popular in Iceland but also widely seen abroad; it was one of the most disseminated Icelandic films prior to the 1980s.[16]

Both Guðmundsson and Gíslason would soon become the pioneers of Icelandic narrative cinema, swapping modes in the late 1940s. Unlike the older and outward-looking Iceland-films, the first narrative features looked only inward.

Early Narrative and the Struggle between Country and City

Two peculiar-looking figures come walking toward the camera. From the film's title we know their names are Jón and Gvendur, although we do not know who is who. Intertitles tell us that they are about to meet a farmer to display their workmanship, presumably to obtain employment at the farm. However, events do not begin well, as either Jón or Gvendur steps on a shovel, his foot framed in a close-up, before falling flat on the ground. More pandemonium seems headed their way as the farmer's daughter is about to arrive on the scene. However, we never find out how Jón and Gvendur get along with the farmer and his daughter because less than two minutes survive of what was a twenty-minute-long film. Despite what little remains of the film, the character of Jón or Gvendur (Tryggvi Magnússon) is modeled on Charlie Chaplin, who has apparently come to visit the Icelandic countryside.

The Adventures of Jón and Gvendur (1923, *Ævintýri Jóns og Gvendar*) is not only the first Icelandic narrative film, but also the only one made prior to the late 1940s when a boom occurs in local feature film production. Loftur Guðmundsson, the director of *The Adventures of Jón and Gvendur*, now returned to his roots in fiction after making several documentaries in between. However, if his first foray into narrative fiction was indebted to the most iconic Hollywood figure of them all, his first Icelandic narrative feature, *Between Mountain and Shore* (1948, *Milli fjalls og fjöru*), was inherently local in approach. Guðmundsson's concerns about how his inexpensive film might have paled in comparison to the glossy products of Hollywood prompted him to apologize for the discrepancy in quality on introductory title-cards.

A poor farmer's son Ingvar (Gunnar Eyjólfsson) is accused of theft by the county magistrate and must clear his name. Along the way he is faced with making a romantic choice between an innocent country girl and a rich seductress, the daughter of the magistrate. The story is set in a far-removed past without any traces of modernity. It takes place during Danish rule, but no hostility is expressed toward the Danish characters (Iceland only became fully independent four years prior to the film). Instead, the film's most benevolent character is a Danish merchant, who has settled in the country and comes to Ingvar's rescue, despite the long-standing historical animosity toward Danish merchants known for exploiting the local population. The actual thieves, on the other hand, turn out to be foreigners of unspecified origin.

Stylistically the film is indebted to the theater. In conversation scenes, all the actors are typically gathered together in the frame and often without any editing. Long and medium-long shots dominate, camera angles are rare, and camera-movement is minimal. In general, the camera is used to convey narrative information rather than contribute to a particular aesthetic style. If this reserved approach worked well for the innately cinematic subjects of the earlier Iceland-films, it is restrictive in the more grounded narrative fiction of *Between Mountain and Shore*. Like other local features of the period, the movie suffers from comparisons with the sophisticated film production of the more technically and professionally advanced national cinemas. But despite the film's many technical drawbacks, it was an outstanding box-office success, breaking all previous attendance records.[17] Evidently the local audience was more than willing to sacrifice the technical standards of Hollywood for the pleasure of seeing a locally made film.

Óskar Gíslason's first feature, *The Last Farm in the Valley* (*Síðasti bærinn í dalnum*), was not only a major success in its initial run in 1950, but also during repeated re-runs.[18] Intended for children, the film makes use of a framing device in which a grandmother recounts certain fantastical events of her youth. The scene of her telling the story dissolves into the events narrated. The setting is a traditional Icelandic farm and a field full of domestic animals. Children are seen playing by the farm in shots ranging from close-ups to long shots. These pastoral images ultimately give way to a darker setting and inclement weather. The audience is told about the destruction of the land: "Desolated ruins of fallen settlement." Based on traditional Icelandic folklore, what follows is a dramatic story about the grandmother and her brother in their youth, struggling against malevolent otherworldly powers over the last farm in the valley. It all ends happily, though, with the promise of "the settlements in the valley blossoming again as the malevolent forces have been laid to rest."

Gíslason makes expressive use of color and various visual tricks to depict the fantastical atmosphere of the story. Most of these are rather simple, like stopping the camera and adding or removing objects from the scene before rolling the camera again to give the impression of objects disappearing or appearing miraculously. Slightly more complicated are scenes of the siblings flying on a magical chest, with point-of-view shots taken from an airplane. However, special effects aside, *The Last Farm in the Valley* is no more dynamic a film than *Between Mountain and Shore*. The acting is rather static, made all the more so from the absence of dialogue during scenes that feature movement or activity, such as characters walking or riding horses. Attention to editing or framing is scant, and again the camera is used to narrate a story without aesthetic flourishes.

What these two first Icelandic features have in common above everything else is their nostalgia for the countryside. If the founding of the Republic in 1944 motivated these productions, unlike the documentaries of the late 1940s, neither film expressed any interest in contemporary Icelandic society or the future of the young Republic. Instead, both *The Last Farm in the Valley* and *Between Mountain and Shore* display a remarkable romantic longing for the country of the past, very much in the manner of nineteenth- and early twentieth-century nationalism. As foregrounded by its title, *The Last Farm in the Valley* reflects the fear of the purported demise of the countryside, with otherworldly powers standing in for modernity and urbanization. Invoking the location of the Icelandic farm with its title, *Between Mountain and Shore* celebrates traditional farming values and offers up the farmer at the ideal Icelander. The tales are indeed far removed from the Reykjavík of the twentieth century.

Raymond Williams begins his classic study of *The Country and the City* by pointing out that: "In English, 'country' is both a nation and a part of the 'land'; 'the country' can be the whole society or its rural area."[19] To a certain extent this is also true of the Icelandic language, as "land" has roughly the same meaning in English and Icelandic, and can indicate both the "country" and the "nation." However, the more commonly used *sveit* does not refer to the nation, although strong affiliations are clearly believed to exist between the two. Even during the rapid modernization and urbanization of the mid-twentieth century, there is little doubt that the countryside was still seen as the heart and soul of the nation. Set on a nineteenth-century farm and displaying stock characters of country fiction, Guðmundsson's second narrative feature and last film, *The Displaced One* (1951, *Niðursetningurinn*), is equally preoccupied with the countryside.

Reykjavík, however, would play a more prominent role in Gíslason's future work. His second feature, *The Reykjavík Adventure of the Bakka-Brothers* (1951, *Reykjavíkurævintýri Bakkabræðra*), occupies a liminal space between the country and the city by updating the folk tales of the Bakka-brothers, whose excessive stupidity now humorously plays out with a visit to the capital. In this new film version, the comedy originates from the brothers' unfamiliarity with city life, having never left the countryside before. The corresponding conflict between past and modernity is manifested in slapstick scenes where the brothers come across various modern gadgets with which they are unaccustomed. Conversely, Gíslason's third and final narrative feature, *New Role* (1954, *Nýtt hlutverk*), was a serious contemporary adult drama set in Reykjavík, but it also dealt thematically with the conflict between traditional values and modern ones.[20] Stylistically, both films are very much along the lines of *The Last Farm in the Valley*: minimal editing, static camera, straight-on shots, and theatrical acting. Whether set in the country or city, the mid-century features of Guðmundsson and Gíslason share an inherently local approach. They rely on well-known Icelandic fairy tales and other traditional sources, the particularities of which are never explained because the films were never intended for foreign exhibition in any form. The basic style or lack thereof and an insistence on narrative clarity rather than aesthetic embellishment also express an internal national consistency rather than any transnational engagement with the medium.

Concerned with the technical shortcomings of local productions, the company Edda-film sought a foreign co-producer for what would become its first and only narrative feature, *The Girl Gogo* (1962, *79 af stöðinni*), although it had previously participated in the Swedish production of *Salka Valka* (1954, Arne Mattson).[21] Danish director Erik Balling and cinematographer Jürgen Skov were assigned to the project, and they arrived with an extensive selection of film equipment from Nordisk Film. The professionalism of *The Girl Gogo* far exceeded that of the earlier features. An exciting film stylistically, it draws from both Italian neo-realism for its location shooting and Scandinavian symbolism for its pictorial compositions. The camerawork includes elaborate but unobtrusive camera movements, careful framing and mise-en-scène design, and dramatic close-ups.

The narrative itself, however, is shaped by the city and country opposition characteristic of the earlier films. Based on the novel by Indriði Þorsteinsson, *The Girl Gogo* is the story of Ragnar (Gunnar Eyjólfsson), a young man who has moved from the country to the city in the early 1950s, where he makes a living driving a taxicab and illegally selling liquor.[22] After driving a drunk American soldier from Reykjavík to the Naval Air Station at *Keflavík*, he meets Gógó (Kristbjörg Kjeld), whom he drives back to the city because her Cadillac has broken down. With her husband hospitalized in Denmark, Gógó begins an adulterous affair with Ragnar, while unbeknownst to him she is also in a relationship with Bill (John Teasy), an American soldier. Ragnar's good friend Guðmundur (Róbert Arnfinnsson) is aware that Gógó is also cheating on Ragnar, but hesitates to inform him despite objecting to the relationship.

Gógó's relationship with these three men plays out as a national allegory in the novel and film, with her having to choose between them. Given his adulterous affair and black-market activities, Ragnar does not arrive at the purity of Ingvar (also played by Eyjólfsson) in *Between Mountain and Shore*, but he still functions as the unspoiled country boy figure who stands in for Iceland. Although the film does not succumb to the easy solution of casting Bill as a villain, it does suggest that the American presence which he symbolizes is undesirable. Finally, despite never being named as Danish, Gógó's husband is identified with Denmark in a number of ways, through the family name Faxen, his absence due to hospitalization in Denmark, and his upper-class social status. Just as Denmark no longer rules Iceland, the husband's time with Gógó is up and he dies midway through the film. The question facing Gógó and the Icelandic nation is whether to uphold the traditional values of the Icelandic countryside or pursue American modernization.

When Ragnar first meets Gógó, she resembles an Americanized city girl through her clothing, nickname (with Ragnar preferring her Icelandic name Guðríður), Cadillac, and bold behavior. To Balling's credit, he resists turning Gógó into an unsympathetic seductress, and instead emphasizes her fragility and unenviable position. Nonetheless, the film upholds the opposition between the spoiled city girl and the innocent country boy. Ragnar is systematically tied to both the countryside and nation, whose mutual affinities are clearly established in a dialogue between Guðmundur and Ragnar in the novel:

- It is good to find the country boy in you, Guðmundur said.
- It has been a long time....
- Still he has lived in me and you and many others.
- There is no reason for him to die, I said.
- No, said Guðmundur. —Not while he preserves some of his renewal in the countryside, in its power and productivity and its hurt pride.
- If he dies.
- Then nobody knows this land anymore, he said.[23]

This exchange is not found in the film; however, Ragnar's parents' farm, where the dialogue occurs, is of great importance to both. Gógó's husband has just passed away and Ragnar goes to the country to clear his head. Striking in their visual and aural differences from the city, the scenes which take place in the country make way for bright panoramas that contrast with the dreary and claustrophobic compositions of Reykjavík. The music becomes more upbeat, and dialogue is withheld for long periods of time as if it would disrupt the country's quaintness. The filmmakers also take advantage of the novel's brief reference to Gógó and Ragnar's cherished visit to Þingvellir, the site of the original Althing parliament and a national symbol par excellence. The scene plays out more extensively in the film and the beautiful natural settings work to redeem their adulterous affair. Rowing a boat on the sunlit lake Þingvallavatn, Ragnar is heard saying: "This land. It is as if it just stepped down from the heavens" (see Figure 2.4). Even while he is in the city, Ragnar is visually tied to the countryside, for instance, when a medium shot

Figures 2.4 and 2.5 In *The Girl Gogo*, Icelandic nature works to redeem the adulterous affair of its two main protagonists, played by Gunnar Eyjólfsson and Kristbjörg Kjeld, here boating on lake *Þingvallavatn* (2.4). Conversely, the Reykjavík cityscape presents a gloomy counterpoint—including the film's ending that leaves Gógó alone on a dark and empty street (2.5). Source: Edda film.

neatly frames his face within a landscape painting, immediately after the audience has been informed of Gógó's affair with Bill.

Gógó eventually chooses Ragnar, but it is too late. He has already found out about Bill, but nonetheless comes to blows with Guðmundur to defend

Gógó's honor. Driving home to the farm in an exhausted state, he pulls over to fill his car with gas. "I am going home," he says to a concerned gas-service man. "Nobody is tired when on their way home." Not long after, he loses control of the car and crashes into a river. Guðmundur and Gógó receive the news of his death on the radio on their way to the farm. A long shot effectively captures their car slowing down to a halt, remaining still for a considerable time, before slowly turning around and driving back. The film ends with Gógó exiting Guðmundur's car only to encounter a dark and gloomy city scene (see Figure 2.5).

The Girl Gogo was the only Icelandic narrative feature made in the span of more than two decades. It was finally followed up in 1977 with *Murder Story* (*Morðsaga*, Reynir Oddsson), the first film set in Reykjavík not to extensively feature the countryside. Often dismissed as an oddity or cult film due to its splatter-like finale, it is first and foremost a parody of the emerging Reykjavík bourgeoisie and modern suburbia. The narrative references and acknowledges its debt to Claude Chabrol, but it perhaps draws more from Luis Buñuel, as in the instance of one sexually charged but ultimately absurd and surreal dinner scene. Its critique of patriarchy connected the abusive father of the household to the general rise of the bourgeoisie and modern business practices. However, in neither its city setting nor its indebtedness to the European art film did *Murder Story* foreshadow what lay ahead when Icelandic film production finally took off in the early 1980s. Aspiring to establish itself as a national institution, Icelandic cinema followed the example of early twentieth-century Icelandic nationalism by turning to the countryside, its past, and its literary heritage. *Land and Sons* (1980, *Land og synir*, Ágúst Guðmundsson), the first major Icelandic film of the 1980s, was based on a novel from the same trilogy as *The Girl Gogo*. Set in an earlier time period, *Land and Sons* nostalgically depicts the countryside before its decline and concludes with the country boy leaving his farm for the city.

Here, the so-called Icelandic film spring of the early 1980s has more in common with the now almost forgotten mid-century narrative features of Guðmundsson and Gíslason than today's Icelandic cinema. Their national aspirations distinguish them from the transnational co-productions of contemporary Icelandic cinema, the global aspects of which have more in common with the older tradition of the Iceland-film.

Tellingly, director Friðrik Þór Friðriksson will take an inward turn with his last feature, *Mamma Gógó* (2010). About his mother Gógó's (also played by actress Kristbjörg Kjeld) struggle with Alzheimer's disease, the film borrows scenes from *The Girl Gogo* to reconstruct the character's past. These images represent Gógó's vague memories, not unlike the way the Icelandic cinema discussed in this chapter conjures up the aura of an Iceland long gone. If this focus on the local is largely suppressed in contemporary Icelandic cinema, Friðriksson's film suggests that such filmmaking tendencies are not fully extinct, and may rise up to the surface at any moment.

3
Adapting a Literary Nation to Film

The year before Friedrich Engels and Karl Marx first met in 1842, Friedrich List, another great but lesser known German scholar of economics, published his magnum opus, *The National System of Political Economy* (*Das Nationale System der politischen Ökonomie*). List claimed that the nation-state was the ideal unit for maximizing economic development. However, for such development to take place, the national population needed to be large and its geographical territory extensive. For him, successful nationhood was contingent upon large nations: "A nation restricted in the number of its population and in territory, especially if it has a separate language, can only possess a crippled literature, crippled institutions for promoting art and science."[1] In other words, List saw the limitations of a small "national economy," resulting in inferior art and culture.

The early 1840s also saw national revival reach new heights in Iceland, with increased demands for secession from Denmark—itself a rather small nation in terms of territory and population. The population of Iceland, at 60,000 inhabitants, barely amounted to that of a modest-sized European town, and although larger in surface than Denmark, the country was mostly uninhabitable. If Iceland thus had none of the national qualifications outlined by List, it ultimately turned his theory upside down by constructing its very national identity on a *separate language* and literature that was understood as anything but "crippled." Language and literature were crucial to the identity of Iceland, which hardly had a national economy, industry, monuments, or other traditional arts of its own. The veneration of this heritage has meant that literature is often the source from which cinema and other forms of art and culture have been compelled to draw, relegated as they are to secondary status.

This chapter broadly addresses the relevance of literature for Icelandic national identity, as a necessary preparation for thinking about film adaptation in the Icelandic context. It moves on to the close examination of two distinct but key examples—the silent-era screen adaptations of plays and novels written by Icelandic neo-romanticists in Copenhagen, and the role played by both the celebrated medieval sagas of Icelanders and novels of Nobel laureate Halldór Laxness on the history of Icelandic cinema.

The Ties That Bind: Icelandic National Identity and Literature

Despite being spoken for a millennium, it was only in the nineteenth century that romanticists and Icelandic nationalists attached a value to the Icelandic language that extended beyond its role in communication. Inspired by German romanticism and national ideology, they felt that Icelandic medieval literature was intrinsically tied to the national character. Admittedly the nation had fallen on hard times, but one only had to look to its literature to discover the ideals of the original golden age of the Viking period. Heterogeneous in form, this literature spans poems about Norse gods and Germanic heroes to prose narratives of European knights, Scandinavian kings, and Icelandic bishops. But the sagas of the Icelanders (also known as family sagas) were the most admired by the romanticists, and it is not difficult to understand why they were singled out.[2] Not only were they stories about the Icelanders themselves, they were also open to strong national interpretations. In the most celebrated of them, *Njal's Saga* (*Njáls saga*), the hero Gunnar decides in the end against exile in Norway, despite knowing that remaining in Iceland will cost him his life. About to escape in his vessel, Gunnar looks back over to his farmland, and has a change of heart: "So lovely is the hillside that it has never before seemed to me as lovely as now."[3] The romanticists interpreted Gunnar's decision as a patriotic one—a national declaration. Nowhere is this more pronounced than in Jónas Hallgrímsson's poem "Gunnar's Holm" (*Gunnarshólmi*), in which the hillside becomes Iceland itself: "'Never before has Iceland seemed so fair.' [. . .] For Gunnar felt it nobler far to die / than flee and leave his native shores behind him."[4] If "Gunnar's Holm" has been explicitly mobilized to develop a sense of Icelandic national identity, it is also typical of the broad role the sagas have played in this construction. Gísli Sigurðsson explains:

> The sagas civilized the landscape by imparting some meaning to it through their events and place names, many of which refer back to the settlement period, thus establishing a direct link through the land back into the dark past when the heroic ancestors created the nation. The sagas and the role

played by the Icelandic landscape were thus of major significance in the development of the romantic sense of national identity among Icelanders.[5]

The site where Gunnar is believed to have turned away from the sea is now a popular tourist attraction, continuing to serve as a landmark that bridges the golden age and contemporary Iceland.

The authorship and historical accuracy of the sagas of the Icelanders remain contested; however, the qualities they share with the novel are unquestioned. Expansive in scope, the sagas are prose fiction focusing on character interactions. Robert Scholes and Robert Kellogg have argued that no other medieval literature went as far in combining romance and history, leading "the way from epic to the novel."[6] In fact, following Benedict Anderson's well-known thesis on the intrinsic ties between novel and nation, the sagas might be the most convincing argument for asserting a pre-modern Icelandic nationhood.[7] Not unlike Timothy Brennan's claims about the novel, the sagas articulated "the 'one, yet many' of national life, [...] by mimicking the structure of the nation."[8] The sagas of the Icelanders present Icelandic society broadly with their complex character interaction, but just as importantly, they distinguish it from other "nations."

But the novel itself arrived quite late on the Icelandic literary scene—or not until national revival was in full bloom, offering further support for the strong ties between nation and novel. The first Icelandic novel, *A Boy and a Girl* (*Piltur og stúlka*) by Jón Thoroddsen, was published in 1850, the year before the pivotal national assembly in which Icelandic delegates, under the leadership of independence hero Jón Sigurðsson, refused to adopt the Danish constitution. However, the novel first rose to prominence in the twentieth century with Halldór Laxness, whose first book was published the year after the establishment of a sovereign state in 1918. Following the publication of his major novels in the 1930s and 1940s, the novel became the national art form par excellence. The only cultural event of the twentieth century of greater significance than Laxness being awarded the Nobel Prize in 1955 was the return of original manuscripts of the medieval sagas from Denmark beginning in 1971. Scholars have amply pointed out Laxness's role in tying the novel to Iceland's literary heritage:

> Laxness helped make the novel a significant genre in Iceland. Through his [novels of the 1930s] he changed the shape of literary history, creating a new artistic mirror of national importance [...]. Laxness was of course

making his own entrance into literary history by first elevating the genre of the novel, and then bringing about a kind of settlement of saga and novel [...], He became the champion of a national epic identity, which was defined by history but rejuvenated through his modern, realist narrative.[9]

The connections are found in his own fiction—for example, the old manuscripts are at the center of *Iceland's Bell* (*Íslandsklukkan*), and the saga heritage is rewritten and parodied in *Wayward Heroes* (*Gerpla*)—as well as with his controversial publications of the sagas in modern spelling in the 1940s.

Halldór Guðmundsson opens his influential biography of Laxness by claiming that he "was Europe's last national poet."[10] However hyperbolic this assertion might appear, Laxness's reach within the nation was exceptional. Even after his death in 1998, his work lives on in conversations and debates that transcend the boundaries of literary circles. One suspects these arguments over Laxness's life and work are this spirited because they are about Icelandic national identity itself.[11] To address these interrelations of literature and national identity in an international context, I turn to Pascale Casanova's essential *The World Republic of Letters* (*La République mondiale des letters*). One of the numerous merits of her work is the explication of an "international literary space" that explains how national literatures are evaluated through international competition, and where there is great inequality found between large and small nations. Casanova defines small countries by their marginalized languages and absence of a literary tradition (as compared to English or French). In consideration of her first criterion, Iceland may be small, but its long and voluminous literary heritage carries weight in the international literary space: "In the world republic of letters, the richest spaces are also the oldest, which is to say the ones that were the first to enter into literary competition and whose national classics came also to be regarded as universal classics."[12] The active promotion of the literary heritage abroad is an attempt to further center Icelandic literature (and by implication the nation) in the international literary space: "In proclaiming the antiquity of their literary foundation and stressing the continuity of their national history, nations seek to establish themselves as legitimate contestants in international competition."[13] Thus, as with many other things, national pride is generated by foreign appreciation.

Casanova's model applies equally well to the intrinsic ties between the national revival in Iceland and the rise of romanticism in the nineteenth century, along with that of the novel in the twentieth. As she says: "In the case of 'small' countries, the emergence of a new literature is indissociable from the appearance of a new nation."[14] The Icelandic romanticists produced a "nascent literary space" by turning what were "merely" stories, oral or written, into literature through a process Casanova defines as *littérisation*: "Ancient legends and traditional narratives, unearthed and ennobled, gradually came to inspire countless poems, novels, stories, and plays."[15] Hallgrímsson's "Gunnar's Holm" is a textbook example of this process that culminated in the novels of Laxness, whose international pedigree further enforced his national pedigree and cultural capital. It is worth pointing out that the novels by Laxness (save for his late modernist period) have arguably more in common with the nineteenth-century novel than early twentieth-century European modernism. Again, Casanova's historical model usefully explains that only after a national tradition has established itself can formal revolts take place: "Whereas national writers, fomenters of the first literary revolts, rely on the literary models of national tradition, international writers draw upon this transnational repertoire of literary techniques in order to escape being imprisoned in national tradition."[16] The novel had just managed to establish itself as the national medium in Iceland at the mid-twentieth century, and the arrival of modernism was accordingly delayed. Laxness's own novel *Under the Glacier* (*Kristnihald undir jökli*) was part of a larger formal revolt in Icelandic prose that took place in the 1960s. However, with its inauguration in the early 1980s, Icelandic national cinema took little notice of it, reverting instead to older traditions. Indeed, films that focused on national stories had established a precedent long ago, in the early twentieth century—but with a notable twist.

The Neo-Romantic Varangians: Awesome Nature in Theater, Novel, and Film

Although the romanticists had developed an Icelandic literary space, a country of less than a hundred thousand inhabitants—most of whom were poor farmers—offered little in the way of writing careers. Jónas Hallgrímsson and most of his fellow romanticists were students in Copenhagen who composed poetry in their spare time. When in the first decades of the twentieth century a new generation of aspiring writers decided to devote themselves fully to literature, it was only logical that they should try their luck in

Copenhagen—they were, after all, Danish citizens. The belonged to the neo-romanticism of the early twentieth century, and have been grouped together in Icelandic literary history as the Varangians, evoking the travels of Vikings during the golden age.[17]

Jóhann Sigurjónsson, Guðmundur Kamban, and Gunnar Gunnarsson were the most prominent of the neo-romantic Varangians. Although not technically transnational, their work dealt almost solely with Iceland but was written in Danish, and involved the staging/narration of one nation for the audience/readership of another.[18] As a result, the national status of the neo-romanticists was—and remains—shrouded in uncertainty. These writers inhabit a marginal place in Icelandic literary history since they wrote primarily in Danish, and have been largely erased from Danish literary history since they were Icelandic. They are excellent examples of what Pascale Casanova has named the tragedy of translated men:

> As "translated men," they are caught in a dramatic structural contradiction that forces them to choose between translation into a literary language that cuts them off from their compatriots, but that gives them literary existence, and retreat into a small language that condemns them to invisibility or else to a purely national literary existence.[19]

Considering their quasi-transnational status, it is not surprising that their work should be the first "Icelandic" literature to be adapted to the global medium of cinema.

Jóhann Sigurjónsson was the first of these writers to come to prominence with his play *The Outlaw and His Wife* (*Bjærg-Ejvind og hans hustru*).[20] Based on the life of the eighteenth-century Icelandic outlaw and legend Mountain-Eyvindur (Fjalla-Eyvindur), it became a major hit upon its premiere in Copenhagen in 1912. In the play, Eyvindur, hiding under the name Kári, works as a laborer at a farm owned by the rich widow Halla, and the two soon become romantically involved. However, Halla is also being pursued by the county magistrate Björn, who exposes Kári's real identity when the widow refuses Björn's marriage proposal. Halla and Eyvindur escape to the mountains where, despite considerable hardship, they live happily for years along with their daughter Tóta and fellow outlaw Arnes. When their hide-out is eventually discovered by Björn and his posse, Halla and Eyvindur again escape, but not without a sacrifice. At the play's climax, Halla throws Tóta, now three years old, down a waterfall rather than have her be captured by Björn.

The final scene shows Halla and Eyvindur in their old age, having grown distant from one another and suffering from hunger as a blizzard rages outside their shelter.

In addition to its setting and characters, *The Outlaw and His Wife* is full of references to Iceland. It alludes to the sagas, locates Eyvindur's hideout in *Hveravellir*, and invokes the national cuisine with the presence of shark and the spirit *brennivín*. Icelandic nature is also mapped onto the play's larger-than-life characters. Eyvindur proclaims: "I am king of the hills! The fire on my hearth never dies, day or night. The country is mine, as far as my eyes can reach. Mine are the glaciers that make the streams! When I get angry, they swell, and the stones gnash their teeth against the current."[21] This exotic primitivism was common to the representation of Iceland in the works of the Varangians.

Following its success in Copenhagen, *The Outlaw and His Wife* was widely translated and performed in Europe. In Sweden it was directed by Victor Sjöström, who also played the role of Eyvindur. Sigurjónsson encouraged Sjöström, who had already directed a number of films, to adapt the play. The 1917 film was a key work in the international breakthrough of Swedish cinema, and helped launch the career of Sjöström, who a few years later made the shift to Hollywood. Sjöström's film adaptation is remarkably faithful, down to the intertitles' fidelity to the original dialogue. This results in a film that is more theatrical than cinematic at times; however, it does come into its own during the mountain scenes. The film's representation of nature is ultimately what sets it apart, considering that the script's dramatic natural environment is too challenging to reproduce in the setting of a stage play. For example, a rather detailed scene at the beginning of the third part involves a deep river canyon, a waterfall, a glacier, and lava formation. Sjöström's film, on the other hand, can and does record nature itself. The First World War made traveling to Iceland nearly impossible, so Sjöström filmed in the Lapland of northern Sweden instead. Sigurjónsson himself acknowledged how *The Outlaw and His Wife* (1917, *Berg-Ejvind och hans hustru*) captured the exalted natural settings of his play in a manner not possible on stage:

> [The] heaven above [Eyvindur and Halla.] The stars. The night. The morning with its gentle light and the day with its long shadows. Sjöström has penetrated deeply into the heart of the poem before translating it to the screen, so as if to give it back to me, enriched and saturated with beauty […]

I have no hesitation in declaring what Victor Sjöström has succeeded in doing here as metteur-en-scène and director, as being a work of genius.[22]

In a review of the film, the influential French critic (and soon-to-be major filmmaker) Louis Delluc also lingered on the cinema's particular ability to capture nature:

> And the public is swept away with emotion. For the public is awestruck by the barren landscapes, the mountains, the rustic costumes, both the austere ugliness and the acute lyricism of such closely observed feelings, the truthfulness of the long scenes which focus exclusively on the couple, the violent struggles, the high tragic end of the two aged lovers who escape life through a final embrace in a desert-like snowscape.[23]

The few changes Sjöström made involved enacting scenes that the play had only referenced through dialogue. Most dynamic of these is the scene in which Eyvindur is hanging from a high and steep cliff, while Arnes (Nils Arehn), infatuated with Halla (Edith Erastoff), flirts with the idea of cutting his rope. The film scene is a tour de force of staging high drama in an awesome natural setting, while in the play Arnes only tells Halla about the incident.

A comparable scene forms the climax of Guðmundur Kamban's play and film *Hadda Padda*. Working as a playwright and stage director in Copenhagen, Kamban had his first and greatest success with the staging of *Hadda Padda* in 1914. Although set in contemporary Iceland, *Hadda Padda* was clearly influenced by *The Outlaw and His Wife* in the romantic correlation it makes between Iceland's barren nature and the emotional extremes of its characters. Kamban then moved on to more cosmopolitan and modern themes, setting many of his plays in New York, but he returned to *Hadda Padda* (1924) for his directorial film debut ten years later. The title character (Clara Pontoppidan) is devoted to her parents and fiancé Ingólfur (Svend Methling), while her younger sister Kristrún (Alice Frederiksen) mischievously swaps one boyfriend for another. Hadda Padda's character quickly transforms after Ingólfur is seduced by Kristrún and breaks off their engagement. In the narrative's s climax, a distraught Hadda Padda throws herself down a sheer cliff, attempting to take Ingólfur with her.

Although Kamban was Icelandic, the film and play were predominantly Danish productions. The film's indoor scenes were shot in a Copenhagen studio and bear a much greater resemblance to Danish interiors than Icelandic ones. However, in correspondence with the work's romanticization of Icelandic nature, outdoor scenes were shot in Iceland. As with the earlier case of *The Outlaw and His Wife*, stage directions created various challenges for theatrical productions, so that the play almost was not staged at all. It is difficult, for instance, to imagine how a theatrical space might accommodate the play's fourth act, or the final encounter between Ingólfur and Hadda Padda set in a deep ravine, complete with a waterfall and receding mist.[24] The composition and camerawork of the scene in the film version remain theatrical, but the images fully capture the awesome natural setting (see Figure 3.1). Ingólfur and supporting character Steindór (Paul Rohde) help Hadda Padda rappel down a ravine with a rope tied around her waist after she claims to have dropped a jewel over the edge. Her devious and desperate plan is to pull down Ingólfur, who has the other end of the rope wrapped around himself, with her, uniting them in death as they had been previously in life. Pulled toward the edge, Ingólfur and Steindór finally realize her intentions. The latter calls out to Ingólfur: "You must let go of the rope. That's all you can do. It is better that she falls alone, than that she drags both of us with her. You must let go. Or I'll let go."[25] Ingólfur will not hear of it, but when he is about to succeed in pulling Hadda Padda back to safety, she cuts the rope with a knife and falls to her death.

The similarities between this scene and that in *The Outlaw and His Wife* are striking: the sublime natural setting, the central character hanging on a rope off a sheer cliff, the question of letting go of the rope, and closer views of the knife cutting at the rope (see Figure 3.2). The first two major Icelandic successes on the Danish stage, then, appealed to audiences by using Icelandic nature to represent or externalize the emotional intensity of their characters. The recording capacity of film most fully articulated these parallels, and nature has continued to be a defining character of Icelandic cinema ever since.

In the long run, the most successful of the Icelandic writers in Copenhagen was novelist Gunnar Gunnarsson. In 1912 he helped Sigurjónsson translate *The Outlaw and His Wife* to Icelandic, and he also published his first novel *Ormarr Ørlygsson*. It would become the first volume in *The Story of the Borg Family* (*Af Borgslægtens historie*), but it was with the third volume *Guest the One-Eyed* (*Gæst den enøjede*) that Gunnarsson made his breakthrough. *The Story of the Borg Family* was eventually translated into thirteen languages.[26] As a family saga observing the state of the nation through three generations, it addresses ties to Denmark and emigration to North America. Although its

Figures 3.1 and 3.2 The camera allowed director Guðmundur Kamban to film scenes from his play *Hadda Padda* in awesome natural settings (3.1). Additionally, editing and close-ups heighten the suspense as Hadda Padda cuts the rope she is hanging from during the film's climax (3.2). Source: Edda film (DK).

national status is complicated by it being written in Danish, it exhibits the extremely strong ties between novel and nation, and presents Iceland with the same romantic characterization as *The Outlaw and His Wife* or *Hadda Padda*. However, it goes further in making explicit what is implicit in the plays. For example, the very opening of *Ormarr Ørlygsson* lists over ten place names in describing its setting. Cultural specificities are described in detail, and the ethnic origins of the Borg family are traced to Norwegians and Celts. It also frequently references the characters' love for both land and nature.

The rich and powerful farmer Örlygur and his two sons, Ormar and Ketill, are at the center of the novel. Ormar, who is ten years older than Ketill, is described as dreamy and lofty in his ambitions but also melancholic and heavy-hearted. The emotional range of the character is romantically attributed to Icelandic nature: "The wistful, dreamy thoughts that burned in his dark, passionate eyes, betrayed that rich and abundant imagination peculiar to the sons of Iceland, fostered by the great solitude and desolate yet fertile grandeur of the land itself."[27] The contradictory aspects of Ormar's character are also mirrored in his equal devotion to both father and farm, and conversely his desire to travel and see the world outside Iceland. Although not supportive of his son's artistic and dreamy disposition, Örlygur arranges for him to go to Copenhagen to study violin. About to conquer the music world with his natural talent during his debut ten years later, Ormar unexpectedly rejects all he has learned and retreats to "primeval nakedness": "Then suddenly there came over him an irresistible desire to jerk [the audience] back to life [...] To tear at their sense, to render their innermost souls, to fling at them, like a fiery volcanic eruption."[28] Having thus forfeited his career by breaking all the rules—however dramatically—Ormar returns to Iceland.

Later, as a respected and extremely wealthy businessman, his second stay in Copenhagen is more successful. His subsequent return to Iceland, however, is marred by his brother Ketill, who is now a pastor married to Alma, a Danish woman, despite having earlier seduced their foster sister Rúna. To save the reputation of his family, Ormar marries the pregnant Rúna and settles at the Borg farm. Wanting Borg for himself, Ketill uses the authority of his religious position to turn the congregation against Ormar and their father Örlygur. However, instead of Ketill's moment of triumph, it is disclosed that he is actually the father of Rúna's illicit child. The discovery leaves his father dead and his wife mad, and Ketill disappears, believed to have committed suicide. The third volume opens many years later with an encounter between Örlygur, the son of Ketill and Rúna, and a highly revered ascetic wanderer, the one-eyed Gestur of its title. Gestur, it turns out, is really Ketill, who has returned to Borg before his death. A changed man, he is redeemed by his faith in God and forgiven by all. Ketill/Gestur can now be linked to the land, like Ormar before him: "He had a peculiarly close relationship with the ghastly and desolate land of the wilderness. It was as if he belonged there and nowhere else."[29]

The unmistakable ties between Ormar and Gestur's perceived Icelandicness and the harsh environment were already suggested by Hadda Padda and Eyvindur. However, Gunnarsson's novel first makes explicit the opposition between a modern and civilized Denmark and an archaic and primitive Iceland, only hinted at by the plays. Ormar's dream of going abroad is equally a dream of encountering modernity, which serves as a foil to the pre-modern working methods and traditional culture of Iceland:

> The great world called to him, and every fibre in him answered to the call. He knew that there, where he was going, were wonderful machines contrived to do the work of men. [...] Think—to fill a room with light by the mere turning of a switch! And talk with people through a wire—which he imagined as hollow. [...] He would live in a city with streets like deep chasms between unscalable cliffs—cave-hollowed cliffs peopled with human beings, instead of giants and goblins.[30]

In fact, Ormar's economic success results from his ownership of a shipping empire that assists in bringing modernity to Iceland from Europe. The definitive image of an Icelander is thus in the end not Ormar, the cosmopolitan businessman who actually gives up his job to become a farmer at Borg. It is Gestur the one-eyed, who, in opposition to modern life, roams the Icelandic wilderness having reached the heights of asceticism.

Icelanders were concerned about the image of the country presented in foreign films, and its real or perceived backwardness was particularly resented. As Helga Kress points out, some Icelanders found the neo-romantic image of Iceland presented in Denmark questionable as well.[31] These stories, after all, were intended to appeal to a Danish audience and readership, rather than an Icelandic one. If this was generally true of Icelandic authors writing in Denmark in the early twentieth century, the second volume of Gunnarsson's novel, *The Danish Lady at Hof* (*Den danske frue på Hof*), took this even further by inscribing Danish reception in the text itself. Although narrated in the third person, it often presents Alma's perspective of Iceland:

It was all so strange to her that now, looking at it calmly, it seemed unreal, incredible. Alma turned cold at heart as she looked. She remembered her first survey of the landscape earlier in the day, from Borg; she had found nothing green in it all save the sea. All the meadows and pastures round the house seemed withered and grey; the autumn green of the field in Denmark was nowhere to be seen.[32]

Similar descriptions of the country are also expressed through dialogue:

[KETILL:]: Well, I'm glad you do not find the country altogether forbidding. Many people do, you know.
[ALMA:]: Forbidding! I feel as if I were under a spell. No will of my own, just a thing in the hands of Fate. And I love the feeling that there are great and distant powers that have taken my life into their hands.
[KETILL:]: You had better be careful, or you will be growing superstitious—it is a common failing among the people here. They believe in all kinds of spirits, portents, omens, fate, and all that sort of thing.[33]

Danish readers, then, are invited to experience Iceland through the character of Alma, sharing in her bewilderment, fascination, and fear. Here *The Danish Lady at Hof* remarkably foreshadows the central transnational strategy of contemporary Icelandic cinema—the bewildered foreigner visiting the country (see chapter seven). This is not the case for contemporary Icelandic literature; even though many novels include foreign characters, the novels themselves are written in Icelandic.[34] Conversely, a number of recent Icelandic films make use of foreign languages to invite a foreign audience (for example, in *Cold Fever* [Friðrik Þór Friðriksson, 1995, *Á köldum klaka*] and *101 Reykjavík* [Baltasar Kormákur, 2000]), following the example established by *The Story of the Borg Family*.

Along with playing an important role in the novel's commercial success, this narrative technique made *The Story of the Borg Family* feasible for adaptation. The film version was made in the summer of 1919 by Nordisk Film, with a primarily Danish cast and crew, including director Gunnar Sommerfeldt, who also played Ketill/Gestur.[35] It achieved a degree of authenticity, however, by filming interior and exterior scenes in Iceland, consulting with Gunnarsson, who joined the crew in an advisory capacity, and casting the Icelander Guðmundur Thorsteinsson in the role of Ormar. The filmmakers faithfully reproduced the epic scope of the novel, resulting in a three-and-a-half-hour movie (at least as it was exhibited in two parts in Iceland). Echoing *The Outlaw and His Wife* and *Hadda Padda*, the film foregrounds natural settings to elaborate on Ormar's character, not unlike the novel. Medium shots of Ormar playing the violin are superimposed over shots of mountains, rivers, and waterfalls (see Figure 3.3). As if not fully trusting the visuals, the filmmakers use intertitles to assert: "With the violin's tones he called forth the beauty and the awesomeness of his land." With this pronouncement, Ormar might very well be the first of Icelandic cinema's many children of nature.

This fascinating period came to an end almost as quickly as it had begun, and although Gunnarsson and Kamban continued to work and write in Danish, they soon parted from their neo-romantic roots. At least two major explanations have been provided for this turnaround. Jón Yngvi Jóhannsson has argued that Danish-Icelandic literature, or the work of the Varangians, functioned as a counter-identity for the Danish audience/readership.[36]

Figure 3.3 Through a series of superimpositions, Ormar's (Guðmundur Thorsteinsson) psychology and subjectivity are interwoven with Icelandic nature in the *Story of the Borg Family*. Source: The National Film Archive of Iceland/Kvikmyndasafn Íslands.

Although there is little doubt that the Icelandic writers themselves played a role in producing and contributing to perceptions of Icelandic primitivism, in the long run, they resented being relegated to the status of regional artists or cultural ethnographers. The establishment of a sovereign Icelandic state in 1918, although under the Danish king, created a variety of political complications and made their works nationally and even politically suspect.[37] Following a narrow nation-state demarcation, Danish-Icelandic literature was nothing but Danish, but after 1918 a broader horizon included destinations outside Copenhagen. If you wanted to make it in the big world, why not go to Hollywood? That is what Halldór Laxness did.

Anxiety of Influence: Laxness and the Sagas

It is fitting that it was during the sovereign year of 1918 that Halldór Laxness, only sixteen years old, wrote his first novel, *Child of Nature* (*Barn náttúrunnar*). As suggested by its title, it was influenced by neo-romanticism, but even though Laxness followed in the footsteps of the Varangians by trying his luck in Copenhagen, where he wrote a few neo-romantic short stories (including "The Thousand Year Old Icelander" ["Den Tusindaarige Islænding"]) for newspapers, he seems to have had little interest in establishing himself as a writer in Danish. He soon traveled to other European countries, and toward the end of 1927 he arrived in Los Angeles ready to make his way in the movies. During his short stay in Los Angeles, Laxness wrote two film treatments, *Kári Kárán* (or *Judged by a Dog*) and *Salka Valka* (or *A Woman in Pants*).[38] Despite hiring an agent, changing his name to Hall d'Or, and networking, Laxness's hopes of getting his treatments filmed were dashed.[39] In a letter written in June 1928, Laxness states that MGM had agreed to film *Salka Valka* that same summer in Iceland.[40] However, nothing came of MGM's plans, and Laxness soon left Los Angeles, disillusioned. His encounter with the American social-realist novel would have a more lasting impact on him than Hollywood, and when Laxness finally returned to California in 1959 it was to visit Upton Sinclair, among other old acquaintances.[41]

Neo-romanticism had run its course in literature and theater, but its melodramatic extremes—expressed in the film treatment of *Salka Valka*—were ideally suited to Hollywood. Laxness's descriptions could well be used to define Icelandic neo-romanticism: "An atmosphere of hard struggle for life, and misery. Uncultivated passions. The characters are rude, naïve and primitive. Nature is phenomenally barren and wild; the sea is usually restless and the psychology of the characters is closely tied together with this wild nature."[42] The orphan girl Salka Valka grows up among boys and must make a living in adulthood, all the while refusing the advances of the upper-class Angantyr and the vulgar brute Arnaldur. The latter saves her from a gang-rape attempt by fighting the culprits, but ends up having an erotically charged fight with Salka Valka himself. Nonetheless, she refuses Angantyr's marriage proposal and is seen "kissing [Arnaldur's whip!] with all the voluptuousness and pathos of the primitive."[43] In general, the treatment follows the neo-romantic portrayal of Icelanders as primitives (and "primitive" is a word that is repeatedly used by Laxness), overdetermined by their harsh natural environment. Laxness, in fact, partly earned a living in Hollywood by giving lectures on Iceland, during which he praised the literary merit of Jóhann Sigurjónsson, Guðmundur Kamban, and Gunnar Gunnarsson.[44] The character of Salka Valka as a strong independent woman defined by her relationship to nature—not to mention her name—owed a lot to both *The Outlaw*'s Halla and Hadda Padda. Such "girls of nature" have also become a cornerstone of Icelandic cinema and were, for example, reincarnated as the characters played by Margrét Vilhjálmsdóttir in both *The Seagull's Laughter* (*Mávahlátur*, 2001, Ágúst Guðmundsson) and *Falcons* (Friðrik Þór Friðriksson, 2002, *Fálkar*).

While in Hollywood, Laxness worked on an English translation of his breakthrough novel *The Great Weaver of Kashmir* (*Vefarinn mikli frá Kasmír*). He harbored hopes of success in the United States as elsewhere, but he does not seem to have been interested in becoming a writer in English any more than in Danish. The distinctions between the film treatment of *Salka Valka* and the novel that was eventually written in 1931–1932 tell us a great deal about the different relationships these mediums have to the nation. Although the film was to be set in Iceland, it offered only a superficial glimpse and stereotypical vision of the country (which could have been substituted by any forlorn place in the world). But then it was a script written for Hollywood with Greta Garbo in mind. The novel, on the other hand, is written in Icelandic and provides comprehensive and elaborate commentary on the nation. Separated from the film treatment's neo-romanticism, and with the "primitive" whip put aside, the fishing village of the novel is a microcosm of Icelandic society experiencing the political turmoil of the early twentieth century. The American title of the novel, *Salka Valka: A Novel of Iceland*

(1936), could not have been more decisive in articulating the medium's relationship to nation building.[45]

Considering the novel's origin in a film treatment, it seems appropriate that *Salka Valka* was the first of Laxness's works to be adapted to film (1954). It was also the first project initiated by Edda-film, a company established with the sole purpose of bringing the national literary heritage to the screen. Directed by Arne Mattson, shot by Sven Nykvist, and starring Gunnel Broström as the adult Salka Valka, the production, however, was ultimately a Swedish one. The film contrasts claustrophobic interior scenes shot in a studio in Sweden with breathtaking panoramas of Icelandic nature, perfectly captured on location by Nykvist. The climax of the film features the reunion of Salka Valka and Arnaldur (no longer the brute of the film treatment) in the midst of beautiful natural surroundings, accompanied by a lofty musical score. Here *Salka Valka* foreshadows the role of nature in much of Icelandic cinema to come.

The first domestically produced film adaptation of a Laxness novel, however, did not materialize until the 1984 premiere of Þorsteinn Jónsson's *Atom Station* (*Atómstöðin*). In the four decades that have since passed, only two more adaptations of Laxness's work, *Under the Glacier* (1989, *Kristnihald undir jökli*) and *Honour of the House* (1999, *Ungfrúin góða og húsið*), have seen the light of day. Both were directed by Laxness's daughter Guðný Halldórsdóttir. And while the novels *Atom Station* and *Under the Glacier* are far more important works than the novella *Honour of the House*, none of them are at the center of the Laxness canon. They may have been chosen because of their temporal and spatial restraints compared to the epic span of the most canonical novels, *Independent People* (*Sjálfstætt fólk*), *World Light* (*Heimsljós*), and *Iceland's Bell*, that have yet to be filmed. Due to their scope, the latter novels are not easily adapted to film without substantial changes.[46] Also, as period pieces, they suggest steep budgets, making them economic challenges for a small national cinema. However, the reverence in which Laxness's key works are held has been equally inhibitive. This reverence would seem to have discouraged filmmakers from developing creative low-budget alternatives to faithful and expensive staging of their epic and historical scope. The novels' apparently inseparable ties to Icelandic history and society also might explain why they have not been embraced by today's transnational European cinema. On the other hand, Laxness guarantees a local audience, and his international renown would benefit foreign marketing.

The serially postponed production of *Independent People*, the most treasured work of modern Icelandic literature, crystallizes some of the challenges and limitations of a small national cinema. Icelandic film producer Snorri Þórisson had aimed for an English-language adaptation as it would allow for a much higher budget. Long the best-selling Icelandic novel in translation, he believed a film adaptation of *Independent People* would have a considerable global potential. Furthermore, Þórisson points out that even though the central character may be "specifically Icelandic, people around the world can relate to him."[47] Scripted more than two decades ago by Ruth Prawer Jhabvala, renown for her work on *A Room with a View* (James Ivory, 1985) and *Howards End* (James Ivory, 1992), the proposed film drew upon the conventions of the English heritage school, famous for its many faithful adaptations. But *Independent People* still awaits filming.

If the works of Laxness have been seriously underexplored by Icelandic filmmakers, the sagas have been almost entirely ignored. A common misconception is that the sagas have played a major role in Icelandic cinema, but only a single saga, *Gisli Sursson's Saga* (*Gísla saga Súrssonar*) in Ágúst Guðmundsson's *The Outlaw* (1981, *Útlaginn*), has been adapted to the screen. Although important to the canon, it never achieved the admiration directed at *The Saga of the People of Laxardal* (*Laxdæla*), *Njal's Saga*, and *Egil's Saga*. *The Outlaw* was a remarkably faithful adaptation of the original source and its historical setting. In fact, the film's narrative is almost incomprehensible without prior knowledge of the saga, making it out of reach for most foreign viewers. In the early eighties the foreign market was of little concern to Icelandic filmmakers, but *The Outlaw*'s domestic box-office success and subsequent place alongside the original *Gisli Sursson's Saga* in the national elementary school curriculum should have provided an impetus for further saga adaptations. However, thereafter only director Hrafn Gunnlaugsson mined the Viking heritage. Originating from an aborted adaptation of *Wayward Heroes*, Laxness's satire about the saga heritage, Gunnlaugsson's *When the Raven Flies* (1984, *Hrafninn flýgur*), was neither a literary adaptation nor a historical re-enactment. It is difficult to know whether its irreverent approach indicates a fearlessness on the part of the director, or if it is intended to sidestep the weight and influence of the saga literature. Regardless, *When the Raven Flies* and its two follow-ups, *In the Shadow of the Raven* (1988, *Í skugga hrafnsins*) and *The White Viking* (1991, *Hvíti víkingurinn*), experienced far greater international success than *The Outlaw*. By partnering with a Scandinavian film company for the last two of these films and successfully depicting Iceland's "primitive" past for outside audiences (Scandinavian, but primarily Swedish), Gunnlaugsson is more than a little reminiscent of the Varangians of the early twentieth century.

Outside of *The Outlaw* and Gunnlaugsson's Viking trilogy, the literary heritage has been all but avoided. Just like the longer novels by Laxness, faithful saga adaptations require expensive budgets. But if *Gisli Sursson's Saga* could be filmed with the meager financial resources of the early 1980s, budget restraints are not the primary obstacle. At the narrative level, the sagas seem to invite adaptation. Their insistently objective third-person narration, in which feelings and emotions are revealed through action and dialogue, is comparable to conventional film narration. Additionally, they are full of dramatic situations, exciting plots, colorful characters, and are set in spectacular natural surroundings—the hallmark of Icelandic cinema. Therefore, the absence of such adaptations might reflect an anxiety that filmmakers experience in daring to approach such revered literary works. More concrete evidence of this comes in the form of exorbitant budgets that filmmakers have argued are required to adapt the sagas. These proposed budgets often become the very obstacles that prevent the projects from materializing. Friðrik Þór Friðriksson's planned Viking epic *A Gathering of Foes* (*Óvinafagnaður*)—a rewriting of the medieval *Sturlunga Saga* by contemporary Icelandic novelist Einar Kárason—would have been the most expensive Icelandic film to date,[48] but as in the case of Þórisson's *Independent People*, the project could not be financed.

It appears that the history of Icelandic saga adaptations is one of broken promises and unrealized projects. As far back as 1923, the plans of Danish director Carl Theodor Dreyer to make two saga adaptations, with Guðmundur Kamban as an advisor, came to naught.[49] But it is the continued deferral of filming *Njal's Saga*, the most venerated of all the sagas, which could be said to constitute a running thread throughout the sporadic production history of Icelandic cinema. Already in 1919, a group of entrepreneurs had plans of filming the *Saga* that never materialized. It came closest to being adapted to the screen during the mid-1960s when Guðlaugur Rósinkranz finished a script intended for an Edda-film production. However, the company failed to secure both foreign co-producers and financial support from the state. Burdened by fidelity, the surviving script displays few attempts to delimit the *Saga*'s epic scope, likely having resulted in a heavy-handed film.[50] If Edda-film never succeeded in adapting *Njal's Saga* into a feature, it did produce the documentary short *Iceland: Island of Sagas* (Rune Lindström, 1954, *Fögur er hlíðin*), which presents some of *Njal's Saga*'s important locations in addition to staging certain key events. The company also took part in the making of the transnational Viking film *The Red Mantle* (Gabriel Axel, 1967, *Den røde kappe*).[51]

Half a century later, *Njalssaga* (2003), another such documentary that mixed educational material with staged scenes, was made for television by Björn Br. Björnsson. Baltasar Kormákur, director of the adaptations *101 Reykjavík* (2000) and *Jar City* (2006, *Mýrin*), both of which achieved a degree of international exhibition and festival success, had ambitious plans of his own for filming *Njal's Saga*.[52] Although by 2008 it had already transformed into a more commercial "Spaghetti-western-Viking movie," with four times the intended budget of Friðriksson's *Gathering of Foes*, the film has still not seen the light of day.[53] Like all the other aspirations for filming a major saga or Laxness novel, it seems to have been permanently shelved.

But Icelandic cinema is not lacking altogether in adaptations. In fact, many of its most successful films at the local box office and some of its noteworthy international breakthrough films have been adaptations. Interestingly, two adaptations of Indriði Sigurðsson's novels, *The Girl Gogo* (Erik Balling, 1962, *79 af stöðinni*) and *Land and Sons* (Ágúst Guðmundsson, 1980, *Land og synir*), bridge the era of Nordic co-productions and the explicitly national cinema of the early 1980s. Its early years were also distinguished by faithful and reverent adaptations, including Þorsteinn Jónsson's *Dot Dot Comma Dash* (1981, *Punktur punktur komma strik*) and *Atom Station*. The heavy reliance on literature during the early 1980s might be understood as a strategic alignment with the national form par excellence. Chapter eight elaborates on this trend by taking a much closer look at *The Outlaw* and *When the Raven Flies*. It also addresses a major shift in the approach to adaptation during the 1990s that I will be referring to as transnationalization.

The space this chapter devotes to films that have never been produced makes for an unorthodox adaptation study. But in the case of Iceland—no matter how paradoxical it may seem—these are arguably the most illuminating adaptations. The fact that the canonical sagas and novels by Laxness have yet to be filmed is more revealing of the encounter between Icelandic cinema and literature than the adaptations that actually have been made. The overall anxiety in facing the literary heritage is symptomatic of a cinema that belongs to a nation whose identity is deeply interwoven with its language and literary heritage.[54]

4
A Cinema of Fire and Ice

The opening shot is a spectacular panorama of a sublime wintery mountainscape. It appears to be a world far removed from that of humans, but soon a vehicle enters the frame from the right. A closer view reveals a Toyota Land Cruiser equipped for glacial driving, struggling across the terrain in almost zero visibility, surrounded by a range of white tones. The inevitable happens and it gets stuck, and out jumps a man while a woman looks on with her head out of the open window. He is able to dig them out and guide them further up the snowy mountain range, where they ultimately exit the vehicle by a pitch-black lava range that provides the first color contrast. And then, as they reach the top, we finally see them together, taking in the wondrous sight of a fiery red volcanic eruption. This is the pre-credits scene of *Fire of Love* (Sara Dosa, 2022), a documentary about the French volcanologists Katia and Maurice Krafft, which became an unexpected popular and critical hit, earning an Academy Award nomination for best documentary. The film's broad appeal is understandable. It presents the dramatic love story of the couple, touring volcanoes all over the world, until they tragically perished in Japan's Mount *Unzen* eruption of 1991. The promotional poster foregrounds the film's striking volcano imagery, with the Kraffts standing before a bright red wall of fire in their aluminized suits. But why begin the film in a snowy Icelandic landscape far removed from such volcanic imagery, in a country that plays a relatively small role in the film?

The narrator of *Fire of Love* provides an answer to that question, accompanied by a shot of golden sunlight that transitions us from a world of ice to a world of fire: "In a cold world, all the watches started to freeze. The sun came and went between blizzards and gusts which erased all bearings. In this world lived a fire. And in this fire two lovers found a home." Poetically, the voice-over explains that volcanoes provided the Kraffts with a refuge from the rest of the (cold) world, but it also evokes the familiar reference to Iceland as the "land of fire and ice," a description that would have been familiar to the film's director Sara Dosa, whose previous documentary, *The Seer and the Unseen* (2019), was about elves in Iceland. Whether intentional or not, the

Light in the Dark. Björn Norðfjörð, Oxford University Press. © Oxford University Press 2025.
DOI: 10.1093/oso/9780197762141.003.0005

centuries-long association between Iceland and its contrary elements seems to compel the filmmaker to begin with the country and its volcanoes and join them to their icy counterpart.

The title of another recent English-language documentary, *Fire and Iceland* (April Anderson and Martin Chytil, 2022), about the 2021 eruption in Mount *Fagradalsfjall*, also summons this terminology. Following a series of shots that depict the eruption from varying perspectives, singer/actress Guðrún Ýr Eyfjörð raises a familiar subject: "People in Iceland—we are so connected to nature. We have had to experience really bad eruptions. It's so powerful and it's built in every Icelandic person to respect that." Clinging to platitudes about the close ties between Icelanders and nature—and in this case, volcanoes in particular—the film mostly shuns volcanologists and other geological experts for artists whose work engages with volcanic imagery, or members of search and rescue teams. But Werner Herzog's *Into the Inferno* (2016), which examines the impact of volcanoes around the world, offers the most passionate argument regarding nature's impact on Icelanders. His typically dramatic voice-over concludes an extensive segment on the country's volcanoes:

> These primordial occurrences influenced the mythical poetry of the Icelanders. There is a text that defines the spirit of the people. It exists only in a single manuscript. [...] In 1971, Denmark returned it to Iceland. Knowing it constituted the soul of the country, the Codex was put on Denmark's largest battleship and escorted by a whole fleet.

Over a close-up of the *Codex Regius* manuscript, Herzog continues: "In the opening passage, called 'The Prophecy of the Seeress,' there is an apocalyptic vision of the end of the pagan gods. This seems to describe a huge volcanic event."[1] He proceeds to read a lengthy quote from the poem that is supplemented with images of volcanic eruptions. Herzog's anachronistic association between nation, nature, and literature harkens back to nineteenth-century romanticism (see chapter three). Nonetheless, old ideas persist, kept alive not only by great dramatists of exoticism like Herzog but also by many Icelanders, as interviews in *Fire and Iceland* suggest.

In this chapter we take a closer look at the role that volcanic imagery has played in Icelandic cinema. The overview begins with the filming of the great eruption in Mount *Hekla* in 1947 and then covers the oeuvre of Ósvaldur Knudsen, the greatest filmic chronicler of Icelandic volcanoes. We will continue to trace this history all the way to the present-day eruptions at *Reykjanesskagi* that have become headline news around the world. In doing so, we will raise the question whether there is such a thing as a volcano film, and if so, what it consists of. But we will not neglect the other half of the "fire and ice" dyad by introducing also documentaries focusing on ice and glacial imagery. Lastly, we will jump ahead a bit in our chronology and consider the relevance of fire and ice for Icelandic filmmaking today.

Mount *Hekla* and the Emergence of the Volcano Film

Iceland experienced four major eruptions in the twentieth century. In October 1918, Mount *Katla* erupted with such force that it extended the southern coast of Iceland by a few miles, and caused extensive glacial flooding over large parts of the southern region. A little further to the west, Mount *Hekla*, the most famous of all Icelandic volcanoes, erupted in March 1947 with a strength not witnessed since 1104. In one of the major eruptions anywhere in the twentieth century, *Hekla* continued to erupt until April of the following year. An even longer-lasting eruption began below sea level, close to the *Vestmannaeyjar* archipelago just southwest of Iceland, in November 1963. It soon rose to the surface, with an island forming early in the following year and with volcanic activity continuing into 1967. And, perhaps most dramatically, Mount *Eldfell*, which is located on *Heimaey*, the only inhabited *Vestmannaeyjar* island, erupted in January 1973, leading to a quick and successful evacuation. *Hekla* would erupt twice again before the end of the century, but these were minor compared to the great 1947 eruption. More noteworthy were the numerous eruptions of *Krafla* in the Northeast during the years 1975–1984, some of which provide the backdrop for the promotional poster of *Fire of Love*.[2]

The eruption of *Katla* occurred just before the renewed filmmaking activity of 1919, and it is unlikely there was any equipment in the country to film it. Most of the eruptions in the twenties and thirties belonged to volcanoes located in the remote central and northeastern highlands, including the *Askja* caldera and the subglacial *Grímsvötn* (part of *Vatnajökull* Glacier), and were therefore not easily accessible to the few aspiring filmmakers. On the other hand, the location and timing of the *Hekla* eruption were fortuitous. Not only is *Hekla* relatively close to Reykjavík, but its activity coincided with a remarkable growth in filmmaking and improved access to film material following the end of World War II. The depiction of its eruption also benefited from the arrival of color film to the local scene.

Among the established Icelandic filmmakers at the time, both Kjartan Ó. Bjarnason and Vigfús Sigurgeirsson filmed the eruption, but they approached it differently. In Bjarnason's lengthier work, *Rangárvallasýsla* (1948), about the eponymous county in which *Hekla* is located, the eruption serves as the climax to a film that focuses on farming and popular tourist sites in the region. A segment devoted to the mountain valley Þórsmörk concludes with a female traveler taking in the view from a high cliff, before the film cuts to an aerial shot of the eruption. The change in perspective is much too extreme for the audience to connect it directly with the traveler, but it nonetheless functions as a tacit subjective shot. In fact, Bjarnason's representation of the eruption privileges the views of travelers and the region's farmers, capturing the volcano from ground level before gradually offering closer views motivated by the various groups approaching it. Images of the lava are withheld until people have actually reached the volcano, and by this time, individuals are often featured amidst the eruption itself. The film even includes a shot of a man using the flowing lava to light his cigar. Ultimately, the whole process is repeated with another group traveling the same route in wintry conditions, before the film concludes with an overview shot not unlike the one that opens the volcano segment. In general, the film is a regional travelogue rather than a volcano film per se, which begs the questions of what is meant by volcano films.

It is certainly not a genre category that either film enthusiasts or scholars make use of, but the internet is home to a surprising number of lists charting the supposedly best volcano films. It is a hodgepodge of extremely different films that simply share the inclusion of volcanoes. Most prominent are historical films set in Pompeii, disaster films, and a few documentaries, including *Fire of Love*, which tops many of the lists.[3] As no attempt is made at defining the films included, let me try to explain a little what I mean by a volcano film. It is a film that displays an interest in volcanoes in and of themselves—often a specific eruption—and thus would not include films such as Roberto Rossellini's *Stromboli* (1950), where the volcano is a catalyst for character psychology, or *Volcano* (Mick Jackson, 1997), where it could be replaced with any other force of nature, or Bjarnason's film, where the volcano is part of a regional survey. In other words, formally and aesthetically, volcano films make use of the medium to capture something about the essence and power of volcanic eruptions that is difficult or impossible to put into words.

First shown in late 1947 or before the end of volcanic activities in *Hekla*, Sigurgeirsson's film is solely devoted to the eruption itself, lasting about ten minutes, or just shorter than the corresponding segment in Bjarnason's film. The film begins with an aerial shot of the complete eruptive column, followed by closer views tracing the column by restrained tilting or panning as the camera is severely constrained by the small size of the airplane whose wing and motor are often visible in the frame as well. These shots are proceeded by extreme long-distance shots that provide a good overview of the eruption from the ground. But it is not until more than a third of the way into the film that we get the first closer views, many showing rivers of lava flowing down the mountain. And more than half the film is over before we see the first humans, who play a small role until near the end when we see farmers clearing ash from their fields. Here the pure spectacle of the eruption has made way for more conventional documentary footage focusing on the extensive cleanup. The film unexpectedly concludes with a series of close views of flowing and splashing lava against a fully black background accentuating its fiery red and orange colors, resembling abstract paintings. The location and presence of the striking final images are not easily explained by other elements of the film. It could be that more lava oozed after ash was cleared from the fields, but it is more likely that the scenes are out of sequence and lacking a thematic or formal explanation. This is exactly the challenge of the volcano film: how to arrange the spectacle of the natural phenomenon into a work of art that lives up to the splendor of its subject. The incongruity between the pure spectacle of the opening and concluding images and the conventional documentary footage of human activity (cleaning up the lava) constitutes, as we will see, the battle lines of the volcano film.

In his magnum opus *Theory of Film*, Siegfried Kracauer has argued that the particular properties of cinema (especially photographic movement) were ideally suited to capture certain subjects that the traditional arts could not (see chapter two). In other words, cinema can reveal that which we are blind to, from the movement of plants to that of the urban masses.[4] Admittedly, volcanic eruptions were not among the topics discussed by Kracauer, but then again, they are unlikely to be on the radar of a modern urban intellectual living in Frankfurt and later New York. But there are few phenomena that better support his thesis than the striking colors, unruly movements, and mysterious sounds of these eruptions—the power of raw nature that written texts or still images simply do not come close to capturing. And that is precisely the claim made by Jean Epstein—the one classical film theorist who not only discussed volcanoes but also filmed an eruption. It is a great loss that his proto-volcano film of the 1923 Mount *Etna* eruption, *La Montagne infidèle* (1923), has not survived. His vivid description of the "blazing spectacle" hints at the way volcanic eruptions capture something essential about the film medium: "Glorious volcano! I have never seen expressions comparable to yours."[5]

Given this early historical interest and the more recent and developed work on ecocinema, which focuses on the broader relationship between film and the environment, it is surprising that film scholars have paid such little attention to volcano films. Elena Past is one of the few to have analyzed a film in such a context, not surprisingly in a study of Italian ecocinema. She makes a strong case for the interrelations between cinema and volcanoes:

> As one of the most dramatically visible testaments to the fact that our earth is on the move, volcanoes quite fittingly have a privileged relationship to the kinetic language of cinema, that art of moving pictures. Sharing our impulse to mobility and visibility, a cinema that turns its gaze to volcanic landscapes finds a world that speaks its language.[6]

I would contend that a volcano film displays this "privileged relationship" and uses its "language" to capture its visual counterpart. In the comparison between Bjarnason and Sigurgeirsson we see a clear difference between a filmmaker whose primary interest lies in the visuals of the volcano and one who uses it as a backdrop to document something else, in this case a region and the people living and traveling within it. But a newcomer on the Icelandic film scene would go much further than Sigurgeirsson by exploring the *Hekla* eruption in aesthetically innovative ways, attempting to develop "a language" that speaks the "truth" of volcanoes.

Ósvaldur Knudsen: Nature, Animals, and People

Ósvaldur Knudsen's *Fire in Hekla* (1949/1972, *Eldur í Heklu*) is a synthesis of Vigfús Sigurgeirsson and Kjartan Ó. Bjarnason's different approaches, but it also adds many new elements. Relying on petic intertitles and shots of nature, animals, and even turf houses, it opens like a traditional Iceland-film before arriving at the site of *Hekla* prior to the eruption. Not unlike the female traveler in Bjarnason's *Rangárvallasýsla*, a male hiker walks up a cliff and takes in the view—the camera panning frequently and providing a panorama of the region. It is only now that the first eruptive column is introduced from a great distance, but it is soon followed by a few brief closer views of burning lava. The remainder of the forty minutes long film is faithful to the chronology of the eruption, and also resembles the structure of Bjarnason's film by foregrounding the perspective of travelers and scientists making their way to, and ultimately exploring, the eruption. But Knudsen's film also differs in important ways. It provides a brief historical overview of *Hekla*, it includes maps to situate the audience, and describes in more detail the chronological development of the eruption, with the aid of both intertitles and a voice-over.[7]

The unusual combination of explanatory intertitles and voice-over together might be explained by Knudsen's continuous development of his footage. It is instructive to compare the version released in 1949 to the "final version" completed in 1972, after Knudsen had mastered his approach to the volcano film. In some ways it is simply a shorter but more sophisticated version of the original; however, halfway through it unexpectedly moves into a different filmic register. The voice-over cuts off and the film privileges pure spectacle—lingering on plumes of smoke and the ejection of volcanic rocks. Another such scene occurs near the end of the film that includes shots of red lava flows against stark black backgrounds (see Figure 4.1). This is plainly different from anything presented in the original version, although a simpler version of the second scene is also found in it. However, there the narrator explains that it is an overview of things that most impacted travelers during the eruption. One can also retroactively point to scenes that have the potential for such disruptive spectacle, but which are not developed in that direction. But even the 1972 version, apart from these two scenes, adheres to a more conventional documentary mode than the other films about the *Hekla* eruption.[8]

By comparing the different versions of *Fire in Hekla*, we can see how Knudsen is developing an aesthetic strategy—"a language"—to not only inform the viewer but also capture that volcanic element that cannot be put into words. After the *Hekla* eruption he would have to wait some eighteen years to film another eruption and further develop his approach. In the meantime, he filmed a variety of subjects, becoming a major chronicler of people and places in Iceland until the arrival of television in the late sixties.

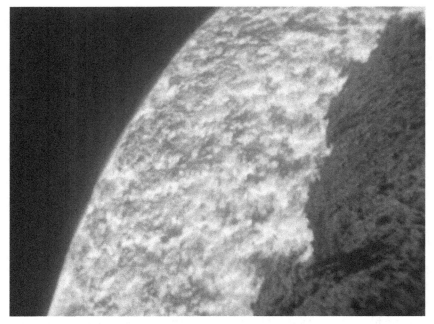

Figure 4.1 In Ósvaldur Knudsen's *Fire in Hekla* shots such as this prioritize the spectacle of fiery lava. Source: The National Film Archive of Iceland/ Kvikmyndasafn Íslands.

Following upon *Fire in Hekla*, he made his only fiction film, the short *Tents in the Woods* (1949, *Tjöld í skógi*), the same year the first Icelandic narrative feature was released. A depiction of romanticized nature and ideal boyhood, it tells the story of two boys who spend the summer camping in Þrastarskógur woods, where they study and live in close harmony with nature. They pick berries and fish for trout while the camera captures the beauty of their surroundings with close-ups of plant and animal life. Interestingly for a fiction film, *Tents in the Woods* describes the activities of the boys through a voice-over narration rather than dialogue, and the film borrows in other ways from documentary, or what would become Knudsen's preferred mode of filmmaking.

Outside his volcano films, Knudsen's oeuvre can be divided into two groups of films, all of them fifteen to thirty minutes in length. The first kind, his environmental films, are set in specific locations where nature, animals, and people coexist. Knudsen's *Hornstrandir* (1956) is a good example, and like *Sogið* (1954) and *Þjórsárdalur* (1967), it is named after the location, in this case an isolated region in the northernmost part of the already remote Westfjords. The film opens with dramatic nature footage of dark clouds, steep snow-covered mountains and forceful ocean waves, before narrator and archaeologist Kristján Eldjárn interrupts the musical score to draw attention to how "sea and land" have shaped the people of this region.[9] He describes "the mysterious beauty" of the harsh and isolated environment in which "no car has ever been seen." By providing a look at this unchanged region, the film also offers a glimpse into Iceland's past as the traditions of *Hornstrandir* are characterized as similar to "when the land was first settled ten centuries ago." The first example of this involves the large-scale amassing of driftwood that fills the shores of *Hornstrandir* and that is used for everything from fence posts to ornamental storage chests. Despite this, the narrator has to admit that more modern machinery has arrived to the region, and corresponding images reveal wood being cut up on a professional power-saw deck. Similarly, after a long dramatic scene of bird and egg collecting in high and steep cliffs, we are informed that the farms by the cliffs are abandoned and that the egg collectors are in fact all visitors.[10] This somber note is punctuated with numerous shots of deserted farm ruins surrounded by a majestic mountain landscape. The film ends on a single piece of driftwood rolling on the waves of a "deserted beach."

Footage from this elegy for Iceland and its disappearing traditions finds its way into Friðrik Þór Friðriksson's *Children of Nature* (1992, *Börn náttúrunnar*), where it stands in for the memories of the main female protagonist, who longs for the place of her youth. Not unlike the films Loftur Guðmundsson made decades earlier (see chapter two), *Hornstrandir* and most of Knudsen's output provide rare documentation of an Iceland that no longer exists. Television would take over that role starting in the late 1960s, but without his contributions the visual history of Iceland in the two previous decades would have been much the poorer. *The Country between the Sands* (1964, *Sveitin milli sanda*), Knudsen's most celebrated film of this type, refers to a rural region in the Southeast, long isolated by sandy beaches and wide rivers that had only just been bridged when the film was made. Similar to *Hornstrandir*, it focuses on the farmers, livestock, and wildlife inhabiting the dramatic natural environment just south of the glacier *Vatnajökull*. Knudsen's work was not confined to rural environments, however, and with *Reykjavík 1955* (1955), he drew his attention to the emerging modernity of Iceland's capital. But more to the point, not all of the films were devoted to locations, whether rural or urban.

The other type of movies Knudsen made might be described as "portraits" or brief sketches, reflected in the title of his 1965 film *Sketches* (*Svipmyndir*). The film opens with celebrations on Independence Day, and while it includes official events, it focuses on more mundane activities, such as views of everyday people encountering the city, before shifting its attention to some of the most celebrated artists, painters, composers, and writers in Iceland. Instead of interviews or traditional biographies, the emphasis is on producing "sketches" of them, whether at work or leisure. Apparently recorded without sound, the film is again narrated by Eldjárn, who identifies many of the celebrities attending the seventy-fifth birthday of author Gunnar Gunnarsson (see chapter 3). The film engages with the political and especially cultural elite of the country, but for the most part, it addresses them in the same modest manner that it does the farmers in the regional documentaries.

Most of the films in this category are devoted to a single artist, but the approach remains remarkably similar. Knudsen's film *Þórbergur Þórðarson* (1961) opens with the writer on his daily walks in a wintery landscape just outside Reykjavík, before traveling to the Southeast to the farm of his youth, where he serves as a kind of guide to the countryside. It is worth pointing out how little the film highlights Þórðarsson's writing career, instead creating a portrait of the man that focuses on everyday activities, such as taking a walk or a nap, exercising at the beach, and so on. Equally important to the film is its emphasis on beautiful landscapes or close-ups of animals in the countryside segment, so much so that even in Knudsen's portrait films, nature and the environment remain central. First and foremost, as "sketches," these movies are even further removed from conventional documentaries than the volcano films. Admittedly the film *Halldór Kiljan Laxness* (1962) opens with a celebration of the author's Nobel Prize award and includes ample footage from the 1955 ceremony and subsequent celebrations, where Laxness meets Swedish royalty and Arne Mattson, the director of the film adaptation of *Salka Valka* (1954), among other guests. The film features part of the author's own reception speech and also those given by a variety of artists and politicians upon his return to Iceland. Nonetheless, ten minutes into the twenty-four-minute film, Knudsen reverts to the strategies informing his other films. Laxness is seen hiking, playing the piano, swimming (see Figure 4.2), or reading from some of his books, and everyday objects in his home at *Glúfrasteinn* are singled out with close-ups. The rather stiff and quasi-official celebrations of the film's opening, then, are replaced by the director's

Figure 4.2 Nobel laureate Halldór Kiljan Laxness relaxes in his swimming pool in one of Ósvaldur Knudsen's many documentaries devoted to celebrated Icelandic writers and artists. Source: The National Film Archive of Iceland/ Kvikmyndasafn Íslands.

sketch mode. Interestingly, the film about Þórðarsson is characterized by a similar split, but it concludes rather than opens with a party honoring him—even echoing the voice-over in *Sketches*, with which Eldjárn identified the esteemed guests at Gunnarsson's celebration. The division is of a different nature than that of Knudsen's volcano films, but it is significant that they should also be characterized by such opposing extremes.[11]

Two years before Knudsen completed *Sketches*, an underwater eruption began just southwest of Iceland that would last four years, ultimately forming the new island of *Surtsey*. Knudsen's chronicle of the process from start to finish would form the basis of two of his major volcano films. The Icelandic title of the first, *Surtur fer sunnan* (1965, "Surtur travels south"), is far more poetic than the descriptive English title, *Birth of an Island*. It refers to the formidable giant Surtur, whom the new island, *Surtsey* (literally "island of Surtur"), is named after. Surtur brings fire and destruction to the battle of Ragnarök in "The Prophesy of the Seeress," the very same poem that Werner

60   LIGHT IN THE DARK

Herzog quotes in *Into the Inferno*. The film begins with images and sounds from the eruption that continue during the opening credits, but when they conclude, the film reverts back to a conventional documentary. Maps display the active volcano zones in Iceland, and narrator Alan Boucher directs us to the *Vestmannaeyjar* Islands.[12] We are given a few glimpses of peaceful life in *Vestmannaeyjabær*, the town named after the archipelago, framed with the volcano *Helgafell* behind it. A map reveals the location of the eruption in relation to the *Vestmannaeyjar* Islands, followed by shots of the eruption taken from them: "The eruption was an impressive sight from the Islands and from a closer view it was overwhelming." At this point the narration fades out, providing time to take in that very sight. In its early stage as a submarine eruption, there is no eruptive fire or flowing lava typical of land eruptions. Instead, the encounter between lava and sea produces powerful explosions of black and white mass. After providing cartographic representations of the new island, the film cuts to footage of the first expedition to the site. Instead of moving to the traditional documentary aesthetics, as one might have expected, *Birth of an Island* does something surprising. The first visitors take in the spectacle before them and again Boucher's voice-over disappears, inviting viewers to concentrate on the eruption itself. Shortly the humans disappear from the frame altogether, replaced with an experimental musical score by Magnús Blöndal Jóhannsson, its dissonant tones working in concert with images of the eruption. The film has now abandoned documentary for experimental cinema: the constantly shifting shape of the gigantic eruptive column, the struggle between black and white explosions, the dramatic compilation of discordant viewpoints, and shots too close to provide any situational context (see Figure 4.3). Two and a half minutes pass before the expository voice-over returns, but it struggles to compete with the musical score and visual spectacle. Almost halfway through the film, the voice-over reveals that in April 1964 the new land had formed, implicitly promising a new visual splendor that comes with actual lava flow.

The filmmakers now join a group of scientists visiting the new island to take in its astonishing landscapes, only to be followed by another scene of pure cinema, which includes shots of unusual rock formations and vibrant lava erupting or flowing against stark black backgrounds (see Figure 4.4). The subsequent close-ups of the exploding lava river, accompanied by Jóhannsson's score, might constitute the first images of an avant-garde cinema in Iceland, providing a breathtaking example of what the film medium can capture.[13] Perhaps what makes these sequences so surprising

Figures 4.3 and 4.4 *Birth of an Island* is the culmination of Ósvaldur Knudsen's experimentations with volcanic imagery and sound. The constantly shifting columns create a formalistic struggle between black and white (4.3). Essentially, the interplay between pure form, color, and movement results in the first avant-garde aesthetics of Icelandic film history (4.4). Source: The National Film Archive of Iceland/Kvikmyndasafn Íslands.

is how they alternate with scenes mobilizing conventional documentary strategies, in what is not only a fundamental aspect of Knudsen's films but also, I would argue, a defining feature of the volcano film. In other words, this type of film might be characterized by the contradictory impulses toward both visual pleasure and the need to explain it. And indeed, Buchner will return briefly to explain the lava river to us, but his voice is inobtrusive and often gives way to the pure spectacle and experimental score. We might very well call these extended scenes "volcano montage," and the final one in *Birth of an Island* appropriately returns us obliquely to the beginning by showing us the clash of lava and sea as the lava now flows off the new island and into the ocean surrounding it.

Land Out of the Ocean (1973), Knudsen's other film about *Surtsey*, also refers to Norse mythology in its Icelandic title, *Jörð úr Ægi* ("Land out of Aegir"), in this case a giant associated with the ocean. Despite their similarities, the two films deviate from one another in important ways. While *Birth of an Island* avoids showing people in relation to the eruption until they arrive at the island, *Land Out of the Ocean* begins with them traveling on boats toward the eruption. The latter film recycles some shots of the eruption from the former film; however, as a kind of sequel, it is far more invested in what happens after. A couple of other islands are formed from new volcanic activity but both soon sink below sea level, while new small craters emerge on *Surtsey* itself. These become the material for volcano montage sequences comparable to those found in *Birth of an Island*. But the latter half of the film is devoted to post-volcanic activity, including scientists now conducting research in their laboratories rather than on the island. Rather interestingly, the representation of the emerging life on the island—flocks of birds in long shots and various plants in close-ups, shifts us into the territory of Knudsen's environmental films, in an attempt to capture the coexistence of nature, animals, and people (if only scientists).

Both *Birth of an Island* and *Land Out of the Ocean* repeatedly identify the *Vestmannaeyjar* Islands on the maps that they feature due to the archipelago's proximity to *Surtsey*. The footage of the town *Vestmannaeyjabær* in *Birth of an Island* provides a peaceful foil to the violent eruption nearby. No one could have anticipated that in 1973, *Heimaey*, the inhabited island of *Vestmannaeyjar*, would experience the most dramatic Icelandic volcanic eruption in terms of risk posed to human lives. Knudsen's *Fire on Heimaey* (*Eldur í Heimaey*), released only a year later, begins with the eruption, but it soon travels back in time to provide a chronological timeline of life before, during, and after the eruption. The successful evacuation includes dramatic footage of workers rescuing valuables while houses burn or pumping seawater to slow the flow of lava, slag and ash fallout covering large portions of the town, and cemetery crosses sticking out of the ash. More houses are destroyed when the lava breaks through a barrier, but by the end of winter, the eruption subsides and the extensive cleanup begins. Miraculously no one is killed, and the film ends happily with the renewal of grass and the return of children—and in a stroke of good luck, the land formed by the lava flowing into the sea makes for a much better natural harbor than what was there before.

Fire on Heimaey bears the signature of Knudsen, but it also stands apart in a number of ways. The film contains visually striking shots of volcanic activity, but they are shorter than the drawn-out volcano montages of his previous work. The lava flows captured in the *Surtsey* films are pure spectacle, given that little information is provided about their timing, location, or larger role in the eruption. The lava flows in *Fire on Heimaey*, on the other hand, are typically supplemented with narration. For example, upon a change in direction, the audience is notified that "the lava is flowing away from town." This is understandable considering that *Fire on Heimaey* is not solely about a volcanic eruption; it is also about the dangers facing an entire community and its miraculous rescue. As a result, it lacks the visual and sonic experimentation of Knudsen's other works. Still, it reflects the aesthetics of the volcano film more than *Days of Destruction* (1973, *Eldeyjan*), the other major film about the Heimaey eruption, by Ernst Kettler, Ásgeir Long, and Páll Steingrímsson. Admittedly, *Days of Destruction* also opens with images of a volcanic eruption, but they are supplemented with an explanatory if incongruous voice-over that does not correspond with the images we are watching. More perplexing is the film's narrated overview of other historical ordeals, including a pirate raid that took place in 1627, during which many islanders were abducted and sold into slavery. It is as if, unlike Knudsen, the filmmakers do not trust the images to stand on their own. Despite a few visually and sonically experimental moments, the emphasis is rather on evacuees, including many close-ups that reveal their distress and anxiety during a meeting on the mainland.

The *Heimaey* eruption also finds its way into a surprising number of non-Icelandic films. The narrator of Chris Marker's *Sans Soleil* (1983) evocatively compares footage of the eruption shot by the Kraffts' mentor Haroun Tazieff with older footage from *Vestmannaeyjar* in 1965. The poetic voice-over in

Marker's film seems also to have influenced the narration of Sara Dosa's *Fire of Love*, a film that also has footage of the *Heimaey* eruption during which the Kraffts were working with Tazieff. Herzog's documentary tribute, *The Fire Within: A Requiem for Katia and Maurice Krafft* (2022), includes footage the Kraffts filmed of the eruption, as well as images of Maurice contemplating the eruption. At another point in the film, with the Kraffts filming volcanoes in Hawaii, Herzog declares: "They are no longer volcanologists. They are artists who carry us, the spectators, away in a realm of strange beauty. This is a vision that exists only in dreams. There is nothing more that can be said. We can only watch in awe." Like those of Knudsen's narrators, Herzog's voice-over fades away, inviting us now to linger on the volcanic images.[14] Herzog describes their footage correctly as breathtaking, but it is hardly any more so than Knudsen's volcano montages and it is regrettable that they are not better known.

Knudsen, as a chronicler of volcanoes, finds his counterpart in Magnús Jóhannsson (not to be confused with Knudsen's composer), who began his career by filming glaciers. *A Winter Trip* (1952, *Vetrarferð*) documents the journey of a Bombardier snowmobile crew traveling from Reykjavík to *Akureyri*, by way of the Highlands. The voice-over narrator explains that the goal of the expedition is both to test the snowmobile in the most challenging of circumstances and to satisfy the travelers' desire for adventure. Jóhannsson's follow-up film, *Glacial Adventure* (*Björgunin á Vatnajökli*), tells the story of a remarkable rescue operation on the *Vatnajökull* Glacier during the winter of 1951. It opens with a prologue about the beauty of Iceland's glacial Highlands. The narrator questions whether Iceland should have been named "Fireland" ("Eldland") in light of its mild climate and geothermal heat, eventually confirming the accuracy of its "cold" name due to the country's many large glaciers. Following the prologue, the film informs us of a rescue mission conducted by the US Air Force Air Rescue Service, then based at the *Keflavík* Naval Air Station, in which a Douglas DC 3 airplane landed on *Vatnajökull* with the help of skis rather than wheels. Unfortunately, the three-man crew was not able to take off from the glacier, leaving nine rather than six individuals stranded, who would then have to be rescued by land. *Glacial Adventure*'s main focus, however, was on the retrieval of the plane itself near the end of that winter. The mission took twelve men four weeks to accomplish, with extensive footage capturing these most challenging circumstances.

Jóhannsson's next film, *The Highlands of Iceland* (1954, *Hálendi Íslands*), is a survey of popular locations around the country, including Lake *Mývatn*, *Geysir*, and the waterfalls *Gullfoss* and *Dettifoss*. Despite the film's title, most of the sites it tours are actually not located in the Highlands. Notably, there is also an absence of glacial imagery, with the now historically distant 1947 *Hekla* eruption added to the mix. Moreover, in stark contrast to the opening of *Glacial Adventure*, the narrator here concludes that Iceland has "rightly earned its name as land of frost and fire."[15] It is also instructive to compare the original *Glacial Adventure* to a new version made a couple of decades later that maintains the overall structure but includes significant alterations.[16] The prologue is now less focused on glaciers, and it features hot springs and volcanoes in order to strike a balance between elements of fire and ice. This time the film's travels from Reykjavík to the rescue in *Vatnajökull* Glacier include a stopover at Mount *Hekla* that uses footage from the 1970 eruption. While Jóhannsson's early documentaries might be understood as a foil to Knudsen's volcano films, his later work increasingly replaces ice with fire.

If there is such a thing as a golden age of Icelandic volcano cinema, it comes to an end with the *Heimaey* eruption. We might attribute this to the fact that an eruption of comparable drama has not occurred since, and that Knudsen passed away a year after completing his film about it. More importantly, television gradually took over the role of reporting on and documenting volcanic eruptions. The evening news could communicate daily events far more quickly than film, and television in Iceland would usurp cinema in the production of documentaries.[17] Most ambitious in that regard was the six-part television series *Living with Violent Earth* (Jón Hermannsson and Guðmundur E. Sigvaldsson, 1989, *Hin rámu regindjúp*), which traveled beyond Iceland, touring major volcanic sites all over the world. While news reports and this kind of documentary production had some benefits, television did not carry over the aesthetic approach of the films it replaced, which seemed guided by discovering the "natural" meeting place of cinema and volcanoes.

That does not mean that volcanic eruptions disappeared altogether from cinema. Knudsen's work lived on with his son Vilhjálmur Knudsen, who was co-credited as director of *Fire on Heimaey* and who had worked closely with his father for some time. He continued to film eruptions all over the country and even began exhibiting their films for tourists in their Reykjavík theater under the name *The Volcano Show*. But he was much less productive than his father in making use of his voluminous total footage, and the rare film

Villi Knudsen's Iceland demonstrates a markedly different approach from his father's. Influenced by *The Volcano Show*, the film is in English and made with foreign viewers in mind. Knudsen plays a central role on screen as well as behind the camera, and he seems to have regularly updated the film by frequently incorporating new footage. The film begins with him walking with a camera and tripod through a wintery landscape, before he addresses the camera in a close-up, introducing himself and referencing his father's previous work. The film that follows is much closer to a conventional Icelandfilm (see chapter two)—albeit almost solely focused on volcanoes—than his father's work. However, the personal narrative and voice-over are distinctly his own. As he travels around the country, Knudsen repeatedly features lengthy footage from his father's films. For example, during his stop in *Surtsey* in 1988, he tells us it was the first eruption he witnessed when working on the film with his father in 1963, and then moves into footage from *Birth of an Island*. His own film displays none of the characteristics of their prior work, resembling instead material intended for the tourist market. Indeed, on home video formats it competed with countless other such items in tourist shops, including coffee table books that contained work by some of Iceland's best-known photographers.[18] Rather, Steingrímsson, who also got his first filmmaking credit shooting the *Heimaey* eruption, might be a closer heir to Ósvaldur Knudsen, especially considering his continued engagement with Icelandic nature, animals, and people in numerous documentaries up to the present day.

Twenty-First-Century Fire and Ice

The new century has seen two major volcanic eruptions. In 2010 the eruption of the glacier *Eyjafjallajökull* generated such a powerful ash cloud that European air space was repeatedly closed, causing the largest air traffic disturbance since World War II. On the other hand, it had little impact upon domestic air travel. Instead, it turned out to be gratis global advertisement for the tourism industry—a territory that proponents of Icelandic cinema have often claimed for their own. The second major eruption is actually an ongoing series of eruptions originating from the same region on *Reykjanes* Peninsula; first in *Geldingardalir* Valley in 2021, then Mount *Fagradalsfjall* the following year, and two eruptions in 2023, one at Mount *Litli Hrútur*, and another at *Sundhnúkar*, just north of the town of *Grindavík*.[19] These eruptions were not powerful on any scientific scale, but their impact has been considerable because of their location on *Reykjanes*, not far from the capital Reykjavík and close to the international airport at *Keflavík*. The first three have been aptly referred to as "tourist-eruptions" as they presented little risk, and domestic and international travelers visited the site in large numbers. Conversely, the fourth one was preceded by extensive faulting, responsible for severe cracking through the town of *Grindavík*. Fearing the eruption could literally happen in the town itself, the authorities quickly evacuated its 4,000 inhabitants—the first such evacuation since the *Heimaey* eruption. Although the eruption occurred two and a half miles north of the town, subsequent *Sundhnúkar* eruptions in 2024 reached the edge of town and it was only the erection of defensive walls that prohibited further damage by directing the lava flow away from *Grindavík*.[20]

While the twenty-first-century eruptions have received plenty of media attention in Iceland and elsewhere, not many films have been made about them. There is the already discussed *Fire and Iceland* that deals with the *Reykjanes* eruptions, but the most ambitious film about the *Eyjafjallajökull* eruption is Herbert Sveinbjörnsson's feature-length documentary *Ash* (2013, *Aska*). The film begins with dramatic images of the volcanic eruption, but it is first and foremost about the struggles of a few farming families living right under the volcano. Although clearing the ash from their farms is no easy task, one farmer admits it is nothing like the financial difficulties they suffered due to the economic collapse two years prior. While some families depart, owing to the double blow of the collapse and the eruption, the farmers at Þorvaldseyri resourcefully turn their farm into a tourist center. *Ash* ends up being a conventional documentary that captures the farming families in their daily lives and in straightforward interview set-ups, but its interest in the eruption itself is limited. *Eruption on Mount Fimmvörðuháls* (Hrafnhildur Gunnarsdóttir, 2010, *Gos á Fimmvörðuhálsi*), a very brief film that consists of a single volcano montage sequence without any documentary context, is arguably closest to an outright volcano film. It prefigured the profusion of amateur films of the *Reykjanes* eruptions that were shot using drones, which flooded *YouTube* and comparable platforms. The most popular of these have been viewed over millions of times, and along with stationary cameras whose feed can be viewed live online at any time, they are another challenge to the existence of volcano films proper.

Although its future prospects may be uncertain, there is no doubt that the volcano film has been crucial to Icelandic documentary cinema. In comparison, one is struck by the marginal role volcanoes play in Icelandic feature filmmaking.[21] It was not until *Volcano* (Rúnar Rúnarsson, *Eldfjall*) was released in 2011 that an Icelandic film focusing on an eruption appears to have emerged. The powerful opening credit sequence begins with documentary footage from *Fire on Heimaey*, accompanied by "Hear, smith of the heavens" ("Heyr himna smiður"), a somber Icelandic funeral hymn. But the film thereafter focuses on a character who lives in Reykjavík, having departed the island during the evacuation. Despite its title or opening sequence, then, the rest of the film focuses on the trauma of being forced to leave one's home—the cause, whether a volcanic eruption or something else, matters little. More recently, the Icelandic remake of the Italian comedy *Perfect Strangers* (Paolo Genovese, 2016, *Perfetti sconosciuti*) cleverly incorporated the *Geldingardalir* Valley eruption into the plot of a dinner party gone sour when the guests decide to share their revealing cell phone conversations. In *Wild Game* (Elsa María Jakobsdóttir, 2023, *Villibráð*) the eruption begins during the party and it advances the dramatic buildup of the plot as the evening progresses. In its brief epilogue, one of the male characters admits to having had a second phone, and thus having cleverly hidden his secrets during the dinner party. The film ends with him destroying the evidence in the lava of the volcano he is visiting with his buddies from the party. But more than any film, it is the series *Katla* (Baltasar Kormákur, 2021) that makes the greatest use of volcanoes in its plotting. An eruption in the eponymous volcano has left the town of *Vík* mostly empty of inhabitants. As the *Mýrdalsjökull* Glacier, on which *Katla* is located, begins to melt, mysterious beings emerge, leading from one strange event to another. *Katla* is without a doubt the most ambitious attempt to incorporate the topic of volcanoes into a popular miniseries format. Whether due to the presence of the volcano or not, its genre boundaries are unusually fluid, with melodrama, romance, fantasy, folklore, mystery, horror, and science fiction all in evidence. At the opposite end of the spectrum, *Godland* (Hlynur Pálmason, 2022, *Volaða land/Vanskabte Land*) uses footage from the *Geldingardalir* eruption to depict the 1875 *Askja* eruption. But the volcano is never specified and plays no role in the film's plot. Instead, the footage unexpectedly makes its way into the film halfway through, mirroring the aesthetics of Ósvaldur Knudsen's documentaries. For a little while, we are invited to forget all about the narrative and just take in the visual splendor of a volcanic eruption.

These three features and the series *Katla* engage compellingly with volcanoes, but overall their contributions might be considered rather meager for the "land of fire and ice."[22] Although hardly common, ice plays a slightly larger role than its counterpart. Arguably the ultimate Icelandic Arctic film, Friðrik Þór Friðriksson's *Cold Fever* (1995, *Á köldum klaka*) follows the Japanese visitor Hirata (Masatoshi Nagase) as he travels around the wondrous winterscape of Iceland. The strange world of *Noi the Albino* (Dagur Kári, 2003, *Nói albínói*) is characterized by an "ice blue" color palette. In general, there is a strong correlation between the representation of exciting nature imagery and an appeal to global audiences. Thus films like *Cold Fever*, *Agnes* (Egill Eðvarðsson, 1995), *Cold Light* (Hilmar Oddsson, 2004, *Kaldaljós*) and, to a certain extent, *101 Reykjavík* (Baltasar Kormákur, 2000) make pronounced use of Arctic landscapes rarely seen in the locally produced cinema. Arctic imagery is likewise found in films indebted to Hollywood genre cinema like the glacial-thrillers *Cold Trail* (Björn Br. Björnsson, 2006, *Köld slóð*), *Frost* (Reynir Lyngdal, 2012), and *Operation Napoleon* (Óskar Þór Axelsson, 2023, *Napóleonsskjölin*). Standing alone in its realistic engagement with nature, *The Deep* (Baltasar Kormákur, 2012, *Djúpið*) is a factual account of a local fisherman (Ólafur Darri Ólafsson) who miraculously managed to swim ashore after his vessel and fellow crew sank six kilometers from land during high winter, with ice, snow, and the Northern Lights on full display (see chapter eleven for a fuller discussion of Arctic imagery in Hollywood runaway productions filmed in Iceland).

In documentaries, on the other hand, the dominance of fire might be explained by the unique drama and movement of volcanic eruptions, offering a dynamism not shared by the transformation of glaciers, which is too slow to witness with the human eye. One suspects this is one reason why Magnús Jóhannsson gradually shifted from glacial to volcanic imagery. Of course, glaciers are melting as a result of global warming, and in *Chasing Ice* (Jeff Orlowski, 2012), American photographer James Balog is shocked to discover just how much *Sólheimajökull* Glacier (an outlet glacier of *Vatnajökull*) has shrunk. In an effort to document the loss, he launches the Extreme Ice Survey project, in which two dozen cameras in Iceland, Greenland, Canada, and the United States (Alaska) are timed to take one photograph every hour. Balog believes the visual evidence his film can provide is far more impactful than the statistics, graphs, or scientific evidence more typically used to argue the reality of climate change. *Chasing Ice*, it seems, is another vivid example of Siegfried Kracauer's theory that cinema can help us see what remains hidden to our eyes.[23] However, the accelerated glacial footage is not enough to carry the documentary; the filmmakers also add excitement by featuring dogsleds and helicopters to reach the distant camera sites. *Chasing Ice* also relies on Balog's own visually arresting glacial photographs, along with unrelated news sequences of extreme weather around the world. The most visually and aurally arresting, though, are scenes of glacial calving when gigantic ice blocks break off from their glaciers and the climax of the film—along with the results of the sped-up camera footage of glacial shrinking—is powerful footage of "the largest witnessed calving event."

The two closest Icelandic candidates to *Chasing Ice* are *Glacial Land: A World of Changes* (Gunnlaugur Þór Pálsson, Anna Dís Ólafsdóttir, and Jóhann Sigfússon, 2016, *Jöklaland: Veröld breytinga*), which focuses on climate change and glacial shrinkage in Iceland, and *Last Days of the Arctic* (Magnús Viðar Sigurðsson, 2011, *Andlit norðursins*), which follows celebrated photographer Ragnar Axelsson as he traverses some of the same region as Balog. However, RAX, as the photographer is best known, is just as interested in the people as in their environment (the literal meaning of the Icelandic title is "Faces of the North"). Composer Jóhann Jóhannsson's experimental *End of Summer* (2014, *Sumarlok*), filmed at the opposite end of the globe, is also relevant here. Composed of lengthy black-and-white 8mm shots, it depicts penguins and a few sea lions in their environment before the Arctic imagery takes on an almost abstract form. If *End of Summer* shares a certain kinship with Knudsen's formally innovative volcano sequences, Jóhannsson's images of snow also provide an antithetical aesthetics in its slow pace. Also unlike the dissonant and jarring score by composer Magnús Blöndal that accompanied Knudsen's vibrant volcano imagery, Jóhannsson's music (composed with Hildur Guðnadóttir and Robert A. A. Lowe) is moody and atmospheric. *End of Summer* leads naturally to Jóhannsson's *Last and First Men* (2020), whose synthesis of Olaf Stapledon's classic science fiction novel and Yugoslavian war memorials is about the end of mankind; it is arguably the most formally ambitious Icelandic film since the days of Knudsen's volcano montages.

5
Overview II, 1980–1999

As we have seen, the history of documentary filmmaking prior to 1980 is in many ways quite lively, with something akin to continuous production dating back to at least the mid-1930s, but that picture is much altered when addressing narrative features. Nonetheless, we did come across a few in the first part of this work; some were solely shot in Iceland or were adapted from Icelandic literary works, while others were clearly local productions. It would thus be inaccurate to claim that Icelandic features only emerged with the introduction of the Icelandic Film Fund in 1978. Nonetheless, the Fund marks a historical turning point by guaranteeing systematic film production—even though ultimately it assisted with only a fraction of production costs. We should not take it as given that a small country like Iceland should make films systematically; indeed, without the Fund we might not have an Icelandic cinema to speak of. In other words, filmmaking existed in various forms in Iceland prior to the 1980s, but it is only after the Fund that we can speak of a national cinema proper.

Although the state initiated public radio broadcasts in 1930 and television in 1966, and maintained a monopoly of both until 1986, it never established an official film body until the Icelandic Film Fund was founded in 1978. The rationale for it echoes the long-standing and continuous support of national culture and arts dating back to the mid-twentieth century, including the founding of the National Theater and the Icelandic Symphony Orchestra in 1950, the Icelandic Ballet in 1973, and salary funds for writers and other artists in 1975 (with earlier precedents). Establishing the Fund was an effort to protect and support Icelandic culture, and there was a tacit understanding that the arts could not thrive in such a small country without state support. In regard to cinema, it was considered important for the well-being and continuous independence of the nation to make films in Icelandic, about Icelandic society and history, and by Icelandic filmmakers who had long fought for the right to practice their craft. Perhaps the argument for national filmmaking was further motivated by the fact that Icelanders visit film theaters in record numbers, but watch almost solely Hollywood films. The presumption was therefore that the state-supported films should have a national focus, as the films of the early 1980s were to do.

The two key films of the first year of what was soon to be referred to as the "Icelandic film spring" shared this national approach. Ágúst Guðmundsson's *Land and Sons* (*Land og synir*) and Hrafn Gunnlaugsson's *Father's Estate* (*Óðal feðranna*) were filmed in Icelandic by local crews, and they addressed nationally specific topics—focusing on the relationship between the capital Reykjavík and rural farming communities.[1] The national emphasis during the early 1980s was also evidenced by the numerous adaptations of prestigious literary works, including *Dot Dot Comma Dash* (Þorsteinn Jónsson, 1981, *Punktur punktur komma strik*), *The Outlaw* (Ágúst Guðmundsson, 1981, *Útlaginn*), and the two Halldór Laxness adaptations, *The Atom Station* (Þorsteinn Jónsson, 1984, *Atómstöðin*) and *Under the Glacier* (Guðný Halldórsdóttir, 1987, *Kristnihald undir jökli*). But this prioritization of literary adaptations did not last long, and there is little to suggest that adaptations are more common in Icelandic cinema than in other national cinemas—if anything, they are rather rare. Another common misconception about Icelandic cinema is the supposed influence of the Old Norse literary heritage, but the fact is *The Saga of Gisli Sursson* (*The Outlaw*) remains the only saga adaptation to this day. However, Gunnlaugsson's trilogy *The Raven Flies* (1984, *Hrafninn flýgur*), *In the Shadow of the Raven* (1987, *Í skugga hrafnsins*), and *The White Viking* (1991, *Hvíti víkingurinn*) undeniably lends the decade something of a Viking impression, even though the director's role models were sought outside that heritage just as much as they were within.

The films of the spring far surpassed the pioneering efforts of Loftur Guðmundsson and Óskar Gíslason in professional sophistication, but they were similarly modest in their aesthetic approach. The emphasis was on the story itself, and directors typically presented it in a straightforward manner to the audience. Comedies—often considered the most local of genres—dominated, including the box-office hits *On Top* (Ágúst Guðmundsson, 1982, *Með allt á hreinu*), *The Icelandic Shock Station* (Þórhildur Þorleifsdóttir, 1986, *Stella í orlofi*), and the *Life-Trilogy* (Þráinn Bertelsson, 1983–1985). Women filmmakers made huge contributions to this first decade of Icelandic national cinema, with Guðný Halldórsdóttir, Kristín Jóhannesdóttir, Kristín Pálsdóttir, Róska, and Þórhildur Þorleifsdóttir debuting their feature films. Unfortunately, women have played a less prominent role ever since, and this absence has diminished the diversity of Icelandic filmmaking, which has been undeniably male-centered. Women are not only more likely to tell stories about women, but during this foundational decade their films were also more aesthetically ambitious and wide ranging than those of their male counterparts. Finally, in terms of production, the new Film Fund focused its limited resources almost entirely on narrative feature filmmaking, thus marginalizing documentaries. Nevertheless, the decade saw extensive work done on Icelandic fishing history by Sigurður Sverrir Pálsson and Erlendur Sveinsson, while a couple of music documentaries by Friðrik Þór Friðriksson caught the spotlight—and he was to become the most celebrated Icelandic filmmaker of the following decade.

Important changes also took place around film exhibition. The first multiplex opened in 1977, but in the 1980s they multiplied and began making inroads in the suburbs. In response to this expansion, the large single-screen downtown theaters began adding smaller screens. However, step by step they made way for suburban multiplexes. Currently the only downtown theater is the original 1977 multiplex, now refashioned as a cinematheque that relies on various kinds of financial support. It is worth noting that the Americanization of theatrical exhibition began in the midst of the very national film spring of the 1980s.

Many of the decade's early films were immensely popular at the box office—some were seen by a quarter and even a third of the national population. Attendance numbers were not collected as systematically as they are today, but the case has been made that *On Top*—the most popular of all the spring films—was seen by close to half the national population.[2] These stunning numbers did not hold up as the novelty of seeing Icelandic films began to wear off. During this period, directors typically produced films at their own financial risk, and since the Fund's contribution was small, it only took one box office flop for filmmakers to jeopardize their future careers. As attendance numbers continued to drop throughout the eighties, the future prospects for Icelandic filmmaking were not particularly promising at the end of the decade.

It was the introduction of foreign film funds, especially the Nordic Film and Television Fund and the pan-European Eurimages, that came to the rescue. In stark contrast to the locally funded film of the prior decade, Icelandic films of the nineties received considerable finance from abroad, which included both film funds and co-producers. However, this trend did not undermine the primary role of the Icelandic Film Fund because foreign support was typically contingent upon a prior financing promise from the Fund. Nevertheless, this new financial environment would transform Icelandic filmmaking throughout the nineties.

During the eighties all paradigms had been national: films centered on local stories (many drawing upon canonical literature), were often set in the countryside, and were filmed for a national audience. The typical film of the nineties, on the other hand, could just as well take place abroad, was influenced by the European art film, and was made with the international film festival circuit and foreign audiences in mind. More than any other film, it was Friðriksson's *Children of Nature* (1991, *Börn náttúrunnar*)— the first Icelandic film to be nominated for an Academy Award—that heralded this shift. The film's international paradigm became even more conspicuous in the director's next two films, *Movie Days* (1994, *Bíódagar*) and *Cold Fever* (1995, *Á köldum klaka*)—the latter an English-language film focusing on American and Japanese travelers in Iceland. This international shift was far from limited to Friðriksson: Hilmar Oddsson left an isolated Icelandic fjord in *The Beast* (1987, *Eins og skepnan deyr*) for Nazi Germany in *Tears of Stone* (1995, *Tár úr steini*); Halldórsdóttir traveled from the *Snæfellsnes* Peninsula of *Under the Glacier* to Germany with *The Men's Choir* (1992, *Karlakórinn Hekla*); and the French visit Jóhannesdóttir in *As in Heaven* (1992, *Svo á jörðu sem himni*) and Gísli Snær Erlingsson in *Behind Schedule* (1993, *Stuttur Frakki*).

The foreign financing of Icelandic cinema, then, has consequence for both the films' subjects and aesthetics. In some cases, this new approach worked well, but in others, it resulted in a perfunctory narrative structure designed to fulfill co-production stipulations. As time passed, such stipulations eased, especially as continent-wide criticism of opportunistic co-productions— increasingly referred to as Europuddings—emerged. At the same time, Icelandic filmmakers became increasingly skilled at hiding such foreign contributions, by directing them behind the camera rather than placing them conspicuously in front of it. One result is the disproportionate role played by foreign cinematographers in Icelandic cinema beginning in the nineties.

Interestingly, Friðriksson himself took a U-turn in the latter half of the decade with two immensely popular adaptations of contemporary Icelandic novels, *Devil's Island* (1996, *Djöflaeyjan*) and *Angels of the Universe* (2000, *Englar alheimsins*). Their success at the local box office also confirmed that Icelandic audiences preferred local productions over those intended for the international market—and that remains the case to this day. Two surprising box-office hits at the beginning of the nineties introduced other novelties. Even though they sought models from abroad—North American rather than European—their tenor was local. Both *Remote Control* (Óskar Jónasson, 1992, *Sódóma Reykjavík*) and *Wallpaper* (Júlís Kemp, 1992, *Veggfóður*) told humorous stories of young people in Reykjavík entangled in criminal subplots, with soundtracks that privileged popular music, and in doing so made contemporary Reykjavík central to Icelandic cinema for the first time. A similar emphasis shaped *Dream Hunters* (1996, *Draumadísir*) by Ásdís Thoroddsen, the only new woman filmmaker of the decade, and although her debut *Ingaló* (1992) was a much more serious affair, both films focused on young women.

In the next chapter I will closely analyze two pioneering films of the early 1980s, *Land and Sons* and *Father's Estate*, and the role of the countryside more broadly, before looking at the shift to the city a decade later. Chapter seven then focuses on the transnational turn in Icelandic cinema. I begin by looking at the authorship of Friðriksson and his extensive contribution to Icelandic cinema during this period, and then consider other relevant examples of transnational filmmaking in Iceland. The last chapter of this part looks closely at adaptation. Resembling the trends of Icelandic cinema more broadly, adaptation also shifts from a national emphasis during the 1980s to a transnational approach at the end of the century that was to continue into the new one. This becomes apparent when comparing the adaptation of the saga heritage in *The Outlaw* and Gunnlaugsson's Viking trilogy with explicitly transnational adaptations like *101 Reykjavík* (Baltasar Kormákur, 2000) and *Cold Light* (Hilmar Oddsson, 2004, *Kaldaljós*). The latter not only are European co-productions but also develop narrative strategies to address foreign audiences directly.

6
The Countryside versus the City

In *The Country and the City*, Raymond Williams observed that English literature remained rural long after England had been transformed by urbanization.[1] Although urbanization occurred much later in Iceland, the same phenomenon can be observed regarding Icelandic literature. While most villages grew in size during the early decades of the twentieth century, it was only Reykjavík that developed into a city. But if Reykjavík had become the center of commerce, culture, and politics in Iceland, in addition to housing close to half the population at mid-century, it was not until "the seventies [that] Reykjavik finally [became] the capital of Icelandic fiction."[2] As a modern craft centered in the capital, one might have expected Icelandic filmmakers to follow the recent literary shift toward the capital when Icelandic national cinema was established in the early 1980s. What happened was everything but, as Icelandic filmmakers turned to the past, the countryside, and the national literary heritage, in the tradition of conservative Icelandic nationalism dating back to its roots in the mid-nineteenth century. The desire to convince the local population and the state of the national relevance of indigenous filmmaking is likely to have been an underlying motivation.

Conflict in the Countryside

There is a certain risk in generalizing too broadly the emphasis on the countryside, as it varied greatly from film to film. The breakthrough films of 1980, Ágúst Guðmundsson's *Land and Sons* (*Land og synir*) and Hrafn Gunnlaugsson's *Father's Estate* (*Óðal feðranna*), both deal with a generational shift regarding rural Iceland. Both also display its dire economic situation and the urge to leave it for the city, and both reach a narrative climax with symbolic scenes involving horses. Nonetheless, they ultimately offer fundamentally different perspectives on the countryside. In the hope of capturing the range within this national emphasis on the countryside, this chapter will engage in a close analysis of these two pioneering films before addressing the belated arrival of the city to the scene a decade later.

As a literary adaptation set in the countryside of the past, *Land and Sons* epitomizes what, in the context of English cinema, Andrew Higson has defined as the heritage film:

> a genre of films which reinvents and reproduces, and in some case simply invents, a national heritage for the screen. [. . .] One central representational strategy of the heritage film is reproduction of literary texts, artifacts, and landscapes which already have a privileged status within the accepted definition of the national heritage.[3]

The emphasis on heritage in *Land and Sons* and many other films of the eighties is not surprising considering the decade's emphasis on Icelandic cinema as a national institution intended to counter the pervasive influence of Hollywood filmmaking.

Although published in 1963, the novel by Indriði G. Þorsteinsson had come to occupy in 1980 a place in the national literary canon, and the film's reverence for its source was manifested in the opening credits, as Þorsteinsson was first to receive credit. Einar (Sigurður Sigurjónsson) lives alone with his father Ólafur (Jónas Tryggvason) at their farm in the mid-1930s. Despite lifelong hardship, Ólafur is devoted to the countryside, but his son sees no future in continuing the struggle. After his father passes away, Einar sells the land and slaughters the stock to cover his debts, against the wishes of his girlfriend Margrét (Guðný Ragnarsdóttir) and her father Tómas (Jón Sigurbjörnsson). Margrét ends up breaking her promise of leaving with Einar and the film concludes with him departing alone. It may be worth noting that this story is continued in *The Girl Gogo* (Erik Balling, 1962, *79 af stöðinni*) (see chapter two), although both novel and film had appeared prior to the release of *Land and Sons*—making it a prequel.

The filmmakers followed the novel's narrative accurately and filmed key dialogue scenes with minimal alterations. As Þorsteinsson's prose relies more on objective descriptions than subjective meditations, the accurate rendering of the novel does not result in heavy-handed literariness. In director Guðmundsson's own words: "The novel has a certain cinematographic feel to it. It almost reads like a screenplay."[4] In fact, the film's many cinematic scenes, capturing its natural settings with the help of atmospheric sunlight and mist, have already been laid out in the novel, even when nearing the

Figure 6.1 The mise-en-scène of *Land and Sons* nostalgically evokes the farming countryside of the past. Tómas (Jón Sigurbjörnsson) and Einar (Sigurður Sigurjónsson) get ready for the annual sheep gathering. Source: Ísfilm.

subjective: "[Ólafur] always became eloquent when it came to land and sky and light, and sometimes he had tried to convince his son about the beauty found in these three."[5] If the cinematography excels in capturing the beauty of the countryside, it is also mostly subjected to it, and camera movements and editing are used modestly. In taking such a visual but static approach to its pictorial scenery, *Land and Sons* also epitomizes the visual qualities of the heritage film. As Higson points out, they tend to be visually engrossing period dramas, despite often drawing upon celebrated literary works.[6] The same certainly applies to *Land and Sons*, whose reproduction of the past is constructed through a pictorial mise-en-scène, costume design, and, perhaps most importantly, in the primary use of the colors brown, green, and white (see Figure 6.1). The result is a nostalgic longing for the country of the past.

Land and Sons, like its predecessor *The Girl Gogo*, revolves thematically around the divide between countryside and city, although Reykjavík is never used as a setting in the later film. The countryside is linked to the nation, as is well manifested in a dialogue exchange between Ólafur and Örlygur (Þorvarður Helgason), a poet who has briefly returned to the country after moving to Denmark (which otherwise does not figure in the film):

ÖRLYGUR: The peasants' society is history.
ÓLAFUR: You have never been much for farming.

ÖRLYGUR: Dear friend. It happens everywhere and it is inescapable. And when the change happens here it will no doubt be ludicrous and fanatical. [...]
ÓLAFUR: How have you been?
ÖRLYGUR: I don't need to complain.
ÓLAFUR: Denmark is a good foster mother.
ÖRLYGUR: What do you mean?
ÓLAFUR: Nothing except that it is good to live there.
ÖRLYGUR: What should I have done here?
ÓLAFUR: Compose [poetry] in Icelandic.

If Örlygur's leaving for Denmark is presented as betrayal, Einar's departure to Reykjavík is more ambiguous. His decision to leave is unfortunate, but not unreasonable. The climax of the film, and its most vividly shot and explicitly symbolic scene, has Einar shoot his treasured white stallion, as he cannot bear the thought of selling or leaving it behind: "If you leave. All of you leaves." Einar's departure is not caused by his ambition or desire for a different life elsewhere. Unlike Örlygur, he is not opposed to farming, but the impoverished and archaic ways of the country: "There exist efficient machines, but we don't get them. We mow with a scythe. [. . .] Here everything is in decay. Here is nothing but damned misery." To a certain extent, his perspective on the countryside is endorsed by the film, but its demise is seen as tragic. The nostalgic mise-en-scène and the beautifully captured country setting work against the critique and in the end overcome Einar's harsh verbal denunciations.

Ultimately, *Land and Sons* is a mournful eulogy to the countryside. Along the lines of traditional Icelandic nationalism, it locates national values in rural areas, whose loss it mourns. It comes closest to offering a critique of that ideology during Ólafur's funeral, in which the priest, played by novelist Þorsteinsson himself, delivers a clichéd speech describing the deceased as being "poor of worldly goods, but richer than most other men in ideals." If the speech remains somewhat unclear in its intentions and hardly offers a critique of the farmers' subjection to nationalist ideology, the funeral that begins *Father's Estate* and precedes its opening credits leaves no room for ambiguity.

Relatives and friends have gathered at the deceased's estate (a rather flattering noun for the decaying farm). A well-dressed gentleman, who turns out to be a member of parliament, asks to be heard. He begins to reminiscence about the past:

> The spirit of patriotism and the struggle for independence were sustained by young men who believed in the countryside and were proud to be Icelandic and Hafsteinn [the deceased] was one of them. [...] He was one of those men that believed in the sheep and knew the importance of keeping the countryside settled.

The two sons of the deceased, Helgi (Jóhann Sigurðsson) and Stefán (Jakob Þór Einarsson), leave the room as they can no longer bear listening to the pompous speech. Helgi enlightens his younger brother and the audience alike: "Old dad, a romantic fool that allowed himself to be taken advantage of. He had no clue about what sort of society he lived in—where the capital lies."

The opening scene sets the tone for the film's sustained critique of the traditional patriotic celebration of rural Iceland, and some of its economic and political implications. Stefán's aspirations of studying in Reykjavík seem doomed after Helgi is critically injured early on and their mentally handicapped sister Helga (Guðrún Þórðardóttir) becomes pregnant after being raped by a farmhand (Sveinn M. Eiðsson). Stefán's attempts to convince his mother Guðrún (Hólmfríður Þórhallsdóttir) to sell the farm and move to Reykjavík come to naught when they are cheated out of their salmon-fishing rights, which leaves the estate worthless. Stefán no longer has any choice of leaving and is framed in the final scene, high up on a ladder, painting the farmhouse, followed by a high-angled point-of-view shot of the bus leaving for Reykjavík without him. Unlike *Land and Sons*, the tragedy is found in the protagonist being stuck in the countryside instead of leaving it. The camerawork is also devoid of any romantic and nostalgic longing for the countryside so characteristic of *Land and Sons*. Despite mostly taking place in the countryside and sometimes filming in beautiful locations, the natural settings are neither lingered on nor elevated. The camerawork is generally unobtrusive, relying extensively on close-ups, with few flourishes of its own. *Father's Estate* is no heritage film.

The way in which the two films approach similar subjects differently is well exemplified in a scene where Stefán's horses are being castrated. It is overtly symbolic of his own castration and ultimately symbolizes his inability to leave the countryside. In its gruesome explicitness, the castration scene itself has none of the tragic romanticism of the horse being shot in *Land and Sons*. Narratively the scenes have the same function, but they are executed in fundamentally different ways, as is true of the films at large.

A direct translation of the original title of *Father's Estate* is *Fathers' Estate*, but this small shift in position of the possessive apostrophe makes the allegorical intent of the title much clearer. Like *Land and Sons*, it is not only a film about the demise of one family but the demise of rural Iceland at large. It is from this perspective that the rather fanciful conspiracy plot of the pompous parliament member joining hands with the director of the county's National Cooperative and a rich businessman from the capital, in cheating Stefán and his mother out of the estate's salmon-fishing rights makes sense. It is an allegorical rendering of how the patriotic celebration of the countryside subjected farmers to the extensive economic interests of the Cooperative and businessmen and politicians located in the capital. It is therefore little wonder that *Father's Estate* caused a considerable stir on its release and was extensively debated in the media, while *Land and Sons* aroused no such hostile response.

Despite these fundamentally different perspectives on the countryside-city divide, the films have in common an explicitly local approach. The plot of *Father's Estate* takes as a given certain basic knowledge of the former National Cooperative and its twentieth-century history, which is an implicit subtext of *Land and Sons*, and thus not easily followed by a foreign audience. The same is true of other national specificities of the divide. A good example is provided by Gunnlaugsson himself when explaining why he did not make the appearance of Reykjavík more appealing in the film:

> If I had done so *Father's Estate* would probably have had a wider appeal, and possibly been more international in scope and no doubt dramatically more effective. But just as soon would the raw Icelandic reality, which I was describing, have been altered and fictionalized and I am not sure the film would have kept its credibility.[7]

Similarly, Guðmundsson says about his own approach to landscape:

> *Land and Sons* was made solely for an Icelandic audience. I never even gave it a thought that it might later be transmitted on television overseas or shown at film festivals. [...] In hindsight I can say that my first two films show a certain tendency to make proper use of the Icelandic landscape, as if we were trying to create our own visual language. But even that was more for the locals than the rest of the world, *at least in those days*.[8]

It is quite clear that the breakthrough films of the year 1980 were solely addressed to Icelanders, and that their respective production processes took no notice of any export designs.

There exists no empirical method for measuring the local, national, or global attributes of a text, and such evaluations must remain to a certain extent a subjective interpretation. However, let me suggest something akin to a local/global litmus test. Let us try to "measure" the financing, production, distribution/exhibition, narrative, and address of these two films. *Land and Sons* was solely financed by Icelandic sources; *Father's Estate* received some Swedish funding during post-production, which thus was of little influence. Both were solely made by locals in Iceland. The films were first and foremost distributed locally, along with exhibitions at special screenings and some festivals abroad, but attempts to distribute *Father's Estate* in Sweden soon faltered. The narratives were set entirely in Iceland and had principally no foreign characters. And as already stated, both films were solely addressed to Icelanders and made no attempts to describe their considerable local specificities to a foreign audience. The results of the test are altogether one-sided. We will do some more testing in the upcoming chapters of this part of the book as we progress toward the globally bent cinema of today.

In terms of craftsmanship and professionalism, *Land and Sons* and *Father's Estate* share little with the features made at mid-century. Unlike Loftur Guðmundsson and Óskar Gíslason, who acquired no formal film training, Gunnlaugsson and Guðmundsson had studied the craft in European film schools, like most of the other maverick directors of the early 1980s. However, their approach remained quintessentially local in every regard. Despite increased sophistication and professionalism, aesthetics continued to be subjected to narrative, and there was little in the way of style transcending the local specificity of their subjects. The same is broadly true of Icelandic cinema during the 1980s, which consisted mostly of adaptations of canonical Icelandic literature, comedies characterized by local humor, and stories set in the countryside and the distant past. Guðmundsson epitomized all of these as he followed up *Land and Sons* with a faithful adaptation of the medieval *Gisli Sursson's Saga*, before turning his hand to comedies. Gunnlaugsson, on the other hand, did something uncharacteristic with his next film, *Inter Nos* (1982, *Okkar á milli: Í hita og þunga dagsins*), as it was a formally adventurous narrative based upon an original script and set in contemporary Reykjavík. Furthermore, his subsequent Viking films approached the heritage in a much more cavalier manner than Guðmundsson, comparable to their different handling of the countryside (both will be analyzed in chapter eight). Gunnlaugsson was also the first director to experience anything akin to a foreign success, most notably with his first Viking film *When the Raven Flies* (1984, *Hrafninn flýgur*), which was a commercial success in Sweden and also won him the *Guldbagge* (akin to a Swedish Oscar) for best direction. But rather than pursuing a career in Sweden, Gunnlaugsson felt a strong need to return to Iceland as he did not feel at home in making Swedish/foreign narratives. The same sentiment of making films "at home" is echoed by Guðmundsson.[9] In other words, the directors who began their careers in the 1980s felt a strong need to engage with Icelandic culture and society, and their aspirations of making films abroad seem to have been limited. They also had in common a considerable reverence for the craft that was not challenged until the following decade.

The City: A Shift in Setting and Sensibility

Icelandic literature arrived belatedly to Reykjavík, but it certainly arrived much earlier than Icelandic cinema. It was not until the 1990s that the capital began to rival the countryside as the central source of narratives and settings for Icelandic cinema, beginning with the box-office successes of Júlíus Kemp's *Wallpaper* (*Veggfóður*) and Óskar Jónasson's *Remote Control* (*Sódóma Reykjavík*) in 1992. It should be noted, though, that they were far from being the first films set in Reykjavík. Two comedies directed by Þráinn Bertelsson, *A Policeman's Life* (1985, *Löggulíf*) and *Magnus* (1989, *Magnús*), were both set in the city, as were (to a considerable extent) two heritage adaptations directed by Þorsteinn Jónsson, *Dot Dot Comma Dash* (1981, *Punktur punktur komma strik*) and *Atom Station* (1984, *Atómstöðin*). But these films stood out from the general output of the 1980s, which was mostly located in the countryside. Of the thirty Icelandic features made, beginning with *Land and Sons* in 1980 and ending with *As in Heaven* (Kristín Jóhannesdóttir, 1992, *Svo á jörðu sem á himni*), the last film released prior to *Wallpaper* in 1992, only seven were set in the capital (23%). However, eighteen of the twenty-six feature films made during the remainder of the nineties took place in the capital (69%)—an almost inverse ratio.[10] This shift is remarkable not only in its extensive scope but also in its abruptness, as the last film set in the city prior to *Wallpaper* was *Magnus* from 1989.

Equally important to the shift in location was an altogether new filmic sensibility, characterized by a more cavalier approach. Whether taking place in the city or the countryside, the films of the 1980s were characterized by an extensive reverence for the craft (even the comedies are only partial exceptions, as many are intended to be important commentaries on Icelandic society). For example, the earlier city films *Dot Dot Comma Dash* and *Atom Station* drew upon the same traditional aesthetics as films set in the countryside, in addition to being period dramas. Despite rarely following art film conventions, Icelandic cinema of the 1980s aspired to establish itself as a respectable national institution. It would be inaccurate to describe it as pompous, but it was broadly serious in tone and was clearly seen to belong in a different cultural realm than that of Hollywood entertainment. In their debut films, Kemp and Jónasson broke with this tradition of respectability.

The shift in location from countryside to city was therefore also a turn toward a more contemporary and urban sensibility. The original Icelandic title of *Remote Control* (*Sodom Reykjavík*) is suggestive of these changes; *Sodom* of its cavalier approach and *Reykjavík* of the shift in location. The imaginative plot has its central character Axel (Björn Jörundur Friðbjörnsson) search for his mother's (Þóra Friðriksdóttir) remote control as she threatens to empty their bathtub that is filled with his goldfish. The search takes the young protagonist into Reykjavík's underworld, where a gang war rages between Moli (Helgi Björnsson) and Aggi (Eggert Þorleifsson), the owner of the club Sodom Reykjavík. Aggi goes after Axel, whom he believes to be Moli, with the help of his two dim-witted assistants (Stefán Sturla Sigurjósson and Þröstur Guðbjartsson), dressed up in Roman costumes no less.

To a considerable extent, the appeal of the film is found in placing the American criminal world as pictured in Hollywood films in an Icelandic context—their striking incompatibility. Moli wears a traditional Icelandic woolen sweater, while his colorful gang family, including infants, plays the board game *Monopoly* in their secret hangout. Aggi, inspired by a comic-story, decides to do away with Axel by placing his feet in a tub full of concrete, but the concrete does not dry and the river is too shallow. American cinema is evoked by numerous car chase scenes, with the camera lingering on Axel's Trans Am as he drives around the capital. The imaginative plot and its many surreal visual situations can be said to invite a global appeal. However, in many other regards the humor is locally specific, for example in various comic references to local institutions, companies, and commercial products.

Remote Control is not only a comedy set in Reykjavík but a film about the city itself—studying it narratively and visually. Accordingly, knowledge of the characters' location within the city is of considerable importance, as Axel's search for the remote control takes him from one end of Reykjavík to the other, with the camera detailing the traveled distances. The film is fascinated with Reykjavík as a modern metropolis, or at least an aspiring one. Numerous aerial shots capture and document its increasingly sprawling size, extensive wide roads, and large crossings (à la America/Hollywood) (see Figure 6.2).

Furthermore, the city's geography has a considerable importance for the plot development. The referencing of various suburbs and specific streets is hardly accommodating to foreign spectators. The film's narrative climax involves the address of Axel and his mother's apartment, which through a series of misunderstandings becomes a party destination and criminal hideout. Walking home late at night, Axel is taken by surprise in recognizing the numerous characters driving past him. The suspenseful buildup of the scene, which involves the timing of characters arriving at the apartment, Aggi's pursuit of Axel, and the fate of his mother, is based upon the constantly shifting geographic locations of the characters. These locations are never explained to spectators unfamiliar with the city.

Figure 6.2 In its evocation of the Hollywood crime film, *Remote Control* aspires to present the growing city of Reykjavík as a sprawling metropolis. Source: Skífan ehf. and Moli hf.

And even though the film's soundtrack is modeled on the Hollywood norm of incorporating various songs and also releasing them on their own for retail, the approach is localized by including only Icelandic songs. The film's actors, Björn Jörundur Friðbjörnsson, Helgi Björnsson, and Sigurjón Kjartansson, were better known as musicians, with Kjartansson also composing the score. In addition, he performs along with his band *HAM* at the film's club Sodom Reykjavík. Many of the soundtrack's songs became popular (particularly the title song by the band *Sálin*) and thus helped promote the film along the lines of Hollywood's synergistic model. *Remote Control* also followed Hollywood trends in targeting a younger audience than had been customary with Icelandic films.[11] The same is true of *Wallpaper*, whose marketing was also boosted by a popular soundtrack that was most effectively incorporated into the narrative, as its heroine, Sól (Ingibjörg Stefánsdóttir), is a country girl aspiring to make it as a singer in the city. And with so many live performances of well-known local bands, the narrative structure was not unlike that of a musical. If both films drew upon Hollywood traditions in terms of entertainment values, use of soundtrack, and certain narrative traditions, they did so in a thoroughly local manner that made few attempts to address a foreign audience. According to our local/global litmus tests, they are also both solely financed and produced in Iceland, though *Remote Control* did receive some very minimal distribution abroad. Finally, the narratives are limited to Iceland. In fact, the very last shot of *Remote Control* offers an extensive aerial overview of Reykjavík, which concludes by framing Aggi's two lackluster assistants in the act of escaping on a cruiser from Reykjavík's harbor. But the joke is that they are going no further than the nearby town of *Akranes*, which is surely lost on foreign audiences unfamiliar with the town and the ferry.

Gísli Snær Erlingsson's *Behind Schedule* (1993, *Stuttur Frakki*) shares many similarities with the pioneering city films of 1992. It is a debut film whose plot makes extensive use of the capital, and revolves around a big concert with established Icelandic performers. However, it has one fundamental difference—the *Short Frenchman* of the Icelandic title. The journalist André (Jean-Philippe Labadie) arrives in Iceland on a cultural mission to cover the concert, but gets lost and can find neither the stadium nor the Icelandic girl Sóley (Elva Ósk Ólafsdóttir) whom he has fallen in love with. As a result, there is considerable English dialogue in the film and a brief scene shot in Paris, and various peculiarities of Icelandic culture are introduced. Accordingly, the narrative and address aspects of our local/global litmus test are beginning to be affected. However, the financing, production (despite having a small French unit), and distribution/exhibition remained primarily national. Perhaps most importantly, just like *Remote Control* and *Wallpaper*, it remained essentially local in terms of aesthetics. If *Behind Schedule* reached outside its national borders narratively, it showcased little interest in the norms of the European art film and thus stood little chance of breaking into the festival circuit.

To summarize, despite having left the countryside for the city, the filmmaking approach remained inherently local. This refutes the somewhat prevailing notion that the transfer to the city and the internationalization of the industry went hand in hand. The fact is that Reykjavík had become the capital of Icelandic cinema long before the international success of *101 Reykjavík* (Baltasar Kormákur, 2000), whose title no doubt helped it receive the spotlight in this context, but the internationalization itself originated with films set in the countryside. To trace the shift from the local to the global, we need to look elsewhere.

7
The Transnational Imperative

As in many other small countries (and admittedly many large ones as well), Icelanders are close to being obsessed with their own nationality. A case in point is the travelogue *Dear Icelanders* (*Góðir Íslendingar*) by Huldar Breiðfjörð, published in the late 1990s, whose title is the traditional greeting offered by pompous officials when addressing the nation on lofty occasions (not unlike "fellow Americans"). Unhappy with his life in Reykjavík, Breiðfjörð took a two-month road trip around the country in midwinter. The result is a subjective portrayal of the national character, which epitomizes the local and introverted character of Icelandic literature. But when restless yet again in Reykjavík, having quit smoking, Breiðfjörð decided to walk the Great Wall of China. The result can be found in *The Wall in China* (*Múrinn í Kína*) that conversely is global and extrovert in scope, describing encounters between Breiðfjörð and the Chinese as well as other nationals.[1] Thus even if stylistically similar, these two travelogues are literally worlds apart. In between these two books, Breiðfjörð wrote a film script in Icelandic called *Næsland*, whose title playfully spelled out in Icelandic the English pronunciation of "niceland," which obviously also referenced the name of Iceland. However, when released in 2004 it had become an English-language film titled *Niceland*, which was no longer set in Iceland, but in some unspecified "nice land."[2]

We will return to *Niceland* at the end of this chapter, but we begin with a close look at its director Friðrik Þór Friðriksson and Iceland's arguably most important filmmaker. In delineating his career in some detail, we also tell the overall story of how Icelandic cinema shifted quite abruptly from being an inward-looking national institution to one closely integrated into European cinema. This is the process I am describing as the transnational turn of Icelandic cinema. After covering the career of Friðriksson, I address the key contributions of other directors participating in the turn, especially Guðný Halldórsdóttir, Hilmar Oddsson, and Baltasar Kormákur.

Friðrik Þór Friðriksson and the Transnational Turn

In the 1990s, Friðriksson became Iceland's best-known filmmaker at home and away, and more than any other filmmaker his career marks the crucial transition from local to global interests in Icelandic cinema. However, instead of focusing solely on Friðriksson as a director of narratives that increasingly work out relatively complex global relations, I am also interested in him as a producer, a festival organizer, and an industry spokesperson. Throughout the 1990s, he became the largest producer of Icelandic films and even began co-producing foreign films, in addition to lobbying extensively for increased state support for local film production and later for tax incentives as well.

Friðriksson's began his career with the experimental film *Burning-Njal's Saga* (1981, *Brennu-Njáls saga*), which was an extremely playful take on Iceland's literary heritage. The film consists of nothing but a burning copy of *Njal's Saga*, often referred to as *Burning-Njal's Saga* in Icelandic, making it ripe for Friðriksson's cruel wordplay. The film's meaning is clearly directed to Icelanders alone, as it is virtually impossible for an audience little familiar with Icelandic culture to understand the thrust of the film's critique of the celebration of the national literary heritage. Another key experimental film, *The Circle* (1985, *Hringurinn*), uses time-lapse photography to film Highway One from the "perspective" of a driving vehicle. Considering the abstract nature of much experimental filmmaking, *Burning-Njal's Saga* and *The Circle* are unusually rooted in a particular locale. Also, one can already see in *The Circle* a foreshadowing of Friðriksson's obsession with the road motif and his somewhat pessimistic take on it. Since Highway One runs in a circle around the island's coastline (explaining its nickname the "Circle"), the film ends where it began—giving a universal theme a distinct specificity. Unlike the American road that conventionally signifies freedom and new beginnings, the Icelandic "Circle" has more somber overtones. The further one drives, the closer one is to getting back to square one—with the North Atlantic on one side and a no man's land on the other.[3]

Friðriksson's two early documentaries were also quintessential local productions. Both document a particular cultural locale: *Rock in Reykjavík* (1982, *Rokk í Reykjavík*) the contemporary rock/punk scene in the capital, and *The Cowboys of the North* (1984, *Kúrekar norðursins*) the first country music festival held in Iceland. And although both are clearly working with the impact of popular Anglophone music traditions on Icelandic culture, neither film foregrounds nor analyzes it in any pronounced way. Both are certainly also addressed to a domestic audience and make no attempts to explain these locales to a foreign audience unfamiliar with both settings and performers.

Similar to the breakthrough films of 1980, *Land and Sons* (Ágúst Guðmundsson, *Land og synir*) and *Father's Estate* (Hrafn Gunnlaugsson, *Óðal feðranna*), Friðriksson's first feature deals with specific domestic political and cultural concerns. *White Whales* (1987, *Skytturnar*) opens with two whalers coming ashore after their last tour and follows them on an erratic and drunken blitz through Reykjavík, climaxing in a fateful shootout with the police. In one sense it is a locally oriented film: it is loosely based upon events that took place in Reykjavík, its city settings are left unexplained, and it is cast by local amateurs (in an attempt to grasp the actuality of both place and characters). In another sense it is one step removed from the local specificity of the earlier films. While the tragedies of the protagonists in both *Father's Estate* and *Land and Sons* resulted from domestic politics, Friðriksson's story is tied to global politics: the highly contested issue of whaling that was very much in the international spotlight at the time. Thus the particular local narrative of *White Whales* is entangled in a global debate.

More important, though, than the issue of whaling is the way in which the film transcends its local specificity by adhering to many of the norms of the European art film, which had been mostly absent from earlier Icelandic cinema. *White Whales* evidences an interest in form and symbolism little evident in the films of the early 1980s. Somewhat obvious parallels are drawn between the whalers (also addressed in dialogue as "fish out of water") and their prey. The film is framed by a flashback of a young boy taking his goldfish out of its bowl and dropping it accidentally to the floor. The opening also lingers on abstract images of whales underwater, later to be cross-cut with industrial images and sounds of the whaling vessel, creating an effective dissonance between nature and industry. Finally, the film relies heavily upon Anglophone music, including songs by the Australian Nick Cave and the American Tom Waits.

Friðriksson aggressively advertised his debut feature at the Cannes film festival, whose importance for the Icelandic film industry he has candidly compared to the importance of international fish markets for the fishing industry.[4] But the role of film festivals has not been limited to the marketing his own films, as they have been instrumental to his broader film activity. He took part in establishing the International Reykjavík Film Festival in 1978, with Wim Wenders among its guests, and subsequently served frequently as its director. According to Friðriksson, Icelandic filmmaking thrives upon a dialogue with other filmmaking traditions, suggesting that a valuable national cinema must be fully global. If not without an element of self-promotion, it seems clear that as an Icelandic director Friðriksson feels he has an obligation to encourage and help develop a diverse domestic film culture: "When I see a good film at a festival abroad it hurts me to know that Icelandic film fans will not have a chance to see it."[5] However, it was not Cannes but Hollywood that put Friðriksson on the world cinema map. The successful run of his second feature, *Children of Nature* (1991, *Börn náttúrunnar*), around the film festival circuit culminated with an Academy Award nomination for best foreign film, which was to help pave the way for transnational productions in Iceland.

Despite having been in many ways an outstanding success with a deep impact upon the cultural environment of the 1980s, the future of Icelandic cinema was by no means certain at the end of the decade. Looking back in December 1989, the film critic Arnaldur Indriðason (and later a celebrated crime novelist, discussed in chapter ten) referred to it as the "Decade of the Icelandic Movie"—suggesting the considerable impact Icelandic film had had on culture and society during the decade.[6] However, a strong concern was raised in the article about the future of the industry based upon interviews with local film talent. Many filmmakers had risked their own financial stability and were either already bankrupt or in dire financial straits. It was clear that the remarkable box-office returns early in the decade were primarily due to the novelty of local filmmaking, and that the domestic exhibition market was too small to profit from. In speculating about the 1990s, filmmakers called for increased cooperation with other countries. Implicitly they were acknowledging that in the long run Icelandic filmmaking, despite reasonable state support, could not survive solely through its own resources.[7]

It was the good fortune of the Icelandic film industry that the 1990s saw an unparalleled rise of co-productions in Europe with considerable financial support from pan-European funds, some of which welcomed small nations and their cultural and lingual specificity. The European Community introduced the MEDIA program in 1987, which, along with its general goal of strengthening audiovisual industries on the continent, offered protection for minority languages. A year later the European Council established Eurimages, a fund geared solely toward co-productions, that was particularly attentive to countries with low film productivity. As Anne Jäckel points out, both MEDIA and Eurimages offered indispensable support for small

European nations, and she pinpoints Iceland as an exemplary beneficiary of both programs.[8]

Children of Nature was one of the first in a wave of Icelandic films to receive support from Eurimages, while additional funding was supplied by the Icelandic Film Fund. Along with Friðriksson's own company, the Icelandic Film Corporation, Max film Berlin and Metro film Oslo were listed as coproducers. However, despite pan-European financing, setting and talent were mostly local. Many key members of the crew were to become part and parcel of Friðriksson's regular team: composer Hilmar Örn Hilmarsson, cinematographer Ari Kristinsson, and writer Einar Már Guðmundsson, who co-wrote the script with Friðriksson. The cast was Icelandic with one notable exception, soon to be addressed.

Veterans of the Icelandic stage, Gísli Halldórsson and Sigríður Hagalín, played an elderly couple, Þorgeir and Stella, who escape their nursing home for a final return to the deserted home of their youth. Relying upon landscape settings along with scenes in Reykjavík, the film is shot in Icelandic and makes use of traditional and contemporary Icelandic music. It is a romanticized city versus countryside tale, but with none of the local specificities that so clearly marked both *Land and Sons* and *Father's Estate*. Indeed, *Children of Nature* is a film about neither the local city and countryside debate nor the social conditions of the elderly in Reykjavík, but rather such universal themes as freedom of the individual, death, nature, religion, and so on. The Icelandic dialogue is minimal, while great emphasis is put on seeing, hearing, and touching (most notably toward the end in a scene where flashbacks are instigated by Stella touching vegetation in the fields of her youth). This emphasis on perception, along with formalistic studies of both characters and nature, can be said to take priority over the rather loose narrative buildup. The camera repeatedly lingers on the faces and hands of Stella and Þorgeir—studying them without any narrative motivation. The film has little narrative thrust and for the most part develops without direct cause-and-effect structure, as is true of much of Friðriksson's work at large. The title itself suggests the universality of the film by its infantilization of the elderly couple as children of nature—figures of innocence in a corrupt modern world. This universality is also evident in shots of Stella and Þorgeir in atmospheric landscape settings, in which the nationality of the characters and the geographical specificity of the settings are irrelevant. A striking example occurs toward the end of the film when Þorgeir, having just buried Stella, walks barefoot up a mountain. This religious motif is then clearly intertwined with the European art film when celebrated German actor Bruno Ganz emerges as the angel he played just four years prior in Wenders's *Wings of Desire* (1987, *Himmel über Berlin*) and prepares Þorgeir for his eventual exit through a visually abstract heaven's gate. Notably, the encounter between Þorgeir and the angel from Berlin takes place in the ruins of an American military structure (see Figure 7.1). It remains an abstract and unexplained intrusion, but American cultural influences were to remain a primary concern of Friðriksson's work throughout the 1990s.

Following its success at various international film festivals, culminating with an Oscar nomination for best foreign film, *Children of Nature* soon became the most widely seen Icelandic film abroad.[9] Thus it is very much a transnational film not only in terms of financing (a European co-production supported by Eurimages) and distribution/exhibition, but also in terms of its narrative, with national aspects being addressed to a global audience. In other words, it is not the lack of nationality that ensures *Children of Nature*'s appeal to a global audience, but its transparent packaging. Part of what makes the film appealing is its foreignness—its "Icelandicness"—but only because it is never allowed to stifle, disorient, or put the foreign spectator at a disadvantage. These are the defining characteristics of the transnational; unlike the international, the transnational does not do away with the national.

Figure 7.1 As *Children of Nature* draws to a close, German actor Bruno Ganz emerges as the angel he played in *Wings of Desire* to prepare Þorgeir (Gísli Halldórsson) for the afterlife. Source: Íslenska kvikmyndasamsteypan.

After the success of *Children of Nature*, Friðriksson turned down offers from Hollywood when denied a final cut. In doing so, he aligned himself with a long tradition of European art cinema—a well-known debate between art and commerce in filmmaking. Jäckel has suggested that it might be appropriate to consider the auteur film "the European film genre par excellence" and adds that the "celebration of the director's [. . .] cultural status" is particularly pronounced in the continent's small countries.[10] By evoking Guiseppe Tornatore's cinephilic nostalgia film *Cinema Paradiso* (1988), and explicitly comparing his next feature *Movie Days* (1994, *Bíódagar*) to Federico Fellini's *Amarcord* (1973), Bille August's *Zappa* (1983), and Woody Allen's *Radio Days* (1987), Friðriksson continued to turn himself into an auteur.[11] Thematic and stylistic concerns were so consistent with his earlier success that the film could justifiably have been titled a "Child of Nature."

The opening scene of *Movie Days* depicts a family going to a theater in downtown Reykjavík in the early 1960s. Soon the film cuts to the iconic MGM logo, which fills the screen as if the actual spectators were watching a classical Hollywood film. The audience within the diegesis watches, mesmerized, a buildup to the crucifixion, suggesting an analogy between cinephilia and religious devotion. As the scene is about to reach its climax with Jesus being nailed onto the cross, the father covers the eyes of his young son with his bowler hat. The screen goes black and the credits of *Movie Days* begin to appear, but the sounds of the Hollywood crucifixion—Nicholas Ray's *The King of Kings* (1961)—continue. Thus, while manifesting a nostalgic devotion to classical Hollywood cinema, the film also asserts the links between Friðriksson and auteur cinema as Ray was a particular favorite of the *Cahiers du Cinema* critics that became the core of the French New Wave and a late collaborator of Wenders.[12] Wenders himself is also quoted again in the film when the other angel from *Wings of Desire*, played by Otto Sanders, appears in a brief cameo. Also typical of art cinema are numerous other self-reflexive scenes of film exhibition, projection, and voyeurism.

Unlike Friðriksson's earlier films that had certain global appeal but hardly constituted a transnational narrative, *Movie Days* is explicitly concerned with global issues. The city versus countryside opposition takes on a transnational angle where Reykjavík has become a site of international flux characterized by American films and television and popular British music, while traditional values and local myths and fairytales are upheld and cherished in the countryside. Midway through the film, its young hero Tómas (Örvar Jens Arnarson), a city boy, has to stay at a farm in the north for the summer. Instead of watching Roy Rogers and television broadcasts from the US Naval Air Station (national television broadcasts only began in 1966) in Keflavík, he must contend with stories told by the elderly at the farm. When he has finally learned to appreciate these, the unexpected death of his father forces him to return to Reykjavík, where the film ends with a freeze frame close-up of him watching the silver screen. It is hard not to think of the famous concluding freeze frame of young Jean-Pierre Léaud in François Truffaut's *The 400 Blows* (1959, *Les quatre cents coups*).

The interrelations between Iceland and the United States, most notably the latter's military presence and audiovisual omnipresence, are addressed in the context of the Cold War's global politics. Despite the weighty subject, the film's tone is lighthearted, for example when, having been scolded for bringing a Pepsi beverage to school, a classmate of Tómas responds to his teacher: "As a free man I decide what I drink and eat." A patriot turns to communism in his desire to oppose the American army presence, and projects for Tómas and his friends Vsevolod Pudovkin's *Mother* (1926, *Mat*) in his basement (that of course also serves as yet another cinephilic reference). An altogether different transnational sequence is found in Tómas's attempts to learn Danish by reading Donald Duck comics, as it was not until the early 1980s that the popular weekly Disney comic began to be published in Icelandic translation.

To an even greater extent than *Children of Nature*, Friðriksson's third feature is financially a transnational product. The most important addition is the funding received from the Nordic Film and Television Fund, which was to become, along with Eurimages and the Icelandic Film Fund, the most important monetary source for Icelandic film production. The impact of these transnational funding practices on Friðriksson's work and Icelandic cinema more broadly culminates with his next feature, where Iceland is offered on a plate like an exotic dish, indicating that Icelandic cinema had in only five years been transformed from an inherently local cultural institution to a fully transnational enterprise.

In *Cold Fever* (1995, *Á köldum klaka*) a young Japanese businessman Hirata travels from Tokyo to a remote corner of Iceland to carry out a ritual ceremony in memory of his deceased parents. Along the way, he must tackle everything from American tourist-bandits to Icelandic cuisine—the national spirit *Brennivín* and smoked sheep-heads. The Japanese actor Masatoshi Nagase stars as the bewildered Hirata, veteran director Seijun Suzuki plays his grandfather, the American actors Fisher Stevens and Lili Taylor play the bandits, and Icelander Gísli Halldórsson plays Hirata's drinking partner, who enables him to carry out the ceremony. The film is produced by Jim Stark, George Grund III, the Icelandic Film Corporation, Film Fonds Hamburg, Sunrise A.G., Pandora Film, Zentropa Entertainment, and Alta Films. Such an extensive list of production partners was unprecedented in 1995 but was to become typical in the new century.

In both *Movie Days* and *Cold Fever*, Friðriksson relied on his longtime Icelandic collaborators: shot by Kristinsson, edited by Steingrímur Karlsson, and composed by Hilmarsson. The most notable addition was American producer Stark, who co-wrote the script with Friðriksson. As Stark was a longtime collaborator of Jim Jarmusch, his participation explicitly tied Friðriksson to the US independent auteur with whom he had often been compared—Nagase even starred in Stark's production of Jarmusch's *Mystery Train* (1989). If it was a project primarily intended for the lucrative but difficult American market, Nagase's presence was to help market it in Japan. Therein lie the reasons for the international cast and transnational narrative of *Cold Fever*.

It is a rather peculiar film as it takes place mostly in Iceland but has no Icelandic dialogue. However, it is technically not an English-language production in which English replaces the respective national/local language. It is "realistic" to the extent that the film depicts foreigners in Iceland speaking among themselves, or addressing locals who must answer in English. Furthermore, the early scenes set in Tokyo are all in Japanese. In fact, the very first scene taking place outside Japan, on board a plane about to land in Iceland, begins with an intrusive passenger asking Hirata: "Excuse me. Do you speak English?" Having received a hesitant confirmation, the passenger goes on: "Is this your first visit to Iceland? [...] You are going to love it. Everybody does." The question is equally addressed to the audience, who like arriving tourists are about to be introduced to Iceland: its spectacular nature and curious customs. The film cuts to the first view of Iceland in the form of a dazzling white wintery mountain scene, by dramatically extending the screen to a much wider aspect ratio, further enforcing the island's grandeur and majesty (as compared to the enclosed spaces of Tokyo and Hirata's restricted point of view).

On his arrival at the national airport, Hirata accidentally joins a bus full of tourists receiving a guided tour. Hirata manages to escape the group at the Blue Lagoon, Iceland's most popular tourist resort, only to end up with a taxi driver equally intent on educating Hirata about local customs. Thus through the character of Hirata, a global audience, unfamiliar with Iceland, is being introduced to Icelandic nature, culture, and society. A particular case in point is Hirata's visit to *Kántríbær* (Country-town) in which he receives a fairly detailed explanation of the oddity of country music being performed in Iceland. Thus Friðriksson has traveled a long distance from his early documentary *Cowboys of the North*, where he solely addressed a national audience, to *Cold Fever*, in which he explains local customs to a global audience in English. If we apply our local/global litmus test from the prior chapter to this film, we find that financing, distribution/exhibition, and address have become overwhelmingly global, while production and narrative are threading precariously between the local and the global. After *Cold Fever*, Icelandic cinema seemed somehow less Icelandic.

Devil's Island (1996, *Djöflaeyjan*), Friðriksson's third film in his three most productive years, returned to the theme of postwar American and Icelandic relations. Based upon Einar Kárason's popular and celebrated novel, the film taps into the heated controversy regarding the Naval Air Station in Keflavík that was established during World War II and would remain there until the United States unilaterally closed it in 2006. *Devil's Island*'s opening text candidly lays out the film's premise:

> Icelandic Vikings found America in the ninth century—But as Oscar Wilde said they had the good taste to lose it again—A thousand years later, during World War II, the US occupied Iceland—But they were so set on not losing it again that they kept a military base there long after the war ended. They moved out of the capital though, leaving behind barracks—for the benefit of homeless Icelanders.

The film begins in one of these barracks with the middle-aged Gógó (Saga Jónsdóttir) marrying an American officer. As the two groups—Icelanders and Americans—are not mixing very well at the wedding party, she shouts: "Don't be so scared of the Americans. O my Gosh they are only Yanks." And this well represents the film's perspective on the American military presence in Iceland. In preferring "Yanks" to "Americans," Gógó—and the film by implication—emphasizes the personal and light-hearted rather than the geopolitical. And compared to the powerful and robust Gógó, her new husband and the other officers appear not only harmless, but almost just as awkward and shy as the Icelandic guests.

In Gógó's two grown-up sons from her first marriage we find a familiar opposition between countryside and city in Icelandic cinema being played out in a novel form. Baddi (Baltasar Kormákur) returns transformed from a visit to the United States, wearing a black leather jacket, speaking in a strange mixture of Icelandic and Hollywood-English, and driving a shiny red Plymouth, and he begins partying and drinking nonstop (see Figure 7.2).

His brother Danni (Sveinn Geirsson) is as introverted as Baddi is extroverted, and is repeatedly linked to the countryside as he flies over some beautiful landscape scenery. He also dies tragically when out in nature, suggesting once again that Iceland's future lies with modernization (and perhaps more specifically Americanization) and that the Iceland of old is slowly disappearing and dying.

But compared to *The Girl Gogo* (Erik Balling, 1962, *79 af stöðinni*) and *The Atom Station* (Þorsteinn Jónsson, 1984, *Atómstöðin*), based upon Halldór Laxness's critique of the Keflavík station in the novel of the same title, the American influence is presented in a more positive light in *Movie Days* and *Devil's Island*. Although the latter has its dark moments, it is American culture that provides much of the excitement—the music, the automobiles, the fashionable clothes and hairstyles. And notably, the film's most likable character does a loving imitation of Chaplin's famous walk. This shift has no doubt much to do with the fact that the Naval Air Station no longer generated

Figure 7.2 Baltasar Kormákur, who would replace Friðrik Þór Friðriksson as the principal representative of the Icelandic film industry in the twenty-first century—and encourage a shift from the norms of Europe to those of Hollywood—appropriately played the Americanized Baddi in the latter's *Devil's Island*. Source: Íslenska kvikmyndasamsteypan.

the same political debates it had in the past, but it is also likely to stem from the increased global outlook of Icelandic cinema. Instead of privileging the national cultural heritage, *Movie Days* and *Devil's Island* situate the country within a global realm by referencing the classics of American and European cinema and making extensive use of American and British pop and rock 'n' roll songs.

In conjunction with his international success, Friðriksson became the unofficial spokesperson for the Icelandic film industry. During the latter half of the nineties, Friðriksson also became more and more involved with producing, and his production company, the Icelandic Film Corporation (whose ironic naming had begun to describe its role rather truthfully), was involved in many key productions of the period. In addition, he acted as an associate or executive producer on foreign productions having to do with Iceland in one form or another, including Lars von Trier's *Dancer in the Dark* (2000), starring Icelandic singer Björk, and Hal Hartley's *No Such Thing* (2001), mostly filmed in Iceland. At home Friðriksson would agitate for further state support, and abroad work toward carving out a space for Icelandic cinema—most dramatically at the Rouen Nordic Film Festival, where he threw his prize statue to the floor in protest over what he viewed as the underrepresentation of Icelandic films at the festival.[13]

I have focused here on Friðriksson's first five feature films since they not only reflect an important shift in his own oeuvre, but also were instrumental in bringing about that shift in Icelandic cinema at large. With each of his feature films, a greater distance was reached from the national specificity of the early 1980s, including the breakthrough films *Land and Sons* and *Father's Estate* and Friðriksson's own documentaries and experimental work. In *White Whales*, Friðriksson took on the European art film; he addressed universal themes in *Children of Nature* and global cinephilia in *Movie Days*; he used a multi-lingual and international cast in *Cold Fever*; and he evoked American popular culture in *Devil's Island*. These films crystallize the most important development in Icelandic cinema since the Icelandic Film Fund was established in 1978.

To Europe Back and Forth

As the countryside made way for the city in the early 1990s in the films of a new generation of directors, including *Wallpaper* (Júlíus Kemp, 1992,

Veggfóður) and *Remote Control* (Óskar Jónasson, 1992, *Sódóma Reykjavík*), more established directors began making more expensive and elaborate films with extensive foreign financial support. Despite occurring during the same time period, this transnationalization of Icelandic cinema had nothing to do with the transfer to the city, as it originated in the countryside. A case in point is Kristín Jóhannesdóttir's *As in Heaven* (1992, *Svo á jörðu sem á himni*), the last film released prior to *Wallpaper*. Unlike *Wallpaper*, which was entirely locally funded, the budget of *As in Heaven* was supplied by various European production funds and companies. The narrative alternates between parallel stories set in the same fjord, *Straumfjörður*, but separated by centuries in time. One takes place in the fourteenth century when the heartbroken sorceress Halla (Tinna Gunnlaugsdóttir) places a curse on the land. The other is set in 1936 as the curse is realized in the shipwreck of the French vessel *Pourquoi Pas?* carrying the famous explorer Jean-Baptiste Charcot and his crew. These two settings of *As in Heaven* have clearly little to do with today's Reykjavík. Friðriksson's most successful films abroad, *Children of Nature* and *Cold Fever*, are contemporary tales, but they are also primarily set in the countryside. Their brief city scenes provide primarily dramatic counterweight to the countryside's traditional way of life, spectacular nature, and mysticism. Prior to *Children of Nature*, only the Viking films of Hrafn Gunnlaugsson, having obviously little to do with modern urbanity, garnered notable attention abroad. Even Jón Tryggvason's thriller *Foxtrot* (1987), the first Icelandic film to be explicitly designed with export in mind, was set in some of the country's most deserted parts.

If a new generation of directors in the early 1990s was responsible for the shift to the city, directors who had begun their careers in the mid-1980s brought about the transnational shift. In addition to Friðriksson, the transformation can be clearly discerned in the careers of Guðný Halldórsdóttir and Hilmar Oddsson, whose films are also mostly located in the countryside. Halldórsdóttir's first feature was an adaptation of Halldór Laxness's *Under the Glacier* (1989, *Kristnihald undir jökli*), which was primarily set in the region near *Snæfellsjökull* Glacier. It was essentially a local production save for some German funding, which is hardly discernible on screen, in the manner of many other films. The celebrated status of Laxness in both Iceland and Germany discouraged comprehensive changes to the original novel, and its foreign funding brought fewer stipulations regarding its use than was customary. Halldórsdóttir's next film, *Men's Choir* (1992, *Karlakórinn Hekla*), about a choir from a small Icelandic town that goes on a trip to Germany, can be seen as occupying an in-between position in the development toward transnational cinema. The film's narrative structure not only incorporated foreign funding by having large portions of it set abroad, but also could adjust to the funding's national origin. As producer Halldór Þorgeirsson put it: "*Men's Choir* could have taken place anywhere. It just depended on who put up the money."[14] In other words, the film's choir could just as easily have traveled to France, Denmark, or the United States, without making any fundamental changes to the narrative. If Halldórsdóttir's adaptation of Laxness's *Honour of the House* (1999, *Ungfrúin góða og húsið*) allowed no such liberties, taking place in both Denmark and Iceland, the filmmakers were quite resourceful in managing the heterogeneous sources of its funding. As Halldórsdóttir and Þorgeirsson point out, while the film appears to be an Icelandic-Danish film, in terms of funding it was primarily an Icelandic-Swedish production. The Swedish contribution could be veiled on screen by using Swedish studios for indoor scenes, having the actors Reine Brynolfsson and Agneta Ekmanner play Icelandic characters, and finally utilizing the craftsmanship of the Swedes Tonie Zetterström (production design) and Per Källberg (cinematography). In other words, the production of *Honour of the House* could take advantage of considerable Swedish funding without changing the film's original narrative design by directing it partly behind the camera, while Swedish actors played Icelandic characters and Swedish studio sets represented Danish settings.

It took Hilmar Oddsson nine years to follow up his debut film *The Beast* (1986, *Eins og skepnan deyr*), which in many ways epitomized the local approach of the 1980s, as it was shot on location in a deserted part of the country by a solely Icelandic crew. Conversely, *Tears of Stone* (1995, *Tár úr steini*) was a pivotal film in ushering in the transnationalization of Icelandic cinema. Its seeds already lay within *The Beast*, as Oddsson was perhaps to an even greater extent than Friðriksson influenced by the European art film. An aspiring auteur, Oddsson not only directed and scripted the film, but also took on the role of composer. Its alienated central character was a writer verging on going mad—a familiar figure in art cinema. *The Beast* was excessively symbolic, made extensive use of pictorial compositions, and thematically investigated questions of artistic creativity. Its handling of music, painting, nature, and Icelandic folklore foreshadowed their more elaborate form in *Tears of Stone* and *Cold Light* (2004, *Kaldaljós*).

On its release in 1995, *Tears of Stone* was a critical triumph and a major cultural event, as it participated in the general re-evaluation of Iceland's best-known composer Jón Leifs, the film's central character. In an unprecedented whole-page review in the country's largest newspaper, *Morgunblaðið*, Erlendur Sveinsson described it as the finest achievement of Icelandic cinema. Writing on the eve of the film spring all the way back in 1981, Sveinsson had suggested that Icelandic cinema belonged to the future, and judging by his review that future had finally arrived.[15] Euphorically, he claimed that Icelandic cinema had for the first time "created world art in the field of cinema which will carry its makers' reputation around the world. As of now the criterion of Icelandic cinema has been changed, a new standard set."[16] Sveinsson may have been right in carving out a special place for *Tears of Stone* in Icelandic film history, but rather than being a culmination of a national development of sorts, it constituted a break with it. Instead of elevating what was a distinguishable Icelandic cinema, *Tears of Stone* not only subscribed to the standards of the European art film but was also primarily a German-language film set in Germany. Herein lie also the contradictions of the review in which the value of Icelandic cinema is found in foreign appreciation and the international norms of the art film. Sveinsson describes *Tears of Stone* as a piece of "world art" with relevance for a global audience, all the while suggesting the film to be essentially an Icelandic production. None of the foreign members of the cast and crew are mentioned in the review, for example, the critical, if brief, performance of the German actor Heinz Bennent, known for his work with many canonical figures of European art cinema. A more striking neglect is found in Sveinsson's discussion of the cinematography: "Sig[urður] Sverrir Pálsson and his camera assistants have contributed more than we realize in forming the work. [...] With [Pálsson] Iceland has acquired a cinematographer comparable to the best in the world."[17] Not a single mention is made of the contribution of Slawomir Idziak, best known for his collaboration with Krzysztof Kieślowski, including *Double Life of Veronique* (1991, *La double vie de Véronique*) and *Blue* (1993, *Bleu*), who not only shot extensive parts of the film but also was instrumental in establishing the film's appearance. Pálsson, on the other hand, only began filming after Idziak was forced to leave the set due to other contractual assignments when the production of *Tears of Stone* was delayed. Similarly, Sveinsson discusses the Icelandic folktale that inspired the film's title, but makes no mention of the extensive Faustian motif of the film.[18]

Tears of Stone focuses primarily on the years that Jón Leifs (Þröstur Leó Gunnarsson) spent in Nazi Germany with his Jewish wife Linda (Ruth Olafsdóttir) and their two daughters. Leifs's public and private aspirations are interwoven in the most difficult of circumstances, with primarily the Nazis showing interest in his work, inspired as it is by Icelandic nature and the Old Norse heritage. The setting of the story in Germany in the lead-up to World War II helped give the film an unfamiliar cosmopolitan sophistication compared to conventional Icelandic productions. Visually the film's yellow color scheme gives an arresting impression of the past and a distinct look aligning it with the European art film, whose influence is also evident in striking visual compositions (see Figure 7.3). Arguably no Icelandic film had followed the established norms of the European art film to this degree.

While Baltasar Kormákur's early work is also indebted to the European art film, it is so on more general grounds. It neither portrays the extreme thematic anguish and alienation of *Tears of Stone* nor manifests its excessively detailed visual compositions, but it is often flamboyantly stylistic, in a more cavalier way, and explicitly addresses questions of sexuality. His debut film *101 Reykjavík* stars Victoria Abril, best known for her roles in the films of Pedro Almodóvar, including *Tie Me Up! Tie Me Down!* (1990, *Atame!*) and *Kika* (1993), who more than any other European auteur has made marginal sexual identities the cornerstone of his authorship.

101 Reykjavík was far from leading the way from the countryside to the city, but it was the first film to replace nature and the countryside with Reykjavík

Figure 7.3 Icelandic composer Jón Leifs (Þröstur Leó Gunnarsson) having coffee with his Jewish wife Linda (Ruth Olafsdóttir) and her parents (Heinz Bennent and Ingrid Andree) in *Tears of Stone*, set in Germany during the interwar years. Source: Tónabíó.

in appealing to foreign audiences. Reykjavík had been transformed during the twentieth century, with today's cosmopolitan culture bearing little resemblance to the small isolated village we find in the oldest extant films of the city. The increased popularity of Reykjavík in the late twentieth century as a destination for European youth, intrigued by its nightlife and music scene mixed with some "Nordic exoticism," had formed an altogether new image of Iceland that filmmakers had made little use of prior to *101 Reykjavík*.

The financing and production of *101 Reykjavík* exemplifies the transnational imperative of contemporary Icelandic cinema. It was a co-production between the Icelandic firm 101 ehf. and four other European companies, Zentropa Productions, Liberator, Filmhuset, and Troika Entertainment, in addition to receiving financial support from the Icelandic Film Fund, Eurimages, and NRW. Hlynur (Hilmir Snær Guðnason) is an unemployed slacker who lives with his mother Berglind (Hanna María Karlsdóttir) and takes a break from browsing the internet to party during weekends.[19] Their daily routines are upset when the Spanish flamenco dancer Lola (Victoria Abril) comes to visit. The comedy revolves around this triangle, as having made love to Hlynur, Lola begins a relationship with his mother. After becoming pregnant, Lola decides to raise the baby with Berglind, with Hlynur suspecting he may not only be its brother but also its father. After going through an extended state of anguish, Hlynur learns to appreciate the new family setup, and as a result of his newfound responsibility takes a job of issuing parking tickets in downtown Reykjavík.

In various comic puns, the film's dialogue indicates a local approach, as they are not easily translated. These word-plays stem from Hallgrímur Helgason's novel upon which the film is based, whose playfulness with the Icelandic language borders on obsession (see discussion of the novel and the adaptation more specifically in chapter eight). However, many of the film's jokes have global rather than local references, including Keith Richards, Domino's Pizza, and Las Vegas. Lola's very name is a reference to *The Kinks* song of the same title, which dealt in fact with a trans woman rather than a lesbian, but otherwise works well for the film. Einar Örn and Damon Albarn, of *Sugarcubes* and *Blur* fame, respectively, have extended the song's melody into the film's overall music schema. Thus, in terms of the soundtrack, *101 Reykjavík* is global in scope rather than local in the manner of *Remote Control*, *Wallpaper*, and *Behind Schedule*.[20]

101 Reykjavík's style and sexual explicitness come together already in the opening scene, as a point-of-view shot of Hlynur's face moves back and forth, imitating the perspective of his girlfriend Hófí (Þrúður Vilhjálmsdóttir) during intercourse. After she removes Hlynur's glasses, the audience is given his perspective with a point-of-view shot of Hófí's face moving in and out of focus, with the first few opening credits subjected to the same treatment. More complex articulations of sexual identity are also presented stylistically in a scene where Hlynur crawls into his mother's bed as a young boy. The camera moves to the right and lingers briefly on his mother and returns to the left side of the bed to find Hlynur now an adult, and when turning right again, his mother has been replaced with Lola—all happening without a single cut. The camera work is in general fluid, and effective use is made of visual bridges. The sets and costumes are extremely colorful, giving the film a distinct and joyful look, supported by various little surreal touches like placing Hlynur and Berglind's bathtub in their kitchen. Finally, the considerable display of nudity is hardly alien to European art cinema.

The title *101 Reykjavík* does in fact refer to the postal code of the city's downtown, but it also exemplifies the film's role as a guide or introductory course on (downtown) Reykjavík. Since Lola arrives to Iceland less than ten minutes into the film, a considerable part of the dialogue is in English. Like Hirata in *Cold Fever*, she receives an extensive introduction to Icelandic society and culture. Hlynur explains to Lola: "No insects. No trees. No nothing. The only reason why people live here is because they were born here. It's a ghost town." The dialogue describes Reykjavík not only to Lola, but also to foreign spectators. In fact, the film continues to explain local specificities even in scenes where Lola is absent. In a scene where Hlynur again ventures uncharacteristically outside of the city center, the following dialogue occurs:

BERGLIND: Hlynur, dear, don't be so glum.
HLYNUR: I always get depressed when I go to the country.
BERGLIND: But this is only *Grafarvogur* [translated as a suburb in subtitles].
HLYNUR: Exactly.

In addition to being a humorous exchange, the scene helps spectators unfamiliar with Reykjavík to understand the characters' location, the local audience needing no such help. In this, *101 Reykjavík* is quintessentially different from *Remote Control*, where no such effort was made despite relying extensively on the city's geography and local peculiarities (see chapter six). As one of the examples given regarding *Remote Control* was the unexplained "getaway" to *Akranes*, it is noteworthy that its location is described in detail in

101 Reykjavík when Lola returns from there after a brief visit. *101 Reykjavík* has a global reception inscribed in its national/local articulations.

To summarize, while *Remote Control* is characterized by a singular address, *101 Reykjavík* has a double address which speaks to both local and foreign audiences. In terms of our litmus test, the film is also verging on the global in financing and production and more importantly in exhibition and distribution as it was a considerable success abroad. The narrative is set in a demarcated locale, but it is given a more global resonance by the inclusion of a foreign central character. Certainly, the film's themes transcend this locale. *101 Reykjavík* is a transnational product par excellence, wrapping up the locally/nationally specific in a global package.

A No Man's Land?

By way of conclusion, let us return to Friðrik Þór Friðriksson, who had his greatest domestic box-office success with *Angels of the Universe* in 2000—seen by four times as many as *101 Reykjavík*, released the same year. It was an adaptation of a popular novel set in Reykjavík by Einar Már Guðmundsson, who had written the script to *Children of Nature* with Friðriksson.[21] It constituted a major U-turn from the presentation of Iceland's mystical nature in *Children of Nature* and *Cold Fever* that had primarily appealed to foreign audiences. And it did not generate much interest abroad, but at the local box office it sold close to 90,000 tickets, like *Devil's Island* had done four years prior. Such numbers had not been seen since the early 1980s.

Then in *Falcons* (2002, *Fálkar*), Friðriksson returned to a thoroughly transnational narrative and the explicit themes of the European art film. To a certain extent, *Falcons* repeated the narrative formula of *Cold Fever*, with the American actor Keith Carradine replacing Masatoshi Nagase as the bewildered visitor. However, midway through the film Carradine's character Simon leaves Iceland for Germany, along with his daughter Dúa (Margrét Vilhjálmsdóttir) and a falcon he hopes to sell in Hamburg. Thus the film narrative incorporates the two most typical transnational strategies by having both a foreigner visiting Iceland and an Icelander going abroad, resulting in a rather aimless plot. Also prevalent are many of Friðriksson's auteur trademarks like the nature mysticism, the road-motif (whose German setting helps evoke Wenders again), and Simon's alienation while Dúa has all the characteristics of a child of nature. The symbolic paralleling of Simon and the caged bird culminates in an elaborate pictorial composition displaying Simon's death and the setting free of the falcon. This time, however, the rubric did not appear to work and the film failed both at home and away.

Friðriksson's next feature, the Icelandic-UK-German-Danish production *Niceland*, went one step further by setting the narrative in a world beyond conventional borders, but whose inhabitants nonetheless speak English.[22] Thus *Niceland* goes even beyond the transnational premise of *Cold Fever* and *Falcons* by doing away altogether with Iceland, whose presence is relegated to the Icelandic accent of some of its supporting cast. It effaces any national/local specificity in the hope of appealing to all—but ended up appealing to very few.

Considering the unparalleled local box-office success of *Devil's Island* and *Angels of the Universe*, the extremely poor performance of *Falcons* and *Niceland* at the local box office was all the more unexpected and dumbfounding. Each film sold only around 5,000 tickets, and abroad they came and went without anyone noticing.[23] This turnaround presents a fundamental dilemma for Icelandic cinema, and likely all smaller national cinemas caught up in the same tension between the local and the global. In appealing to a global audience, one risks losing the local one, while an explicitly local approach closes the door to transnational funding and festival prestige. This may be too neat a formulation, but it is certainly true that Icelandic films primarily shot in English have had limited success at the local box office.[24] While the box-office discrepancy of Friðriksson's films undoubtedly has various causes, including critical reception and the popularity of the novels *Devil's Island* and *Angels of the Universe*, I believe that the failure of *Falcons* and *Niceland* lies especially in their lack of national specificity—abroad no less than at home. If Iceland still contributed to *Niceland*'s financing and production, the film's narrative and address altogether erased it from the picture. By giving up Iceland, the filmmakers lost their biggest pull in the global market of cinema, as the country itself would seem to be a much greater attraction than Friðriksson's auteur reputation or the minor foreign stars cast in *Niceland*, whereas Icelandic nature had been the primary appeal of Friðriksson's own *Children of Nature* and *Cold Fever*.

It is worth reviewing now our earlier local/global litmus tests. The results of both the countryside films of the early 1980s and the city films of the early 1990s were overwhelmingly local. Later in the decade, numerous films showed notably different results, as they seemed to be in an equilibrium between the local and the global. These are the transnational films that typified much of Icelandic cinema during the nineties. Now if we apply the test to *Niceland* we gain yet again remarkably different results. It is only marginally local in terms of financing, production, and distribution/exhibition, and is perhaps the very first "Icelandic" film which neither addresses the nation as an audience nor represents it in one form or another. In this, Friðriksson and the producers of *Niceland* had gone too far, and as Icelandic cinema continued to travel further into the twenty-first century much work went into finding the right balance between the local and the global.

8
Adaptation as Transnationalization

The 1987 novel *Cold Light* (*Kaldaljós*) by Vigdís Grímsdóttir tells the story of Grímur, who as a boy loses his family in an avalanche.[1] In early adulthood, painting and love help him overcome this trauma. *Cold Light* exemplifies the strong ties between novel and nation. Iceland appears as little more than a village in which the outside world has no place, and Grímsdóttir's poetic prose is characterized by notable playfulness with the Icelandic language. The first of the novel's two parts takes place in a small fishing village and presents a traditional image of the countryside. The second half is set in Reykjavík, where Grímur has moved a decade later to study painting—an unpolished talent, developed by nature in the tradition of Ormar Örlygsson from Gunnar Gunnarsson's *Story of the Borg Family* (*Saga Borgarættarinnar*). He soon falls in love with his teacher Bergljót, and their relationship is at the center of the novel's second part. In adapting the novel in 2004, director and script-writer Hilmar Oddsson was most faithful to his source material and went to great lengths in giving equal weight to the novel's two time periods. However, there was one striking difference between novel and film. Bergljót became Linda. And unlike Bergljót, she is English, and Grímur and Linda communicate in English.

In this chapter we will begin by looking at some of the key heritage adaptations of the 1980s—emphasizing the role played by the medieval Icelandic sagas. After being absolutely central to the emergence of Icelandic national cinema during the early eighties, adaptations unexpectedly almost vanish toward the end of the decade. The latter half of the chapter charts their re-emergence toward the late nineties and into the new century, but now fully incorporated into the transnational imperative, as evidenced by our opening example. I therefore describe their adaptation process as one of transnationalization.

To Adapt or Not to Adapt the Literary Heritage

The overt reliance on literary adaptations in establishing Icelandic national cinema in the early 1980s can be seen to stem from at least two important factors. First, there was no film tradition to fall back upon as a model or even as a counter-model. Second, in trying to establish cinema as a national institution, literature was an obvious ally as the national art par excellence. Thus, the novels chosen for adaptation, including Indriði G. Þorsteinsson's *Land and Sons*, Pétur Gunnarsson's *Dot Dot Comma Dash*, and Jökull Jakobsson's *Message to Sandra*, were of considerable cultural esteem. However, they were hardly located at the center of the Icelandic literary canon. Even those filmmakers who did go to the very heart of the canon by taking on the medieval Icelandic sagas and the work of Nobel laureate Halldór Laxness, most notably Ágúst Guðmundsson in adapting *Gisli Sursson's Saga* in 1981 and Þorsteinn Jónsson in adapting Laxness's *Atom Station* (1984, *Atómstöðin*), evaded the most highly esteemed works. Filmmakers clearly revered and felt a strong impulse to film the literary heritage, but that very same reverence left the most canonical works of Icelandic literature untouched (see chapter three). But the novels that were adapted were followed quite closely, and without exception, considerable effort was made to transfer them faithfully to film. Nowhere was this more apparent than in the adaptation of *Gisli Sursson's Saga*.

Like most of the sagas of Icelanders, *Gisli Sursson's Saga* is extensive in scope, both temporally and spatially. It also opens, like most of them, with a lengthy and colorful genealogy before introducing its main characters, Gísli himself (Arnar Jónsson), his brother Þorkell (Þráinn Karlsson), and his sister Þórdís (Tinna Gunnlaugsdóttir), who escape a bloody past in Norway for Iceland in the tenth century. After a brief period of peace in their new home, Gísli is soon in trouble again and headed for a tragic demise. In an attempt to keep the peace, Gísli, Þorkell, Þórdís's husband Þorgrímur (Benedikt Sigurðsson), and Gísli's in-law Vésteinn (Kristján Jóhann Jónsson) decide to pledge their brotherhood. However, midway through the ceremony, Þorgrímur refuses to share blood with Vésteinn, with the result that Gísli pulls out of the peace settlement as well. The situation intensifies when Þorkell leaves Gísli to settle at Þorgrímur's farm after overhearing his wife Ásgerður (Kristín Kristjánsdóttir) acknowledge her intimate feelings for Vésteinn. When Vésteinn is murdered in his sleep while visiting Gísli's farm, Gísli takes revenge by slaying Þorgrímur in similar circumstances. Spurred on by Þórdís, the brother of the slain, Börkur (Sveinbjörn Matthíasson), goes after Gísli, who becomes an outlaw. The remainder of the saga describes Gísli on the run from Börkur and his posse, staying with friends like Ingjaldur (Jón Sigurbjörnsson) and Refur (Bessi Bjarnason). Gísli is finally killed after valiantly fighting fifteen men, led by Börkur's friend Eyjólfur (Helgi Skúlason), and killing many. Numerous subplots also include the slaying of Þorkell by Vésteinn's sons, the marriage of Börkur and Þórdís, and her attempt to avenge her brother's death by killing Eyjólfur. Apart from the opening in Norway, the film adaptation entitled *The Outlaw* (1981, *Útlaginn*) follows this plot outline in every regard.

Should the reader be a little confused by the above plot description, that is exactly the point. It is difficult to follow the original plot and the saga's many characters. However, it is almost impossible for spectators to follow the film's plot unless they are familiar with *Gisli Sursson's Saga*. Even though the main characters are introduced during the film's opening with portraits that explain key familial relations, it is a rare viewer who can keep track of these, as many of the characters enter the action belatedly. It is a task not made easier by the characters' physical resemblance and indistinguishable costumes. The audience would seem to be expected to be familiar with the original saga—the ultimate literary approach to adaptation. As such, it is an explicitly national approach, as the filmmakers could not expect a foreign audience to know the original text. Broadly speaking, director Guðmundsson concurs: "The purpose was not at all to reach foreigners. The purpose was always to reach Icelanders."[2]

As the saga's Norwegian part has not been included, the film begins *in medias res*, with the ill-fated brotherhood ceremony. Despite partly acknowledging that it would have been difficult to include the pre-history in Norway considering the time span of conventional film narratives, Bergljót Soffía Kristjánsdóttir has argued that as a result the film is lacking a convincing explanation for the siblings' rivalry.[3] Thus she regrets its erasure from the film and is critical of new material introduced and any tightening of the plot. As in much of literary-oriented adaptation criticism, the original saga is approached as a literary masterpiece, and most deviations from the original source are seen as problematic.[4] Conversely, I would propose the opposite and argue that the structural flaws of *The Outlaw* stem instead from adhering too closely to the original text, as the saga's episodic trajectory never gels into a fluid film narration. For example, Börkur's villainous role as Gísli's nemesis could have been strengthened by conflating his character with that of Eyjólfur. While such strategies are not uncommon when it comes to adapting extensive and sprawling narratives to film, the extreme literary prestige of the sagas allows little meddling with their original plots and characters. In fact, when forced to add material, the filmmakers have reverted to the literary heritage or other traditional cultural artifacts, for example, in the effective use of the Old Norse poem *Sayings of the High One* (*Hávamál*) during Vésteinn's funeral: "Cattle die, kinsmen die, / the self must also die; / I know one thing which never dies: / the reputation of each dead man."[5]

Finally, *The Outlaw*'s faithful approach is manifested in following the original dialogue to the extreme. Understandably, the saga's many famous lines, some of which have become common sayings, are delivered in the film. However, many dialogue scenes are delivered almost verbatim, as if the saga itself were the script, including the swearing of brotherhood, the plotting of Þorgrímur's murder between Gísli and the slave Geirmundur, the respective funerals of Vésteinn and Þorgrímur, Gísli's escape when imitating the Ingjald-fool, Eyjólfur being ridiculed by Gísli's wife Auður (Ragnheiður Steindórsdóttir), and finally Gísli's last stand. Herein lies to a great extent the film's heritage appeal by faithfully adhering to a classic literary text that represents the nation's golden age on screen.

Considering that *Gisli Sursson's Saga* was adapted in the early 1980s, it is extraordinary that it should still today remain the only saga adapted. While there are undoubtedly many reasons for this omission, *The Outlaw* manifested the difficulty of adapting the saga heritage: the almost incompatible goals of being faithful to the source while making a fluent cinematic narrative. As if responding to this dilemma, Hrafn Gunnlaugsson chose a fundamentally different approach to the heritage and the Viking era in making *When the Raven Flies* (1984, *Hrafninn flýgur*). It is of interest that *When the Raven Flies* has its origin in an aborted adaptation of Laxness's *Wayward Heroes* (*Gerpla*), whose film option had been bought by Gunnlaugsson's Swedish producer, Bo Jonsson. As such, the film would have brought together in one adaptation the two most revered literary sources, though perhaps not in a happy marriage, as the novel is a biting parody of the literary heritage. According to Gunnlaugsson, they were eventually forced to give up the project as the novel's extensive scope could not be adhered to while staying within the budget.[6] Instead, Gunnlaugsson ended up writing an original script inspired by the saga heritage, and while it is lacking Laxness's satire, it shows little of *The Outlaw*'s reverence.

When the Raven Flies begins with a short prelude set in Ireland, where plundering Vikings kill the parents of a young boy and kidnap his sister. Twenty years later, he arrives in Iceland as the mysterious stranger Gestur (Jakob Þór Einarsson), literally meaning a "guest," in search of revenge. Gestur turns his enemies against one another, with the Viking chief Eiríkur

(Helgi Skúlason) ultimately killing his longtime friend Þór (Flosi Ólafsson) and most of his clan. He then turns his attention to Eiríkur, who is now married to Gestur's sister (Edda Björgvinsdóttir), and kills him in a duel. The film ends with Gestur's young nephew handling the weapons used by Gestur in slaying his father, thus suggesting that the revenge cycle is about to repeat itself once again—all in all, a much simpler plot than that of *The Outlaw*, a direct cause-and-effect narrative focusing on a few well-established characters. Furthermore, the noble and handsome Vikings of *The Outlaw* have made way for grotesque and dirty figures dressed up in outlandish costumes. The film is clearly intended to de-romanticize the Viking period, and the characters do not think very highly of Iceland and would return to Norway if they were not political outlaws.[7]

Although not a direct sequel, Gunnlaugsson's next feature, *In the Shadow of the Raven* (1988, *Í skugga hrafnsins*), continued his exploration of the time period, with religion now added to feuds and bloody revenges. And in *The White Viking* (1991, *Hvíti víkingurinn*) religion took center place, as its more historically grounded narrative delineated the Christianization of Norway and Iceland. It has become commonplace to liken this trilogy, and especially *When the Raven Flies*, to the westerns of Sergio Leone and the samurai films of Kurosawa Akira. While there is little doubt that the basic plot structure of *When the Raven Flies* is borrowed from *Yojimbo* (1961) and *A Fistful of Dollars* (1964), there is good reason to question how closely Gunnlaugsson actually resembles the two auteurs. Bjørn Sørenssen has analyzed the interrelations of the three directors and arrived at some rather bold conclusions by grouping the samurai films of Kurosawa and the westerns of Leone together with the sagas themselves as they all share a generic "action orientation." Accordingly, "a movie like *When the Raven Flies* does not appear as a cheap pastiche of Kurosawa or Leone but as an appropriate way of transposing this specific literary material into cinematic form."[8] However, the connections Sørenssen ends up making between the sagas and the two auteurs are extremely broad, for example in stating that the "world of the saga, the Italo-western, and the samurai film is multifaceted, complex and volatile" and characterized by an "unbridled materialism."[9] Apart from the similarity of the plots in *When the Raven Flies*, *Yojimbo*, and *A Fistful of Dollars*, little support is given to Gunnlaugsson's supposed indebtedness to the two auteurs. In fact, Sørenssen acknowledges that Gestur is fundamentally different from the protagonists played by Clint Eastwood and Toshiro Mifune in that he is driven by a "fanatical need for revenge."[10] As such, the plot of *When the Raven Flies* owes at least as much to Leone's *Once Upon a Time in the West* (1968) as to *Yojimbo* and *A Fistful of Dollars*.

The comparison to Kurosawa strikes me as particularly tenuous, and I find that Gunnlaugsson's Viking trilogy shares little with Kurosawa in terms of visual compositions and general themes. Leone is, on the other hand, at least marginally present in Hans-Erik Phillip's Ennio Morricone–influenced score of *When the Raven Flies*, and perhaps also in the dirtiness and gruesomeness of the characters. More generally, the western tradition is evoked by Gunnlaugsson's choice of weapons, with swords and axes making way for bows, arrows, and knives. Moreover, the small blades Gestur throws at his opponents function like a revolver, allowing for duels of the western type (see Figure 8.1).

But in terms of aesthetics and Leone's excessive visual style, little comparable material is to be found in the Viking trilogy. The scene that I find most evocative of Leone in Gunnlaugsson's oeuvre is actually not found in the Viking trilogy at all, but in the contemporary setting of *Father's Estate* (1980, *Óðal feðranna*) when a departing bus reveals an arriving stranger, just as a departing train revealed Charles Bronson's character Harmonica in *Once Upon a Time in the West*—both with a comparable dramatic emphasis in the music score.

Figure 8.1 The duel between Gestur (Jakob Þór Einarsson) and his nemesis Eiríkur (Helgi Skúlason) in *When the Raven Flies* recalls the western more than traditional Viking battle scenes. Source: F.I.L.M.

Nonetheless, it would seem clear, and certainly Gunnlaugsson himself leaves little doubt in this regard, that Kurosawa and particularly Leone served as partial models in the making of *When the Raven Flies*.[11] By drawing in such a manner on foreign models, the director broke with the national inscription of *The Outlaw* and Icelandic cinema of the early 1980s, which might explain why it became the first Icelandic film to have some success abroad. If Gunnlaugsson's two Viking follow-ups were in many ways consistent with *When the Raven Flies* in terms of style and mise-en-scène, they were hardly indebted to Kurosawa or Leone in any meaningful way. However, they were the first films to transcend Iceland in terms of both narrative and production. *In the Shadow of the Raven* was an Icelandic-Swedish co-production, with outdoor scenes shot in Iceland but studio work conducted in Sweden. The crew was somewhat equally divided between Icelanders and Swedes, with a Danish composer thrown in the mix, and although primarily cast by Icelandic actors, the Swede Reine Brynolfsson played the main character. And despite drawing upon the saga heritage, its central source was the romance *Tristan and Isolde* and thus not of Icelandic origin.[12] Furthermore, the narrative revolves to a great extent around the conflict between Christianity and paganism, and thus thematically transcends its specific local setting. That conflict was also to become the main theme of Gunnlaugsson's third Viking feature, *The White Viking*, which dealt with King Ólafur Tryggvason's christening of first Norway and then Iceland. Shot in both countries, it was a pan-Nordic production made for film and television.

Thus, in terms of both narrative and production, Gunnlaugsson's Viking trilogy far transcended the national specificity of *The Outlaw*, whose adaptation of *Gisli Sursson's Saga* did away with both its Norwegian part and the thematic conflict between Christianity and paganism. However, it would be mistaken to group the trilogy with the transnational productions that began transforming Icelandic cinema during the 1990s. Indeed, director Gunnlaugsson himself asserts that he was not thinking "internationally" when making the trilogy.[13] Although the production context of the latter two films may of course undermine such intentions, Gunnlaugsson's assertion would seem both accurate and consistent with his broadly local oeuvre. Both films were made within a solely Nordic context whose regionalism far predates the transnational imperative—as evident by the historical subject of the trilogy itself, nota bene.

However, there is no questioning the fundamental difference between *The Outlaw* and Gunnlaugsson's trilogy, a difference that ultimately regards the national. Gunnlaugsson has not only constructed more conventional film narratives by drawing broadly upon the literary heritage rather than faithfully adapting specific texts, but also made his films somewhat available to a foreign audience. Conversely, *The Outlaw* almost demands an extensive knowledge of the literary heritage and particularly that of *Gisli Surrson's Saga* in its dedicated adherence to the original saga. In this, Gunnlaugsson's trilogy can be said to anticipate the explicit transnationalization so typical of subsequent Icelandic film adaptations, if only by steering away from direct saga adaptations. As a matter of fact, the trilogy was made during a period of Icelandic cinema in which adaptations all but disappeared.

Adaptation as Transnationalization

Considering the strong ties between Icelandic national identity and literature, one might expect adaptations to be unusually frequent in Iceland. However, nothing could be further from the truth, as they are actually comparatively rather rare.

Looking back over the first two decades of continuous film production in Iceland, a clear pattern emerges regarding adaptation. There is an overt reliance on literary sources in the establishing of national cinema in the early 1980s, most notably in 1981, when all three features were adaptations. But if Icelandic filmmakers felt thus compelled to draw upon the literary heritage, it would appear as if they soon became anxious about cinema being subordinated to literature. One thinks, for example, of Friðrik Þór Friðriksson's refusal to "make illustrations complementing the heritage."[14] In asserting the independence of cinema, literature was put aside. A ten-year drought between 1985 and 1994 followed: only one play, *Rust* (Lárus Ýmir Óskarsson, 1990, *Ryð*), and one novel, *Under the Glacier* (Guðný Halldórsdóttir, 1989, *Kristnihald undir jökli*), were adapted out of thirty films produced.

In trying to appeal to the local audience, comedies, rarely drawn from literature, become more frequent in this ten-year period than any other before or after.[15] At the other end of the spectrum, but with the same result as regards adaption, directors influenced by the European art cinema, like Friðriksson and Hilmar Oddsson, emerged with a more global vantage point. Icelandic cinema became increasingly transnational through this period, and the explicit national inscription of Icelandic literature may have appeared ill-suited to such productions. But the solution to this literary problem was just around the corner.

Toward the end of the 1990s, adaptations began surfacing again. To begin, filmmakers reverted to the heritage tradition established in the early 1980s by adapting canonical texts in numerous period pieces. Ágúst Guðmundsson directed his first film in fourteen years, *The Dance* (1998, *Dansinn*), which was adapted from a short story by William Heinesen. It remains the only outright Icelandic film adapted directly from a foreign source, but as such had not traveled far away from home, as Heinesen was a Faroese author who wrote in Danish.[16] Indeed, in terms of narrative and mise-en-scène, it could have taken place in a small Icelandic village in the early twentieth century. A year later, Hrafn Gunnlaugsson filmed Pastor Jón Magnússon's classic seventeenth-century account of his tormented sufferings in *Witchcraft* (*Myrkrahöfðinginn*), whose approach was actually far more local than the director's earlier Viking trilogy. After all, Iceland was much more isolated in the seventeenth century than it had been during the Viking period. That same year, the first Laxness adaptation in a decade, *Honour of the House* (Guðný Halldórsdóttir, *Ungfrúin góða og húsið*), opened, although the novella upon which it was based was hardly canonical. Despite following all the typical hallmarks of the heritage approach in its period setting and costumes, high-brow aesthetics, and alignment with the literary heritage, the film *Honour of the House* was fundamentally different from the original novella in one important regard.

Honour of the House tells the story of Þuríður (Tinna Gunnlaugsdóttir) and her younger sister Rannveig (Ragnhildur Gísladóttir), who returns pregnant from a lengthy stay in Copenhagen. To save the honor of the house, Rannveig is deprived of her child, leaving her an emotional wreck. Pregnant again, she is married to the social outcast Hans (Reine Brynolfsson), but her daughter is born sickly and dies at the age of ten. Although Copenhagen plays a considerable role in the novella, it appears only through dialogue and letters. The third-person narrator never describes events as taking place in Copenhagen, but presents them solely as second-hand accounts in the village. The filmmakers, on the other hand, have developed the references to Copenhagen into extensive scenes of comparable relevance to the Icelandic village setting itself. Not only is Rannveig's stay depicted in much more detail than in the novella, but a second visit by Þuríður to Copenhagen is added that ultimately changes the course of the narrative. Thus, a mostly local story of a small Icelandic village has been transnationalized into a film boasting a pan-Nordic cast and taking place in both Denmark and Iceland.

The narrative of *Honour of the House* is confined to Iceland and Denmark, but as regards financing and production it is primarily an Icelandic-Swedish film. The adaptation has clearly been affected by its production arrangements, but it would be inaccurate to say that they dictated the end result. The novella is often evasive and sparse in descriptions and thus gives the filmmakers ample opportunity to "film in" the blanks. Director Halldórsdóttir herself describes the novella as one akin to a good story sketch that gives her the freedom to develop it further on her own.[17] Nonetheless, it would seem apparent that the option of extending the narrative to Denmark made the novella a practical choice for a transnational production.

Although the adaptation of *101 Reykjavík* (Baltasar Kormákur, 2000) did the exact reverse by doing away with a section of the novel taking place abroad, it is one that exemplifies better than any other the process of transnationalization so typical of Icelandic adaptations at the turn of the century. The novel by Hallgrímur Helgason both draws upon Western pop culture and makes extensive use of the English language, which may of course also help explain why it was chosen as source material for this particular production. *101 Reykjavík*'s contemporary city setting sets it apart from earlier adaptations that were typically period pieces, and almost invariably located in the countryside. Finally, *101 Reykjavík* belonged to a new breed of Icelandic novels, whose adherence to popular entertainment showcased little of the highbrow features typical of Icelandic literature.

The novel offers a satirical take on contemporary Reykjavík, especially idle young males. The anti-hero Hlynur (Hilmir Snær Guðnason) spends his weekends partying, and weekdays flipping through television channels and browsing the internet, while a job remains pretty much out of the question. Hlynur's daily routines are turned upside down, though, when his mother Berglind (Hanna María Karlsdóttir) comes out as lesbian and his friend Hófí (Þrúður Vilhjálmsdóttir) becomes pregnant. The prose of *101 Reykjavík* makes extensive use of English, which Hallgrímsson spells in Icelandic: "Gró öpp!" "Maíkul Djakkson," and "Djísus Kræst."[18] In fact, Hlynur opposes the use of "Jesus Christ" on grounds of it being American and suggests Icelanders take up "Halldór Laxness" instead.[19] The Icelandic language is also accented for comic effect when dealing with immigrants and tourists. Often the text's comedy involves mixing Icelandic and English, for example when Hlynur translates various Icelandic place-names into English: "*Kidafell*. The Kid

That Fell. *Ingunnarstadir.* Ingunn's Place. *Saurbær.* Shit Farm. *Geldingaá.* Castration River."[20]

Popular Western culture is found in endless references to British music and American films and television—often very lengthy, like the extended debate on the ethnic origin of Anthony Quinn—while the novel itself is a playful rewriting of *Hamlet*.[21] The comedy also often involves placing Iceland in the context of international pop culture (e.g., subtle changes of well-known film titles: "A Reykjavik Werewolf in Gardabaer" and "Things to Do in Iceland When You're Alive").[22] To a certain extent, this unflinching tirade of language games and pop references ultimately turns the novel itself into the object it sets out to ridicule. *101 Reykjavík* does not so much parody MTV as it becomes MTV. As such, the novel was an ideal choice for a film adaptation intended to have a global appeal, and many of these references and jokes have been included in the film.

But the novel equally relies on a plethora of unexplained local references that would confuse most foreign readers and viewers, which have accordingly not made their way to the film. These include references to Icelandic cinema, literature, and local public figures ranging from sports broadcasters to politicians.[23] The film adaptation not only strategically avoided such local specificities and privileged international ones, but went one step further by changing the nationality of Berglind's girlfriend Lolla—now Lola (Victoria Abril)—from Icelandic to Spanish, and as a result, extensive portions of the film are in English. Furthermore, being a visitor unfamiliar with Iceland and Reykjavík, Lola is introduced to local specificities throughout the film, and by implication a foreign audience is receiving a guided tour through Reykjavík. In this, the film is fundamentally different from the novel, which despite its obsession with both the English language and Western pop culture, never addresses a foreign readership (and was only translated into English after the international success of the film). The novel's title "101" simply refers to the local postal code of downtown Reykjavík, but in the film it signals a brief introductory course on Reykjavík for foreigners (as "101" has no such connotations in Icelandic). *101 Reykjavík* has been transnationalized.[24]

Kormákur's second feature, *The Sea* (2002, *Hafið*), adhered closely to the transnational pattern laid out in *101 Reykjavík*. It was adapted from a locally focused play by Ólafur Haukur Símonarson that, despite being inspired by Shakespeare's *King Lear*, was set in a small Icelandic fishing village, had no foreign characters, and was in Icelandic only.[25] In unchanged form, *The Sea* was ill-suited to the new transnational imperative of contemporary

Icelandic cinema. However, the dilemma was solved by simply turning two of its characters into foreigners. Well-known after the international success of *Elling* (Petter Næss, 2001), the Norwegian actor Sven Nordin played an immigrant who speaks in accented Icelandic. More important, though, was the character of Lóa, who became the Frenchwoman Françoise (Hélène de Fougerolles), who is introduced in English to Icelandic customs in a similar manner to Lola in *101 Reykjavík*. The adaptation of *Cold Light* also made use of this technique, as discussed in the opening of this chapter. However, not all adaptations reverted to such obvious *trans*formations in appealing to a foreign audience, but went through a process of transnationalization nonetheless.

While *101 Reykjavík* was the most successful of these adaptations abroad, they were all easily outdone at the local box office by Friðriksson's *Angels of the Universe* (2000, *Englar alheimsins*). It was based on the popular and highly acclaimed novel of the same title by Einar Már Guðmundsson, who also wrote the script for the film.[26] Despite being a transnational production financed by companies and institutions from across Europe, *Angels of the Universe* was a faithful adaptation that made no concessions regarding the use of English or transnational narrative elements. The novel's first-person narrator Páll looks over the course of his life from beyond the grave, having committed suicide after suffering from depression and schizophrenia. The film, on the other hand, is concerned only with his adulthood and focuses in particular on the interrelations between Páll and other inmates at *Kleppur*—Reykjavík's oldest mental institution and a historical landmark. However, as Guðni Elísson has pointed out, the symbiosis between Páll's schizophrenia and the national turmoil of the latter half of the twentieth century is lost by erasing the early period of his life: "[Páll's] life reflects the nation's history. Páll is born March 30th 1949, the day Iceland joined NATO and his life ends a little over 40 years later with the fall of the Berlin wall."[27] Thus, the character's life no longer functions as an explicit national allegory in the film. In fact, writer Guðmundsson and director Friðriksson have gone out of their way to efface the novel's period settings in favor of a more abstract and universal one.[28] These changes help give the film a more global applicability as compared to the explicit national inscription of the novel. This semi-transnationalization of *Angels of the Universe* is equally apparent in its adherence to the European art film, its visually stunning look (shot by Dane Harald Paalgard), universal themes of anxiety and mental suffering, and its study of colorful social outcasts.

Even Guðmundsson, who directed the explicitly local adaptations of *Land and Sons* and *Gisli Sursson's Saga* in the early 1980s, adhered to a more global approach two decades later in his adaptation of Kristín Marja Baldursdóttir's novel *The Seagull's Laughter* (2001, *Mávahlátur*). The novel is set in a small Icelandic village in the postwar period, where the return of Freyja (Margrét Vilhjálmsdóttir) from America—or "Emiríka"—turns the village upside down. Now a widow, having lost her American husband, Freyja moves back to the working-class household of her youth, filled with women: her mother, aunt, and three cousins—the only man of the house usually out at sea. The women are all entranced by the many commodities Freyja has brought with her—most notably an endless variety of colorful dresses and a perfume like the one used by "Ríta Heivúrt."[29] The novel's third-person narration is mostly restricted to Agga (Ugla Egilsdóttir), the youngest girl of the household, and the one who harbors misgivings about the American intruder. She believes these are confirmed when the abusive husband of Freyja's friend Dísa (Bára Lyngdal) dies in a fire under suspicious circumstances. However, the police officer Magnús (Hilmir Snær Guðnason), with whom Agga confides, does not believe a word she says, as he is infatuated with Freyja, as are most other men in the village. However, Freyja ends up marrying high above her class status when she weds the affluent and respected Björn Theodór (Heino Ferch), resulting in a most strenuous relationship between Freyja and her stepmother (Jónína Ólafsdóttir). Magnús finally begins to listen to Agga's eyewitness testimony when Björn Theodór also dies under suspicious circumstances. However, when she herself reaches womanhood, Agga comes to realize that she is better off siding with her own sex than the law of patriarchy and dismisses her earlier testimony as a lie.

As in his earlier adaptations, Guðmundsson has remained faithful to his literary source and tampered with neither settings nor characters. If in this *The Seagull's Laughter* is very much in line with *Land and Sons* and *The Outlaw*, it is most different in other respects. It is a transnational production, financed by various production companies and institutions around Europe. But the filmmakers have mostly succeeded in veiling its transnational financing by steering foreign contributions behind the camera, including Peter Joachim Krause's cinematography, Tonie Jan Zetterström's production design, Henrik Møll's editing, and Ronen Waniewitz's jazzy score. It is perhaps only in the casting of Heino Ferch as Björn Theodór, whose dubbing is quite apparent, that the film's mise-en-scène can be said to show visible traces of its transnational funding.

Despite its local period setting, the narrative of *The Seagull's Laughter* has a much greater global applicability than Guðmundssons's early adaptations. Present throughout both novel and film is mythical America—the source of modern fashion, commodities, and cinema itself. Hollywood is present in numerous references to stars, fan magazines, and going-to-the-movies, as Agga's understanding of adult relations is seen to stem from Hollywood films: "Movies in which misunderstanding, hopelessness and tears preceded reconciliation and kisses, quenched a little [Agga and her friend's] thirst for a knowledge of a world that hitherto had remained hidden to them."[30] Further parallels are drawn between cinema and Agga, who investigates the world hidden away from the unfolding action.

The Seagull's Laughter has not done away with local and national elements, but has wrapped them up in global packaging—a quintessential transnational strategy. This is very much evident in the character of Freyja. On the one hand, she stems from the tradition of strong Icelandic women explicitly tied to nature, like Hadda Padda and Salka Valka, who were also expected to appeal to a foreign audience (see chapter three). Repeatedly, she is seen out walking late at night and becoming one with the lavascape surrounding the village. Conversely, as the lady from "Emiríka," Freyja also represents modernity, commodification, and possibly women's independence. This transnational character of Freyja as both national and foreign is perfectly captured in a scene depicting festivities on Independence Day. Freyja, her cousin Dódó (Edda Björg Eyjólfsdóttir), and Dísa arrive to the scene wearing immaculate red, white, and blue dresses, respectively. As these are the colors of the Icelandic flag, their ties to the nation are being privileged, at the cost of Freyja's blandly dressed upper-class rival Birna (Halldóra Geirharðsdóttir). However, these are the dresses Freyja brought with her from America, which also make up the colors of the American flag. In their dual nature, the dresses crystallize much of the transnational character of contemporary Icelandic cinema (see Figure 8.2).

The transnationalization typical of Icelandic adaptations at the turn of the century could take various forms. It includes everything from subtle changes, like downplaying the national allegorical aspects of the protagonist's life in *Angels of the Universe* and the introduction of colorful aesthetics and a jazzy score in *The Seagull's Laughter*, to explicit alterations in narrative, by either adding scenes taking place abroad, as in *Honour of the House*, or more typically by changing the nationality of characters so as to have recourse to English, as in *101 Reykjavík* and *The Sea*. When compared to the adaptations

Figure 8.2 Dressed in the colors of white, red, and blue, Dódó (Edda Björg Eyjólfsdóttir), Freyja (Margrét Vilhjálmsdóttir), and Dísa (Bára Lyngdal) simultaneously call forth the Icelandic and the American flags in *The Seagull's Laughter*. Source: Ísfilm.

discussed in the opening of this chapter, which in their faithful adherence to the adapted text made no attempts to reach out to a global audience, the overall differences could not be more pronounced. The Icelandic film industry of the early 1980s was inherently local and bent on making films for a domestic audience. Only two decades later, it had become immersed in the transnational imperative of world cinema that called for narratives addressed to audiences around the world. This shift clearly fundamentally altered the adaptation process of Icelandic novels at the turn of the century.

There will be no outright chapter devoted to adaptations in the third part of this book for the simple reason that their role in Icelandic cinema continued to dwindle. One might even go as far as to state that they are suspiciously absent from Icelandic cinema in the first two decades of the twenty-first century. No saga or Laxness novel has been adapted in the new century, and even the dream of making one seems to have evaporated. The few remaining film adaptations now stem primarily from popular literature rather than canonical classics, and we will consider some of these in our broader discussion of crime films and television series in the next part. Indeed, following the shift from the local to the global, we also increasingly see a shift from the highbrow to the popular in the new century.

9
Overview III, 2000–2020

The new century welcomed Icelandic cinema with open arms as an unusually high number of films were released in the centenary year. *Angels of the Universe* (*Englar alheimsins*) was the most successful in terms of critical reception and box office, further cementing the leading position of its director, Friðrik Þór Friðriksson. But change was in the air as well, as four of the films were debuts, notably set in Reykjavík and characterized by playful approaches that harkened back to the 1992 duo *Remote Control* (Óskar Jónasson, *Sódóma Reykjavík*) and *Wallpaper* (Júlís Kemp, *Veggfóður*). These were Ragnar Bragason's *Fiasco* (*Fíaskó*), Jóhann Sigmarsson's *Plan B* (*Óskabörn þjóðarinnar*), Róbert I. Douglas's *The Icelandic Dream* (*Íslenski draumurinn*), and Baltasar Kormákur's *101 Reykjavík*. Although the cheeky comedy *The Icelandic Dream* was by far the most profitable at the local box office, directors Bragason and especially Kormákur were to have the most impact on Icelandic filmmaking in the new century. *101 Reykjavík* was the only successful film abroad, and soon Kormákur would replace Friðriksson as the leading figure of Icelandic cinema.

The pioneers of the early 1980s, on the other hand, had faced various difficulties and had looked back nostalgically to that golden era of Icelandic cinema referred to as the "film spring." Ágúst Guðmundsson directed a belated sequel to his all-time box-office hit, *On Top* (1982, *Með allt á hreinu*), called *Ahead of Time* (2004, *Í takt við tímann*), while Guðný Halldórsdóttir revitalized another eighties hit, *The Icelandic Shock Station* (Þórhildur Þorleifsdóttir, 1986, *Stella í orlofi*), with *Stella for Office* (2002, *Stella í framboði*). After the box-office bomb *Witchcraft* (1999, *Myrkrahöfðinginn*), Hrafn Gunnlaugsson directed his last film, *A Revelation for Hannes* (2003, *Opinberun Hannesar*), which caused a media sensation due to accusations of questionable financing from the Icelandic Film Fund.[1] More consequential, though, in the long run was the bankruptcy of Friðriksson's production company, the Icelandic Film Corporation, that had been so instrumental to filmmaking in Iceland throughout the nineties. It was a sign of the times when Friðriksson directed *Niceland* (2004) for the production company Zik Zak Filmworks. Since then, he has directed only one more feature, while Zik Zak has become an integral part of the Icelandic film scene. Even though *Niceland* was an aesthetic and commercial failure, it signified a shift from director-centered film production toward one with a clear separation between producers and directors, as Zik Zak developed projects in-house for others to direct. The border between the two, though, is not always clear. For example, the production company Blue-Eyes has primarily produced works by Kormákur, but it is currently experiencing an expansion under the name of Rvk. Studios. The firms Pegasus and Saga Film are better examples of this shift, as both produce television series, advertisements, and feature films, while also servicing foreign runaway productions. Thus in the twenty-first century the film scene has been utterly transformed, and arguably, it only now makes sense to speak of an Icelandic film industry.

This altered industrial environment had considerable impact on the kind of films that were made in Iceland during the aughts. In short, the art cinema that characterized the nineties soon made way for genre films along the lines of Hollywood. It is worth keeping in mind that this shift is not limited to Icelandic cinema, but follows trends already in place in the other Nordic countries and elsewhere in Europe. In fact, Icelandic cinema could still be understood as being influenced by European filmmaking, which was itself drawing upon Hollywood to a greater extent than in the past.

Notably, Dagur Kári was the only new director to emerge during the decade who was working within the parameters of art cinema, and his debut film *Noi the Albino* (2003, *Nói albínói*) was a major hit at the international film festival circuit. He continued to work in this mode while alternating between languages in the Danish *Dark Horse* (2005, *Voksne mennesker*) and the English-language film *The Good Heart* (2009), while other filmmakers turned their backs on art cinema. After the duo *Children* (2006, *Börn*) and *Parents* (2007, *Foreldrar*), intense and critically acclaimed dramas shot in black and white, Bragason turned to television comedy. His success culminated in the spin-off feature *Mr. Bjarnfredarson* (2009, *Bjarnfreðarson*), one of the decade's biggest hits at the local box office. After his art cinema follow-up to *101 Reykjavík*, the *King Lear*–inspired *The Sea* (2002, *Hafið*), Kormákur made the crime films *A Little Trip to Heaven* (2005), an English-language production starring American actor Forrest Whitaker, and *Jar City* (2006, *Mýrin*), whose popularity at home and abroad would help him replace Friðriksson as the country's leading filmmaker.

It was not the first time that Icelanders made crime films, let alone comedies, but the genre films that took over Icelandic cinema during the aughts now imitated the plots, formulas, and aesthetics of Hollywood genre films in ways they had not done prior. Crime films were by far the most conspicuous representatives of this shift, including *Cold Trail* (Björn Br. Björnsson, 2006, *Köld slóð*), *Reykjavík Rotterdam* (Óskar Jónasson, 2008), and *Higher Force* (Ólafur Jóhannesson, 2008, *Stóra planið*), in addition to numerous television series, while other examples include the fantasy *Astropia* (Gunnar B. Guðmundsson, 2007, *Astrópía*), the horror film *Reykjavík Whale Watching Massacre* (Júlíus Kemp, 2009), and the adventure children's film *The Big Rescue* (Bragi Þór Hinriksson, 2009, *Algjör Sveppi og leitin að Villa*).

Documentary films also returned to the fore during the decade, but they had been long neglected by the Icelandic Film Fund, which had directed its limited resources to establishing a national cinema that prioritized narrative feature filmmaking. Several documentaries released in theaters generated extensive buzz in the media. These include: *Lalli Johns* (Þorfinnur Guðnason, 2001), about a well-known outsider in Reykjavík; *In the Shoes of the Dragon* (Hrönn Sveinsdóttir og Árni Sveinsson, 2002, *Í skóm drekans*), an exposé of Iceland's major beauty pageant; *Last Stop* (Ólafur Sveinsson, 2002, *Hlemmur*), about homeless alcoholics and other outsiders dwelling at the capital's major bus stop; and *Shining Star* (Ólafur Jóhannesson, 2004, *Blindsker*), about Iceland's most celebrated singer, Bubbi Morthens. The global economic collapse of 2008, which hit Iceland especially hard, and the 2010 volcano eruption of *Eyjafjallajökull* would greatly impact the focus of Icelandic documentaries at the end of the decade. In rare cases, documentaries also began addressing foreign audiences—*Dreamland* (Þorfinnur Guðnason and Andi Snær Magnason, 2009, *Draumalandið*) is a particularly pertinent case in its examination of big industry and environmentalism. As evidence of this new golden era, the Skjaldborg Film Festival has been held at *Patreksfjörður* since 2008, showcasing a plethora of new documentary films every year.

If the novelty of the first decade of the twenty-first century was the introduction of Hollywood genres and aesthetics into Icelandic filmmaking, the most striking novelty of the second decade was the arrival of Hollywood itself. There was a precedent for earlier runaway productions, including the two James Bond films *A View to a Kill* (John Glen, 1985) and *Die Another Day* (Lee Tamahori, 2002). However, it was only in the teens that the number and scope of such productions reached a point where they began to impact conventional Icelandic filmmaking and had to be considered an instrumental part of the Icelandic film industry. In the summer of 2012 alone, film crews were traveling all over Iceland to shoot material for the Tom Cruise star vehicle *Oblivion* (Joseph Kosinski, 2013), the Marvel superhero film *Thor: The Dark World* (Alan Taylor, 2013), Darren Aronofsky's biblical epic *Noah* (2014), and Ben Stiller's *The Secret Life of Walter Mitty* (2013), where Iceland was also actually part of the plot as well, among other projects.

It is impossible to tell with any certainty whether a new and different understanding of the nature of Icelandic national cinema paved the way for the extensive role of Hollywood in the twenty-first century, as regards both its aesthetic influence upon local genre films and its very own runaway productions, or if it is only after the fact that we find ourselves needing to rethink the meaning of Icelandic cinema. The Icelandic Film Fund was established in the late 1970s on cultural grounds and as a counterweight against the omnipresence of Hollywood films. It was considered important to make films in Icelandic, about Icelandic topics (including literary adaptations), for Icelanders and by Icelanders. In other words, the films were intended to be artistic and national and thus diametrically opposed to Hollywood. But incrementally, with its emphasis on generic filmmaking and commercialism, Hollywood became the model for an Icelandic film industry now prioritizing entertainment, productivity, job creation, profits, and tourism. To a certain degree, filmmaking in Iceland simply responds to the expansion of neoliberalism, but the industry's representatives have also played their part in this shift by emphasizing financial gain over national, cultural, and aesthetic priorities, in their argument for renewed financial support from the state. To summarize, Icelandic cinema is now broadly defined in industrial rather than cultural terms, and on that basis, it matters little whether the product is Icelandic or American.

It is worth emphasizing that the different paradigms characterizing each decade of this historical survey (the national cultural focus in the eighties, European art cinema in the nineties, Hollywood genres in the aughts, and finally runaway productions in the teens) do not replace one another but instead augment the plurality of Icelandic national cinema. Indeed, the popularity of Icelandic crime films continued unabated in the teens, as exemplified by *City State* (Ólafur Jóhannesson, 2011, *Borgríki*), *Black's Game* (Óskar Axelsson, 2012, *Svartur á leik*), and *The Oath* (Baltasar Kormákur, 2016, *Eiðurinn*), along with TV series like *Trapped* (Baltasar Kormákur, 2015-2021, *Ófærð*) and *Stella Blómkvist* (Óskar Axelsson, 2017-2021).

While Ólafur Jóhannesson and Óskar Axelsson drew upon international crime formulas in their films, Kormákur literally directed a couple of successful Hollywood crime films—the Mark Wahlberg star vehicles *Contraband* (2010) and *2 Guns* (2012), joined by Denzel Washington in the latter. Kormákur also added real-life survival narratives to his authorial repertoire—the local production *The Deep* (2012, *Djúpið*), before making *Everest* (2015) and *Adrift* (2018) in Hollywood. Other genre films include the horror films *Frost* (Reynir Lyngdal, 2012), *Rift* (Erlingur Óttar Thoroddsen, 2017, *Rökkur*) and *I Remember You* (Óskar Axelsson, 2017, *Ég man þig*) and the animated features *Legends of Valhalla: Thor* (Óskar Jónasson, Toby Genkel, and Gunnar Karlsson, 2011, *Hetjur Valhallar: Þór*) and *Ploey* (Árni Ólafur Ásgeirsson, 2018, *Lói: Þú flýgur aldrei einn*). Along with Baldvin Zophoníasson's melodramas *Life in a Fishbowl* (2014, *Vonarstræti*) and *Let Me Fall* (2018, *Lof mér að falla*) and the Sveppi series (2010–2014) of children's films by Bragi Þór Hinriksson, the decade's most popular films—*Black's Game*, *The Oath*, *I Remember You*, and to a certain extent *The Deep*—all stem from genre productions.

A sharp generational shift also took place during the teens. Friðriksson made his last film with *Mamma Gógó* (2010), while Guðmundsson directed the comedy *Spooks and Spirits* (2013, *Ófeigur gengur aftur*), which shared little with his prior work. In addition to the prolificacy of Kormákur, the decade was characterized by the arrival of new directors. Axelsson, Benedikt Erlingsson, Guðmundur Arnar Guðmundsson, Grímur Hákonarson, Jón Atli Jónasson, Þór Ómar Jónsson, Reynir Lyngdal, Hlynur Pálmason, Rúnar Rúnarsson, Hafsteinn Gunnar Sigurðsson, Bjarni Haukur Þórsson, Marteinn Þórsson, and Zophoníasson, all made their debuts early in the decade. What is striking, however, about this long list is that it does not include a single female director. Thankfully that changed toward the end of the decade as four women released their debut features: Guðrún Ragnarsdóttir's *Summer Children* (2017, *Sumarbörn*), Ása Helga Hjörleifsdóttir's *The Swan* (2017, *Svanurinn*), Ísold Uggadóttir's *And Breathe Normally* (2018, *Andið eðlilega*), and Ásthildur Kjartansdóttir's *The Deposit* (2019, *Tryggð*). These films testify to an important gender shift onscreen as well, with female characters figuring more prominently than ever before. The latter two films also address the issue of ethnicity, which has been conspicuously absent in Icelandic cinema. *And Breathy Normally* also focuses on queer characters, as do several other recent pictures, such as the horror film *Rift* and the teenage drama *Heartstone* (Guðmundur Arnar Guðmundsson, 2016, *Hjartasteinn*). On the whole, these films suggest that contemporary Icelandic cinema is slowly but surely becoming more diverse.

Although hurting in comparison to local genre fare at the box office, art cinema also remained an integral part of the national cinema with a number of films doing well at the international film festival circuit. Most strikingly, Icelandic filmmakers won the Nordic Council Film Prize three times over a five-year period, having never won it previously (the prize was first awarded in 2002). Erlingsson also became the second director, after Thomas Vinterberg, to receive the award twice, with his first two films, *Of Horses and Men* (2013, *Hross í oss*) and *Woman at War* (2018, *Kona fer í stríð*). Kári received the same award for *Virgin Mountain* (2015, *Fúsi*), which also won the main prize at the Tribeca Film Festival. Hákonarsson's debut feature *Rams* (2015, *Hrútar*) was awarded the Un Certain Regard Prize in Cannes, and was later remade under the same name in 2020 by Jeremy Sims. Sigurðsson followed his debut film *Either Way* (2011, *Á annan veg*), remade as *Prince Avalanche* by David Gordon Green in 2013, with *Under the Tree* (2017, *Undir trénu*), which somewhat unusually became a hit both at home and abroad. Interestingly, Pálmason's debut feature *Winter Brothers* (2018, *Vinterbrødre*) and third film *Godland* (2022, *Vanskabte Land/Volaða land*) were both nominated by Denmark for the Nordic Council Film Prize, while his second feature *A White, White Day* (2019, *Hvítur, hvítur dagur*) represented Iceland—and while it did not win, the film did have an outstanding international reception. Rúnarsson also made three strong but quite different art films during the decade. With the exception of Kári, all these directors were newcomers during the teens, hinting that art cinema can continue to thrive next to the more popular genre cinema at the local box office.

The upcoming chapter focuses on the overwhelming popularity of the crime genre, which exemplifies the influence of generic Hollywood filmmaking during this period. It provides a survey of the crime genre's history while looking more closely at prominent examples. The chapter also continues our investigation of adaptation as two of its three primary case studies, *Jar City* and *Black's Game*, are adaptations, while the third, *Reykjavik Rotterdam*, was remade in Hollywood as *Contraband*. Chapter eleven, "Hollywood Does Iceland," addresses Hollywood runaway productions and their impact upon Icelandic national cinema. It also places the films in a larger historical context that considers Iceland's exotic image abroad, going all the way back to Jules Verne's *Journey to the Center of the Earth*. Chapter twelve, "Icelandic Women's Cinema," looks at the contributions of women to Icelandic filmmaking, especially the four debut directors of the late teens. Through close analyses of all of their films, the chapter not only describes each director's particular impact, but also examines the applicability of women's cinema to contemporary Icelandic cinema. The last chapter of the book takes us back to the beginning by turning its attention to the revival of nature in Icelandic films. However, as the chapter details, the new films depart from the earlier focus on landscape to consider issues related to animals and their interactions with humans. An epilogue follows that assesses the status of Icelandic cinema today while also drawing attention to how it has belatedly become attentive to its own past as Icelandic filmmakers have at last discovered their own history.

10
Crime Fiction, Film, and Television

Under the banner of noir, Nordic crime fiction, film, and television have become a globally recognized phenomenon. Nordic crime novels top bestselling lists around the world while television series are being remade outside the region—overshadowing crime films proper. Although typically traced back to the pioneering police procedurals by writer-couple Maj Sjöwall and Per Wahlöö, Nordic noir really took off as a global phenomenon with the spectacular success of Swedish novelists Henning Mankell and especially Stieg Larson, and film and television adaptations of their respective *Wallander* and *Girl with Dragon Tattoo* series. Denmark joined the fray with *The Killing* (Søren Sveistrup, 2007–2012, *Forbrydelsen*) before partnering with Sweden in the making of *The Bridge* (Hans Rosenfeldt, 2011–2018, *Broen/Bron*). Although there can be no doubt about the leading role played by Sweden and Denmark, the other Nordic countries have played an important role in Nordic noir as well—including Iceland, as this chapter will make clear.[1] Arnaldur Indriðason, Yrsa Sigurðardóttir, and Ragnar Jónasson are among the Icelandic writers that have experienced success in translation (only the novels of Nobel Prize laureate Halldór Laxness compare when it comes to global distribution of modern Icelandic literature). Crime television series have changed the local screen landscape, and *Trapped* (Baltasar Kormákur, 2015–2021, *Ófærð*) has followed in the global footsteps of *The Killing* and *The Bridge*. Finally, Icelandic crime films have topped the domestic box office repeatedly and even have done well abroad, winning top prizes at festivals and being remade in Hollywood. It is therefore no exaggeration to say that crime has taken over Icelandic popular culture.

In this chapter I will begin with an overview of the Icelandic crime phenomenon before analyzing its first major film hit, *Jar City* (Baltasar Kormákur, 2006, *Mýrin*), and then turning to *Reykjavík Rotterdam* (Óskar Jónasson, 2008) and its American remake, *Contraband* (Baltasar Kormákur, 2012), before wrapping up with *Black's Game* (Óskar Axelsson, 2012, *Svartur á leik*) and the television series *Trapped*. Both *Jar City* and *Black's Game* are adaptations of popular novels, but the intertextual borrowings of all these texts are much more complex than the one-way model of adaptation suggests. For that reason I will also be delving into broader questions regarding the topic and will devote specific sections of the chapter to adaptation, remakes, and intertextuality, respectively. The chapter thus aims to not only give an overview of Icelandic crime fiction, film, and television, but also consider some key issues in adaptation theory through these specific case studies.

A Belated Sea Change

Crime fiction arrived belatedly to the Icelandic literary scene—perhaps due to the fact that Iceland did not have much of a crime scene. Even in the early twenty-first century, only two murders were committed on average annually, and rarely did they involve any mystery. But these numbers are a bit deceiving because of Iceland's small population, and the murder rate per capita is actually similar to those of Germany and Denmark and a bit higher than those of Italy and Norway.[2] Thus while the actual numbers themselves remain small, they do not explain the early lack of crime fiction in Iceland while it was blooming in the other Nordic countries—including Norway. The explanation is more likely to be found in the particular role that literature played in forming Icelandic national identity, and the high esteem in which Icelandic language and literature are held to this day. Novels signaled cultural elevation rather than entertainment. As a consequence, paperback fiction was frowned upon: both the material (novels were almost solely published as hardbacks) and the content. Maj Sjöwall and Per Wahlöö probably slipped through the cracks (in hardcover) as their novels offered a social critique elevating them above the charge of being pure entertainment.[3] But they did not help establish crime fiction as an integral part of the Icelandic literary scene, as elsewhere in the Nordic countries. Moreover, Icelandic crime fiction was virtually nonexistent until the late 1990s, and translations of the Scandinavian variety were rare—even the internationally renowned Henning Mankell was not translated until 1998, a year after the Icelandic breakthrough author Arnaldur Indriðason wrote his first novel. In the twenty-first century, however, Scandinavian crime fiction began to crowd the local bestselling lists, including novels by Tom Egeland, Karin Fossum, Anne Holt, Jørn Lier Horst, Mons Kallentoft, Jens Lapidus, Unni Lindell, Camilla Läckberg, Liza Marklund, Jo Nesbø, Jussi Adler-Olsen, Leif GW

Persson, Vidar Sundstøl, and Johan Theorin, not to mention the global phenomenon of Stieg Larsson's Millenium trilogy.[4]

As regards Icelandic crime fiction, it can be broadly divided into three categories. The first is characterized by writers like Yrsa Sigurðardóttir, Viktor Arnar Ingólfsson, and Óttar Norðfjörð, whose work is based on fanciful plotting and sometimes also supernatural elements. A good example is Sigurðardóttir's *I Remember You* (*Ég man þig*), which intertwines a ghost story with a more conventional crime mystery. The second is inspired by hard-boiled fiction of the American kind and includes writers Stella Blómkvist (pseudonym), Árni Þórarinsson, and Stefan Máni—author of *Black's Game*, analyzed later in this chapter. Outright private detectives, however, hardly exist in Iceland and would seem to constitute the verisimilitude borderline: fanciful murders are acceptable, but not private detectives. Instead, lawyers or journalists typically take on the role of the private detective. The third and largest group consists of police procedurals written by, among others, Ævar Örn Jósepsson, Ragnar Jónasson, and Indriðason. It is also this group that is most influenced by the socially conscious Swedish authors Sjöwall and Wahlöö and their heir Mankell. Indeed, Indriðason's Detective Inspector Erlendur bears an uncanny resemblance to his Swedish predecessors Martin Beck and especially Kurt Wallander. Both Erlendur and Wallander are divorced and suffer from various ills, including a past trauma, face constant familial problems centered on their relationship with their daughters, and are somewhat old-fashioned and troubled by today's society. Society is the central concern of these police procedurals, as the crime and its investigation invariably also uncover one social problem or another.

It did take a few years for Icelandic filmmakers to catch up and take advantage of this dramatic change in the publishing realm. However, when they finally did so, midway through the aughts, it was to constitute a most dramatic shift as genre cinema—and primarily that of crime—took center stage in Icelandic filmmaking for the first time. Although Scandinavian (and British) influences can be detected, particularly in crime series made for television, this was the first time that Hollywood served as the primary model for Icelandic filmmaking. Certainly, crime had surfaced as a subject earlier, but only rarely in the genre-specific manner that became the dominant trend in Icelandic cinema around the middle of the decade.[5] In addition to *Jar City*, such prominent films were made as *A Little Trip to Heaven* (Baltasar Kormákur, 2005), *Cold Trail* (Björn Br. Björnsson, 2006, *Köld slóð*), *The Higher Force* (Ólafur Jóhannesson, 2008, *Stóra planið*), and

Reykjavík-Rotterdam. Perhaps even more striking was the swift introduction of crime series on television and their rapid ascendancy to dominance over other fiction series. Examples of such series during the aughts include *Every Colour of the Sea Is Cold* (Anna Th. Rögnvaldsdóttir, 2005, *Allir litir hafsins eru kaldir*), *Black Angels* (Óskar Jónasson, 2008, *Svartir englar*), *I Hunt Men* (Björn Br. Björnsson, 2008, *Mannaveiðar*), *Press* (Óskar Jónasson, 2008, *Pressa*), and *The Cliff* (Reynir Lyngdal, 2009, *Hamarinn*).

Remarkably, when Óskar Jónasson, one of the more prominent directors of the crime wave, directed his debut film, *Remote Control* (*Sódóma Reykjavík*), in 1992 it was a comic spoof of the crime genre, which profited from the incongruity between Icelandic society (mostly devoid of organized crime) and Hollywood genre conventions. When making *Reykjavík-Rotterdam* and the television series *Black Angels* and *Press* fifteen years later, this incongruity would seem to have evaporated altogether as Icelandic society was placed firmly within these genre conventions. As already noted in relation to Icelandic crime fiction, this is less likely to stem from changes taking place in the Icelandic "crime scene" itself than from a different cultural sensibility privileging entertainment over highbrow art. It would be misleading, though, to separate the cultural realm here from the sphere of economics, as during this same period neoliberalism transformed the Icelandic film and television industry. As in many other Icelandic institutions, filmmaking became subject to such neoliberal criteria as efficiency, privatization, and profitability; acceptance and popularity were now to be gained from genre cinema and television serial production. And as the Hollywood business model replaced earlier norms, it brought its narrative formulas, generic patterns, and even ideological baggage.

Jar City and Adaptation

Jar City was not only the most successful of all the crime films that flooded Icelandic film screens in the aughts, but the biggest overall hit at the local box office during the decade. Furthermore, it did very well abroad where it was able to transcend its genre constraints and cross over into the festival circuit: most notably winning the main award at Karlovy Vary in 2007. To a certain extent, its success can be attributed to the original novel, as Arnaldur Indriðason was then, and remains, the most successful of all the Icelandic crime novelists. He is the pioneering figure of this literary phenomenon and its most popular representative in Iceland and abroad. In addition to drawing upon the popularity of the original novel, the film was given a marketing and distribution campaign modeled on Hollywood, including a wide release of the kind typically reserved for the biggest of Hollywood blockbusters. But what is rather striking about the film's international success is that *Jar City* was primarily a local production, unlike the earlier transnational films that garnered success outside Iceland partly by catering to a foreign audience, including director Baltasar Kormákur's own adaptations of Hallgrímur Helgason's novel *101 Reykjavík* in 2000 and Ólafur Haukur Símonarsson's play *The Sea* (*Hafið*) in 2002. Unlike these earlier adaptations, no catering to art cinema or narrative changes occur in the adaptation to make the film more accessible to a foreign audience.

Two quintessential themes shape the crimes committed in the novel *Tainted Blood*.[6] One is the conception of their being uniquely Icelandic; the other is that these are crimes committed primarily against women. The film has faithfully adapted the prior element while engaging in some fundamental and problematic alterations as regards the latter. The changes made are symptomatic of the different economic models, aesthetic norms, and political implications of Hollywood filmmaking as compared to not only European art cinema but also Scandinavian crime fiction. Thus, a close reading of the adaptation helps shed light on what is at stake in the twenty-first-century transformation of Icelandic cinema.

Tainted Blood was Indriðason's third entry in his series on Detective Inspector Erlendur (Ingvar Sigurðsson), who despite being born in the remote Eastfjords of Iceland lives and works in the capital Reykjavík. On the police force, Erlendur is assisted by both Elínborg (Ólafía Hrönn Jónsdóttir), a female partner, and Sigurdur Óli (Björn Hlynur Haraldsson), whose American influence provides a counterpoint to Erlendur's rather old-fashioned local customs: "Sigurdur Óli was [. . .] a graduate in criminology from an American University. He was everything that Erlendur was not: modern and organized."[7] Although these three provide the core of Erlendur's team, numerous other characters enter the fray, as is typical of the police procedural: forensic experts, pathologists, retired colleagues, and meddling supervisors.

The plot of *Tainted Blood* is quite complicated as it involves numerous crimes—two murders, two rapes, and a case involving child sexual abuse. It turns out that the murder victim found at the beginning of the novel, an older man named Holberg (Þorsteinn Gunnarsson), had back in 1974 murdered a former friend, Grétar, who had been blackmailing him, and whose mysterious disappearance is solved when a body is discovered, buried under Holberg's floor. It is also discovered that Holberg had raped two women at an earlier time, resulting in their respective pregnancies. Unbeknownst to him, he had carried a genetic disease, which led to the early death of Auður, the daughter of his first rape victim, Kolbrún, who subsequently took her own life. The second rape victim, Katrín (Kristbjörg Kjeld), raised her son Einar/Örn (Atli Rafn Sigurðsson) as if he were one of the children she had had with her husband. While Einar showed no signs of the disease, he unknowingly passed it on to his daughter, who died of it. After her death, Einar began a secret investigation at his workplace, the national Genetic Research Centre. Having discovered the truth of the matter, he confronted his real father, Holberg, and killed him, unpremeditatedly, before ultimately committing suicide at the grave of his half-sister Auður. The complex and intriguing plot also draws parallels to Erlendur's personal life, for his daughter Eva Lind (Ágústa Eva Erlendsdóttir) is a drug addict facing numerous difficulties, including an unexpected pregnancy. Eva Lind also encourages Erlendur to look for her friend Dísa Rós, who has disappeared; Erlendur discovers that her disappearance is a consequence of having suffered prolonged sexual abuse by her father. The social problems uncovered and highlighted in this expansive narrative concern widespread and multifaceted gender-based injustice.

Although Reykjavík is the scene of the murder at the opening of *Tainted Blood*, the crime investigation reaches throughout Iceland. Interestingly, at least one English publication of the novel includes four maps to help situate the reader: one of Iceland, one of *Reykjanes* Peninsula (the southwest corner of Iceland), and two of Reykjavík. Many of these settings call for a local knowledge that is not easily translated, and while the novel's geography has been simplified in the film adaptation by limiting it to Reykjavík and *Reykjanes* (e.g., by relocating one of the rapes from *Húsavík* in the far northeast to *Reykjanes* and thus closer to Reykjavík), locations are otherwise true to the novel. Although prior familiarity with the setting remains helpful, I suspect locations are more easily apprehended in the film than in the novel, as the mise-en-scène speaks volumes. Reykjavík, including the modern office building of the Genetic Research Centre, often resembles any other Western city, in opposition to the countryside, typified by the rustic house and cemetery by the coast. It is also worth pointing out that the landscape in *Jar City* differs significantly from the majestic and tourist-friendly imagery typical of transnational Icelandic cinema. Atmospheric though it may be, the lavascape of *Reykjanes* Peninsula and the gray Atlantic Ocean appear gruesome and cold; the harrowing wind, bleak skies, and relentless rain contrast with conventional tourist imagery (see Figure 10.1). Unlike many of the earlier transnational films in which the landscape was the ultimate national signifier, in *Jar City* the landscape functions primarily as background, even if it does have some narrative importance and may still generate some exotic appeal abroad. The novel involves an altogether different national motif—the not so typical Icelandic murder—to which the film adheres faithfully. This motif was to arouse considerable interest abroad.

The incongruency between crime fiction and the Icelandic "crime scene" is explicitly addressed in relation to the murder of Holberg at the opening of *Tainted Blood*:

"Isn't this your typical Icelandic murder?" asked Detective Sigurdur Óli who had entered the basement without Erlendur noticing him and was now standing beside the body.

"What?" said Erlendur engrossed in his thoughts.

"Squalid, pointless and committed without any attempt to hide it, change the clues or conceal the evidence."

"Yes," said Erlendur. "A pathetic Icelandic murder."[8]

Sigurdur Óli's complaint about the murder's apparently crude obviousness speaks to the lack of "exciting" crimes in the Icelandic context. As a genre,

Figure 10.1 The police procedural *Jar City* forgoes more typical tourist-friendly landscapes for gloomy weather and the somber lava fields of *Reykjanes* Peninsula. Source: Sögn ehf.

crime fiction of course requires complicated crimes with their clues, evidence, and investigations. In the end, this murder will also turn out to be a complicated one, and therefore not a typical Icelandic crime at all, yet nonetheless quintessentially Icelandic. Step by step, Erlendur and his colleagues begin to realize the unusual nature of the murder: "I know Icelandic murders aren't complicated, but there's something about this one that doesn't fit if you just want to put it down to coincidence."[9] As it turns out, the solution to the crime is found in the genes of the Icelandic nation as a whole, which by implication raises relevant questions regarding contemporary Icelandic society:

> The Genetic Research Centre had recently begun collecting medical data about all the Icelanders, past and present, to process into a database containing health information about the whole nation. It was linked up to a genealogy database in which the family of every single Icelander was traced back to the Middle Ages; they called it establishing the Icelandic genetic pool. [...] It was said that the homogenous nation and lack of miscegenation made Iceland a living laboratory for genetic research.[10]

Having first discovered to his dismay that Auður's brain has been kept in a jar for research purposes in the so-called Jar City, a bio-sample bank from which the film takes its name, Erlendur is in for another shock when he realizes the extent of personal information gathered in the database of the Genetic Research Centre. Face to face with one of its directors, Erlendur rants: "And you keep all these secrets. Old family secrets. Tragedies, sorrows and death, all carefully classified in computers. Family stories and stories of individuals. Stories about me and you. You keep the whole secret and can call it up whenever you want. A Jar City for the whole nation."[11] Thus the riddle first solved by Einar and only subsequently by Erlendur, the complex web untangled by tracing the hereditary disease from Holberg down to Einar's daughter, is presented as just one emblematic secret in the vast database. Or rather, the database is a web made out of the family secrets that comprise the Icelandic nation—"that little community, Iceland, where everyone seem[s] related or connected in some way."[12] It is as if the national character itself is being uncovered or "decoded." "'Paternity,' Sigurdur Óli said, putting on his rubber gloves. 'Can we ever be sure about that in Iceland?'"[13]

The murder mystery is thus embedded in the Icelandic nation's genetic code, its obsession with family trees and origins, and the attempt of corporations to turn the nation into a profitable guinea pig. In adapting the novel, Kormákur has kept faith with and emphasized these national elements, ranging from the typical Icelandic murder to the genetic database. Considering the extensive nationwide debates regarding the controversial deCODE Genetics, upon which the Genetic Research Centre is explicitly modeled (and whose founder and director Kári Stefánsson even plays himself in a small role in the film), *Jar City* has much in common with what Andrew Nestingen has defined as a "medium concept cinema" in contemporary Scandinavian filmmaking, and which he considers a key product of its neoliberal shift. In particular, he emphasizes the national or regional topical nature of medium concept:

> Medium concept can be understood as filmmaking that involves the adaptation of genre models and art-film aesthetics; an engagement with political debates, lending the films cultural significance; and that integrates with these elements a marketing strategy designed to reach a specific audience. [. . .] Medium-concept films are a type of popular fiction that uses crime narratives and other violent genres to stage conflicts over notions of individualism.[14]

Jar City would seem to be an exemplary case of medium concept, as topical questions of individual rights are addressed by tightly interweaving the genetic database with a crime narrative, resulting in a remarkable local and foreign box-office success. However, the film also deviates from the concept, as an important part of Nestingen's definition is a blending of genre and art cinema elements.[15] Unlike classic Scandinavian crime films, such as the Norwegian *doppelgänger* study *Insomnia* (Erik Skjoldbjærg, 1997)—and one of Nestingen's key examples—*Jar City* is mostly devoid of traditional art-cinema aesthetics. As a local film garnering such interest abroad, due to a topical national theme rather than art cinema aesthetics, *Jar City* seems to undermine what had appeared in the Icelandic context as a rather straightforward distinction between national films and transnational ones. Closer analysis suggests, however, that rather than undermining that distinction, *Jar City* complicates it. A film that encourages foreign viewers to obsess over the genetic pattern of the Icelandic nation is surely an exemplary case of the transnational. In any case, *Jar City* is hardly a typical local film; it is simply that its global register is of an altogether different nature, stemming from the now universal crime genre, with a notable slant toward Hollywood rather than European art cinema as had been customary.

As noted, Kormákur's adaptation remains true to the characters, setting, and the "national" theme of *Tainted Blood*. As regards the plot, Kormákur has rearranged it in such a manner as to tell simultaneously the story of the crime and the story of the investigation—to recall Tzvetan Todorov's well-known two-part definition of detective fiction.[16] Although the distinction is not explicitly stated or explained, the alert viewer can gather from the blue-gray color palette used to portray the story of the crime that its scenes are set in the past, unlike those of the investigation, which are shown in a more ordinary palette. Since so much of the plot is set in the past, it would have been cumbersome to convey these elements solely with dialogue and/or more conventional flashbacks. In fact, extensive information regarding the genetic theme provided late in the novel, including Einar's long explanatory confession before he shoots himself, is arguably somewhat heavy-handed.[17]

Evaluating the success of particular adaptations is to a considerable extent a matter of interpretation rather than objective analysis. As Brian McFarlane has pointed out in his influential study of adaptation, it is especially important to treat with care the issue of fidelity. He observes:

> Fidelity criticism depends on a notion of the text as having and rendering up to the (intelligent) reader a single, correct "meaning" which the filmmaker has either adhered to or in some sense violated or tampered with. [. . .] The critic who quibbles at failures of fidelity is really saying no more than: "This reading of the original does not tally with mine in these and these ways."[18]

In place of such naïve and subjective fidelity criticism, McFarlane proposes a more rigorous and objective method of analysis, based on Roland Barthes's "Introduction to the Structural Analysis of Narrative."[19] McFarlane distinguishes between those elements of the narrative that must be adapted, and thus remain subjective to interpretation, and those that can be transferred, and therefore can be evaluated objectively. Central to the latter are so-called cardinal functions (Barthes's term) or key events that constitute "the irreducible bare bones of the narrative."[20] McFarlane's conclusion in this regard: "The filmmaker bent on 'faithful' adaptation must, as a basis for such an enterprise, seek to preserve the major cardinal functions."[21]

The extensive restructuring of the plot does not in and of itself alter the novel's cardinal functions as they are simply distributed differently. What is curious, however, is that in a film adaptation that otherwise would seem to aspire to fidelity (even avoiding the transnationalization typical of Kormákur's earlier adaptations *101 Reykjavík* and *The Sea*) and was presented and marketed as such, the crimes—the most salient cardinal functions of any crime narrative—at the heart of *Tainted Blood* have been fundamentally altered. Although the novel's two murder victims were male, *Tainted Blood* is ultimately about crimes against women. Grétar and Holberg generate little sympathy, particularly the latter, who is himself guilty of raping two women in a gruesome manner. Attention is likewise drawn to the difficulty that women face in pressing charges for sex crimes and the poor handling of such cases by the police force. Furthermore, the novel includes the subplot of Dísa Rós, who suffers extensive sexual abuse by her father. These elements have fallen by the wayside during the adaptation process. No doubt it could be argued that subplots such as the one regarding Dísa Rós are quite typically sacrificed due to constraints of space. However, the issue of space is irrelevant to the film's most questionable alteration, that, if anything, makes its plot more convoluted and unconvincing. In *Jar City*, Einar's mother Katrín is "guilty" of cheating on her fisherman husband while he is out at sea, rather than being a victim of a horrendous crime. Thus, the narrative no longer emphasizes crimes against women, but rather a woman's "crime." This is what makes *Jar City* a suspect adaptation as regards its gender politics.

In a pivotal scene, Einar confronts his mother about his paternity, finding her half-naked; this unmotivated nudity directly follows a scene in which old black-and-white photographs of Katrín making love to Holberg surface among the rats and bones in Grétar's grave. The nudity in the confrontation scene would seem to serve little other purpose than to associate the female body with crime and death. During Einar's confrontation with his mother, Katrín leads her son to believe that she was raped, thus prompting Einar's murder of Holberg and his own suicide. The adaptation thus acquits Holberg of the rape and by implication indicts Katrín for the death of her granddaughter and her son's suicide. The origin of this family tragedy is now to be found in Katrín's promiscuity, as it is her affair with Holberg that brings the bad gene into the family tree. It is this association of sex and death that ties Katrín to the figure of the *femme fatale*, although her appearance has little of the glamour and seductiveness of her more famous and younger Hollywood cousins, the old photographs notwithstanding.

As already noted, Indriðason's police procedurals are very much an heir to the Swedish prototype in which the genre is used as a tool for social critique. Kristín Árnadóttir has pointed out that: "it is clear that Indriðason wants to address with his stories the problems of modern society in a realistic manner and explain them sociologically."[22] In the novel *Tainted Blood* the problem addressed is the social violence perpetrated against women—not merely a single crime but systematic gender-based injustice. In the film *Jar City*, the social critique of the Scandinavian police procedural has given way to rather questionable genre elements of the Hollywood prototype—the sinful femme fatale. A murderous psychopathic villain, a prison escape, and a chase add further familiar Hollywood genre elements. The novelty of these elements in Icelandic cinema, along with *Jar City*'s wide release and marketing campaign, is indicative of the shift toward genre cinema and the Hollywood model, stemming from the broader introduction of neoliberalism.

Reykjavík Rotterdam and Remakes

Two years after *Jar City*, the versatile Baltasar Kormákur played the main role in another crime film, *Reykjavík Rotterdam*, whose remake he was to direct in Hollywood four years later under the name *Contraband*. This remake raises most interesting questions regarding the perceived differences between Hollywood and Icelandic cinema, but also challenges some common assumptions regarding remakes. In what follows, I begin by tracing the plot of *Contraband* before comparing it to the "original"—as we will see, there is every reason to make use of scare quotes—and finally ponder *Contraband*'s relevance for the study of remakes, in particular transnational remakes where Hollywood appropriates a "foreign" text as its own.

In New Orleans, Chris Farrady (Mark Wahlberg) is forced to return to his old criminal world of smuggling after his younger brother-in-law Andy (Caleb Landry Jones) drops a drug "package" intended for gang leader Tim Briggs (Giovanni Ribisi). Chris then travels on board a large cargo ship to Panama City, purchases counterfeit money to smuggle back to the United States, and gets caught in a violent hold-up, which also leaves him unknowingly in possession of a Jackson Pollock painting. Meanwhile, Tim violently harasses Chris's wife Kate (Kate Beckinsale) and their two sons to make sure Chris not only brings back the money but also the drugs Andy has bought in Panama City. Before returning to New Orleans, Chris discovers that it is really his longtime friend Sebastian Abney (Ben Foster) who has orchestrated the whole thing; what he cannot know on his return is that Sebastian is about to bury Kate alive, believing he has accidentally killed her. Chris lays a trap for Tim and his gang, resulting in their arrest as well as the arrest of his old nemesis, the ship's captain (J. K. Simmons). Finally, Chris rescues Kate as cement is being poured over her at Sebastian's construction site. The film concludes with serene images of the reunited family.

Contraband is in many ways a faithful remake of *Reykjavík Rotterdam*. Indeed, the plot outline delineated above holds for the original film—all one needs to do is change names and locations. Such minor details as Sebastian's Ford pickup truck, the unexpected appearance of Tim's daughter, a close-up of Kate's twitching finger, the hiding place on board the freighter, and the escape route from the hiding place are likewise found in the original—Icelandic actor Ólafur Darri Ólafsson even plays the same role in both films. Nonetheless, numerous alterations reshape the plot and the tone of the remake. Notably, *Contraband* is almost half an hour longer than its predecessor. That time is used to fill out various aspects of the narrative, to deepen familial relations, and to extend action scenes.

In *Reykjavík Rotterdam*, Chris/Kristófer (Baltasar Kormákur) was primarily motivated by his financial difficulties and had little sympathy for the plight of his brother-in-law; in contrast, his return to smuggling in *Contraband* is solely to bail out Andy. Thus the two narrative threads of crime and family are much more tightly interwoven in *Contraband*. Furthermore, Sebastian/Steingrímur (Ingvar Sigurðsson) used to be Kate's/Íris's (Lilja Nótt Þórarinsdóttir) lover, and is clearly motivated by a desire to get her back, while in *Contraband* Sebastian is trying to make sure Chris brings back the drugs he desperately needs for financial reasons. Important secondary characters have also been added, such as Chris's jailed father (William Lucking) and a ruthless crime boss (David O'Hara), who is putting the squeeze on Sebastian. The latter addition makes Sebastian more sympathetic than in the original, where he acts alone. Other changes include making the inscrutable captain corrupt, the heist bloodier and more violent, and, perhaps inevitably, enlightening Chris about the value of the Pollock painting. At the end of *Reykjavík Rotterdam*, his predecessor is seen using it as a floor cover while the family paints its new apartment.

While it is relatively straightforward to note changes in plot, it is harder to pinpoint and account for changes in tone and effect—in the language of narratology, this is essentially the difference between narrative/story and narration/discourse. Or in Seymour Chatman's influential definition: "What is communicated is *story*, the formal content element of narrative; and it is communicated by *discourse*, the formal expression element."[23] Thus, in our example, the two films communicate for most purposes the same story, but deliver it in somewhat different terms. One way of differentiating the two texts is to define *Contraband* as an action film, but *Reykjavík Rotterdam* as a crime film. Although the crime and action genres do intersect in a variety of ways, there are important distinctions to be made, as the latter has "a propensity for spectacular physical action, a narrative structure involving fights, chases and explosions, and in addition to the deployment of state of the arts special effects, an emphasis in performance on athletic feats and stunts."[24] *Contraband* fits this definition much better than *Reykjavík Rotterdam*, as it prioritizes spectacular physical action scenes in numbers, length, and design. Conversely, the emphasis of *Reykjavík Rotterdam* falls on criminal orchestration and it lies closer to the "quirky" criminal film, especially in the Rotterdam section that comes across as pure parody (see Figure 10.2). But ultimately it is truly the strong affinity between the films that is striking, rather than their differences: they share an emphasis on family scenes, broken friendship, and local environments—and for an Icelandic film, *Reykjavík Rotterdam* does have plenty of action. And it is this affinity that is perplexing: What kind of Icelandic film would Hollywood remake faithfully?

Contraband challenges many common assumptions about remakes and particularly non-American films remade in Hollywood, including the perceived familiarity/popularity of the original, the struggle involved

Figure 10.2 Petty Icelandic criminals, played by Baltasar Kormákur and Þröstur Leó Gunnarsson, encounter trouble in the quirky crime film *Reykjavík Rotterdam*, later remade in Hollywood by Kormákur as *Contraband* and starring Mark Wahlberg in his role. Source: Sögn ehf.

in tackling (the reputation of) the original, the transformation from art to genre, an accompanying dumbing down, and, most importantly, an overall assumption of a one-way relationship. It is far from easy to situate *Contraband* on three- or four-tier remake scales, such as Thomas Leitch outlines in his essay "Twice-Told Tales," that assess different types of remakes.[25] Leitch emphasizes the familiarity of the source film as a classic, while in the case of *Contraband* most spectators are unlikely to be aware they are watching a remake. Further, the notion that the filmmakers engage in some sort of Oedipal struggle in dealing with the presence of the original would be farfetched. After all, director Kormákur was highly involved as the main star and producer of the original film. This is without a doubt unusual. Even Robert Eberwein's typology of fifteen kinds of remakes (many with up to four subgroups) has no room for a star-to-director remake.[26] However, *Contraband* does fit categories "4d" of "a foreign film remade in the United States" and "7a" of "a remake that changes the cultural setting of the film."[27] These types match Hollywood's increased interest in remaking foreign films, and could arguably be categorized as "transnational remakes." Yet as a specific category, such films have received little scholarly attention.

An important exception is Lucy Mazdon's *Encore Hollywood: Remaking French Cinema*, which shows that France has been Hollywood's most popular source for remakes (if increasingly rivaled by crime films and television series from the Nordic countries).[28] In her book Mazdon opposes the tendency to define the French film as an original and the American remake as a generic, commercial copy. It is her contention that the basic opposition in popular remake discourse and even theory—original and copy—must be rethought considering the reality of global film production:

> Indeed, it is one of the central paradoxes of the remake that while demonstrating the *transnationalism* which lies at the heart of cinematic production it is also mobilised to reinforce the *national* identities which continue to dominate much discussion of film and film industries. [...] The location of both films in a global industry along with the various forms of exchange and interaction immanent to the practice make the remake a thoroughly *transnational* undertaking.[29]

One of Mazdon's key examples is *Breathless* (1983), Jim McBride's much maligned remake of Jean-Luc Godard's *Breathless* (1960, *À bout de souffle*), chastised for being a bad copy and an Americanized one to boot. But as Mazdon reminds us, although not a direct remake, Godard's film itself is a multifaceted reworking of Hollywood film tradition and thus already a "copy" of American cinema.

While *Reykjavík Rotterdam* shares neither the prestige nor the popularity of Godard's *Breathless*, it is similarly invested in and modeled upon American cinema, and arguably more closely, as it lacks Godard's Brechtian distantiation techniques. This point is essential to any consideration of *Contraband*'s status as a remake: How can it be considered a "copy" of an Icelandic film when the "original" is an outright copy of Hollywood cinema in the first place? It is clear that when analyzing transnational remakes (and perhaps many others) we must divest the words "original" and "copy" of any evaluative meaning, and think of them as constituting a two-way rather than a one-way relationship. If anything, the "American" in *Reykjavík Rotterdam* is much more discernible than the "Icelandic" in *Contraband*—it is as if *Reykjavík Rotterdam*'s liminal national identity destined it to be remade in Hollywood.

In this, Kormákur's remake is arguably no different from most transnational remakes. Interestingly, however, its plot can be said to reflect the inner workings of such remakes. *Contraband* is not only about crossing borders but specifically about crossing borders with goods—some legitimately, others clandestinely, and still others even accidentally. Something similar happens in the process of filming remakes: certain things are carried over legitimately, others are smuggled, and yet something always travels accidentally. In fact, the central plot of *Contraband* involves a crew that departs from the United States to Panama to bring back counterfeit American money, just as its film crew brought a "counterfeit" American film made in Iceland back to the United States. Notably, Kormákur himself played the contraband leader in the original film, and it is no exaggeration to state that in his Hollywood films, very much unlike his Icelandic ones, he is preoccupied with contraband and crossing borders. Made between the two films, *Inhale* (2010) deals with organ trafficking between the United States and Mexico, while the Hollywood follow-up to *Contraband*, the much more cavalier *2 Guns* (2013), revolves around drug trafficking across the same border. Placed between those two Hollywood films, and sharing so much with them thematically and aesthetically, it would be truly a stretch to see *Contraband* as a one-way copy/remake of *Reykjavík Rotterdam*.

Black's Game, *Trapped*, and Intertextuality

As Baltasar Kormákur was making forays into Hollywood, the local crime scene continued to get bloodier during the teens, if anything: Ólafur Jóhannesson directed two films on the *City State* (2011/2014, *Borgríki*), Óskar Axelsson's debut film *Black's Game* was a major hit at the local box office rivaling *Jar City*, and he went on to direct the thriller *I Remember You* (2017, *Ég man þig*) based upon Yrsa Sigurðardóttir's bestselling novel.[30] And in-between Hollywood projects, Kormákur found time to contribute the thriller *The Oath* (2016, *Eiðurinn*) and the series *Trapped* that became a major success at home and abroad. In this section I will focus on *Black's Game*, an adaptation of Stefán Máni's novel, and *Trapped*, a remake of sorts, but I want to expand upon the terms "adaptation" and "remake" and consider such texts in their larger intertextual configurations.

Although remakes like *Contraband* and adaptations like *Jar City* and *Black's Game* have much in common, the quintessential difference is that in the latter process the new version appears in a different medium. Also, unlike remakes, which have only recently begun to garner theoretical interest, adaptations were being analyzed long before the advent of the discipline of film studies itself. Quite understandably, the focus of such studies has involved close analyses of the texts in question and an assessment of the specific relationship manifested between them. Julie Sanders offers this wide-ranging list: "Version, variation, interpretation, continuation, transformation, imitation, pastiche, parody, forgery, travesty, transposition, revaluation, revision, rewriting, echo."[31] This variety notwithstanding, adaptation studies have typically—one could say it is in their nature by definition—privileged the relationship between novel (or other "original" texts) and film (or other "secondary" texts) at the cost of other intertextual relations. As a corrective, Robert Stam has suggested that the scope of "adaptation" should be expanded with the help of Gérard Genette's *Palimpsests* and its five categories of intertextual relations (or what Genette terms "transtextuality").[32] In particular, Stam draws our attention to "hypertextuality" in which a new text, which Genette names "hypertext," is grafted upon an older text, named "hypotext" (note, though, that Genette's definition does not include a change of medium). However, it is the other four categories that are most helpful in transcending the delimited focus on novel and film, as "architextuality" refers to the overarching influence of genre or modes, "paratextuality" involves extratextual matter like forewords, illustrations, and book covers, "metatextual" relations go uncited and unacknowledged, while the fifth and final category, rather confusingly named "intertextuality," involves in Genette's narrower definition citations and allusions and other such references.[33] In what follows, I will begin by analyzing the hypertextuality of *Black's Game* before moving to its other intertextual relations.

The novel *Black's Game* was published in 2004, and while it must be considered part and parcel of the Icelandic literary crime wave, it also has its own unique and distinct qualities, both in terms of narrative material and structure. It is told from the perspective of criminals rather than police officers, private detectives, or journalists attempting to solve crimes. Events, not least criminal ones, are also rendered in unusually explicit and brutal terms, while the author tries to incorporate street language in his characters' dialogue. As such, it lies closer to hard-boiled fiction or even the gangster genre than the dominant police procedural. The narration travels back and forth in time over an extended period, making the plot a somewhat complicated puzzle. Briefly summarized, it involves the fall and rise of a criminal organization in Reykjavík with the lives of key members, including leaders Tóti and Brúnó and "the girl" Dagný, traced back to their youth, save for the newcomer Stebbi.

The film deviated from the novel by following a much more linear narrative with a clear-cut single main protagonist, Stebbi (Þorvaldur Davíð Kristjánsson), whom we follow as he climbs the gang's ladder before things get out of hand and it all comes crashing down. This streamlining was due to various factors and not only the difficulties involved in adapting the complexity of the novel to a feature film of standard duration. There was an awareness that an Icelandic audience might not be ready for an unorthodox crime film considering the lack of a domestic "tradition" regarding the genre, and thus a more "typical film" had to be produced. The low budget also made it difficult to include the multiple time periods, which resulted in a faster and more compact narrative. And although most of the financial support came from Icelandic sources (in addition to the Nordic Television and Film Fund), the film's producer Zik Zak Filmworks always intended it for the foreign market as well. It was hoped that the film's local manifestations of familiar crime genre elements would appeal to foreign audiences.[34]

The plot streamlining notwithstanding, the filmmakers made extensive efforts to remain faithful to the novel (underscored humorously perhaps by having author Máni play a police officer) by shooting at locations given in the novel, referencing narrative material that could not be directly staged, giving a glimpse of characters' youth with old photos during the opening credits, and so on. They were also assisted by the novel's own appropriation of the film medium. A case in point is the scene where the narrative transitions directly from the gang practicing a bank robbery to its execution, and the novel's so-called zero hour, a clairvoyance occurring at critical moments, which is literally likened to photographic stillness in the novel.[35] Director Axelsson also makes extensive use of other arresting film techniques, like slowing down and increasing the film speed, fast editing, irises, and various split screens—most of which serve to increase the pace of the narrative.

Despite the examples given above, like the "zero hour," where a specific film technique has a hypertextual origin, most of *Black's Game*'s stylistic features are of an architextual nature—stemming from a film genre or mode rather than the original novel. Any fan of international crime cinema should feel quite at home in watching *Black's Game*, as its intertextual ties are very much global in nature. Even its paratextuality helped emphasize such connections, with the poster, for example, depicting the generic trademarks of Hollywood thrillers. The inclusion of Danish crime auteur Nicolas Winding Refn among its executive producers tied the film to the popular cycle of Scandinavian crime films.[36] Nonetheless, the architextual crime elements only tell half the story, for *Black's Game*'s metatextual indebtedness to *Trainspotting* (Danny Boyle, 1996) is equally instrumental. The metatextual relations are established at the very beginning of the film as a voice-over addresses the audience, just as Renton (Ewan McGregor), *Trainspotting*'s central character, famously opens the "original" film, and begins speaking over the credits before the music takes over. The photo-montage introductions of *Black's Game*'s central characters also function in a way similar to the frozen frame introductions of *Trainspotting*'s characters roster, and Renton's wild run down a street is echoed in the high-octane opening of an intoxicated Stebbi, shown through a first-person view with the help of an iris, ultimately assaulting a boy at a club.[37] Also, clubbing, alcohol, and drug intoxication—and the pertinent use of music and subjective film perspectives—turn out to be almost as important as the crime elements. And although *Trainspotting* is hardly a conventional crime film, its narrative trajectory ends with a crime that is uncannily like the one concluding *Black's Game*—a bag full of drug money that the main protagonist decides to keep for himself.

All in all, the intertextuality of *Black's Game* far transcends its original Icelandic novel, and the additional ties are mostly international in nature.[38] If *Jar City* relied primarily on the regional Nordic noir tradition in its transnational appeal, *Black's Game* broadens that approach further afield. This global inscription is even clearer in Ólafur Jóhannesson's *City State*, another popular crime film released early in the teens. Indeed, its multifarious interconnected narrative levels of crime, corruption, and brutal violence give most Hollywood crime films a good run for their money. Icelandic gang members cheat Serb immigrant Sergej (Zlatko Krickic) out of his car repair garage before beating him up, along with his wife, who suffers a miscarriage as a consequence. Looking for revenge, Sergej decides to take over the gang's "business" with the help of some fellow nationals, well prepared from their participation in the Yugoslav wars. Around the same time, the gang's boss Gunnar (Ingvar Sigurðsson) has a health scare and decides to sell out, but British crime lord Jimmy (Jonathan Pryce) loses interest when Gunnar's holdings come under threat from the Serbs. To complicate matters still further, police officers Rúnar (Björn Thors) and Andrea (Ágústa Eva Erlendsdóttir) begin an investigation into the gang's activities, but Gunnar and corrupt police chief Margeir (Sigurður Sigurjónsson) respond by having them roughed up. The "lesson" leaves Rúnar paralyzed, but Andrea forms her own police militia gang and begins handing out the same treatment. Finally, Gunnar lays a trap for Sergej with the assistance of Margeir, but the Serb escapes capture and comes out on top against the Icelanders, and the film concludes with him and his wife finally coming to terms with the loss of their unborn child.

Remarkably, this complicated and stretched plot with its multiple characters is delivered in a relatively short film (82 minutes, including final credits). In other words, *City State* is characterized by a rapid pace, even surpassing the narrative speed of the Hollywood films whose norm it takes as a model. Scenes are short, and the film shifts back and forth in space and time, and editing relies heavily on the now common technique of fast cutting with little motivated changes in shot perspective: even the gobbling up of a hamburger is shot in a number of quick bursts from a variety of angles and distances. Other stylistic effects and plot elements familiar from what we might now call the international crime film, with clear roots in Hollywood, include shaky camera (even traditional shot/reverse shots are constantly fluctuating), intermittent shots depicting the city from above, stylized character name introductions (far into the film), extreme violence (e.g., cutting of a finger with big shears), eccentric crime bosses, stereotypical Eastern European criminals, unsavory locations such as strip clubs and brothels, along with the generic spaces of financial institutions, hotels, hospitals, harbors, car parking houses, and so on. Save for the language, nothing in *City State* (note how its title also evokes the general rather than the specific) could be said to be particularly Icelandic.

Despite the presence of a police team, *City State* has little in common with the police procedural. The police officers do not work as a team but against one another; in fact, they are either working with criminals or reverting to explicitly criminal methods (and privileging revenge over solving crimes). Neither does the film shares much with the noir tradition; for example, it is lacking altogether in character subjectivity, despite the slippery line between criminals and police officers. Instead it is primarily indebted to the gangster genre. In this *Reykjavík Rotterdam*, *Black's Game*, and *City State* are quite representative of the Icelandic crime film; they sway toward the hard-boiled if not outright gangster cinema. In fact, despite the tremendous success of *Jar City*, not a single Icelandic police procedural was released on the big screen during the teens. The only film with a police officer as main protagonist was *A White, White Day* (Hlynur Pálmason, 2019, *Hvítur, hvítur dagur*), but he is not involved in solving any crimes. Instead, while grieving his recently deceased wife, he begins to look into her private life while on compassionate leave and turns criminal himself as he kidnaps and threatens to kill her former lover. The setting is equally telling, as unlike Icelandic crime films that typically take place in Reykjavík, it is set in the countryside. In the end, *A White, White Day* is an art film far removed from the crime genre.

Icelandic television crime series, on the other hand, typically stay within the parameters of the police procedural, although *Stella Blómkvist* (2017–2021) is an interesting exception, a playful take on the hard-boiled heritage helmed by *Black's Game* director Axelsson. Other television series, many directed by key filmmakers, include *Season of the Witch* (Friðrik Þór Friðriksson, 2011, *Tími nornarinnar*); *The Cliff: Depth of Darkness* (Reynir Lyngdal, 2014, *Hraunið*); *Case: Ritual of Abduction* (Baldvin Zophoníasson, 2015, *Réttur*); *Prisoners* (Ragnar Bragason, 2017, *Fangar*); *The Flatey Enigma* (Björn Br. Björnsson, 2018, *Flateyjargátan*); and *The Valhalla Murders* (Þórður Pálsson, 2019, *Brot*). But it was Kormákur's *Trapped* that was by far the biggest success of the decade's many series, especially internationally, where it was often placed in the same category as *The Killing* and *The Bridge*.

Trapped was a super-production from the very beginning, aimed for the international market, with many key figures of the Icelandic film industry joining the cast and the crew. And like Kormákur's own *Jar City*, it is an interesting transnational production. It has the appearance of a national—if not local—production while aesthetically and structurally drawing upon the most globally successful recipes of Nordic noir. The paratextuality of the series emphasizes this complexity. One poster shows the three main characters lined up together and looking us directly in the eye—along the lines of a Hollywood action film, a connection further supported by the top text line, stating: "From the director of *2 Guns* and *Contraband*." A speeding motorboat below further underlines the Hollywood connection, while the Scandinavian indebtedness is indicated by the text at the bottom introducing "a new crime series from Scandinavia," even though Iceland is not Scandinavian. And the village depicted below the three main characters is located in a dark winter landscape setting whose white and blue colors signify the North broadly and Iceland specifically, albeit never mentioned on the poster.

While the architextual model of *Trapped* stems from the crime genre and the police procedural broadly, the series also draws in much more specific ways on *The Killing* and *The Bridge*. While admittedly male, its main police protagonist, Andri (Ólafur Darri Ólafsson), shares numerous characteristics with his Scandinavian female predecessors. He stands out in many ways and is a loner in both his private and professional life. He is recently divorced and has a difficult relationship with his oldest daughter. Similarly, *The Killing*'s main protagonist Sarah (Sofie Gråbøl) is a single mother, and even though *The Bridge*'s Sara (Sofia Helin) does not have a family of her own, her male sidekicks all have broken familial relationships. Andri also has two sidekicks, Hinrika (Ilmur Kristjánsdóttir) and Ásgeir (Ingvar Sigurðsson), in the small police force in the village in which the film is set, while his relationship with the police force in the capital is most tenuous (in a similar manner to Saga and Sarah, who often clash with their superiors in the police force). And despite the isolated fjord setting, *Trapped* borrows the explicit transnational setup of *The Bridge*—the title itself refers to the bridge connecting Denmark and Sweden—by placing a Danish passenger ferry at the harbor that becomes anchored when a body is discovered in the village. Among its passengers are two West African sisters who are being smuggled by a Lithuanian crime gang, and in that manner the geopolitical tragedy of human trafficking is brought into this small Icelandic fishing village. *Trapped* thus very much utilizes the now familiar structure of many intersecting plotlines: Andri's domestic life, Hinrika's private drama, the refugees, the

Danish ferry crew, mysterious villagers and political corruption (inspired by the economic collapse of 2008).

All in all, these connections to *The Killing* and *The Bridge* are of a much more specific nature than those suggested by architextuality. Perhaps the series could be described as metatextual along the lines of *Black's Game*, but *Trapped* draws much more obviously upon its Nordic predecessors than *Black's Game* does on *Trainspotting*. I would therefore argue that hypertextuality best explains the relationship between the two, where *Trapped* is "grafted upon" *The Killing* and *The Bridge*. In fact, if we rely on the broadest categories of remakes offered by Leitch or Eberwein, the case could be made that *Trapped* is ultimately an Icelandic remake of said Nordic series—although that may be stretching the concept a bit far for some.

In *Trapped*, the Scandinavian crime series narrative template has been given an Icelandic mise-en-scène, which probably played as big a role in its success as the borrowed plot structure. Along the lines of *Jar City*, the series adeptly brings together generic crime elements and the specificity of its Icelandic locations. This is visually stated in the opening credits scene itself that intercuts close-ups of a corpse and an Icelandic landscape, seamlessly erasing the difference between the two (see Figures 10.3 and 10.4). The particular circumstances of the murder are also seen as specifically Icelandic, as all the characters—whether local or visiting—are "trapped" in the village because of a snowstorm and bad road conditions (this is the specific meaning of the original Icelandic title *Ófærð*), and visually the series revels in atmospheric wintery scenes.

As Kristín Loftsdóttir, Katla Kjartansdóttir, and Katrín Anna Lund point out, the *Trapped* series thus follows a long tradition of defining Icelandicness in terms of nature—and what they describe as a "long-standing association of Icelandicness with maleness."[39] They pinpoint Andri as the most representative figure in the series in this regard: "He is an integral part of the portrayed landscape, one which is authentically molded by the forces of nature which shapes its people."[40] While their overall analysis of the series is convincing, the representation of nature and national identity in *Trapped* strikes me as somewhat uncharacteristic of Icelandic cinema and television in two important ways. One, Icelandic "children" of nature have typically been female rather than male. Notable examples range from *Hadda Padda* (Guðmundur Kamban, 1924) to the *The Seagull's Laughter* (Ágúst Guðmundsson, 2001, *Mávahlátur*)—not to mention the aptly titled *Children of Nature* (1992, *Börn*

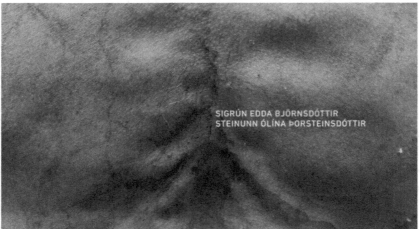

Figures 10.3 and 10.4 Graphic matches connecting Icelandic landscapes (10.3) to close-ups of a corpse (10.4) in the opening credits of the series *Trapped* foreground national specificity in this crime narrative. Source: RVK Studios.

náttúrunnar) and its director Friðrik Þór Friðriksson's oeuvre more broadly (see chapters three and seven). Second, nature is almost without exception presented on screen in summer rather than winter clothing. As such, nature is typically about certain kinds of elevation and freedom (for example, from the constraints of the city), often found in bright open spaces and thus the exact opposite of being "trapped." It is interesting that the two most obvious exceptions to this, *Noi the Albino* (Dagur Kári, 2003, *Nói albínói*) and

Cold Light (Hilmar Oddsson, 2004, *Kaldaljós*), are not only set in winter but deal with the deadly impact of avalanches (on their male protagonists, nota bene). In other words, the case could be made that representations of nature are gendered in Icelandic cinema, where women typically represent summer and men winter.[41] Nonetheless, Andri can hardly be considered a typical representative of either Icelandic nature or masculinity—considering his bulky size and uncharacteristic gentleness—although the two clearly come together in his persona.

But there can be no doubt that the ways in which the series was seen to be specifically Icelandic contributed to its global success. In that sense, I consider it to be an exemplary transnational production: serving up one nation as a feast for others with a plate full of global implications. The producers enhanced the formula in the second season with a plot focused on the environment and national extremism, while the third, entitled *Entrapped*, focused on drug trafficking and cast well-known Danish actor Thomas Bo Larsen as Danish Hopper, the leader of the criminal bikers' gang. Furthermore, *Entrapped* was made in partnership with global streaming giant Netflix, which was also the case with Kormákur's fantastical volcano series *Katla* (2021) and prior Þórður Pálsson's crime series *Valhalla Murders* in 2019. The differences between its modest Icelandic title *Brot* (meaning "violations" or "fragments") and the dramatic over-the-top English title speak to the need for a catchy national cliché to grab the attention of Netflix streamers. Just like its cinema, Icelandic television has traveled far from its explicit national origin.

The pioneering crime films of 2006, *Jar City* and *Cold Trail*, take place in a quintessentially Icelandic environment. But one of the most striking things about the Icelandic crime films is how quickly this national emphasis makes way for a global outlook: the apparent desire to make Icelandic crime appear like any other crime, especially so in *City State* and *Black's Game*. This may also explain why *Reykjavík Rotterdam* lends itself so well to a Hollywood adaptation in *Contraband*. Interestingly, *Trapped* returns to the quintessential Icelandic environment of the early crime films, but does so by placing it in a geopolitical context. The isolated Icelandic fishing villages of old have apparently become central to our interconnected globe.

11
Hollywood Does Iceland

We approach Iceland from above, glimpsing it through the clouds. Steam rises from the barren landscape, which is draped mostly in black and gray, with no green in sight. These overhead shots form abstract patterns, and the introduction of ice prompts new color combinations. As we travel over the land vis-à-vis smooth camera movements, lakes and rivers enhance the spectacle before we finally arrive at the powerful and majestic waterfall *Dettifoss*. One might be inclined to believe that one was watching a tourist promotional video of Iceland, albeit an unusually artful and breathtaking one. But as we travel now upstream toward the waterfall from below—lo and behold—a spaceship hovers over it. And walking toward the cliff's edge is an alien, manifest as a mythical creature about to give life to humanity.

Most viewers of Ridley Scott's *Prometheus* (2012) do not see Iceland in the film's prologue, but prehistoric earth, a place signifying universality rather than the particular. The film's opening illustrates the capacity of Iceland to stand in for other places, real or imaginary. *Prometheus*, in fact, builds on a long tradition of depicting Iceland as alien or untamed. Steaming geysers, harrowing mountains, and icy glaciers prevail over culture and history, with few visitors traveling to Iceland in search of monuments or other historical markers. This aura of otherworldliness helps illustrate Hollywood's desire to appropriate the Icelandic landscape for its fantastical mise-en-scène, in not only *Prometheus*, but so many other productions.

In examining Iceland's relationship to runaway productions, my approach in this chapter shares much with geocriticism, which according to its founder Bertrand Westphal, "places *place* at the center of the debate."[1] Westphal certainly does not erase "the text," but situates it on equal and interactive footing with place. In order to achieve a complex and deep understanding, one must interpret place through not only numerous texts but also a variety of sources that even include "tourist guides and the advertising rhetoric of travel brochures."[2] Although the role of Iceland in runaway productions can vary considerably, it is typically limited to a specific scene or sequence in the completed film, and it most often stands in for other places.

Its function as a substitute undermines the long-held presupposition that an image (photographed or filmed) represents the actual place captured: you are actually looking at Iceland and not the Himalayas. In addition to the textual questions it raises, Iceland's engagement with runaway productions also invites an examination of the environmental and global factors at play, with the globe's most powerful film industry mingling with a particularly small national cinema.[3] In both cases—the textual and the industrial—Iceland's runaway productions provide fascinating examples of transnationalism. With global appeal in mind, Iceland literally stands in for another place, and its image is created by a foreign film industry.

Iceland's twenty-first-century image has a long prehistory, and its origins can be charted by exploring an early example, Jules Verne's *Journey to the Center of the Earth*, as well as subsequent Hollywood adaptations of the novel. Hollywood's current unparalleled activity in Iceland in regard to its runaway productions borrows from and contributes to the archive of exotic nature imagery about the country established by earlier works. The "Picturesque," where local specificity makes way for generic exoticism, will help explain some of the strategies involved in this undertaking. In addition to some of these aesthetic concerns, the chapter will also survey the economic features of these overseas productions. with the help of film commissioner Einar Hansen Tómasson. Finally, I will turn briefly to locally produced films to ask how Icelandic cinema itself has been affected by this alien visitor.

The Outermost Limits of the World

In *Iceland Imagined*, historian Karen Oslund catalogs the tropes of European travel literature about Iceland, noting their similarities and differences with those of European Orientalism. The Orient signified a geographic and ideological otherness, while "in the North Atlantic, a region considered both 'close' and 'small' in the European imagination, the categories of 'self' and 'other,' 'home' and 'away' became less distinct."[4] Oslund describes the travel literature, whether written by scientists or poets, as obsessively attempting to define Iceland and its inhabitants' differences from "normal" continental Europeans. Although the country has undergone dramatic transformations throughout the centuries, Oslund argues that these centuries-old traditions are central to Iceland's more recent whaling and genetic controversies.

I would add that both controversies locate Iceland in terms of natural specificity, and in the latter case, the unique DNA of Icelanders themselves.[5]

Given that Iceland is consistently singled out as one of the most progressive and modern nation-states, it is striking how it continues to be depicted as wild and uncharted.[6] Even Oslund's own description of the country invokes its purported otherworldly qualities:

> This fact leaves, at the beginning of the twenty-first century, a sensation that travelers in the eighteenth century would have found familiar: a sense of confusion, of disorientation bordering on illness, when arriving in Iceland for the first time. This confusion is one of the ways in which the traveler realizes that he or she has arrived at borderlands, a place that is just slightly off the edge of the map of the known world.[7]

Thus despite its complete modernization, Iceland is still perceived as having a special relationship to nature that isolates it from the rest of the world. Oslund's own wording, "slightly off the edge of the map of the known world," echoes the language provided by the narrator of Jules Verne's *Journey to the Center of the Earth* as he looks back from the "barren shores of Iceland and the outermost limits of the world!"[8] The novel, in fact, serves as the perfect bridge from such traditional accounts of Iceland to their modern manifestation in the Hollywood blockbuster.

Verne's remarkable novel was published in 1864, and although it is typically associated with fantasy and science fiction, it has arguably more in common with travel literature. The author was fascinated by the Arctic and drew extensively on actual travel literature in describing Iceland. Although he never visited the country, he had traveled to Scotland, Norway, and Denmark. Until its protagonists begin their descent into the earth midway through the work, *Journey to the Center of the Earth* could be understood as a rigorous account of Icelandic geography, history, language, culture, and customs—if somewhat colorful.[9]

The narrative, on the other hand, indulges in the fanciful. The narrator Axel travels to Iceland with his uncle, Professor Lidenbrock, after the latter discovers a coded message written in runes by medieval scholar Arne Saknussemm (presumably modeled on the manuscript collector Árni Magnússon), hidden inside an old Icelandic manuscript of the canonical medieval saga *Heimskringla*. The decoded message states that Arne had discovered an entrance to the center of the earth on top of the glacial volcano

Snæfellsjökull. Along with their trusted Icelandic guide Hans, Axel and Lidenbrock travel deep into the earth, where they find a prehistoric world full of now-extinct vegetation, mammals, and humans, before a volcanic eruption all the way in Stromboli propels them out again. The fantastic narrative elements overshadow the extensive sections of the novel that describe nature, habitat, and customs in Iceland, which are themselves quite exhilarating, if not comparable to sightings of sea monsters and gigantic ancestors of mankind.

After considerable preparation and a long journey, Axel and Lidenbrock arrive on the boat *Valkyrie* at Reykjavík harbor in mid-June. While the scholarly minded uncle heads straight to the library, Axel takes in the sights:

> To get lost in the two streets of Reykjavik would have been difficult. [. . .] I had soon finished my tour of these bleak, depressing avenues. From time to time I caught sight of the scrap of faded lawns, like an old woollen carpet threadbare through use, or else some semblance of an orchard. Its rare produce—cabbages and lettuces—would not have seemed out of place on a table in Lilliput. [. . .] In three hours, I had visited not only the town but even its surroundings. Their appearance was especially dismal. No trees, no vegetation to speak of. Everywhere the bare bones of the volcanic rock. [. . .] The men seemed robust but heavy, like blond Germans with pensive eyes. They must feel slightly outcast from humanity: exiles on this frozen land, whom nature should really have made Eskimos when she condemned people to live on the Arctic Circle.[10]

Axel's first impressions of Reykjavík and its surroundings are illuminating—almost like a summary or storehouse of ideas about Iceland and its inhabitants. The Lilliput analogy foregrounds the otherworldly aspects of this place, while also dramatically emphasizing its absence of vegetation. The place is described as hardly habitable, so there is little surprise that the capital itself has only two streets. The passage also contains racial undertones: Eskimos [sic] naturally belong here, but people of Germanic origin can hardly be expected to live there—and it has made them weary. The resulting stoicism of the Icelanders is described throughout the novel and personified in the character of Hans "[a] man from the extreme West, but ruled by the fatalistic resignation of the East,"[11] and whose emotions cannot be aroused even by sea monsters. In that sense the people are antithetical to the wild nature that has thus formed them.

160 LIGHT IN THE DARK

Indeed, it is the island's exalted nature that offers a redemptive counterpoint to Axel's gloomy encounter with the sights of Reykjavík. Having reached the top of *Snæfellsjökull*, shortly before beginning his descent toward the center of the earth, Axel offers a description that reflects the novel's general attitude toward the Icelandic landscape and one that continues to inform how we envision Iceland to this day:

> In the morning we woke up half-frozen by a glacial temperature but in the rays of a fine sun. I got up from my granite bed to go and enjoy the magnificent spectacle laid out before my eyes. [...] The panorama extended over most of the island. [...] On my right were endless glaciers and repeated peaks, some of them plumed with light smoke. [...] I plunged into that high-blown ecstasy produced by lofty peaks, without feeling dizzy this time, as I was finally getting used to these sublime contemplations. My dazzled eyes bathed in the clear irradiation of the sun's rays. I forgot who I was, where I was, and lived the life of elves and sylphs, the imaginary inhabitants of Scandinavian mythology.[12]

Once more, Verne's mid-nineteenth-century account of Iceland seems strikingly contemporary—or perhaps it would be more accurate to describe contemporary imagery of Iceland as strikingly archaic. Panoramic vistas, otherworldly landscapes, and transcendental experiences all work to inscribe Icelandic nature with a transformative power. The film, music, and tourist industries continue to recycle and capitalize from this archive so much that we might understand the prologue to *Prometheus* as an uncanny iteration of the spectacle described by Alex. But what have filmmakers done with Verne's tableau when adapting his novel into film, and what kind of process does the Icelandic landscape undergo when it is transformed into cinematic spectacle?

In the classic Hollywood adaptation of *Journey to the Center of the Earth* (Henry Levin, 1959), the depiction of Iceland remains mostly intact, despite changes made to the narrative. Here Professor Lindenbrook (James Mason) of Edinburgh University and his student Alec (Pat Boone) face competition from two rivals; the splendidly named Swedish Professor Göteborg (Ivan Triesault) of Stockholm University, and the film's villain (Thayer David), a descendant of Saknussemm himself. Hans remains the ever-reliable sidekick, now accompanied by a quacking duck named Gertrude. Played by the tall and blonde Icelandic athlete Peter Ronson (Pétur Rögnvaldsson), he speaks in Icelandic throughout the film. Thankfully, Göteborg's widow Carla (Arlene Dahl), who joins the expedition after Saknussemm murders her husband, is fluent in Icelandic and can translate for Lindenbrook and Alec. Despite the revised or additional characters, the narrative progresses in much the same manner, toward the center, before being propelled out at Stromboli.

Despite thus remaining faithful to Iceland's role in the narrative, even hiring a native for the role of Hans, if one much more talkative than his counterpart in the novel, the Iceland that appears on screen has little in common with the comparatively faithful account provided by the novel. With one dissolve we travel from Lindenbrook's library in Edinburgh to the top of *Snæfellsjökull*, which like most of the film's landscape is constructed out of paintings and studio sets, appearing nothing like a glacier (see Figure 11.1).

Reykjavík likewise is staged in a studio, bearing little resemblance to the local environment. The landscape scenes populated by horse-drawn carriages would have been more at home in the Wild Wild West than in Iceland. As such, the representation is consistent with standard Hollywood practice, not least the 1950s cycle of adventure films that relied on outlandish stories taking place in exotic settings. And if Hollywood productions traveled occasionally offshore, it was more likely to be for financial reasons rather than out of concern for capturing authentic locations. One of the few exceptions to these studio-bound productions is the 1956 adaptation of Verne's *Around the World in 80 Days* (Michael Anderson) whose lush mise-en-scène was

Figure 11.1 Professor Lindenbrook (James Mason) and his student Alec (Pat Boone) at the top of *Snæfellsjökull* Glacier. Source: 20th Century Fox.

used to showcase the technical superiority of the Todd-AO 70mm process, but alas Phileas Fogg's route did not include Iceland.

Despite being one of the early entries of the short-lived twenty-first-century 3D craze in Hollywood, the most recent film adaptation of *Journey to the Center of the Earth* (Eric Brevig, 2008) actually did involve traveling to Iceland. As part of a clever updating of the novel, Verne's text itself takes the place of the old *Heimskringla* manuscript and its runic message. The novel in the diegesis is now actual rather than fictional, with true believers referred to as "Vernians." Scientist Trevor Anderson (Brendan Fraser) travels with his nephew Sean (Josh Hutcherson) from Boston to Iceland in search of his brother and fellow volcanologist Max (Jean-Michel Paré), who disappeared there while researching *Snæfellsjökull*. In Iceland they are joined by Hannah, a female version of Hans, who is likewise played by an Icelander, Anita Briem. Soon after beginning their descent, the threesome comes across an old mine, which they playfully acknowledge is nowhere to be found in Verne's novel. From that moment on, the film indulges in sheer 3D fantasy, beginning with the simulated coaster ride on the tracks of the mine. Ultimately, the characters are lifted out of another volcano, Vesuvius this time around, before Trevor and Sean head back home to Boston.

It is a little puzzling as to why the film crew went through the trouble of filming in Iceland. Despite Trevor and Sean traveling with Icelandair and driving through the countryside, amusingly attempting to pronounce a few unfamiliar Icelandic words, the film scarcely makes use of Icelandic locations. Even the mountain they climb appears to be an ordinary hill rather than the majestic *Snæfellsjökull*. The time spent in Iceland is also much shorter than in the novel or the 1959 adaptation, and unlike Verne, the filmmakers apparently had no interest in Iceland per se; it serves only as a brief stopover before the underground extravaganza takes over. Further examination of Hollywood runaway productions in Iceland suggests that this lack of interest is common across the board.

Behind the Image

The meltdown of Iceland's financial infrastructure in 2008 was remarkable for a variety of reasons. Notably, it was the first time in history that Iceland became the focus of media attention for something other than its nature.[13] Iceland, and Reykjavík more specifically, made headline news with two rather different meetings involving the Cold War superpowers. In 1972, Boris Spassky and Bobby Fischer competed in Reykjavík for the World Chess Championship title, and in 1986, Mikhail Gorbachev and Ronald Reagan met there to debate disarmament and the nuclear arms race, but in both cases the city merely accommodated events that might as well have taken place elsewhere. The financial crisis of 2008 was a different story altogether.

Even though Icelandic financial institutions had borrowed and invested money all over the world, with the financial system far outsizing its national parameters, Iceland played a far larger part in media depictions of the meltdown than its financial size/role warranted.[14] In some ways, Iceland became a symbol for the crisis. The swiftness with which the financial crisis emerged there and its far-reaching national impact may have something to do with the disproportionate media attention the country received. Whatever the reason, the coverage undermined the more typical imagery the world had used to view Iceland.

Previously, Iceland was not a country that came to mind when discussing global financial systems, even though its aggressive financial executives were increasingly celebrated in the years leading up to the collapse for their apparent successes in the international marketplace (often and without irony represented as modern-day Vikings). But following the collapse, the disparity between their many scandals and shady deals, and the relatively clean image of Scandinavian civic values, reflected just how rotten the global economy had become—or perhaps had always been. We see the country's new role, for example, in the Academy Award–winning documentary *Inside Job* (Charles Ferguson, 2010), which opens in Iceland with narrator Matt Damon explaining how the government introduced a "broad policy of deregulation that would have disastrous consequences. First for the environment and then for the economy." It is worth noting that the film's prologue emphasizes nature and the economy equally. It concludes with breathtaking aerial shots of various types of landscapes, not unlike those found in the *Prometheus* prologue. In *Inside Job*, however, these shots are followed by two bleak images of environmental destruction (from the construction of the controversial *Karahnjúkar* dam). Here nature apparently stands in for the Icelandic, and perhaps global, economy, as the opening credit sequence leads us to Wall Street and a broader view of the 2008 collapse. Thus while the image of Iceland remains stubbornly associated with nature, it has also dramatically shifted in meaning. For those who admired and visited Iceland for its clean and beautiful environment or distance from the rest of the world, it was hard to fathom how Iceland took on the weight of the financial crisis in *Inside Job*.

But only two years later, with the banks collapsed and their global ambitions extinguished, the eruption of the glacial volcano *Eyjafjallajökull* put Iceland in the headlines again, now for the greatest disruption of air travel in peacetime. Once again, Iceland became the exotic place just beyond Europe, ruled by uncontrollable nature. Instead of the somewhat difficult names of financial institutes such as *Landsbanki* and *Kaupþing*, news anchors around the world now had to grapple with the much harder *Eyjafjallajökull*—whose pronunciation seemed as volatile as the eruption itself. Iceland was back on familiar ground in the global imaginary.

Both the economic crisis and the volcanic eruption had a considerable impact on filmmaking in Iceland. While the local film industry faced budget cuts in state subsidiaries, the collapse of the Icelandic currency *króna* made the country a more competitive location for runaway productions (just as it helped increase tourism). Even more consequential was the *Eyfjallajökull* eruption which, according to Film Commissioner Einar Hansen Tómasson, functioned as a great advertisement, *gratis*, for location shooting in Iceland.[15] However, the elevated interest in location shooting originates much earlier, as far back as 2001, when the government introduced the "Film in Iceland" project. Its purpose was to attract international film productions, largely by means of cost-reimbursement incentives, as many location managers are not even allowed to consider other options.[16] Appealing to foreign film crews is a highly competitive endeavor, as nation-state and municipal representatives spanning the globe, including Arctic neighbors both east and west of Iceland, try to attract jobs and external currency, or promote national prestige and tourism. In the promotional material distributed online and at international conventions, glossy landscape photos leave little doubt about Iceland's greatest pull. An introductory text entitled "Scenery you won't get elsewhere" exploits this draw:

> Black sands, imposing glaciers and snowcapped mountains, otherworldly lava fields, majestic waterfalls, lakes and lagoons with floating icebergs, the stark highland interior, tundra, moors patched with blue ponds, steam emitting red and yellow sulfur mountains, active and dormant volcanoes or scenes of serene beauty. In Iceland this spectrum of scenery is all within easy reach.

> Iceland's stark landscape and amazing range of geological and natural phenomena stem from the active forces of nature still sculpting this geologically young island, sitting on the top of the North-Atlantic ridge where the continental shelves of the Americas and Europe are drifting apart. The land of contrasts, fire and ice, midnight sun, northern lights and lingering twilight welcomes you.[17]

At first sight, this promotional text might not seem particularly illuminating, recycling as it does many clichés about Iceland. It does, however, signpost the reasons for Iceland's popularity with overseas film productions. The language emphasizes conventional Arctic nature scenery like glaciers, snowcapped mountains, floating icebergs, and northern lights, but goes further to suggest the varied uses of Icelandic landscape in recent films.[18] Tómasson explains: "First filmmakers were attracted by the ice. Most everything was shot by [the glacial lake] *Jökulsárlón*. But now the black sands have come in strong. This 'volcano look'— 'another planet look.' And now they have realized the potential of the waterfalls, and other such opportunities."[19] In Iceland these varied landscapes, promotional material points out, are "all within easy reach" and not far from the capital Reykjavík.[20] The "short" distance from Reykjavík to mainland Europe or the United States is equally foregrounded: "From New York the flying distance to Iceland and San Francisco is about the same."[21] In a roundabout way, this also characterizes Iceland as that exotic place that is not distant enough. Unlike, for example, the "mysterious Orient" that in both the past and present represents a fundamentally different world, Iceland, despite its Arctic exoticism, is still part and parcel of Europe. No doubt that is one reason why Iceland figures so rarely as a location in the narratives for which it provides the mise-en-scène. It may be practical to film there, but Iceland is much too close for Hollywood exoticism, unlike say Siberia or the Himalayas—both places that Iceland has stood in for many times.

The Hollywood Picturesque

Economic, logistic, and environmental factors all help to clarify the increased interest in Iceland as a film location. However, they do not explain why Hollywood does not simply rely solely on computer-generated imagery (CGI) but instead goes to the trouble of visiting Iceland or other offshore locations. Nor do they tell us much about the aesthetics of the final product. The concept of the "Picturesque," as described by Malcolm Andrews, is helpful here: "Picturesque taste favors natural scenery for its untouched status, its remoteness from the world of art and artifice—it delights in the result of accident, the traces of agency and time and organic growth, it celebrates what is alien and wild and spontaneous."[22] Though Andrews is analyzing an earlier historical period and pictorial traditions, he describes the "Picturesque" as an ethos that is "part of common experience." Shooting on location offers such an authenticity, removed from the "art and artifice" of CGI (although actual location footage is frequently intermixed with CGI). As a matter of fact, filmmakers working in Iceland have often spoken of the authenticity they achieve from filming at some of the island's "alien and wild" locations, even for the most outlandish of scenes.[23] The result, however, can hardly be considered "spontaneous." After all, such film expeditions are prepared in minute detail and the captured imagery is so carefully processed that it ultimately appears generic and familiar. Such scenery becomes, by means of the Picturesque, "domesticated—it is accommodated within our daily experience both as an artistic experience and as a tourist amenity; it is aesthetically colonized. [. . .] The formulae derived from Picturesque conventions reduce novelty and variety to secure conformity. The Picturesque makes different places seem like each other."[24] Similarly, Hollywood imagery of Iceland brings together—almost schizophrenically—the authentic and the generic. The Hollywood Picturesque diminishes the specificity of Icelandic locations and other exotic sites so that "different places seem like each other." To do so, it paradoxically needs the authenticity of actual natural locations, so that Icelandic Arctic scenery, for instance, stands in for other "icy" settings such as the Himalayas. Through Hollywood's search and capture of the novel or the exotic and the actual, it engages in a process of "aesthetic colonization" that transforms diverse locales into a universal spectacle. Place becomes space, so to speak. Here I follow Yi-Fu Tuan's influential distinction in which place is a lived space—the latter being more abstract and devoid of local specificity. Of course most of the Icelandic settings are not places where people actually live, but these locations are meaningful to the local populations in a variety of ways that dissipate when they are transformed to "abstract" spaces or scenery. Indeed, Tuan's concept of place is quite broad: "When space feels thoroughly familiar to us, it has become place."[25]

These two qualities of authenticity and genericity (by which I mean familiarity and sameness, as well as reliance on Hollywood genres) are abundantly displayed in most of the Hollywood films, whether Iceland figures diegetically in the narrative or provides the mise-en-scène for other settings. Different locations end up looking identical, while the same locations are also used repeatedly, as reflected in the screen time awarded the glacial lake *Jökulsárlón*. An early runaway production, *A View to a Kill* (John Glen, 1985), opens with a panoramic shot of the lake before finding James Bond (Roger Moore) on a snow-capped mountain above it. Spotted by Soviet soldiers, he begins an exhilarating descent, swapping skis for a snowmobile, and even a makeshift snowboard, while fighting the soldiers. Having reached the lake, he shoots down a helicopter before entering one of the glacial islands—a British submarine in disguise. Through seamless intercutting with mountain scenes shot in Switzerland, the Icelandic footage helps create an exotic, adventurous, and rather farfetched Siberian setting. This popular tourist destination also figures prominently in *Lara Croft: Tomb Raider* (Simon West, 2001), where *Jökulsárlón* stands in for Siberia again—an icy and adventurous mise-en-scène for the title character (Angelina Jolie) and her party as they head on dog sleds toward "the ruined city" that shelters the secret to time itself. An equally fanciful Russian setting is found in *The Fate of the Furious* (F. Gary Gray, 2017) as Dom (Van Diesel) and his driving buddies head to a military base in the imaginary "Vladovin" to prevent the theft of submarine nuclear missiles. In the film's final and most extended car chase, a gigantic submarine comes roaring up through the ice, catapulting the car from below. The material shot in the wintery landscape of Iceland is intermixed with CGI and studio filming in a way that makes it hard to distinguish what is "authentic" and what is artificially generated—which is another hallmark of the Hollywood Picturesque. And nobody, save for a few Icelandic spectators, will wonder what a no trespassing sign in Icelandic ("óviðkomandi bannaður aðgangur") is doing in faraway Russia.

Although prominent, Russia does not hold a monopoly in terms of the locations Iceland stands in for, but they were long, almost without exception, icy or snowy and typically mountainous, if not glacial. In *Batman Begins* (Christopher Nolan, 2005) *Svínafellsjökull* Glacier stands in for the Himalayas, where Bruce Wayne (Christopher Bale) overcomes a childhood trauma and is taught to fight by the League of Shadows, led by the mysterious Henri Ducard (Liam Neeson). The wide-open blue vistas make a powerful counterpoint to the claustrophobic and dark city of Gotham (see Figure 11.2).

More than a decade later, the camera glides over another wintery Icelandic mountainside before finding a solitary figure riding across the harsh

Figure 11.2 Bruce Wayne (Christian Bale) and Henri Ducard (Liam Neeson) prepare for a duel on the ice in *Batman Begins*, where the open spaces of the Himalayas—here represented by Southeast Iceland—provide a welcome change from dark and claustrophobic Gotham City. Source: Warner Bros. Pictures.

landscape, soon revealed to be Bruce Wayne (now played by Ben Affleck). He has traveled all this way to find Aquaman (Jason Momoa), who lives in this isolated fjord, which, although never specifically named, is inhabited by stereotypical Icelanders, dressed in traditional wool sweaters, with one of them even speaking a complete sentence in Icelandic. If less icy than typically, Iceland also provides some of the background for the *Justice League* (Zack Snyder, 2017), but now standing in for Russia once again.

From here on, it is only a small step to pure fantasy. *Judge Dredd* (Danny Cannon, 1995) resorts to Iceland to conjure up the "poisoned scorched earth, known as the 'Cursed Earth,'" outside the futuristic cityscape of Mega City One, to which Dredd (Sylvester Stallone) and Chief Judge Fargo (Max von Sydow) are exiled. In *Stardust* (Matthew Vaughn, 2007), Icelandic settings add atmospheric touches to the fantasy world of Stormhold. The black sands of Southern Iceland represent the earth in the year 2077 in *Oblivion* (Joseph Kosinski, 2012), which has been destroyed by earthquakes, tsunamis, nuclear war, and an alien invasion, but is also decorated with a few well-known American landmarks in ruins, courtesy of CGI. As drone repairman Jack Harper, Tom Cruise plays one of the last people left on earth, allowing for some spectacular Picturesque landscape scenes. In *The Midnight Sky* (2020), director George Clooney also plays one of the last people to leave an earth devastated by global disaster. But in *Interstellar* (Christopher Nolan, 2014,) southern Iceland provides the mise-en-scène for two unnamed and contrary planets—one filled with water and the other ice—that astronaut Joseph Cooper (Matthew McConaughey) is hoping can replace a dying earth. For a more traditional apocalypse, a greener part of southern Iceland became the biblical setting for *Noah* (Darren Aranofsky, 2014) in the days leading up to the Flood. The television show *Game of Thrones* (David Benioff and D. B. Weiss, 2011–2019) makes extensive use of Icelandic landscape to depict first the icy world north of "the Wall" (a key geographical barrier in the narrative), but also increasingly greener spaces in later seasons. Iceland stands in for the planet Lah'mu where Jyn (Felicity Jones) is in hiding with her parents at the beginning of *Rogue One: A Star Wars Story* (Gareth Edwards, 2016) while also providing the background for other Picturesque scenes later on in the film. As all these films prove: fantasy is the logical result of the Hollywood Picturesque—a non-place.[26]

But Iceland has also provided on occasion a realistic setting for other places. *Flags of Our Fathers* (Clint Eastwood, 2006), for example, uses *Reykjanes* in the southwest of Iceland to stage the invasion of the black beaches of the volcanic island Iwo Jima. In many ways the aptly titled *Arctic* (Joe Penna, 2018) is an unusually minimalistic and realistic take on the Arctic ice and glacial setting, with the stranded pilot Overgard (Mads Mikkelsen) trying to reach safety with an unnamed and mostly unconscious Thai woman (María Thelma Smáradóttir) in tow. However, the actual location is never specified—it is simply some generic Arctic world—nor is the unlikely presence of a Thai plane in the region ever explained. Worth mentioning in this context as well is the British series *Fortitude* (2015–2018, Simon Donald), set in a fictional town on Svalbard (ostensibly Norwegian but very much an international community) but with exteriors shot in the village of *Reyðarfjörður* in the Eastfjords of Iceland. It is not as bizarre, though, as the Norwegian film *Dead Snow 2: Red vs. Dead* (Tommy Wirkola, 2014) that has Iceland stand in for its Norwegian outdoors. The ways of international film financing can be mysterious indeed.

Ironically, it is much rarer for Iceland to depict itself when it comes to runaway productions. On the few occasions that it has, as was the case with the 3D *Journey to the Center of the Earth*, the approach is often not at all different, and is characterized by exotic nature and the absence of local specificity. Perhaps Iceland's turn was bound to come up at some point, considering the insatiable demand for exotic locations in the James Bond films, but *Die Another Day* (Lee Tamahori, 2002) is also suggestive of the circumscribed qualities of Iceland's exoticism. Despite its capacity for outlandishness, it is too close to the British home of the franchise. Unlike North Korea and Cuba, the film's other exotic countries, Iceland appears only as mise-en-scène. No Icelandic is spoken, and not a single Icelandic character is found in the film. The land simply appears out of the blue as we fly low over an icy setting before finding James Bond (Pierce Brosnan) driving his Aston Martin in a wondrous winterscape toward a fanciful ice palace. The film's stereotypically depicted villain Tan-Sun Moon (Will Yun Lee) is Korean but is disguised as the English entrepreneur Gustav Graves (Toby Stephens) through the process of futuristic plastic surgery. He keeps his latest gimmick "Icarus," which not entirely unexpectedly turns out to be a terrible secret weapon in disguise, amid this unidentified winterscape. After a brief buildup, one of the franchise's over-the-top action scenes follows. Bond and Zao (Rick Yune), the villain's right-hand man, chase after one another at high speeds between icebergs on *Jökulsárlón*, before driving into the now melting ice palace. Notably, its interiors are modeled on "Ice Hotels" found in Lapland, suggesting how the setting is a composite of geographical locations that form an imaginary ice world.

Ben Stiller's *The Secret Life of Walter Mitty* (2013) might at first sight appear different from these films, as its title character actually visits Iceland, where he meets numerous locals who speak to him in English (with language misunderstandings being part of the plot) but also occasionally among themselves in Icelandic. However, Iceland also stands in for Greenland and the Himalayas and reserves for them the most mountainous and glacial locations, thus designating again Iceland as a generic wintery space rather than a specific place. There was really no particular need to go there, as any exotic country could have established Mitty's desire for adventure and excitement in his life (the Mitty of James Thurber's original short story does not travel anywhere). And there are some interesting curiosities about Iceland in this film. After shooting *Nuuk*, Greenland, in the village of *Stykkishólmur* on the *Snæfellsnes* Peninsula, the filmmakers name the Icelandic village where Mitty arrives in Iceland *Stykkishólmur*, even though it is actually a different and far removed fishing village on the other side of the island. This is perhaps the ultimate example of place becoming interchangeable space. Films like these not only evacuate the actual shooting location from the diegesis, but their Picturesque aesthetics turns places into spectacles divorced from local specificity.

The most obvious exception to this is the rare film that deals with real events in which Iceland plays a direct role or provides the backdrop in one way or another. *Pawn Sacrifice* (Edward Zwick, 2015) is an interesting example, as much of it is focused on the famous encounter between Fischer and Spassky in Reykjavík. But remarkably, the filmmakers have not staged any of their scenes in the city, and declined the opportunity to film at least the exteriors of the venue that actually housed the duel. Instead, almost all the material shot in Iceland is located out in nature, far from the capital, where the film inaccurately shows Fischer staying (rather than the actual hotel suite he stayed in in Reykjavík), including numerous shots of him walking and driving in atmospheric landscape settings. In other words, even when Iceland is the historical location, filmmakers privilege nature rather than realism when shooting there. Although unable to resist staging a scene in the Blue Lagoon, Iceland's most popular tourist destination, the filmmakers behind *The Fifth Estate* (Bill Condon, 2013) have, unlike *Pawn Sacrifice*, also filmed scenes at their actual locations, including the Parliament building in downtown Reykjavík. The film follows the globetrotting Julian Assange (Benedict Cumberbatch) over an extended period of time, so it would have been difficult to ignore Iceland altogether, considering the extensive role it played in the history of WikiLeaks, and Icelander Birgitta Jónsdóttir (Carice van Houten) is an important character in the film.[27] Real-life local news anchor Bogi Ágústsson is also present to deliver news of the leaked documents. It is much harder to make sense of the role Iceland plays in *Money Monster* (Jodie Foster, 2016) where finance television host Lee Gates (George Clooney) is taken hostage on live television after promoting a dubious investment scheme gone wrong. The film is focused on the hostage situation but makes brief use of three international locations, South Korea, South Africa, and Iceland, as Gates's producer Patty Fenn (Julia Roberts) tries to trace the money. *Money Monster*'s Icelandic setting is arguably the most uncharacteristic of all those discussed in this chapter, as there is no nature, no landscape, in fact not a single exterior shot. Instead, it shows two computer nerds playing video games in a gloomy apartment that are ultimately called upon by Patty and her television crew to gather information about the plot through online hacking, which they successfully do. Why they had to be Icelandic is by no means clear, but they are actually played by Icelandic actors who speak to one another in their native tongue. Prior to the financial crisis of 2008, I assume audiences would have found this ludicrous, but Iceland's image had been transformed through the scandals of its shady financiers and the hacking tied to WikiLeaks.

Arguably, the only feature not based upon actual events that could be described as locally specific is Hal Hartley's *No Such Thing*, made back in 2001. An unconventional take on *Beauty and the Beast*, the film is about an American reporter Beatrice (Sarah Polley) who visits a monster (Robert John Burke) living at *Heimsendir* (End of the world) in Iceland. The inclusion of such well-known film actresses as Helen Mirren and Julie Christie, in addition to Polley, is balanced by an extensive Icelandic cast representing both realistic local city people and fishermen and fantastical figures in the countryside. The film's urban mise-en-scène also has a strong local flavor, and the landscape scenes are mostly devoid of the Picturesque. In other words, the representation of Iceland in *No Such Things* is of Icelandic rather than Hollywood origin.[28] Something similar could be said about the series *Sense8* (Lana Wachowski, Lilly Wachowski, and J. Michael Straczynski, 2015–2018) despite its overall premise being the exact opposite. The series has a rare global emphasis, with its many central characters inhabiting places all over the world, including Nairobi, Seoul, Mexico City, and San Francisco. Despite *Sense8*'s lofty ambitions of suggesting their interconnectedness, it often succumbs to national stereotyping and overt exoticism in presenting its many locations. It is therefore rather surprising to see how locally specific the approach to Iceland is, incorporating Icelandic folklore and even a traditional lullaby into its storyline.[29] Apart from the casting of the main Icelandic character Riley (Tuppence Middleton)—and here the actor's English nationality could be justified by the fact that she is living as a DJ in London as the series opens—all the other actors are Icelandic and the parts set in Iceland remain true to both local interiors and exteriors. Iceland also plays an increasingly large role in the narrative, and the climax of the first season takes place there, with all the main characters together on an Icelandic fishing boat—while the music of the band *Sigur Rós* provides atmospheric accompaniment.[30]

But this is all rather exceptional. Whether appearing as Iceland itself or standing in for real or fictional places, the filmic results typically combine authenticity with genericity. Rarely can it be said that there was a particular need to film in Iceland, as even those films set in Iceland use it solely as interchangeable background. They have rarely anything to say about Iceland as a place or locale; their authenticity is solely found in offering a "real" generic setting.

The Land of Cinema?

The number of runaway productions reached new heights in 2012, a true watershed year that included unusually expansive projects like *Noah*, *Oblivion*, *The Secret Life of Walter Mitty*, and *Thor: The Dark World* (Alan Taylor, 2013). According to Einar Hansen Tómasson, the influx of projects remained steady throughout the decade, taking into account annual fluctuations.[31] Even the COVID-19 crisis of 2019 had no significant impact, as special measures were taken to keep the country open for visiting film crews. The biggest variant is the unstable Icelandic currency, whose value can change so much more quickly than that of the dollar, the pound, or the euro, and thus can quickly alter any budget calculations. At the time, Iceland was also outdone by some of its competitors despite the generous 25% reimbursements of costs generated while filming in Iceland. Neighboring Ireland, for example, was offering over 30% and also had the advantage of proximity to London and being an English-language country. This helps explain why *The Vikings* (2013–2020) television series was filmed in Ireland rather than Iceland, let alone Norway.[32] Similarly, *The Northman* (Robert Eggers, 2022) was also mostly filmed in Ireland despite being primarily set in Iceland—although the production team found it necessary to film a few exteriors shots in Iceland where Ireland's landscape was "lacking." As a response, Iceland is now offering up to 35% refund payments.

Another major development is the augmented range of activities. No longer are these runaway productions limited to simply shooting landscape scenes, as the local film industry now also includes companies specializing in visual effects, animation, and other post-production work—even taking on assignments for films, television, and games that are not shot in Iceland at all. Iceland had long been hampered by a lack of studio facilities that could complement all the exterior shooting, but in the early 2020s Baltasar Kormákur's RVK Studios opened at the outskirts of Reykjavík, offering the first 3,200 m² sized stage, followed by a couple of 1,600 m² ones. Still more is needed if Iceland wants to truly compete for studio production in addition to exterior location shooting. While there can be no doubt that studio facilities could be a boon to the Icelandic film industry, it is likely that exterior shooting will remain the primary draw for the foreseeable future. Indeed, the range of such productions continues to grow. Earlier in this chapter, I quoted my interview with film commissioner Tómasson from 2012, where he pointed out that no longer were such projects limited to ice and snow. The *Game of Thrones* series, in fact, serves as a splendid example, as the producers were initially drawn to Iceland for the show's wintery world north of the Wall, but enlarged its scope south of it as well when the production team understood the range of landscapes in Iceland. As I revisited Tómasson in 2020, this range had expanded still further, with more interest shown in filming in the capital Reykjavík and smaller fishing villages around the country.[33]

At the risk of stating the obvious, these runaway productions have completely transformed the Icelandic film industry, but the question of how they affect Icelandic national cinema remains open. Separating national cinema and industry in this manner might seem a matter of semantics, but their economic, political, and cultural priorities are completely different. Indeed, as I argue in this book, it is crucial to distinguish between film production in Iceland and films that are culturally Icelandic in the sense that they are made by Icelanders and for Icelanders (even if they may be intended for foreign distribution as well). However, there are links between these two worlds, and the latter has been affected by the former in many ways.

Addressing the watershed year of 2012, the Sunday magazine cover of the newspaper *Morgunblaðið* provided under its main headline "Land of Cinema" (*Bíólandið*) an image of Iceland constructed from photographs of many of the international film stars and directors who had recently worked there.[34] The image illustrates how Icelandic filmmaking (at least domestically) is increasingly defined by foreign productions, which now equal the number of local feature films made annually but that far outweigh their economic impact. Notably, this description of Iceland as a "Land of Cinema" does not even include local film productions. Furthermore, film crews were for the most part unavailable for local productions during the summer of 2012. But given that Hollywood productions provide additional work at a very competitive salary, advance professionalism in the industry, and link local filmmakers to the outside world, there has been little antagonism between domestic filmmakers and overseas productions so far. However, there are signs that things may be about to change. When the Icelandic government introduced major budget cuts to the Icelandic Film Fund in 2022 soon after celebrating its largest ever reimbursement project, the fourth season of HBO's *True Detective* (Issa López, 2024), many spokespersons from within the industry finally expressed their deep concerns. After all, the allotted state contribution to the Fund in 2023 was less than half the expected reimbursement designated for *True Detective*.[35]

Such a state of affairs begets questions regarding the unequal status of national cinemas, their access to creative labor, facilities, and nature/land. As far as economics are concerned, this may be no different from Iceland selling its hydroelectric power to foreign aluminum corporations with global reach, or efforts to increase tourism for valuable foreign currency. However, in the case of cinema, the product itself is a representation, and ultimately quite different from local ones; indeed, the locale has been emptied out. No longer a place, Iceland becomes Picturesque scenery.

12
Icelandic Women's Cinema

Women played in an instrumental role in the establishing of Icelandic cinema as a national institution in the early 1980s. The first to direct a feature was Róska, but her film *Sóley* (1982), made with Manrico Pabolettoni, was made outside the parameters of the emerging film community. It belongs more properly to the experimental art world that both Róska and Pabolettoni came from, and the film never had a conventional theatrical release. The following year, two films directed by women were released: Kristín Pálsdóttir's *Message to Sandra* (*Skilaboð til Söndru*) and Kristín Jóhannesdóttir's *Rainbow's End* (*Á hjara veraldar*), and the latter remains arguably to this day the most radical Icelandic film feature as regards formal aesthetics. In 1986, Þórhildur Þorleifsdóttir scored a big hit with the comedy *The Icelandic Shock Station* (*Stella í orlofi*), and a year later, Guðný Halldórsdóttir directed her debut feature *Under the Glacier* (*Kristnihald undir jökli*). However, it was only Halldórsdóttir who was to have an extended film career, as the spontaneity and experimental phase of the early 1980s made way for a more regulated and organized industry.

Ásdís Thoroddsen was the only female newcomer of the 1990s, but after directing two films during the decade, she has not returned to the chair. More than a decade passed before another woman directed her debut film in Iceland, when Silja Hauksdóttir made *Dís* (2004). Additionally, Sólveig Anspach made her first outright Icelandic film with *Back Soon* (*Skrapp út*) in 2008, having started her career in France during the 1990s. The same year, editor Valdís Óskarsdóttir also returned to Iceland to direct her first feature, *Country Wedding* (*Sveitabrúðkaup*), which she followed up with *King's Road* (2010, *Kóngavegur*). However, she was hardly a newcomer, having already edited such key works of world cinema as *The Celebration* (Thomas Vinterberg, 1998, *Festen*) and *Eternal Sunshine of the Spotless Mind* (Michel Gondry, 2004).[1]

Óskarsdóttir's international success in editing has since been emulated by Elísabet Ronaldsdóttir, whose long-standing partnership with Baltasar Kormákur, including *Contraband* (2012), paved the way for a successful

Hollywood career, including editing the extremely fast-paced action hits *John Wick* (Chad Stahelski, 2014), *Atomic Blonde* (David Leitch, 2017), and *Bullet Train* (David Leitch, 2022). Arguably most successful in the long run, though, of all Icelanders working in Hollywood is makeup artist Heba Þórisdóttir, especially renowned for her work with Quentin Tarantino dating back to *Kill Bill* (2003/2004). She even plays a makeup artist with a recognizable Icelandic accent in Tarantino's *Once Upon a Time in Hollywood* (2019). And on the music front, Hildur Guðnadóttir skyrocketed to fame with her score for the television series *Chernobyl* (Craig Mazin, 2019), winning Emmy, BAFTA, and Grammy awards, and *The Joker* (2019, Todd Phillips), winning Golden Globe, BAFTA, and Academy awards. She was thus not only the first Icelander to win an Oscar but also the first woman to be awarded one for Best Original Score. In her accepting speech, she encouraged women to take on the male-dominated field: "To the girls, to the women, to the mothers, to the daughters who hear the music bubbling within, please speak up. We need to hear your voices."[2] True to her word, she soon wrote another two celebrated scores for films investigating gender violence and discrimination, *Women Talking* (Sarah Polley, 2022) and *Tár* (Todd Field, 2022).

It is not clear—and perhaps unlikely—that these international careers and successes are in any way a response to the lack of opportunities in Icelandic filmmaking. Indeed, the editors Óskarsdóttir and Ronaldsdóttir had long successful careers in Iceland before making the transition to foreign projects. Also, international success has not been limited to women, and Guðnadóttir's achievement was preceded by the work of Ólafur Arnalds, Atli Óskarsson, and especially Jóhann Jóhannsson, who received an Academy Award nomination for both *The Theory of Everything* (James Marsh, 2014) and *Sicario* (Denis Villeneuve, 2015). And outside of music, Karl Júlíusson has had a long illustrious career as production designer, including *Dancer in the Dark* (Lars von Trier, 2000) and *The Hurt Locker* (Kathryn Bigelow, 2008). Nonetheless, it is noteworthy how much more successful than their male colleagues Icelandic women have been internationally. The standout exception is director Kormákur, but the dearth of Icelandic women directors abroad should not come as a surprise considering the topic of this chapter.

At the home front, things were certainly much gloomier, and the years passed one by one after Óskarsdóttir directed her features without a single new film directed by a woman seeing the light of day, until finally a transformation occurred at the very end of the teens.[3] It is that transformation I will be delineating in this chapter. But let it first be clearly stated that the lack of

Icelandic women filmmakers during the three decades from the late 1980s to the late 2010s has been acutely felt, if not always noticed. Not only were their films of the early 1980s more formally adventurous than the work of their male counterparts, but they approached Icelandic society from a very different perspective, as they were, for example, much more likely to focus on female protagonists than male directors. One can only speculate what Icelandic cinema might have looked like with greater gender equality during these three long decades.

It was in 2017 that the pipe finally burst, when Guðrún Ragnarsdóttir's *Summer Children* (*Sumarbörn*) and Ása Helga Hjörleifsdóttir's *The Swan* (*Svanurinn*) were released in quick succession in the fall. They were soon followed by Ísold Uggadóttir's *And Breathe Normally* (2018, *Andið eðlilega*), Ásthildur Kjartansdóttir's *The Deposit* (2019, *Tryggð*), and Silja Hauksdóttir's *Agnes Joy* (2019). Apart from *Agnes Joy*, Hauksdóttir's second film (having directed *Dís* fifteen years prior), all the films were debut features, but that does not mean all the directors were newcomers to the field. Strikingly, all five films focus on female protagonists: the first two deal with the growing pains of young girls, and the latter three with adult women in Iceland's increasingly plural society. Neither had previously played any significant role in the work of male directors. However, some male directors were also affected by this gender shift at the end of the decade, as they made films focused on female characters and experiences, most notably Baldvin Zophoníasson's *Let Me Fall* (2018, *Lof mér að falla*) and Benedikt Erlingsson's *Woman at War* (2018, *Kona fer í stríð*).

In what follows, I will begin by addressing the only non-debut film, *Agnes Joy*, and place it in the context of Hauksdóttir's much earlier film *Dís*, before moving on to the two debut films of 2017, and finally lay out the new social vision presented by women filmmakers at the end of the decade, with a particular focus on Uggadóttir's career. Ultimately, I will raise the question whether the aesthetics and thematic focus of their films are different enough from the main output of Icelandic cinema to warrant grouping them together under the distinct rubric of "women cinema."

From *Dís* to *Agnes Joy*

Silja Haukdsóttir's 2004 debut feature was an adaptation of the novel *Dís* that she wrote in partnership with Birna Anna Björnsdóttir and Oddný

Sturludóttir. Both film and novel purposefully replaced the dominant male perspective of Reykjavík with a female perspective.[4] In many ways, it was *101 Reykjavík* all over again, except that it was narrated from the perspective of the other sex (see analysis of *101 Reykjavík* in chapters seven and eight). The title character is in her early twenties, lives in downtown Reykjavík, postal code 101, and is going through an existential crisis—figuring out what to do with her life. As if to acknowledge its indebtedness to *101 Reykjavík*, the film adaptation of *Dís* begins where the former concluded. Two male tourists come walking up the street *Bankastræti*, exactly where Hlynur in his new job was giving out parking tickets at the end of *101 Reykjavík*, before turning into a café. Inspired by the myth of the promiscuity of Icelandic women, they sit down next to Dís (Álfrún Örnólfsdóttir) and her best friend Blær (Ilmur Kristjánsdóttir). However, they get something very different than they bargained for, as the girls give them a good lecture on the independence of Icelandic women throughout the ages, and the two tourists take their leave, embarrassed under the gaze of the women in attendance. Thus, the very opening of *Dís*, a film about young women in Reykjavík, is a strong response to a degrading stereotype of Icelandic women (sometimes explicitly marketed as such by the tourist industry) that would seem equally directed to foreigners and locals.[5]

Dís was produced by *101 Reykjavík* director Kormákur, and in addition to the similarities found in the novels, the two films also have a similar music score and were both extremely colorful in sets and costumes. The key difference, however, is that *Dís* is very much a local production devoid of the transnational elements that shaped *101 Reykjavík*.[6] For example, the character of the American photographer Jamie Kooley (Ylfa Edelstein) is given considerable screen time, but she is neither systematically guided through Reykjavík in the same manner as Lola in *101 Reykjavík*, nor is she played by a recognizable star of world cinema comparable to Victoria Abril. Also, in the novel, Dís had a Spanish boyfriend who visits her in Iceland, but that character has been erased in the film. Retaining him would have allowed a further developing of its transnational angle, but instead Dís has relationships with two Icelanders. As *Dís* was a low-budget film, shot on digital video (at the time still something of a low-budget alternative), financed and produced solely in Iceland, it had no creative or financial need to make use of a foreign talent or film parts of it abroad, and accordingly there was less incentive to develop the transnational potential of the narrative. While these differences may not seem directly related to gender, the contrasting scope of these two productions is hardly coincidental. These were both debut films, and there is a certain risk in having Kormákur's subsequent big-budget Hollywood career muddy the waters. While not necessarily the only factor, gender is pivotal in explaining the differences between the two productions.

Agnes Joy (2019), Hauksdóttir's belated second feature, is equally a local production. It received no foreign funding, was made by a fully local crew, and shies away from any catering to a foreign audience, through either narrative or aesthetics. Obvious potentials for developing the plot outside Iceland's borders are shunned, and it is formally normative (by which I mean conventional for Icelandic cinema and devoid of typical genre or art cinema traits). In that sense, not much has changed in-between the two films. But this local depiction is fundamentally different from the one found in *Dís* fifteen years earlier. For one, the title character (Donna Cruz) is a nineteen-year-old girl who was adopted from the Philippines. But this not an identity exploration, familiar from world cinema, as Agnes has absolutely no connections to her country of birth and refuses to travel there with her parents, who have long planned to take her there for a visit. The point is rather that Agnes Joy is no different from any other Icelandic teenage girl. She struggles at home and at school, is developing her first serious relationships, and desires to move to the city (a familiar trait in Icelandic cinema).

But even though Agnes is presented as any other Icelandic girl, the film is far from color-blind. Moreover, a key subtext throughout delineates how immigration and ethnicity divide a prejudiced Icelandic society. It draws attention to how "workers' rentals" (*starfsmannaleiga*) are used to avoid legalized minimal wages and do away with labor benefits for foreign workers under the guise of "modern business methods," and it repeatedly shows us immigrant women holding various low-wage service jobs. Most strikingly, Agnes is patronizingly told that she speaks very good Icelandic (as due to her ethnicity she is assumed to be an immigrant) and then after twice being assumed to be a prostitute (again apparently because of her ethnicity) she has had enough and powerfully asserts: "Excuse me. I'm not a whore. My name is Agnes Joy Einarsdóttir. And I'm from *Akranes*." As regards gender, there is a certain similarity here with Agnes's statement and the opening scene of *Dís*, but now ethnicity adds another layer to the assumption about women's sexual roles. There is also a bit of local humor in her response, as the fishing town *Akranes* is typically perceived to be anything but exotic.

The depiction of gender is also made more complex by the inclusion of three generations of women, as Agnes's grandmother and especially mother also play large roles in the film. In fact, the film could just as well have been named after the mother, Rannveig (Katla M. Þorgeirsdóttir), as the daughter. A strong middle-aged woman who has taken over the running of the family firm after her father died unexpectedly, she finds herself increasingly unhappy in both her professional and private life. Her relationship with her husband Einar (Þorsteinn Bachmann) has reached an impasse, as he seems more interested in watching Netflix series than her attempts at rekindling their love life. In a telling scene, she ends up drinking and dancing by herself in a mood of nostalgia, helped by the classic eighties song "Draumaprinsinn" (whose literal meaning, "The Dream Prince," is a familiar Icelandic phrase that means something similar to "Mr. Right"). And her real-life romantic interest (Björn Hlynur Haraldsson), the actor from Reykjavík who moves in next door, betrays her feelings most violently as he also develops a relationship with her daughter. And interestingly, after Agnes seems to have learned from her experiences and found some sort of peace, Rannveig leaves her job, and the film concludes with her looking out her living room window. We cannot gauge her facial expression as we see her only from the back, but a somber note is added with the song "Draumaprinsinn" returning for the film's final credits. It conjures up a bittersweet nostalgia, as Rannveig never found the dream prince of the song, or has lost him through a difficult marriage, while the new candidate turned out to be a nightmare instead a dream. Judging by *Agnes Joy*, it would seem as if both mothers and daughters will have to rely on themselves if they are to find fulfillment in their lives.

Through Young Girls' Eyes

Opening within a month of each other in the fall of 2017, *The Swan* and *Summer Children* together asserted that the long wait for an Icelandic film directed be a female newcomer was finally over. Interestingly, both films focused subjectively on young girls forced to grow up fast due to difficult circumstances. As Ása Helga Hjörleifsdóttir's *The Swan* does this through a remarkable approach to nature and animals, I discuss it in detail in the following chapter, which is specifically devoted to that topic. But albeit an adaptation of a novel written by canonical male author Guðbergur Bergsson, the film offers an unusually pronounced gendered perspective; most of it is presented through the subjectivity of the main protagonist, a young girl called Sól (Gríma Valsdóttir) who is forced to live at a farm far removed from her family. A secondary female character plays a key role as well: Ásta (Þuríður Blær Jóhannsdóttir), a young woman who returns to the farm from Reykjavík, trying to regain her footing. Films set in the farming countryside tend to focus on male characters and experiences, but *The Swan* is most unusual in having two female protagonists that also—if in quite different ways—challenge male customs and ideas at the farm.

Guðrún Ragnarsdóttir's *Sumarbörn* shares the narrative focus on a young girl forced to grow up fast when she is sent to the countryside for a summer stay. In both films the young female protagonists also say goodbye to their mothers before leaving on a bus for the countryside. Eydís (Kristjana Thors) is younger, though, than *The Swan*'s Sól, and she is traveling with a still younger brother Kári (Stefán Örn Eggertsson), whom she also takes responsibility for, and they are staying at a children's home rather than a farm. They belong to the summer children of the film's title and as such are distinguished from the winter children who stay all year long at the home. As we learn later in the film, the siblings' mother has been hospitalized and is recovering from severe domestic abuse, while the children have been told their father is abroad building a palace. The caretakers, led by the extremely stern Pálína (Brynhildur Guðjónsdóttir), are everything but welcoming, and the siblings are desperate to leave from the very first day. The only male worker at the farm gives the young girls candy and ultimately exposes himself and masturbates in front of Eydís, while the exact nature of his abuse to the other girls is left open. The only welcoming and kind presence at the home is found in a German immigrant (Guðlaug Ólafsdóttir), who speaks in broken Icelandic, and is ultimately let go for playing with the children. This environment, especially the character of Pálína, may be felt to be overtly villainous, but the extreme appearance can be explained in two rather different ways. First, systematic abuse at such homes in the past was exposed early in the twenty-first century in a series of scandals, and *Summer Children* take place during the 1950s.[7] Second, much of the film is presented from Eydís's perspective, and the over-the-top depiction of Pálína can be understood to stem from the child's feelings. Indeed, if in quite different ways than *The Swan*, the film is mostly presented through the young girl's subjectivity.

We learn early that Eydís is an imaginative girl who loves to play and sing, but soon her creativity begins to turn to outright fantasy and even hallucinations. During the night, she imagines her mother visiting, and Eydís encourages her brother to stay up for their mother's visits. Even more strikingly, she begins to see and play with a mysterious boy with a horse that no one else seems to see. One of the caretakers suggests it may be the ghost of a boy who was lost to the elements. The exact identity is left ambiguous, but the friend whom she calls Gunnar is clearly different from the other children; dressed up in old-fashioned clothing (including a traditional wool sweater), he never speaks. Whether a figment of her imagination or not, the boy is clearly not of this world. The audience sees him simply because Eydís does so. Other striking moments of such visual subjectivity are point-of-view shots from Eydís's perspective as she imagines herself flying, and we even see her briefly leaving the ground as if she really could fly. However, there is little indication that she can actually do so, and we are instead simply witnessing the exterior world through her subjectivity. However, toward the end of the film, there occurs a remarkable conflation of her subjective imagination and the objective real world.

When at risk of becoming winter children or, even worse, separated, when a visiting couple shows interest in adapting Kári, the siblings decide to make their escape to find their mother again in Reykjavík. And they are helped by none other than Gunnar, who brings his horse that carries them over water as its hoofs tread on a lake barring their way as if on solid ground. And chasing after them, Pálína turns into a giant eagle and the land takes on a sinister appearance watching the children on the run (see Figure 12.1).

No longer are these simply Eydís's imaginings, as the children would not have been able to make their way back to Reykjavík on their own—where they are ultimately reunited with their mother. In this way, something extraordinary happens at the end of the film, where a child's subjectivity (desire, fantasy, and imagination) is able to overcome the real world of adults

Figure 12.1 Seen through the eyes of the runaway siblings in *Summer Children*, the landscape comes frightfully alive at night. Source: Ljósband ehf.

and the film's otherwise realistic mise-en-scène. It is a moment of rare magical realism in Icelandic cinema, and it is important that it stems from a female director depicting the character of a young girl who has been struggling against institutional violence throughout the film. Albeit a pleasurable moment, the reunion with the mother does not necessarily bring the film to a happy conclusion. It is by no means clear if the mother will be able to take care of her two children, and the golden sunlight hue engulfing them as the film concludes has a dreamy like feel to it—perhaps suggesting that the idyllic scene is simply too good to be true. However, in watching this film, one should not underestimate the power of a young girl's wish fulfillment.

Ísold Uggadóttir and Diversity

In both their debut films, Guðrún Ragnarsdóttir and Ása Helga Hjörleifsdóttir focused on the female subjectivity of young girls who were forced to grow up far too quickly toward the gendered world of adults. However, neither film could be said to be a commentary on gender and other identity formations in Icelandic society, but that was to be the focus of the films that followed in their wake. As I turn to these films, I want to enlarge my scope a bit and also think about the role of the female practitioner—the woman filmmaker—to consider how these filmmakers themselves are also working in a gendered environment. In doing so, I draw upon the career of Ísold Uggadóttir, whose career got off to a great start with the short *Family Reunion* (*Góðir gestir*) in 2006, but only released her first feature more than a decade later—significantly later than many of her male colleagues.[8]

Like Uggadóttir at the time, the main character of *Family Reunion*, Katrín (Aðalbjörg Árnadóttir), is a young woman living in New York. The plot of the film revolves around her visit to Iceland for her grandfather's (Grétar Snær Hjartarson) seventieth birthday. Unbeknownst to her family and former boyfriend, Katrín is living with a woman in New York, and the film repeatedly emphasizes the heteronormative expectations she faces during her stay in Iceland. Her mother (Hanna María Karlsdóttir), for example, realizes through frequent cell phone use that her daughter is in a serious relationship and ponders the nationality and the race of her partner, but never suspects that it could be a woman. Toward the end of the film, Katrín fears her "secret" is out, and through a series of misunderstandings expects her grandfather to reveal it at his birthday party—the family reunion of the title. However, the clever twist of the story is that it is he himself who is coming out of the closet on his anniversary, and he introduces his partner to the birthday guests, who, unlike Katrín, are mostly in the know already. Although a short film, *Family Reunion* was an elaborate production that included many established actors, and was well received not only in Iceland but around the world, where it did especially well at the queer/LGBT circuit while also making it into the Sundance Film Festival. No doubt the film's success had much to do with the clever plot twist, but it was also a remarkably assured debut and in the Icelandic context a pioneering work as regards queer identity. The film also draws attention to racism in Iceland, as the mother hopes Katrín's imaginary boyfriend is not Black. Certainly, in her first feature Uggadóttir offers a much more diverse picture of social identity than most Icelandic features.

Stylistically her second short, *Committed* (2008, *Njálsgata*), was fundamentally different: the film showcases the handheld camerawork and abrupt editing characteristic of the Dogme movement.[9] Focusing on a young couple, Eva (Dóra Jóhannsdóttir) and Viðar (Jörundur Ragnarsson), who have just moved in together, it shows their relationship quickly unraveling due to Viðar's jealousy after Eva befriends a new co-worker Þórir (Darri Ingólgsson) at the call-in information agency where she works. And the twist in this film as that it is Viðar, rather than Eva, who ends up having an affair. The Dogme style works remarkably well here and helps lend the film both dread and suspense; even the tedious work environment at the agency becomes filled with suspense. The realistic style may also suggest the film to be first and foremost a personal drama, but a larger commentary is also being made about gender relations, as the male partner ends up committing the offense he accuses his female partner of.

After making *Committed*, Uggadóttir worked on various summer productions in Iceland. But during the winters she stayed in New York, having now joined the film program at Columbia University for an MFA in film production, where she made her first English-language short. Although relying on similar handheld aesthetics as *Committed*, *Clean* (2010) was completely different in being an American production focusing on substance abuse. For her final project, however, she returned to Iceland to make *Revolution Reykjavík* (2011, *Útrás Reykjavík*), where she continued the focus on substance abuse but placed it now in the context of the economic collapse of 2008. At the start of the film, the middle-aged Guðfinna (Lilja Þórisdóttir) has everything under control and gives her daughter (María Heba Þorkelsdóttir) a hard time about her life and the upbringing of her two children. But when Guðfinna loses her bank position, her private life quickly spirals out of control. Unable to confide in her daughter, she turns to drinking when she can no longer pay her bills. What is especially noteworthy about this early foray into the consequences of the economic collapse is the lack of men in the film. Notably, Guðfinna's superior at the bank is male, and so is the prime minister on the television, but she lives alone and her daughter is a single mother. And although this "lack" is not explained, one cannot but notice how the difficult circumstances of the female characters stem from the decisions and failures of men in power. It is difficult not to conclude that this perspective has much to do with the gender of the director. All the main protagonists of Uggadóttir's shorts are women who face various private and public challenges.

After a decade-long stay in New York, Uggadóttir moved back to Iceland in 2011, with the specific goal of making her feature there rather than in the United States. She now expanded her range by working as a production and field coordinator, including the Icelandic portion of Michael Moore's *Where to Invade Next* (2015). However, while such projects can provide beneficial experiences and good salary, they also risk delaying one's own personal film projects.[10] Additionally, the film script took a long time to develop and Uggadóttir participated in workshops both in Mexico and Los Angeles, where the original idea of a struggling young Icelandic woman was broadened with the global refugee crisis. Financing and production obstacles delayed the project further, and it was not until the fall of 2016 that the film went into production. In some ways it was a typical transnational production with Swedish and Belgian partners. Although shot in Iceland, the crew was multinational and post-production was divided between Sweden and Belgium. What was strikingly different, though, from the typical transnational film production was the role played by women in the production; Uggadóttir purposefully filled most of the key positions with women, including cinematographer Ita Zbroniec-Zajt, editor Frédérique Broos, and production designer Marta Luiza Macuga. The emphasis on women's roles was equally reflected on screen as well.

The story of *And Breathe Normally* is about two women who at first sight appear to be mirror opposites that come together and see themselves reflected in one another. Lára (Kristín Þóra Haraldsdóttir) is a single mother down on her luck. She is broke, battling substance abuse, and in a relationship with a woman that is drawing to an end. The only silver lining is a new job at the *Keflavík* international airport passport control. Early on in her job, she spots a counterfeit passport belonging to the film's other main character. Claiming to be French, Adja (Babetida Sadjo) is actually from Guinea Bissau and is trying to make her escape to Canada. Separated from her daughter and sister who have made it through passport control, Adja is subsequently driven to prison by a police officer, with Lára accompanying them. After this the plot begins to follow the two of them separately as their different plights reach new heights. Lára is evicted from her apartment in the *Keflavík* region, and she and her son Eldar (Patrik Nökkvi Pétursson) begin sleeping in her car as they have no one to turn to for help. Meanwhile, Adja is imprisoned and later taken to a rundown apartment house for asylum seekers. As their paths are about to cross again halfway through the film, there is increased crosscutting between the two plotlines. Adja discovers that Lára and her son are homeless and takes them in, and when she herself is denied asylum (as she cannot prove that her life is in danger because of her sexuality), Lára waves her through passport control. It is a scene that is a clear reversal of the early scene in which they first meet: now emphasizing mutual recognition and caring, despite the glass barrier separating them (see Figure 12.2).

The local and global meet in *And Breathe Normally* in quite interesting ways. On the one hand, it is a film about the global refugee crisis, as one of the two main characters is traveling from Africa to North America with a forced stopover in Europe. On the other, it is very local and limited spatially to the area around the *Keflavík* airport and the small town of the same name (the film's apartment house neighborhood is actually the one left behind by the former US Naval Air Station that was located by the airport) and

Figure 12.2 A close-up of a passport passing between hands symbolizes an unlikely alliance in *And Breathe Normally*. Source: Zik Zak kvikmyndir.

even Reykjavík is only glimpsed in the distance. Lára herself has never left Iceland and she and her son speculate how warm it might be in countries that the passengers are departing to in the planes they watch fly above their car. As with the production, *And Breathe Normally* is in one sense a typical transnational narrative, but in another an unparalleled one in Icelandic cinema.

The film's mise-en-scène is telling in this regard. It is the exact opposite of the approach that typified the first wave of transnational films, most spectacularly in *Cold Fever* (Friðrik Þór Friðriksson, 1995, *Á köldum klaka*), and their exotic depiction of Iceland (see chapter seven). First, we are in a region far removed from both the kind of landscape that typically appeals to foreign audiences and the cosmopolitan city of Reykjavík. Second, it is presented in terms that avoid the typical visual appeal of Icelandic landscape and locations. Uggadóttir herself states that she wanted to avoid making a summer film, to avoid it being "green and beautiful."[11] Indeed, the weather is exceedingly drab: gloomy, cloudy, rainy, misty, and windy. Many scenes also take place in darkness or early morning when there is little visibility. Presumably, this is not a place many would want to visit after watching the film. The Icelandic authorities are also shown to be most hostile toward Adja: male characters (including her lawyer) approach her plight with striking triviality, and even though the women characters put on a more sympathetic face, they ultimately also represent the state power that denies asylum as "standard procedure."

As regards race and national background, the two main characters could not be further apart: one is a Black African and the other a white European. However, as they discover throughout the film, they have much more in common than separates them. They are both single mothers, lesbian, and lacking in privilege: and they are willing to help each other out as they realize social institutions will not do so. Despite numerous minor characters, the plot is solely devoted to these two women and young Eldar, while there are no fathers in the film. As such, *And Breathe Normally* draws upon many aspects of Uggadóttir's shorts: female protagonists, sexuality, economic hardship, and substance addiction. In *And Breathe Normally*, Uggadóttir combines all these elements in a drama about refugees and immigration—a topic that Icelandic cinema had barely touched upon. Notably, the other film to delve into this topic in the late teens was also directed by a woman, and if anything, it offered an even stronger critique of immigration and Icelandic society.

From Gender to Ethnicity

The experienced Ásthildur Kjartansdóttir, whose documentary credits include a film about the radical artist *Róska* (2005) discussed at the beginning of the chapter, waited still longer than Ísold Uggadóttir to direct her first feature. Based upon a novel by Auður Jónsdóttir, Kjartansdóttir's debut feature, *The Deposit* (*Tryggð*), tells the story of Gísella (Elma Lísa Gunnarsdóttir), who lives alone in a beautiful large house she has inherited from her grandparents in an old and treasured neighborhood of Reykjavík. Everything speaks to her upper middle-class status, including clothing and the arrangement and decorations of her rooms. At the beginning of the film she quits her newspaper job, tired of the editor's meddling with her work and the paper's frivolous approach to the news. Instead, she joins a critical leftist journal for the specific purpose of writing an exposé on immigration and housing. Doing some preliminary research, she meets two women, Maria (Raffaella Brizuela Sigurðardóttir) from Columbia and Abeba (Enid Mbabazi) from Uganda, living in a small room in rundown industrial housing. Dismayed by their lot, she decides to invite them to stay and rent with her instead. While she is clearly acting out of genuine concern, the offer is not without self-motivation, as her finances are tied up in an investment and having quit her job she is not able to keep up with payments. She is also charmed by Adeba's daughter Luna (Claire Harpa Kristinsdóttir) and we later learn in the film that Gísella has lost her own daughter.

It seems to be an arrangement that works to everyone's benefit—an ideal female community. Maria and Adeba have wonderful new living quarters, and Gísella is enjoying their company and especially Luna's, whom she takes care of while her mother is at work. In addition to getting their own rooms, Maria and Adeba share the kitchen and other living quarters with Gísella, who even encourages them to wear her own nice clothes. They also decide to split household chores and groceries. But soon some minor problems emerge—like untidiness—and the four of them work out together some house rules. The situation continues to unravel nonetheless. Adeba is increasingly concerned about Gísella's investment in her daughter, which is clearly self-serving. She also has a secret that Gísella discovers when she takes Luna to a doctor: they are illegal immigrants. And Gísella feels more and more uncomfortable as the newcomers make the house their home, bringing male friends to stay overnight and even holding a party. She begins to add new house rules on her own, even though, as Maria and Adeba discuss, she does not follow them herself: "She never cooks—ever." Soon they have had enough and inform Gísella that they are moving out, but as she desperately needs the rent money, she insists that they stick to their contract. But when she receives her investment back with great financial rewards and wants them out, the tables are turned, as her renters now insist that she honor their agreement. After Gísella leaves her own house to stay with a friend, she informs the authorities about Adeba, and in the middle of the night, police officers arrive to remove her from the house. Dismayed, Maria leaves as well, and at the end we find Gísella again alone and in control of *her* house.

As this plot outline suggests, *The Deposit*'s handling of the immigrant question is fundamentally different from *And Breathe Normally* in at least two important ways (that also has implications for the films' respective handling of gender). In the latter film, the focus is geopolitical despite the local setting. Adja has no interest in emigrating to Iceland and is simply stuck there on her way to Canada; nor are we introduced to any established immigrants in Iceland. In *The Deposit*, on the other hand, both Maria and Adeba are well established immigrants in Iceland and speak to Gísella in Icelandic (if often broken). They only revert to English if the Icelandic fails them or they are trying to hide things from Luna. Unlike *And Breathe Normally*, *The Deposit* is a fundamentally local production with no foreign financiers or partners. The filmmakers' local approach is not least manifested in the limited use of English despite ample opportunity.

The other key difference is found in how the realist aesthetics of *And Breathe Normally* makes way for an allegorical narrative structure. Certainly, the mise-en-scène and acting are often realistic in *The Deposit* as well, but as indicated by the plot summery above, the story as such is intended to address Icelandic society and immigration much more broadly. Gísella's house represents the Icelandic nation-state. At the beginning of the film, it appears excessively orderly in a monochrome of blue and white and is filled with artifacts that evoke romantic patriotic belonging—most notably a white eagle or falcon (also specifically the symbol of the right-leaning Independence Party). From the inside of her house, Gísella watches the poor immigrant who picks up her used bottles in the morning, suggesting a real insulation and distance from the outside world and specifically that of immigrants. Her relationship with her renters also allegorically represents the limits of liberalism when it comes to immigration and ethnic and cultural diversity. While outwardly extremely welcoming, she makes clear that the house is hers: "Welcome to my house," she says, and she puts the falcon aside. And she enjoys the newcomers' company while she is in control and they add spice to her monotonous life. At this point, the film emphasizes the diversity and vibrancy the new lodgers bring to the house. In a scene with a clear allegorical intent, they all have fun together in the kitchen, listening to music and most notably dancing an African dance together (see Figure 12.3).

However, when Maria and Adeba insist on "rights to [their] private lives," Gísella suggests they move out. When they respond with the obvious "We also live here," she begins to change the tune of her housing exposé, stating now that "immigrants must adapt." She ultimately gives up on the report and has her lodgers forcibly removed. As she again looks out the window at end of the film—alone and insulated, with the falcon back in its "proper" place—the collector now leaves her bottles untouched as he continues down the street while an African song can be heard on the soundtrack. As the end credits fill the screen, a rather gloomy instrumental version of the romantic patriotic song "Land of My Father" ("Land míns föður"), composed by Jóhannes úr Kötlum to celebrate the Independence of the Republic in 1944, replaces the African song. The implications could not be much clearer.

All in all, the film's allegory suggests that as regards immigration, Icelandic—and more broadly, Western—liberalism is only welcoming as long as the host is in control and benefits from it, through financial gain (rent), service work (cooking and cleaning), and entertainment (song and dance). But as soon as the newcomers insist on sharing the house—having

Figure 12.3 Abeba (Enid Mbabazi) teaches Gísella (Elma Lísa Gunnarsdóttir) and Maria (Raffaella Brizuela Sigurðardóttir) African dances. It is a rare utopian moment in the allegorical film *The Deposit*, which criticizes the treatment of immigrants in Iceland. Source: Askja Films and Rebella Filmworks.

equal rights and duties—that ends the liberal welcome and the immigrants are thrown out.[12] This punishing allegory has also relevance for the film's gender politics, as what looked like an idyllic female community increasingly turns sour. As the focus is very much on the three women and the girl Luna, male characters are relegated to the margins. But most of them are in positions of authority: the two editors, the business man (and former lover) who has tied up Gísella's money, and Maria and Adeba's original landlord. So early on, it feels as if they have established an ideal female community free from male influence; however, it soon becomes clear that race and ethnicity far outdo gender in *The Deposit*. In *And Breathe Normally* the ideal sisterhood between Lára and Adja works at least partly as the latter has no intention of staying in Iceland and the film does not have delve into what that might have entailed. Conversely, the sisterhood in *The Deposit* crumbles as other differences in terms of identity override gender.

There is, though, a certain risk in overstating the differences between the two films. They share much more than separates them: a focus on female characters and immigration and a strong critique of the handling of immigration and refugees. And these are topics that Icelandic male directors have shown little or no interest in, and thus they had barely registered in Icelandic cinema prior. However, there is some suggestion that Icelandic male directors are finally taking notice as well. Nonetheless, male and female directors approach these topics in a very different manner. Having very much aligned himself with the aesthetic tradition of Friðrik Þór Friðriksson, and especially *Children of Nature* (1991, *Börn náttúrunnar*) and its depiction of Iceland of old, at the beginning of his career, Rúnar Rúnarsson made an interesting shift both in turns of form and content with *Echo* (2019, *Bergmál*). Narratively, it is the most formally innovative Icelandic feature since Kristín Jóhannesdóttir's *Rainbow's End*, if in very different ways. While *Rainbow's End* is all about character subjectivity, *Echo* offers a remarkable panoramic view of Icelandic society. It is composed of fifty-six static long takes depicting the Christmas/New Year's period. There is no narrative continuation between the scenes and therefore also no conventional characters. Instead, we are thrown in medias res into one situation after another, depicting a range of social encounters and activities around the holiday period. The camera setups range from symmetrical head-on shots to more elaborate arrangements where characters move within the space and even in and out of the frame—but the camera itself never moves. This expansive social portrayal is particularly attentive to class, and numerous scenes directly or indirectly involve social inequality.

In doing so, Rúnarsson does not neglect the role of immigrants in Icelandic society, including, for example, the role of "worker rentals" in cheating immigrant workers of their legalized pay, as also depicted in *Agnes Joy*, and asylum seekers being apprehended by the police. Most potently, one of the vignettes shows a woman of color breaking down on the phone in the midst of her cleaning job as her former partner is keeping her children away from her for yet another Christmas. However, due to the nature of the film, there is no real narrative investment in these immigrants, any more than there is in other characters. And with so many "echoes," the immigrant experience is marginalized: its actual social marginalization is naturalized through the film's particular aesthetic approach (however formally interesting it may be otherwise). Some of the echoes are also more conservative in nature, especially a scene that seems to offer a direct challenge to the MeToo movement when a woman debating her parking job with a male stranger takes up her phone and starts recording as she accuses him of a made-up harassment.

Considering *Echo*'s unique approach, Ragnar Bragason's *The Garden* (2020, *Gullregn*) is a more telling example of differences in terms of gender and immigration. The film itself is a weird and uncomfortable synthesis of Bragason's serious dramas like *Children* (2006, *Börn*) and *Parents* (2007, *Foreldrar*) and his comedies focused on the character of Georg Bjarnfreðarson (Jón Gnarr), whose success culminated in *Mr. Bjarnfredarson* (2009, *Bjarnfreðarson*), a demeaning stereotype of a politically naïve "lefty" oppressed by his mother. The main characters are the middle-aged Indíana (Sigrún Edda Björnsdóttir) and her now adult son Jónas (Eyþór Gunnlaugsson), whom she has brought up all by herself. Throughout his life she has presented both of them as invalids to cheat disability benefits out of the state, resulting in some social deficiencies in the son. However, at the beginning of the film, Jónas is finally able to begin to separate himself a little from his mother, realizes that there is nothing physically wrong with him, and is ready to start his own life. He falls in love with an immigrant from Poland, Daniela (Karolina Gruszka), and they soon begin living together. For the racist and xenophobic Indíana, the Polish background adds insult to injury. Even before we are introduced to Jónas, we see his mother harassing her Vietnamese upstairs neighbors, whom she insists on calling Chinese, about being too noisy among other things, and later she refuses to have a Black woman assist her at a hair salon. But despite Indíana's outrageous behavior, she step by step wins the battle over her son, who ends up leaving Daniela and moving back in with his mother. As Indíana continues to complain about the noise upstairs, Jónas, now a real mess, loses it altogether and savagely murders the Vietnamese immigrants (as the scene takes place off screen, the details are a bit vague). It is a strikingly brutal ending, considering some of the film's overall comedic elements.

The handling of the immigration theme in *The Garden* could not be more different from *And Breathe Normally* and especially *The Deposit*, whose allegory implicated all of Icelandic society in the abject treatment of immigrants. In *The Garden*, conversely, there is only one outright and over-the-top racist. Apart from Indíana, Icelandic society would seem to be overly welcoming and to harbor well-adapted immigrants who are able to enjoy fruitful lives on equal standing. The brutal murder of the Vietnamese immigrants has nothing to do with systematic racism, but results from the psychological suppression inflicted on Jónas by his crazy mother. And indeed, the two of them are the main characters of the film; we only get to know the immigrant characters through them, and the camera never captures them separately on their own. In this, *The Garden* is fundamentally different from the other two films, and at the risk of stating the obvious, so is the depiction of gender. The role of overbearing and oppressive mothers in Bragason's oeuvre overall is intriguing, but combined here with the overt racism of the mother figure, makes for an even more troubling gender portrayal. To summarize, *The Garden*'s focus is unusual for a film directed by a male director, but the portrayal of immigration, ethnicity, and gender shares none of the progressive and critical vision found in the important work by female filmmakers that has been the focus of this chapter.

Icelandic Women's Cinema?

Due to its lack of female directors, Icelandic cinema has become not only skewed in its gender portrayal, but also more limited in many other ways as regards diversity. Even now, as some male directors begin to approach topics like immigration, they do so in a different and, judged by our admittedly small test pool, more problematic manner. Apart from subject matters and perspective, differences can also be pinpointed as regards genre and aesthetics. This raises the question whether the films of Icelandic women directors are fundamentally different from that of their male colleagues.

In concluding this chapter, I address the notion of women's cinema, that has become increasingly prevalent in not only academic film studies but also mainstream media, and consider its applicability to Icelandic cinema. The idea dates back to the 1970s, when English film theorists Claire Johnston and Laura Mulvey, in two very influential essays, "Women's Cinema as Counter-Cinema" and "Visual Pleasure and Narrative Cinema," respectively, both called for a feminist counter-cinema to break with the conventions of the patriarchal mainstream cinema. Mulvey proposed a new alternative cinema which was to be "radical in both a political and an aesthetic sense."[13] To succeed, women filmmakers had to undermine, and preferably destroy altogether, the visual pleasures of mainstream narrative cinema. And while less suspicious of the merits of popular entertainment, Johnston insisted it should be used as a "political tool" in the struggle for gender equality.[14]

Although hugely influential within academia, it does not seem as if the idea of women's cinema as formulated in the 1970s had a great impact upon filmmaking (save for radical experimental work, including Mulvey's own)—and especially not the mainstream cinema that continued to be dominated by men. Certainly, when Icelandic national cinema took off in the early 1980s with great participation from women filmmakers (somewhat unusual for mainstream filmmaking at the time), they were not influenced by feminist film theory, and there is little evidence that they saw themselves as working in a separate realm or on a different project than their male counterparts. The mutual primary goal was to establish a new national cinema. Nonetheless, many of their films were quite different from those of male directors, not only emphasizing female subjectivity but also in some cases showcasing a more aesthetic experimentation, especially in *Rainbow's End*.

As women directors have played an increasingly larger role in filmmaking around the world throughout the twenty-first century, the idea of women's cinema has become more widespread. No longer does the concept call for the radical formalism and patriarchal critique originally formulated by Johnston and Mulvey, and sometimes it seems to suffice that the films in question have been directed by female filmmakers. More typically, at least in academic scholarship, it is suggested that women's cinema should broadly reflect a female perspective and that the films, through form, narrative, and/or subject matter, should be products of female authorship that differ from the male-centered mainstream. For example, Alison Butler proposed at the turn of the century that the concept of minor cinema was better suited to describing women's cinema than that of counter-cinema: "To call women's cinema a minor cinema, then, is to free it from the binarism (popular/elitist, avant-garde/mainstream, positive/negative) which result from imagining it as a parallel or oppositional cinema."[15] Butler's argument could very much support the idea of a separate women's cinema in Iceland, as women are marginal both in front of and behind the camera. Indeed, she goes on to state that the "assumption of [her] book is that women's cinema is not 'at home' in any of the host cinematic or national discourses it inhabits, but that it is always an inflected mode, incorporating, reworking and contesting the conventions of established traditions."[16] While this is convincing when looking at individual films and the authorship of many female directors, and is supported by my own examples of Icelandic filmmakers in this chapter, there is some risk involved in defining their work as such, as it separates their films from the mainstream cinema and places them in a demarcated and more peripheral category. In other words, we end up with male-oriented filmmaking at the center of the national cinema, while women's cinema is relegated to the margins or beyond altogether. It is for that very same reason, despite this chapter, that I hesitate to group these films together as Icelandic women's cinema, even though they share a focus on female characters and subjectivity that is otherwise rare, and in some cases also different aesthetics strategies—if far removed from the radicalism of the 1970s feminist film manifestos.

Icelandic women directors typically avoid familiar genres, while the allegorical structure of *The Deposit* and the extended formal subjectivity of both *Summer Children* and *The Swan* are most unusual for Icelandic cinema. However, to suggest that these films constitute a separate women's cinema—even as a subgroup within the larger national cinema—risks naturalizing the mainstream male dominance in terms of both production and aesthetics. Conversely, one should exactly describe and demand films such as these to be a normative part of any national cinema, which is exactly what they were in Iceland during the early 1980s. The question is whether that has fundamentally changed now, when women have finally returned to the fore during the past few years. Whether their work will continue to develop and flourish may depend on whether these films are seen as anomalies or a part and parcel of the national norm of Icelandic cinema.

13
Animals and Nature

During the nineties, Icelandic cinema increasingly turned to the capital Reykjavík after the strong rural focus of the eighties. However, the city never gained any stronghold on filmmaking in Iceland, and the pendulum soon swung back to the countryside. Certainly, crime films made their home in Reykjavík, but that had much more to do with the genre's typical mise-en-scène than any interest in exploring the capital thematically or realistically. All the while, art cinema remained devoted to the countryside. However, that does not mean that no change has taken place in the depiction and thematic handling of the country. In fact, I will be arguing in this chapter that the most recent cycle of films set in the countryside—emerging halfway through the teens—approaches their location in an unprecedented manner.

What has not changed is the remarkable incongruency between Icelandic cinema and actual habitats in the country. It would not be unreasonable for foreign viewers to believe that most Icelanders lived either in farms or small fishing villages since the majority of the films (and especially those traveling the international festival circuit) are set in these locations. Although they may include Reykjavík, most films end up privileging the countryside, while the larger towns outside of the capital region, including that of *Akureyri* in the north, almost never provide the setting for Icelandic films. The reality is rather different with two-thirds (228,400) of the national population (364,000) living in the capital area in 2020. Only one out of every ten lived in communities with fewer than a thousand inhabitants (and half of those [21,600] in communities with fewer than 200 inhabitants).[1]

Despite the continuous and unilateral flow of the population to the capital—incidentally, a trend that emerges around the same time as cinema itself—and its central role in every economic, political, and cultural facet of the nation-state, filmmakers still feel compelled to locate their stories in the countryside. The five films I will be focusing on in this chapter are all set in those rural areas of Iceland where less than ten percent of the population reside. Benedikt Erlingsson's *Of Horses and Men* (2013, *Hross í oss*), Grímur Hákonarson's *Rams* (2015, *Hrútar*), and Ása Helga Hjörleifsdóttir's

The Swan (2017, *Svanurinn*) are set in farms or small farming communities; Rúnar Rúnarsson's *Sparrows* (2015, *Þrestir*) is set in a small fishing village; and Guðmundur Arnar Guðmundsson's *Heartstone* (2016, *Hjartasteinn*) is located in a mixture of the two. Save for perhaps *Rams*, none of these films turn to the countryside for any kind of commentary on the national character in the manner of the pioneering films of the early 1980s, particularly *Land and Sons* (Ágúst Guðmundsson, 1980, *Land og synir*) and *Father's Estate* (Hrafn Gunnlaugsson, 1980, *Óðal feðranna*) (see chapter six). Nor do the films revert to the touristic landscape approach, best manifested in films of the mid-1990s like *Agnes* (Egill Eðvarðsson, 1995) and *Cold Fever* (Friðrik Þór Friðriksson, 1995, *Á köldum klaka*) (see chapter seven). Instead, these new films break with representations of the countryside of the past in at least two crucial ways. One is the emphasis on strong personal dramas, enhanced by subjective aesthetics, often focusing on the growing-up pains of young characters. The other involves the novel role that animals play in them; they are no longer simple background material of a broader farming mise-en-scène but absolutely central to both themes and narrative. Sometimes these two elements go hand in hand, but they need not.

In pondering this new role of animals in Icelandic cinema, I draw upon Tiago de Luca's insightful essay, "Natural Views: Animals, Contingency and Death in Carlos Reygadas's *Japón* and Lisandro Alonso's *Los muertos*." Although a detailed analysis of the two specific films referenced in the title, whose explicit sex scenes and animal killing scenes contribute to a hyper-realist aesthetic, de Luca does see these two films as part and parcel of the slow cinema of directors like Lav Diaz, Apichatpong Weersethakul and Béla Tarr. De Luca writes:

> Through realist modes of production based on duration and observation, contemporary slow films arguably postulate a new-found awareness of the *natural world* and testify to a renewed fascination with *rural lifestyles* and the untouched environments, such as villages, jungles and forests. This is exemplified by directors [who] place emphasis on remote spaces whose cyclical, seasonal and artisanal temporalities seem to impose themselves upon the film's own pace, thus opening it up to the vagaries of *nature* and *animal life*.[2]

Although there are ultimately important differences between the films discussed by de Luca and this new crop of Icelandic films, the latter also all express this awareness of the natural world that does not simply serve as a setting for plot and human character action. Perhaps even more important than the strong presence of nature is the role played by animal life in one form or another. What role that is exactly is a bit more difficult to pin down, partly because the films in questions approach and present animals in diverse manner. But the difficulty has also to do with the ambiguity of the cinematic presence of animals more broadly. Because of their differences from us, we have a harder time comprehending their actions and motivations than those of other humans. They constitute something of a representational riddle that Jonathan Burt deals with in his pioneering work *Animals in Film*:

> Although the animal on screen can be burdened with multiple metaphorical significances, giving it an ambiguous status that derives from what might be described as a kind of semantic overload, the animal is also marked as a site where these symbolic associations collapse into each other. *In other words the animal image is a form of rupture in the field of representation.* [...] This rupturing effect of the animal image is mainly exemplified by the manner in which our attention is constantly drawn beyond the image and, in that sense, beyond the aesthetic and semiotic framework of the film.[3]

In other words, the animal constitutes something real that cannot be fully contained by its role in the fictional diegesis and narrative of the film—causing a rupture in the "field of representation." The contained story world of the film is in a certain sense broken and infiltrated by the real; unlike the human actors, the animals cannot pretend or act in make-believe. This is probably one reason why directors invested in hyper-realism, like Alonso and Reygadas, often include animals in their works—and in extreme cases the killing of animals. Allowing for certain relevant differences from the work of these celebrated auteurs of global slow cinema, the inclusion of animals in the Icelandic films discussed in this chapter has resulted in subjects and aesthetics that are mostly unprecedented in the national context. In all of them, this rupturing effect challenges conventional film aesthetics and representation, but the five films do so in two markedly different ways. *The Swan*, *Heartstone*, and *Sparrows* include nature and animals to convey the vagaries and frailty of youths on the verge of adulthood, while *Of Horses and Men* and *Rams* undermine the differences between humans and animals, and the former goes as far as to visualize the subjectivity of animals. Let us begin with the second two films.

Animals Living and Dead

The first Icelandic film to receive the Nordic Council Film Prize, *Of Horses and Men* is composed of a number of story vignettes involving horses, linked through a threadbare general plot set in a small farming community. The opening credits are laid over close-ups of a horse fell, where horses are given credit along with "human" actors. And then an extreme close-up of the horse's eye takes us to the first scene, where we see the main character Kolbeinn (Ingvar Sigurðsson) reflected in the eye before more conventional shots of him bridling the horse follow. The scene then shows him riding the mare to a romantic encounter with neighbor Solveig (Charlotte Bøving) at a nearby farm, but as he is about to head back home after enjoying a cup of coffee, a stallion in heat rushes to the mare and mates with her with Kolbeinn still mounted (this became the iconic image of the film's marketing campaign). Humiliated, Kolbeinn subsequently shoots his treasured mare.

In the story episodes that follow, human characters continue to treat their horses—and each other—with various degrees of harm. One farmer has his horse swim out to a trawler to purchase some homebrew, only to die from the beverage himself. A fight leaves another farmer dead and one blind. A traveling tourist saves his life during a winter storm by cutting open his horse and taking shelter among its intestines. These story vignettes are tied together by the thwarted romance of Kolbeinn and Solveig, whom we see, for example, eye each other during the film's two funerals. Each of these mostly self-contained stories begins with the same type of a close-up of a horse's eye as opened the film. A striking reversal occurs to this principle for a very brief but crucial episode as we cut from a horse to a human eye, and it turns out to be a scene where the stallion of the opening scene is being castrated. It is only after "taming" the horse thus, overcoming the male human's humiliation, that the human romance can blossom. In the final episode depicting the annual roundup of horses that have been let loose over the summer, the tables are turned, with Sólveig and Kolbeinn mating on the grass while he holds onto the stallion's bridle.

The film's Icelandic title, *Hross í oss*, literally means "horses within us," and the film plays with various comparisons between horses and men. The film, however, never falls into the trap of anthropomorphizing the horses, and they remain beyond our grasp and understanding. As Stella Hockenhull notes:

Of Horses and Men represents the animals as sentient beings, but at no point does the filmmaker make the horses "speak" for themselves, either visually through the editing of the film, or by imposing them with human voices. Indeed, the horses in this film do not have an active look that motives the plot, and the director does not provide point-of-view shots or shot reverse shots to present their perspective. Their eyes, in fact, frequently conceal any means of interpretation because of the human reflection retained within.[4]

It is crucial, as Hockenhull notes, that the close-ups of the horses' eyes do not lead to point-of-view shots, but instead we see reflections in their eyes. In this way the film directs our attention to their subjectivity but denies us sharing in it (see Figure 13.1).[5]

Furthermore, discussing similar close-ups of animal eyes, Burt states:

> The animal's eye is a very significant motif on film and we need to ask what it is that the film invokes by delineating this type of contact. [. . .] In that sense the exchange of the look is, in the absence of the possibility of language, the basis of a social contract.[6]

Certainly, *Of Horses and Men* suggests not only that there are many parallels between humans and horses, but also that we have certain moral obligations in our treatment of them.[7] The film makes it clear that just like horses, humans follow their natural instincts, but that they are also ultimately guilty

Figure 13.1 Avoiding point-of-view shots that would give the audience access to the subjectivity of horses, *Of Horses and Men* instead shows the human characters reflected in close-ups of the animals' eyes. Source: Hrossabrestur.

of breaking the social contract to which Burt refers as they take advantage of their dominant position vis-à-vis animals. Their treatment of the horses reveals much about the human characters of the film; the uses they make of horses, their attachment and love for them, but also their brutal treatment. Moreover, numerous horses will pay with their lives in the film, but so do human characters. In one instance we go straight from the burial of a horse to a funeral.

Considering how unprecedented *Of Horses and Men* was in Icelandic cinema regarding the role of animals, it is rather remarkable that *Rams* (2015) was released only a couple of years later (and there is little suggestion that it was inspired by the prior film). Interestingly, it also had a strong international reception that included the *Un Certain Regard* award at Cannes and was ultimately remade in English by Jeremy Sims in 2020. Aesthetically and narratively, it did not go to the extremes of *Of Horses and Men*. *Rams* has a more conventional narrative structure and stylistically does not involve the animals in the same manner (which also means there is little suggestion of their subjectivity). But it does make clear analogies between the two main characters and their sheep, and the animal presence is again explicitly tied to death.

Rams tell the story of two brothers, Guðmundur/Gummi (Sigurður Sigurjónsson) and Kristinn/Kiddi (Theodór Júlíusson), who are not on speaking terms despite sharing neighboring farms. After Kiddi narrowly wins the annual rams stock competition, Gummi discovers suspicious symptoms in his brother's sheep. It is soon discovered that they are inflicted with scrapie and all the sheep in the larger farming community must be put down to stop the spread of the disease. Kiddi accuses his brother of jealousy and falls hard for the bottle as their relationship grows worse day by day (they communicate through letters that Gummi's dog carries between the two farms). Meanwhile, Gummi decides to slaughter his own sheep himself. It is a gesture that emphasizes his closeness to the animals, but it also allows him to hide his cherished ram and a few ewes in his own basement. When they are discovered by the authorities, the brothers finally join hands; the sheep are after all from their cherished mutual *Bólstaðir* stock, and they head with them up to *Hvannalindir*, an oasis far up in the highlands. But on the way they get caught in a fierce snowstorm and Gummi collapses while searching for the sheep in the darkness. After finding him nearer to death than life, Kiddi digs out a shelter in the snow and tries to bring him back to life with his own body heat. There the film concludes, and the audience can only speculate whether the brothers—let alone the sheep—will survive.

Should it not be fully clear that the title equally refers to the brothers themselves as their cherished rams, the film also aligns them visually. The film's opening shot shows us the two farms, surrounded by mountains on each side, and an overcast sky. We also see a farmer on the right walking toward two sheep on the left that head toward him as well. As they meet close to the middle of the screen, the film's first cut takes us to a closer look, but interestingly frames the faces of the sheep and only later moves upward to Gummi's face. His long gray-white hair and beard tie him visually to the two sheep, which he caresses with obvious fondness and compassion (see Figure 13.2). With a comparable beard, but much less hair, his brother Kiddi is first introduced with a sheep in his arms. And when they head out to the county's rams competition, they are both wearing traditional Icelandic wool sweaters. In other words, they are literally wearing the sheep they cherish so much. Men and sheep have never been this close in prior Icelandic cinema.

And like the sheep, they are themselves of the same stock. And the film questions what their duty is to one another as brothers and neighbors. Halfway through the film, a lawyer explains to Gummi, who is the legal owner of Kiddi's farm: "You are responsible for your brother." Clearly, this is a reference to Cain's well-known rebuttal after God asks him about Abel's whereabouts: "Am I my brother's keeper?" By the end of the film, *Rams* answer is very much in the affirmative as Kiddi tries to bring his half-frozen

Figure 13.2 Gummi (Sigurður Sigurjónsson) embraces his cherished sheep in *Rams*. In addition to likening the character's appearance to that of the sheep, the film suggests that the two species may be more similar than we are accustomed to believe. Source: Netop Films ehf.

brother back to life. Unlike *Of Horses and Men*, though, it never asks what their duty is to their fellow animals. Despite their love for their sheep, the real tragedy of the scrapie outbreak is that the farmers will not be able to farm sheep for the next three years, with the result that some will give up farming altogether and leave the countryside. Nevertheless, the sheep help to bring about that overall feeling of loss that characterizes the film.

Although *Rams* does not lend its sheep the same kind of subjectivity as *Of Horses and Men* does its horses, the two films do share, nonetheless, a couple of crucial elements. Both films address somewhat playfully questions of national identity, as both horses and sheep have been instrumental to Icelanders throughout the ages: the sheep to keep the nation warm and alive through centuries of hardship and the horse to connect the corners of the land before modern transportation began to make inroads in the country. For example, the breeding competition in *Rams* gently mocks traditional national associations with sheep farming and the countryside, while *Of Horses and Men* evokes, through mise-en-scène, settings that have been quintessential to Icelandic national identity. This part is overall lighthearted and tongue-in-cheek. However, both films also express a more somber tone, as death is all around. In *Rams* much of the sheep have been slaughtered and the lives of the brothers are at risk, while in *Of Horses and Men* both horses and men die left and right and the film includes two extended funeral scenes. The presence of death and loss more generally is in both films very much tied to the presence of the animals.[8]

Growing Pains

If there is one thing that the other three Icelandic films discussed in this chapter—otherwise in many ways quite different works—share with *Rams* and *Of Horses and Men*, it is the use of animal imagery in capturing a somber feeling of loss. To return to Burt's *Animals in Film*:

> In contrast to the moral dynamics that can be located in images of animal death, it might appear that the opposite impulse, the celebration of the living animal, would produce a different set of associations, one less linked to the brutalistic networks of modernity. I have in mind the emotional simplicity of sentimental family films or the pure delights that can be had from a nature documentary. But, in fact, even here human-animal relations are

closely linked to issues of loss. I am not thinking of the death of pets or the extinction of species, but rather of the place of the animal in larger types of networks: the ways in which the animal may be situated at junctures of emotional attachment and kinship networks, or visual aesthetics and narrative structures.[9]

It is these indirect and subtler connections between humans and animals that shape the other three films. They are also closer to the slow cinema aesthetics that the director Tiago de Luca focuses on in his essay. I would place them somewhere in the middle between conventional narrative features and the extreme long-take aesthetics of directors like Apichatpong Weersethakul and Béla Tarr. Their pace is relatively slow—they often shun conventional continuity editing—and show a marked interest in the aesthetic beauty of the image. All three films also tell a strikingly consistent stories of young characters and their emerging sexuality. All are also set in small rural communities surrounded by a striking natural world in which animals play a crucial role.

The Swan is probably the most literary of all the films analyzed in this chapter—perhaps because it is the only one adapted from a novel. It is also the only one directed by a female filmmaker, the debut feature of Ása Helga Hjörleifsdóttir, and that focuses on a female protagonist. Sól (Gríma Valsdóttir) is a young girl, preteen but mature for her age, who leaves her family in their fishing village to stay with relatives at a distant farm. The reasons for this are never specified, but it is suggested that she is something of a "problem child" in need of a new environment, and the practice of sending children to the countryside was long customary in Iceland. She ends up sharing a room with the farm help, a young man named Jón (Þór Kristjánsson), and they develop a friendship in spite of their age difference. Notably, they share a great interest in words and stories; Sól likes to make up stories, while Jón spends much of his free time writing in his notebooks. When the farmers' daughter Ásta (Þuríður Blær Jóhannsdóttir) returns from her studies in Reykjavík, Sól becomes acutely jealous as she senses a sexual tension between Ásta and Jón. As Sól thus step by step becomes more conscious of the adult world, she is also becoming a more integral part of the natural world around her, not least the farming animals. It is this coming together of Sól and the environment around her that a simple plot summary cannot do justice, as it is presented mostly through the film's formal aesthetic strategies.

The tone is given at the very beginning of the film, as we can hear the sounds of the ocean waves before we see the opening image of the ocean itself from high above, before the camera slowly travels to the shore. The next shot shows us seaweed in a close-up on the shore, and as the handheld camera travels to the left we observe a small hand lingering over it, then a quick cut to an unusually framed shot of a girl's blond hair and dark coat whose colors blend into the shore's background palette. Finally, in the fourth shot we see a close-up of Sól's face as she looks up, and the fifth shot of the waves crashing upon the shore could be understood as her point-of-view. As she walks home to the village from the shore, Sól begins to tell us one of her stories. It is clearly inspired by the environment we have just experienced with her; it is about a girl who likes to swim in the ocean daily, but who almost drowned one day as she became tangled up in seaweed at the bottom of the ocean. It is the first, but far from the last, reference of Sól becoming immersed in nature, and in ways that are far from benign or harmless.

When she soon thereafter leaves for the farm on a bus—a scene typical for male characters in Icelandic cinema but not for young girls—the audience is fully aligned with her subjectivity. First, in a somewhat conventional manner we see other passengers through Sól's point-of-view shots, but soon such images take on added complexity. A flashback shot of Sól with her mother is followed by a shot where Sól places a light blue scarf her mother has just given her over her eyes, and as she looks over the lava landscape through the window it takes on a blue ocean-like complexion, further supported by the sounds of waves before a dissolve literally changes the lava to crushing ocean waves with the scarf still superimposed (see Figures 13.3 and 13.4). In these images, perception, memory, fleeting impressions, and feelings are interwoven together in a subjective manner. Throughout the film, the ocean will provide a link between daughter and mother, who are otherwise separated in space, and we will continue to see the world through Sól's eyes, including point-of-views through her hands or underwater.

The farm is not only located far from the ocean but is enclosed on all sides by steep mountains. The film thus shuns the older exotic landscape scenery approach; the location provides an intense feeling of isolation, if not outright claustrophobia. When filmed from a distance, the land is rarely depicted in sunshine but rather in gloomy weather and darkness. Closer views are typically brighter and sometimes outright sunny, as Sól is repeatedly filmed through tall grass so that she blends in with the natural background. And it is worth emphasizing that her name literally means "sun"—another connection

ANIMALS AND NATURE 207

Figures 13.3 and 13.4 The natural world of *The Swan* is presented through the subjectivity of the main protagonist Sól (Gríma Valsdóttir). Here she is about to look through the blue scarf she will put over her eyes (13.3), which accounts for the tinting of the following point-of-view shot (13.4). Source: Vintage Pictures.

between her and the environment. This approach is not only visual but also almost tactile. Many shots show Sól touching natural and other objects, to get a feel for them. This becomes particularly pronounced as she gets to know the animals at the farm: hens, horses, and cows. Especially relevant is a scene where she witnesses the birth of a calf and helps to "rub the life into him." Much later in the film, a traumatized Sól witnesses the slaughter of that same calf, who is ultimately served for dinner at the family's dining table. Plot-wise it constitutes another rupture in Sól's childhood and her early passing into adulthood. But there is more at stake here, as we are not only shown the calf's blood on the grass, but some of it splashes onto Sól's face and clothing. Notably, in the scene just prior, Ásta has lambasted Sól for always looking at her "with those calf's eyes," and before the calf is slaughtered, a crying Sól asks it to take one last look at the world. The point is not that the calf and Sól are literally or even metaphorically the same, but there is a remarkable coming together here of the protagonist, a farm animal, and nature. The butchering of the calf is akin to the scenes of animal slaughter found in the films analyzed by de Luca—although the exact moment of death is not filmed or presented. Narratively, the calf's killing is also tied to an abortion Ásta has, leaving Sól bewildered and shocked, and later the farmhand disappears as well in an ambiguous manner and Sól fears he may be dead. All in all, from the peril of the fairytale girl entangled in seaweed to the calf's slaughter and Ásta's abortion, death lingers over this film from start to finish.

The final key element of *The Swan* is storytelling itself. As already noted, both Jón and Sól "like to make up stories," and we hear parts of her stories through voice-over. Notably, many of these immerse her character "the dream girl" in the natural environment as she tries to become one with the earth by letting "the grass hug her [. . .] as someone she loved" or having grown such long hair that she begins "slowly sinking into the earth." Jón puts the relationship between nature and storytelling more directly when we hear his voice while he writes in his notebook: "It is good for you to take night walks. It is important for people who want to tell stories to pay close attention to nature. Also at night. Because nature never asks for permission. This unshackled beast." This interlinking of nature, storytelling, and danger is ultimately also tied to death when Ásta tells Sól the story of a lake monster that can take on the appearance of a beautiful white swan that lures people into a lake, where it drowns them. As the film draws to conclusion, Sól heads alone up to the mountains, where she finds the swan in a scene that evokes the opening of the film.

Again alone out in nature, Sól faces the swan as the two gaze upon each other through shot/reverse shots. The whole scene is most ambiguous, but there is much that suggests it is Sól's death scene. In addition to the fairytale told by Ásta about the monstrous swan, that reading is supported by a brief looking-back-at-life-montage that includes Sól and her family and the dead calf. Subsequently, Sól runs after the swan and spreads her hands as if they were wings before the last three shots—the very last one evoking the film's opening shot—show us the land from above, as if the swan and Sól have become one being. Following the fairytale, the swan seems to have seduced Sól to her death, but the scene remains highly ambiguous. What is clear, though, is that Sól's identity, her past loss and unknown future, are bound up with the swan—who has a real presence here and is not a mere artificial symbol.

In this manner, nature, animal, and human blend together in ways without parallel in Icelandic cinema.

Although also boasting a bird's name, Rúnar Rúnarsson's *Sparrows*, very much unlike *The Swan*, entails no sparrows or other birds. Instead, the title refers more generally to the fragility of the teenagers at the heart of the film and especially its main character Ari (Atli Óskar Fjalarsson), who also sings in a choir. Early on in the film, Ari leaves the capital Reykjavík for a small fishing village in the remote Westfjords to live with his father and grandmother. The film depicts Ari's growing pains—his feelings of isolation and loss, having had to leave his mother and the capital behind—and more generally the loss of innocence that follows adulthood. Although devoid of sparrows, other animals are integral to the film's handling of these themes. Having played with a seal cub early in the film, Ari finds himself unable to shoot a grown seal while out hunting with his father. There are clear parallels with the seal here and the calf in *The Swan*. In both cases, a loving bond to an animal signifying childhood innocence is traumatically torn asunder by the cold killing of that animal, ultimately paving a way into the world of adults. In other words, the overall feeling of loss accompanying adulthood is conveyed through the death of an animal. To that point, when Ari's grandmother passes away soon thereafter, we find him once again isolated in a natural mise-en-scène. Although the film proposes certain maturity for Ari as it draws to conclusion, that maturity is full of pain and does little to compensate for the overbearing feeling of loss and spoiled innocence. As in *The Swan* again, this is in many ways accomplished with the role played by human-animal relations that Burt reminds us "are closely linked to issues of loss."[10]

Perhaps this sensibility is nowhere better manifested in Icelandic cinema than in *Heartstone*, the last film I address in this chapter, even though it may be the one where the role of animals appears least pronounced. Indeed, it is the only one that does not include animals in its title, and the plot does not revolve around them as the case is clearly with *Of Horses and Men* and *Rams*. Admittedly, the swan only appears late in the film carrying its name, but it owns the climax of the film. And through its title, *Sparrows* sets up certain expectations involving animal imagery from the outset. *Heartstone*, on the other hand, captures an overall sense of loss through its inclusion of nature and animals while refraining from some of the more explicit elements we have pinpointed in the other films.

Notably, *Heartstone*'s setting combines both the very small fishing village and the farm, with no clear borders between the two or the larger natural world; similar to the farm in *The Swan*, this farm is enclosed by a mountain range that results in a certain isolation and even claustrophobia. The film opens with a scene of four boys, including the two main characters, Þór (Baldur Einarsson) and Kristján (Blær Hinriksson), relaxing on the dock at the village harbor. Suddenly they discover a fish shoal right underneath the dock and begin eagerly to angle the fish. The film depicts both their excitement and pleasure in killing them in a rather brutal manner, by both stepping on them and banging their heads excessively against the dock posts. The death throes of the fish are shown in revealing close-ups. In this manner, the film's opening both reveals the closeness of death in rural communities and fishing villages and the harsh and brutal world of boys turning into adults. In a follow-up scene, we also see Þór proudly bringing a catch of the fish home to his mother, but it later rots outside—evoking an early feeling of waste and loss. There is also a more symbolic component to the opening scene, which does not become fully clear until the very end of the film, as one of the fishes—a shorthorn sculpin—is singled out for being particularly ugly and, while Kjartan wants to let him go, he is brutally killed by Þór.

In addition to his mother, Þór lives with two older teenage sisters, and we are informed that the father has left the family for a younger woman. Kristján conversely is a single child and while still living with both parents, they are having marital difficulties. While all these characters are important to the film, as are many of the two boys' friends in town, the film's focus is very much on the relationship between Þór and Kristján. After the opening scene, we follow them as they move around the village and its surrounding area. The film emphasizes their physicality when fighting one another (typically playfully) or engaging in sexual banter and experimentation. They touch each other's thighs and ultimately kiss one another, and pose closely together with facial makeup for Þór's sister, but it soon becomes clear that what is for Kristján a serious engagement is only a frivolous game for Þór. This is also played out in their relationship with two female friends; while Þór and Beta (Diljá Valsdóttir) move step by step toward full sexual relations, Kristján holds back in his relationship with Hanna (Katla Njálsdóttir). In a compelling scene, he leaves a tent shared by the four early one morning and steps into a small natural pool, where nature seems to emphasize his isolation and suffering: most explicitly as he lets out a scream underwater (heard by no one but reverberated through the water). In an extreme close-up, his face blending in with the murky water, air bubbles stream from his mouth as we can hear the subdued scream.

The scene is indicative of the role the natural world plays in *Heartstone*, which was filmed in *Borgarfjörður eystri*, a fjord celebrated for its natural beauty, but it has clearly not been selected with a postcard landscape approach in mind. Rarely does the sun shine through the almost omnipresent clouds, and often enough it rains outright. Many scenes are also shot in dusk or darkness, further accentuating the heaviness caused by the mountains that physically enclose the village. This somber tone takes on an increasingly ominous atmosphere through the animals in the film. In a scene similar to the opening one, the two boys help farmer Sven (Søren Malling) in the killing of infected sheep, whose burnt carcasses Þór later inspects. He also fears for his life as he goes to collect birds' eggs with his father and Kristján in extremely steep cliffs and the rope becomes briefly loose. In both scenes and their aftermath, death is tied to both animals and a harrowing natural world, but a more explicit connection soon follows as Kristján tries to take his own life. He returns to the farm where they previously shot the sheep and shoots himself in the head with the same gun. In addition to thus mirroring the shooting of a ram earlier in the film, horses play a crucial role as well. Shots of Kristján whimpering and shivering are intercut with a couple of horses, including a brief close-up of one of their eyes. And as his crying gets louder, the horses become increasingly unsettled and respond with neighing.

Kristján ultimately survives and returns to the village after hospitalization in Reykjavík that is not depicted as we never leave the rural setting of the film. However, things are not about to return to what they were before, as his parents are divorcing and he may himself be about to move to the capital. In the film's final scene, Þór wanders down to the harbor, evoking the opening of the film, where he now sees a much younger—and by implication more innocent—boy fishing. After catching a sculpin, the boy lets it go instead of killing it, and in the final shot of the film we follow the sculpin down below, where it belatedly comes alive again and swims away. It seems clear that the sculpin signifies Kristján—the one who is different—and stays alive despite coming close to death. In that sense, it can be seen as a hopeful ending, but it is also a somber one as the sculpin swims alone and away from Þór in the dark ocean world below the surface (the scene of Kristján screaming underwater earlier in the film may be evoked here as well).

Despite providing a powerful ending to the film, the overt symbolism of the final scene goes against the film's overall aesthetics. Up to this point it has allowed nature and animal life to speak for themselves in the sense that their meaning does not appear to be explicitly determined. Instead, they surround the world of the characters, infiltrating it at every turn, and impact meaningfully by implication rather than explicit symbolism. As in *The Swan*, this is accomplished through a noteworthy aesthetic strategy. The typically handheld camera often follows the characters, and whether capturing them from the front or behind, it traverses with them through the film's spaces, sometimes also capturing them through tall grass. It often shows the boys in lingering close-ups, even extreme close-ups, and sometimes this closeness is accentuated by shooting inside a small tent or under a blanket. The resulting sensuality is further emphasized by a haptic approach as the camera captures various kinds of touching; the boys fighting or experimenting with their sexuality, the sisters comforting Þór or touching the first snow of the impending winter—a winter that of course signifies that summer is coming to an end.

Thus, like *The Swan* and *Sparrows*, *Heartstone* is very much a story about the loss of childhood, emerging sexuality, and entrance into adulthood—with the presence of death looming over the whole experience. We are typically not met with straight metaphorical or symbolic relations, but a general presence of death through animals and their role in the village and the natural world surrounding it. It is worth reminding ourselves one last time of Burt's claim that animals evoke loss simply by their place "in larger types of networks: the ways in which the animal may be situated at junctures of emotional attachment and kinship networks."[11] And, indeed, *Heartstone*'s powerful feeling of loss—of childhood, friendship, and life itself—is intractably tied to its animal presence. In the film, fish, birds, sheep, and horses all convey an overall presence of loss and death in one way or another.

In addition to the shared storylines, themes, and natural settings, including the important role played by animals, these three films are also shaped by a similar aesthetic outlook. For example, characters are often almost visually folded into the natural world as the camera captures them through tall sunlit grass. In this way, nature does not merely provide a setting for character action, but infuses everything that takes place in these films. All three are also shaped by a similar slow lingering pace, limited plot drive, soundscape full of animal sounds, especially birds, and those of nature like the wind, and an overall feel for the rhythm and circularity of nature.

To conclude, even though the two types of animal films discussed in this chapter are in many ways markedly different, together they suggest a striking shift in the history of Icelandic cinema. It is as if it discovered the natural world and its rich animal life—and death—for the first time.

Epilogue

Born in Reykjavík in 1974, I have grown up with Icelandic cinema, and I have fond memories of watching some of the breakthrough films of the 1980s as a child in theaters or on television. Ever since, I have kept a close eye on Icelandic filmmaking—its ups and down, moments of aspiration and glory and desperation and despair. But as I complete this book in the fall of 2023, the outlook for Icelandic cinema has never appeared better: it has all the key ingredients for what we might define as a healthy small national cinema.[1] Looking back over its history, we can see how the key components have come together decade by decade.

The so-called film spring of the 1980s, prompted by the newly established Icelandic Film Fund, emphasized local storytelling with local talent in front of and behind the camera. The following decade witnessed the emergence of the European art film in terms of narrative and aesthetics as Icelandic cinema became reliant upon European film funds and partners for financing and production and the international festival circuit for distribution and exhibition. Conversely, the first decade of the twenty-first century saw the broad impact of Hollywood; many Icelandic filmmakers began to make extensive use of popular genres like crime and horror films. And in the following decade, the Hollywood industry itself began increasingly to make Iceland a popular destination for its runaway productions. As we have emphasized in this book, the novelty of each decade did not replace a prior emphasis, but instead added to the diversity of Icelandic cinema. It is hard to imagine it thriving with only one or two of these components in place, as together they support one another, with each contributing something quite specific to Icelandic cinema. Local filmmaking emphasizes stories that frankly no one else will tell—there is no impetus for foreign parties to contribute to them. Apart from regular feature films (often comedies and adaptations of esteemed literary works), these can also include documentaries and children's films. The art film, conversely, is much more international in nature, relying on foreign partners in both financing and production while outward-looking in theme and aesthetics. The paradigm is thus vital in

Light in the Dark. Björn Norðfjörð, Oxford University Press. © Oxford University Press 2025.
DOI: 10.1093/oso/9780197762141.003.0015

connecting Iceland to the world cinema system and transcending national demarcations and limitations. The introduction of Hollywood genres has been crucial for enlarging the domestic box office and attracting younger filmgoers primarily interested in Hollywood cinema. And the Hollywood productions themselves have provided more stable work and a range of professional opportunities for local filmmakers, allowing them to focus on their craft throughout the year. Currently there seems to be a healthy balance between all four paradigms.

The Four Paradigms Today

The back to back *Fishing Trip* films (Örn Marinó Arnarson and Þorkell S. Harðarson, 2020/2022, *Síðasta veiðiferðin/Allra síðasta veiðferðin*) were "old-fashioned" silly comedies made solely for the local box office, where they did all right, if not spectacularly. Local certainly as well was *Wild Game* (Elsa María Jakobsdóttir, 2023, *Villibráð*), but with some foreign flavor, as it was one more international remake of the Italian comedy *Perfect Strangers* (Paolo Genovese, 2016, *Perfetti sconosciuti*). As such, it shows that the most local of categories need not be altogether without transnational elements, and what worked in Italy worked in Iceland as well; *Wild Game* became the biggest hit at the local box office for more than a decade. A couple of children's films opened as well: *Birta* (Bragi Þór Hinriksson, 2021) and *Abbababb!* (Nanna Kristín Magnúsdóttir, 2022), although they were not able to match the box-office success of the popular *Sveppi* series (Bragi Þór Hinriksson, 2009–2014).

In light of the emphasis on adaption in this work, I would like to draw attention to a couple of interesting, if ultimately unsuccessful, adaptions that also emerged early in the decade. As we have noted, the 1980s saw a strong emphasis on faithful adaptations of both canonical classics and celebrated contemporary novels before disappearing mostly altogether toward the end of the decade. When adaptations returned in force at the turn of the century, they had clearly been impacted by the dramatic changes that took place in the meantime and thus reverted to a process that we have termed transnationalization in which the local literary text was made more accessible to a foreign audience, for example by introducing a foreign character so that Icelandic customs and specificities could be explained in English (see chapter eight). And then adaptations mostly disappeared again, only to return in the fall of 2022, when within a month of each other two adaptations of popular and celebrated contemporary novels saw the light of day: *The Letter from Helga* (Ása Helga Hjörleifsdóttir, *Svar við bréfi Helgu*) and *Summer Light, and Then Comes the Night* (Elfar Aðalsteins, *Sumarljós og svo kemur nóttin*).

Interestingly, both avoided the transnationalization process and instead reverted back to the earlier approach that has typically paid greater dividends at the local box office. It is precarious to read too much into ticket sales, and certainly there is no direct link between quality and popularity at the Icelandic box office any more than in the United States, or anywhere else for that matter. But the failure of these two films at the local box office is surprising; Bergsveinn Birgisson's *Reply to a Letter from Helga* had been a bestseller and was adapted into a popular play prior to the film version, while Jón Kalman Stefánsson is one of Iceland's most successful and cherished contemporary novelists. While not suggesting it to be the sole reason for their disappointing reception, neither novel is particularly amenable to a conventional film narrative. In Stefánsson's novel *Summer Light, and Then Comes the Night*, a small village provides the personal narrative voice that ties together numerous episodic stories of its inhabitants. And while Elfar Aðalsteins, director and scriptwriter, has gone to great lengths in remaining faithful to the novel, including making extensive use of a narrative voice-over, the aesthetic qualities of the novel are not easily transferable to film. If that is an example of where something other than a faithful approach was called for, *Reply to a Letter from Helga* insisted on some extensive alterations, as the whole novel is written in the form of a single letter where the main protagonist Bjarni (Þorvaldur Kristjánsson) responds to another letter received from his lover decades prior.[2] In the film, this element is mostly lost, and the few contemporary scenes of the aged Bjarni (Þorsteinn Gunnarsson) are cumbersome, if anything, and the transition from past to present stiff. In other words, the form of this novel resists a smooth transition to film, and its mysterious gaps have been filled in with extended material that is of less interest than the original gaps were in the novel. To summarize, if filming these two novels made sense considering their celebrated status and popularity, they were each in their own way difficult material for film adaptation, and their local approach made them unlikely candidates for success abroad. It is too early to tell if these failures will put an end to this emerging cycle of adaptations—and thus again confirm the actual scarcity of adaptations in Icelandic cinema. As local productions go, the numerous documentaries released annually should not be forgotten, as only very rarely are they made with any kind of export in mind.

Perhaps most surprising on the art cinema front was the return of two maverick filmmakers whose admittedly sporadic work helps connect today's cinema to that of the film spring. The directors in question were the first two to be clearly and explicitly influenced by European art cinema during the 1980s and their new films feel like a throwback to the past. Hilmar Oddsson's black-and-white *Driving Mum* (2022, *Á ferð með mömmu*) was in fact set in 1980 when the aging Jón (Þröstur Leó Gunnarsson) fulfills a promise made to his mother (Kristbjög Kjeld) by driving her—dead—from their home in the isolated Westfjords to her birthplace in the Southwest so that she may be buried there. The film is filled with self-reflexive elements, including Jón's love of photography, his 35mm Pentax Spotmatic camera, and his befuddlement toward the end of the film when he is informed about the brave new world of *Rocky* (John G. Avildsen, 1976) and VCR players. In addition to this self-reflexivity, familiar art film traits are found in the black-and-white cinematography, the road motif, the mysterious interplay of past and present, and dreamlike elements—akin to Federico Fellini's surrealism. The time period of Kristín Jóhannesdóttir's *Alma* (2021) is much more ambiguous, but it could just as well have been set in the 1980s as in the present day, and the film indeed shares much with her debut feature, *Rainbow's End* (1983, *Á hjara veraldar*). It is highly subjective, explicitly dealing with a split personality that literally converses with its other part, excessively symbolic in color and mise-en-scène, with costumes often blending into the background, and to top it off the French art cinema icon Emmanuelle Riva is among the cast in her final role. Thus both films adhere very much to the classic parameters of the European art film and as such look back to its emergence in Icelandic cinema. They are also, as stipulated by the domestic art film convention, set in the countryside first and foremost.

Art cinema is a complex and precarious category, and I have used it broadly in this volume in referring to films that are different from both the local paradigm and the Hollywood genre fare, but it should be clear by now that art films can appear in many forms and that they constantly evolve throughout the course of film history. The film aesthetics of Oddsson and Jóhannesdóttir are different from those of Friðrik Þór Friðriksson's that followed in the 1990s, which are again different from the style and aesthetics of the art film directors that emerged in the new century. It should therefore not come as a surprise that the other art films of the early 2020s, made by directors who have only just started their careers, are in many ways completely different from *Driving Mum* and *Alma*. We will discuss the two most successful of these at the end of this chapter, *Lamb* (Valdimar Jóhannsson, 2021, *Dýrið*) and *Godland* (Hlynur Pálmason, 2022, *Volaða land/Vanskabte Land*), but equally indicative of such differences is Guðmundur Arnar Guðmundsson's *Beautiful Beings* (2022, *Berdreymi*), which continued the subjective exploration of young male bonding, friendship, and sexuality of his strong debut *Heartstone* (2019, *Hjartasteinn*). The key difference of his second feature is the setting which, uncharacteristically for Icelandic art cinema, takes place in Reykjavík, if primarily in the oldest part of the city. Certainly, few twenty-first-century films have made the capital look so much like a village. Nonetheless, it may account for the much darker overtones of the film, as it lacks the natural world so characteristic of *Heartstone*. Instead, an alternative world is found in the clairvoyance, emphasized in the Icelandic title of the film, of the main character Addi (Birgir Dagur Bjarkason) and his mother Guðrún (Aníta Briem), countering the film's otherwise stark realism of various forms of abuse, including domestic and sexual violence.

Notably, *Alma* was only the third feature of Jóhannesdóttir's career, despite now spanning four decades, evidencing the extended gender gap found in Icelandic film history. But as regards new women directors, the promising signs of the late teens appeared to be crystallizing early in the decade when Rannveig Jónsdóttir, Ólöf Birna Torfadóttir, Nanna Kristín Magnúsdóttir, Elsa María Jakobsdóttir, and Tinna Hrafnsdóttir made their debut features. Although rarely explicitly feminist along the lines of *Alma*, which criticized patriarchy at both private and public levels, the films typically emphasize female characters and experiences. For example, Jónsdóttir's *Stitch n' Bitch* (2021, *Saumaklúbburinn*) is about a summerhouse weekend trip by a group of women rather than men, as was the case in *The Last Fishing Trip* films. Hrafnsdóttir's *Quake* (2021, *Skjálfti*) tells the subjective story of a single mother (Aníta Briem) who faces various struggles in her adult life, including memory loss, resulting from a childhood trauma. Like *The Deposit* (Ásthildur Kjartansdóttir, 2019, *Tryggð*), it is another adaptation of a novel by Auður Jónsdóttir offering a view of a female experience rarely seen on the Icelandic screen. It is also unusual in its cold wintery Reykjavík mise-en-scène. Last but not least, Magnúsdóttir's children's film *Abbababb!* (2022) is a colorful and playful musical about a diverse group of kids who are trying to stave off a mysterious threat to their elementary school. Not only do all these films share a focus on female experiences, but they all mostly fall within our first paradigm of local filmmaking. This may have to do with filmmakers' interest and preference, but it could also be explained by continuous financial discrimination, as these films are the least expensive to make. Women's films sometimes veer toward the art cinema paradigm, but the field of outright genre cinema (save perhaps for comedies) remains limited to male directors.

And in that field the production of horror and crime films continued unabated. Many of these were actually low-budget local debut films that did not receive financial support from the Film Fund, including *It Hatched* (Elvar Gunnarsson, 2021), *Redux* (Heimir Bjarnason, 2022, Þrot), and *Wrath* (Arró Stefánsson, 2023, *Óráð*), and made little dent at the box office. But the same cannot be said of Hannes Þór Halldórsson's debut *Cop Secret* (2021, *Leynilögga*), which was a huge hit at the domestic box office, spurred on by a popular cast and the director's renown as the goalie of the Icelandic 2018 World Cup soccer team. And as a matter of fact, he integrated a national soccer match, albeit with the women's team, into the narrative climax of the film. But in most respects, it is a familiar Hollywood-style action fare, with humorous references to both James Bond and Indiana Jones, and a villain who insists on speaking in English because that is what movie villains do. The film's claim to originality is found in making its two hyper-masculine testosterone-filled super-cops male lovers who come out at the end of the film. Otherwise, the film mostly harkens back to *Remote Control* (Óskar Jónasson, 1992, *Sódóma Reykjavík*)—in its local appropriation of Hollywood norms (even the Trans Am car re-emerges here, racing around the capital region)—but what was original and funny in the early 1990s feels less so three decades later (see chapter six).

A second film adaptation of a novel by bestselling crime novelist Arnaldur Indriðason also finally saw the light of day, but with an obvious eye on the international market it shunned the Erlendur police procedural series that began with *Jar City* for the international plotting of the thriller *Operation Napoleon* (Óskar Þór Axelsson, 2023, *Napóleonskjölin*). Glacial shrinking caused by climate change reveals a German World War II aircraft in *Vatnajökull* Glacier harboring a mysterious secret about American and German relations at the end of the war. On the run from ruthless American agents trying to keep the secret a secret, Kristín (Vivian Ólafsdóttir) turns to her former English boyfriend Steve (Jack Fox), who happens to be an expert in the mysteries of World War II. Although an Icelandic-German co-production, it was primarily shot in English; in addition to all the American characters, Steve does not speak any Icelandic, so not only must he and

Kristín speak together in English but also everyone else conversing with them. Unlike Óskar Axelsson's prior genre films, *Black's Game* (2012, *Svartur á leik*) and *I Remember You* (2017, *Ég man þig*), that were clearly inspired by Hollywood genre filmmaking but still in some ways distinctly Icelandic films, *Operation Napoleon* aspires to be an outright Hollywood thriller.

Finally, as regards runaway productions proper, the reliance on Netflix has increased considerably, including the features *Eurovision Song Contest: The Story of Fire Saga* (David Dobkin, 2020), *The Midnight Sky* (George Clooney, 2020), *Against the Ice* (Peter Flinth, 2022), and *Luther: The Fallen Sun* (Jamie Payne, 2023), in addition to the Baltasar Kormákur–led series *Katla* (2021) and *Entrapped* (2021, *Ófærð*). As the other major runaway production of the early twenties were FX/Hulu's *A Murder at the End of the World* (Brit Marling and Zal Batmanglijand, 2023) and HBO's *True Detective: Night Country* (Izza López, 2024), there seems to be a clear shift from conventional film production to streaming and series. Whether this is a new trend or an anomaly remains to be seen. Regardless, one should keep in mind the small size of the local film industry, and there is clearly a practical limit to how many large runaway productions can be serviced annually.

All in all, the four key paradigms pinpointed as essential to the current health of Icelandic national cinema seem to be in good shape as it heads into its fifth decade of continuous film production. But as someone who has long followed and studied Icelandic cinema, I know how quickly things can change, and there are no guarantees when it comes to the stability and future prospects of national cinemas—especially the smaller ones. The balance between these four components is important, and for the first time we are seeing some concerns from the local film industry that state funding that could have supported local filmmaking is being diverted instead to tax breaks for foreign productions. In terms of finance, it is a national cinema that relies upon support from three different sources: national state institutions, European funds, and foreign film and media corporations (especially from Hollywood). Withdraw any one of these and the system risks collapsing. Hollywood is the least reliable of the three since it has no particular commitment to Icelandic cinema and its producers could tire of it as a location or search for better deals elsewhere. Frankly, this is not an unlikely scenario, and the local powerhouse True North is increasingly offering its runaway production services outside of Iceland. A major transformation of the European film funding system in the near future seems more unlikely, but any curtailing of support from either the Nordic Film and Television

Fund or Eurimages could have serious consequences for Icelandic cinema. Most important of course is the national Film Fund (along with the state's reimbursement schema); despite the healthy appearance of Icelandic cinema today, no one should imagine it could survive without state support—without it, the whole system comes crashing down. We would likely be returning to the era of great maverick filmmakers, like Loftur Guðmundsson, Óskar Gíslason, and Ósvaldur Knudsen, that we discussed in the first part of this book. The point is not to be unduly pessimistic about the future prospects of Icelandic cinema when things look as good as they do today, but to understand that much can be learned from studying the volatile history of Icelandic cinema, which has always found itself performing a precarious balancing act.

The Past through the Eyes of the Present

It is too early to tell if the new decade will bring another production novelty to Icelandic cinema like the past four did. The novelty I am concluding this work with is of a different kind but arguably no less important when considering the history of Icelandic cinema. It regards a very belated—but no less welcome—awareness of its own history. The history of the well-established national cinemas is not simply a matter of books like this one but a living tradition that continues to inform filmmaking of the day. Key films (the "classics") constitute mutual points of recognition for the filmmaking community and are sometimes referenced or remade outright; certain locations and events become recognizable through repetition; genre films establish familiar conventions; extended acting careers link different time periods; and many directors look toward the past for inspiration, celebration, and sometimes critique. Though no such historical tradition existed in Iceland, that has begun to change recently. It is arguably another indicator of a "healthy" national cinema.

Most of the early signs involved the work of director Friðrik Þór Friðriksson, especially his breakthrough film *Children of Nature* (1992, *Börn náttúrunnar*), who became the model for a new generation of filmmakers. Even a director like Dagur Kári, who is not directly influenced by his style of filmmaking, has stated, "To me he is the godfather of modern Icelandic cinema. I think he was a pathfinder for the younger generation."[3] Friðriksson himself has participated directly in this process, most notably with the biographical film *Mamma Gógó* (2010) that was partly about the impact of *Children of Nature*, but also utilized footage of the actress Kristbjörg Kjeld from the early "classic" *The Girl Gogo* (Erik Balling, 1968, *79 af stöðinni*) to depict the memories of his mother Gógó (see detailed analysis of the original film in chapter two). In this way Friðriksson interwove the personal story of his mother with the history of Icelandic cinema (and his own role in it). By that time, director Rúnar Rúnarsson had already remade *Children of Nature* in his short *The Last Farm* (2004, *Síðasti bærinn*) and was clearly very much under Friðriksson's influence in his debut feature *Volcano* (2011, *Eldfjall*). More comically, Hafsteinn Gunnar Sigurðsson referenced in *Either Way* (2011, *Á annan veg*) a well-known scene from *Children of Nature* where a Willys Jeep disappears seemingly out of the blue.[4]

Three films from the early 2020s have taken us much further back into Icelandic film history. I have already referenced the self-reflexivity of Hilmar Oddsson's *Driving Mum*, but it is hardly a coincidence that it opens by specifying the year 1980, when modern Icelandic cinema emerged, and the film feels like an ode to Icelandic cinema and its many forms: the picturesque landscape, the isolated farm, the road traveled, the enigmatic and mysterious female figure, and so on. Despite avoiding too specific references, one senses here the presence of everything from *On Top* (Ágúst Guðmundsson, 1982, *Með allt á hreinu*) to *Children of Nature* to *Noi the Albino* (Dagur Kári, 2003, *Nói albínói*). In fact, as regards the last-mentioned film, father and son are reunited here: Jón is played by Þröstur Leó Gunnarsson, who played Nói's father, while Tómas Lemarquis, who played Nói, meets Jón a couple of times on the road as a French tourist. And then the dead (but very vocal) mother is played by *The Girl Gogo's* Kjeld, whose career now ties together more than a half century of cinema.

The other two films, Valdimar Jóhannsson's *Lamb* and Hlynur Pálmason's *Godland*, are of a rather different kind, and it is of particular interest that they should also be the two most successful films outside of Iceland during the early decade (while doing rather poorly at the local box office). Following a splendid reception at the international film festival circuit, including a remarkable fourth Nordic Council Film Prize for Iceland in less than ten years, *Lamb* opened at a record-breaking 600 screens in the United States.[5] There it was marketed by the cutting-edge producer and distributor A24 as an unusual horror film in line with many of its other products, and it was seen as such by most viewers around the world. But what must surely have been lost on many is how *Lamb* also responds quite explicitly to Icelandic film history and especially the key film of the early 1980s film spring, *Land and Sons* (Ágúst Guðmundsson, 1980, *Land og synir*).

Lamb is an eerie synthesis of the Icelandic farm film and international horror cinema. Its specific indebtedness to *Land and Sons* is found above all in its mise-en-scène: the green valley farmland enclosed by a mountainside almost invariably covered by a mist or fog toward the top. Both films were shot in the same region near *Eyjafjörður*, the largest fjord in the northern part of the country, albeit in a different valley. It could be said that *Lamb* upended *Land and Sons* by swapping *Svarfaðardalur* Valley for that of *Öxnadalur* as it is the valley where the most celebrated poet of Iceland, the Romanticist Jónas Hallgrímsson, grew up. Indeed, the iconic mountaintop *Hraundrangi*, repeatedly seen in the film (see Figure 14.1), is found next to Jónas Hallgrímsson on the most valuable Icelandic banknote.[6] It is an atmospheric setting that works splendidly for the film's mysterious narrative, but by choosing this specific valley the film presents itself as a commentary on certain Icelandic traditions dating much further back than *Lands and Sons*.[7]

There are very important and telling differences between *Land and Sons* and *Lamb*. The former is a period film set in a larger farming community, and while focusing on the romantic relationship between main protagonist Einar (Sigurður Sigurjónsson) and Margrét (Guðný Ragnarsdóttir), they live separately at neighboring farms (see chapter six for a detailed analysis of the film). *Lamb* conversely focuses on only very few characters and the action never leaves the farm of the couple María (Noomi Rapace) and Ingvar (Hilmir

Figure 14.1 The iconic mountaintop *Hraundrangi* in the far distance behind farmer Ingvar (Hilmir Snær Guðnason) summons Iceland's most celebrated poet, Jónas Hallgrímsson, who grew up in the *Öxnadalur* Valley, the setting of *Lamb*. Source: Go to Sheep, Black Spark Film & TV and Madants.

Snær Guðnason). But before we are introduced to them, the film opens with an extended point-of-view shot from the perspective of a mysterious being that advances to their farm in a dark wintery landscape on Christmas Eve. It enters the sheep barn and has some sort of intercourse with one of the ewes, as becomes clear later in the film when Ada is born. The reveal of the film is that while the top part of her body is that of a lamb, she is human below the chest or thereabouts. Having lost their own daughter of the same name, María and Ingvar raise her as their own child. Later, Ingvar's brother Pétur (Björn Hlynur Haraldsson) visits and is first much dismayed by the new family member but is ultimately won over by Ada before he returns back to the city on a bus in a scene that evokes the ending of *Land and Sons* when Einar departs the countryside. At the very end of *Lamb* we finally get to see the grotesque being from the opening—a gruesome mixture of man and ram—that shoots Ingvar and takes Ada with him, leaving María all by herself. With this otherworldly narrative we seem to have departed dramatically from the Icelandic farm film and entered the world of fantasy and horror. But this narrative is very much in dialogue with its Icelandic predecessor.

Arguably no Icelandic film includes more animals than *Land and Sons*: sheep, cows, horses, hens, and dogs. But unlike in *Lamb*, they are never given any subjectivity and there is little suggestion that they are sentient beings. When Ragnar shoots his treasured white horse before departing for Reykjavík, the tragedy is not its death but that Ragnar had to depart without it. The horse's role is limited to symbolism; similarly, the slaughtering of Ragnar's whole sheep stock is merely a financial issue. Conversely, even before we meet María and Ingvar, we are introduced to many of the animals at the farm, and the film directs us to their subjectivity as we see them, among other things, looking toward the mysterious visitor. But along the lines of *Of Horses and Men* (Benedikt Erlingsson, 2013, *Hross í oss*), the film typically avoids conventional point-of-view shots and denies us a direct access to their perception and subjectivity. It is a way of saying that these are sentient beings, but that we nonetheless cannot understand them as they are different from us. The same principle holds later for Ada, and there is even a remarkable shot when she sees her biological father for the first time where, just as with the horses in *Of Horses and Men*, we see him only as a brief reflection in a close-up of her eye.[8]

By emphasizing their subjectivity and presenting them as sentient beings, *Lamb* raises some serious questions about farming and how humans treat animals that is simply taken for granted in *Land and Sons*. To watch María and Ingvar eat a piece of lamb is not the same after you have been introduced to Ada, and María is shown to be extremely brutal when she shoots her competitor when the ewe comes looking for her offspring. In this way *Lamb* continues the new animal trend in Icelandic cinema (see chapter thirteen) and arguably brings it to yet another level. But it differs from the other animal films in the way it frames that discussion in the historical context of the Icelandic farm film and national romanticism more broadly.

Remarkably, considering that only one film represents each of the Nordic countries, a second Icelandic film, *Godland*, the third feature of director Hlynur Pálmason, was also nominated when *Lamb* was awarded the Nordic Council Film Prize. Following in the footsteps of Kári and Rúnarsson, Pálmason learned the craft at the celebrated National Film School of Denmark. His first feature, *Winter Brothers* (2017, *Vinterbrødre*), was an outright Danish film, while the second one, *A White, White Day* (2019, *Hvítur, Hvítur Dagur*), was an Icelandic one. And both were nominated for the Nordic Prize for their respective countries, but *Godland* was such a balanced co-production that it could have been nominated for either country. If anything, Iceland seems more appropriate: the director is Icelandic and *Godland* is filmed in Iceland. Before we take a closer look at this remarkable collaboration that far transcends typical and now standard European co-production practices, it should be made clear that *Lamb* is also very much a transnational production. But it is one that aspires to hide the foreign elements (see chapter seven), edited by Pole Agnieszka Glinska, shot by Swede Eli Arenson, starring Swedish icon Noomi Rapace, and with special effects from both Sweden and Poland. But on screen it looks very much like a local Icelandic film, set in an isolated valley far removed from the rest of the world. *Godland* is something else altogether.

The film tells the story of the Danish priest Lucas (Elliott Crosset Hove), who is sent to remote Southeastern Iceland to organize the building of a church in the late nineteenth century. Lucas is an avid photographer and travels with his camera equipment (that includes a portable dark room) on the lengthy journey. During the film's opening we are instructed that it is based upon seven wet plate photographs taken by a Danish priest and discovered in a box. Although a complete fabrication, this premise is the springboard for the most remarkable exploration of Danish-Icelandic relations and the role played by images and representation (and by implication, cinema) in that relationship. The explicit dual nationality of the film is already apparent in its Danish and Icelandic titles, shown side by side, as are the opening and final credits. It is worth noting that both titles are fundamentally different from the misleading English title; the Danish "Vanskabte Land" means something akin to a "malformed land," while the Icelandic "Volaða land" is closer to "miserable land." Translation is moreover a key theme of the film, as Lucas does not speak Icelandic and many Icelandic characters do not speak Danish, while others are bilingual. In an early scene, for example, Lucas's Icelandic translator (Hilmar Guðjónsson) explains to him the many different words for rain, and with the constant and fast switching from Icelandic to Danish and vice versa, it is not an easy film to translate. In this volume we have discussed many transnational Icelandic films where the inclusion of other languages (English most often) was intended to ease and support the foreign marketing and exhibition and/or resulted from financing and production stipulation. That is certainly not the case with *Godland* and rather remarkably it is the first and only Icelandic film that involves extended use of Danish. Despite the long and intertwined history of the two countries, *Godland* is actually the first Icelandic (and appropriately an Iceland-Danish co-production, if French-Swedish as well) film to address and interrogate the colonial relationship between Denmark and Iceland.

Before he departs, Lucas is advised by his superior about the differences between the two countries, everything from the bright nights to volcanic eruptions, and the importance of adapting to the ways of the locals— something that Lucas never accomplishes. His nemesis in the film is the Icelandic guide Ragnar (Ingvar Sigurðsson), who during the first half of the film accompanies Lucas from the shore to his destination. Their relationship is stiff from the beginning, while Lucas sticks to his camera and Ragnar is depicted as knowing deeply the land they are traveling through and cherishing local customs like storytelling and singing rhymes (*rímur*). As we get to know them better during their lengthy journey, we are also encouraged to explore the land and the environment. No Icelandic film has depicted the country quite like *Godland*—and without a doubt it is one of the most spectacular-looking Icelandic feature films ever made. In a squarelike format evoking Lucas's own camera, we are shown shores, rivers, valleys, hills, mountains, cliffs, and glaciers, in all kinds of weather—rain, wind, sunshine, fog, mist—all the while capturing the color palette of Icelandic nature. Martin Lefebvre has helpfully distinguished between landscape that provides the setting for a film's narrative and one that is "momentarily [freed] from its narrative function."[9] On numerous occasions in *Godland* we contemplate such pure landscape where characters and plot are all but forgotten.

For example, a particular landscape is often shown before characters enter the frame, and at other times natural environments are simply depicted on their own, ranging from broader overview shots to close-ups (see Figures 14.2 and 14.3).

Halfway through the film, a remarkable five-minute-long circular shot begins with the traveling group heading off on their horses. The camera continues its slow-paced circling, giving us an extended view of the natural environment with its accompanying soundscape before moving closer and closer to the ground itself, where it ultimately comes to a stop on a close-up of an exhausted and near-to-death Lucas. An abrupt cut now takes us to a volcanic eruption—a striking formal depiction of a new land being formed (a volcano montage along the lines of those discussed in chapter four)—that otherwise plays no part in the film narrative proper. And now another visual shift takes us underwater, where we see the limbs of two sisters searching for kelp—the older and Danish Anna (Vic Carmen Sonne) and the younger and Icelandic Ida (Ída Mekkín Hlynsdóttir). Along with their father Carl (Jacob Lohmann), they make up the remaining main characters of the film. Carl's position is never fully explained, but his social and cultural standing is clearly elevated above the locals. After we have been introduced to Carl and his daughters, Lucas gains consciousness again after being bedridden at their home for a lengthy period. While often looking weak and sickly, he is able to hold his ground against both Carl and Ragnar in traditional Icelandic wrestling (*glíma*) when the locals celebrate a wedding (with Lucas refusing to conduct the ceremony in a half-finished church). These playful, but also clearly very antagonistic, engagements will soon lead to much more serious and consequential altercations.

Having completed his work on the church, Ragnar asks Lucas to take a photograph of him, but when the latter refuses, a heated argument ensues in which Lucas attacks Ragnar and kills him by bashing his head on a rock. As is clear from their argument, the scene's relevance far transcends these two characters and addresses the historical relationship between Denmark and Iceland. Ragnar explains how he was forced to learn Danish as his mother always spoke it on Sundays (as a sign of reverence and respect), but that he himself disliked it and found it an "ugly language." Furthermore, Lucas's refusal to photograph him is also indicative of how Denmark denies Icelanders' representation as they are seen to be secondary and inferior, leading Ragnar to insist, "I'm not an animal." In this way, *Godland* evokes cinema and its early history in Iceland, so shaped by its subjection to Denmark: the Dane is in charge of the camera and decides whom to photograph and how. Lucas

EPILOGUE 227

Figures 14.2 and 14.3 In *Godland*, nature is often presented as landscape independent of its role in the film's narrative. It is captured from great distances (14.2) or in close-ups, as with this example of raindrops falling on rocks (14.3). Source: Snowglobe.

photographs all the members of the Danish family in conventional portraits, while the Icelandic models are exoticized in their natural environment—with Ida somewhere in between, posing playfully on a horse. As Lucas himself explains, he desires "to get to know the land, photograph it and its people." Albeit devoid of explicit references, what is at stake here is the whole history of Danish-Icelandic cultural relations, including the exoticism of the Iceland-films and the national duality of the Varangians (see chapters two and three). *Godland* is a film about language and especially visual representation, and the film articulates and visualizes how Denmark subjected Iceland by the means of both.

But it is also a film about the environment. As already noted, it is one of the most visually stunning Icelandic films ever made, but it also manages to avoid the pitfalls of exoticism and tourist imagery. It displays a deep interest in nature and environment that far transcends their role in the narrative. As regards animals, they are plentiful in the film: horses provide the only means of transportation, lambs and chickens are slaughtered, and Ragnar's dog chases Lucas out of his newbuilt church after his master's death. But despite these elements, *Godland* never prioritizes animals or directs us to their subjectivity in the manner of *Lamb* or *Of Horses and Men*. In part, this has to do with its environmental vision in which both humans and animals are equally seen as part and parcel of nature. At the very end of the film, when Ida finds Lucas's bones, having been murdered by her possessive father, resting like rocks in a green bed of moss, she comforts him and herself when saying: "Soon, flowers and grass will grow and you will be in them . . . and that's beautiful." Related to this are numerous shots of a decomposing horse, filmed from above over a number of different seasons, depicting the integration of animal and environment over time.

While natural imagery is often depicted purely for its own sake, it is also tied to the juxtaposition of Denmark and Iceland in the film. There is a way in which Icelandic characters seem to have a more direct connection to their surroundings, while the Danes are always distant and can only see nature in terms of images. Ida is one with her environment, while her sister Anna finds it "terribly beautiful," as does Lucas, and both long for Denmark. This clash between the two countries becomes inescapable in the enigmatic ending of the film, where Hans Christian Andersen's classic patriotic lyrics in "In Denmark I Was Born" ("I Danmark er jeg født"), extolling the territorial extension of Denmark, the softness of its language, and its victorious flag, are heard over beautiful landscape imagery of Iceland.

To return to where we began our discussion of *Godland*, it is indeed a curious film to represent Denmark in competition against Iceland (and the other Nordic countries). The director himself is an Icelander who learned his craft in Denmark and thus finds himself in a similar position as the Icelandic literary Varangians in Denmark who wrote about Iceland in Danish for Danish readers in the early twentieth century. But that does not mean that nothing has changed. When a Danish crew filmed the *Story of the Borg Family* (Gunnar Summerfeldt, 1920, *Saga Borgarættarinnar*) in Iceland a century ago, the idea of Icelanders making feature films would have been preposterous. But now an Icelandic filmmaker holds a revealing mirror up to that past, offering a critique of that history and heritage. No film evidences better than *Godland* that Icelandic cinema has finally gained a historical consciousness, and that is no less a significant marker of an established national cinema than its four production paradigms.

Icelandic cinema has traveled a long road since the Danes Alfred Lind and Peter Petersen filmed a firemen practice in downtown Reykjavík back in 1906. For decades thereafter, Icelandic pioneers crisscrossed the country documenting its nature and people, and finally at mid-century found the confidence and ambition to turn their hands on narrative features—but often looking to Denmark for support. Finally, governmental funding helped instigate a proper national cinema in the early 1980s that further expanded, decade by decade, by building bridges first to Europe and then Hollywood. Its scope today is quite remarkable considering the small size of Iceland, and it is easy to forget the humble beginnings of this splendid journey. It is a sign of the newfound maturity of Icelandic cinema that so many filmmakers today are taking a look back at the long road traveled.

Notes

Preface

1. For full bibliographic entries, see the Bibliography at the end of the volume. In addition to my own work, thankfully, there have been many other publications on Icelandic cinema since I completed my dissertation. I address these chapters or journal articles about specific films where relevant, but this book is not intended to be a complete overview of the major publications on Icelandic cinema. For that, see my entry on the topic in the *Oxford Bibliographies*, "Icelandic Cinema," in *Oxford Bibliographies in Cinema and Media Studies*, ed. Krin Gabbard (New York: Oxford University Press, 2023).

Introduction

1. It may be worth noting that I have also been working on a book on world cinema that shapes the understanding of this one. Thus this book is not only a study of Icelandic national cinema but also a case study in world cinema.
2. The key corrective to this is Mette Hjort and Duncan Petrie, eds., *The Cinema of Small Nations* (Edinburgh: Edinburgh University Press, 2007). The early theorizing also stemmed primarily from Western national cinemas, and even though the field has diversified enormously since then, it remains focused on larger nations, now increasingly South and East Asian ones, most notably India, China, South Korea, and Taiwan.
3. Andrew Higson, *Waving the Flag: Constructing a National Cinema in Britain* (Oxford: Oxford University Press, 1995), 9–13.
4. Andrew Higson, "The Concept of National Cinema," *Screen* 30, no. 4 (1989): 36–46. Higson's influential consumption thesis—that national cinema studies should focus on what the national audience is watching rather than the films produced nationally—becomes untenable when applied to small cinemas, as such studies would amount to little other than reception studies of Hollywood films (and other foreign films depending on the nation in question) around the globe. While such studies are, of course, not without value, the consumption thesis strikes me as highly suspect when applied to national cinemas. In one sense, such reception studies implicitly enforce Hollywood's hegemonic position, by prioritizing the reception of Hollywood films rather than studying locally produced films.
5. Stephen Crofts, "Reconceptualizing National Cinema/s," *Quarterly Review of Film or Video* II, no. 3 (1993): 49–67. Crofts did update his schema subsequently, but instead of adding a category relevant to small national cinemas, the new category involved "United States cinemas." See "Concepts of National Cinema," in *The Oxford Guide to Film Studies*, ed. John Hill and Pamela Church Gibson (Oxford: University of Oxford Press, 1998), 390.
6. "A Survey on National Cinematography," UNESCO, accessed April 7, 2005, http://www.unesco.org/culture/industries/cinema/html_eng/prod.shtml.
7. "Number of National Feature Films Produced: Countries Compared," *NationMaster*, accessed October 14, 2023, https://www.nationmaster.com/country-info/stats/Media/Cinema/Number-of-national-feature-films-produced#2010. Lists such as these are not fully reliable and can vary from one source to another. For example, the Icelandic Film Centre lists only ten narrative feature films for 2010, with the number going up to thirteen for 2021. "Feature Films," *Icelandic Film Centre*, accessed October 14, 2023, https://www.icelandicfilms.info/films-list/gm/genre/movie.
8. To population, Mette Hjort and Duncan Petrie add gross national product, geographic size, and (historical) subjection to larger nation-states. See "Introduction," in *The Cinema of Small Nations*, ed. Mette Hjort and Duncan Petrie (Edinburgh: Edinburgh University Press, 20017), 4–6.
9. John Hill, "The Issue of National Cinema and British Film Production," in *New Questions of British Cinema*, ed. Duncan Petrie (London: British Film Institute, 1993), 14. Hill's italics.
10. Duncan Petrie, "The New Scottish Cinema," in *Cinema & Nation*, ed. Mette Hjort and Scott MacKenzie (London: Routledge, 2000), 154.

11. The concept of the nation is itself hotly contested. It is a debate I intend to address elsewhere, but it may be worth noting that Iceland is also something of an anomaly when it comes to nations. Critics of the concept typically emphasize the artificiality of national borders and suspect ties between language and nationhood. Iceland conversely has a unique language and has been shaped by its "natural" island borders that have enclosed a homogenous population for centuries.

Chapter 1

1. Ivo Blom, "The First Cameraman in Iceland: Travel Film and Travel Literature," in *Picture Perfect*, ed. Laraine Porter and Bryony Dixon (Exeter: University of Exeter Press, 2007), 68–81.
2. Gunnar Tómas Kristófersson, "Upphaf kvikmyndaaldar á Íslandi," *Ritið* 19, no. 2 (2019): 60–61.
3. The film was long credited to Petersen, but he makes clear in his brief biography that it was Lind who made the film, although he was joined by Petersen in shooting it. "Ævisaga kvikmyndahúsaeigandans P. Petersen," trans. Gunnar Tómas Kristófersson, unpublished (original date 1932).
4. Gunnar Tómas Kristófersson, "Meistari rammans: Um kvikmyndagerð Kjartans Ó. Bjarnasonar," *Skírnir* 197, no. 1 (Spring 2023): 43–44.
5. For this reason, Kristófersson believes Bjarnason has not been given his just due and describes his work as "the probably best kept secret of Icelandic film history." "Meistari rammans," 61.
6. Although the title of Íris Ellenberger's *Íslandskvikmyndir 1916–1966: Ímyndir, sjálfsmynd og vald* emphasizes the Iceland-films, her book is the most thorough overview of documentary filmmaking in Iceland (by both local and foreign filmmakers) up until the arrival of television in the mid-sixties (Reykjavík: Sagnfræðistofnun Háskóla Íslands, 2007).
7. The first film directed by a woman in Iceland was the brief dance film *Flat-Charleston*, made all the way back in 1927. Regarding the film that was shot by Guðmundsson, see Gunnar Tómas Kristófersson, "Ódauðleg dansspor: Ruth Hanson og dansmyndin," *Saga* 54, no. 2 (2021): 7–17.

Chapter 2

1. Iceland still remained under the Danish monarchy but now in a personal union with Denmark. To simplify, it gained autonomy over domestic affairs, but Denmark still had control over Iceland's foreign policy. That finally changed when the country became an independent republic in 1944 with all ties to Denmark severed.
2. Nowhere is the claim on the ontological relationship between film and reality more clearly stated than in André Bazin's well-known essay "The Ontology of the Photographic Image," where he goes as far as to claim: "The photographic image is the object itself." "The Ontology of the Photographic Image," in *What Is Cinema?* vol. 1, ed. Hugh Gray (Berkeley: University of California Press, 1967), 14.
3. Walter Benjamin, "The Work of Art in the Age of Mechanical Reproduction," trans. Harry Zohn, in *Illuminations: Essays and Reflections*, ed. Hannah Arendt (New York: Schocken Books, 1968), 221. However, Benjamin was willing to ascribe a certain aura to early portrait photographs—not only because he considered them related to traditional paintings, but also because of their ability to capture a past moment. Benjamin, "The Work of Art in the Age of Mechanical Reproduction," 225–26. For a more detailed description of early photography and its aura, see Benjamin's "Little History of Photography," trans. Edmund Jephcott and Kingsley Shorter, in Walter Benjamin, *Selected Writings*, vol. 2, eds. Michael W. Jennings, Howard Eiland, and Cary Smith (Cambridge, MA: Harvard University Press, 1999), 507–30.
4. Erlendur Sveinsson, "Frekar bogna en brotna: Um frumkvöðul í íslenskri kvikmyndagerð," in *Enginn getur lifað án Lofts: Loftur Guðmundsson konunglegur hirðljósmyndari og kvikmyndagerðarmaður í Reykjavík*, ed. Inga Lára Baldvinsdóttir (Reykjavík: Þjóðminjasafn Íslands, 2002), 19.
5. An important exception to this is a self-reflexive scene in which Guðmundsson pans to the right following a typical landscape shot and by doing so reveals his own shadow filming on a rock.
6. Siegfried Kracauer, *Theory of Film: The Redemption of Physical Reality* (Princeton, NJ: Princeton University Press, 1997), 60–73. Importantly, Kracauer is not making a distinction between fiction films and documentaries, as he finds that documentary makers can be so "exclusively concerned with conveying propositions of an intellectual or ideological nature that they do not even try to elicit them from the visual material they exhibit." Kracauer, *Theory of Film*, 207. As already pointed out, the early Icelandic films make few attempts at manipulating reality and convey no explicit ideological messages. Earlier, Kracauer had also argued for concrete relations

between cinema and nation in his classic study of German national cinema, *From Caligari to Hitler*, if on different grounds, namely cinema being a collaborative cultural product made for the masses. *From Caligari to Hitler: A Psychological History of the German Film* (Princeton, NJ: Princeton University Press, 1947). If Kracauer did not continue his work on cinema and nation, the interrelations of history and cinema were to remain integral to his later work. In his last and incomplete book, *History: The Last Things before the Last*, Kracauer went as far as analogizing history and cinema: "Small wonder that camera-reality parallels historical reality in terms of its structure, its general constitution. Exactly as historical reality, it is partly patterned, partly amorphous—a consequence, in both cases, of the half-cooked state of our everyday world." *History: The Last Things before the Last* (Princeton, NJ: Markus Wieners, 1995), 58.
7. Kracauer, *Theory of Film*, 60.
8. Sveinsson, "Frekar bogna en brotna," 31.
9. Already in 1901 the periodical *Þjóðólfur* claimed: "There is no doubt, that if film exhibitions [of films about Iceland] were held around the globe, they would considerably increase tourism to the country. It would therefore be important, if we ourselves, could guarantee the quality and variety of these films." Quoted in Eggert Þór Bernharðsson, "Landnám lifandi mynda: Af kvikmyndum á Íslandi til 1930," in *Heimur kvikmyndanna*, ed. Guðni Elísson (Reykjavík: Forlagið, 1999), 817–18.
10. For a systematic overview of the Iceland-films of the 1920s and 1930s (many of which are lost), see Ásgeir Guðmundsson, "Ísland í lifandi myndum: Áform um kvikmyndatöku á Íslandi á 3. og 4. áratug 20. aldar," *TMM* 62, no. 4 (2001): 48–59. Guðmundsson also lists a number of projects that never materialized, due to the state's unwillingness to contribute financially or otherwise. He explains that the state's lack of enthusiasm was related to its dire financial situation, but also concerns regarding the nation's image abroad (with the state demanding in some cases what would be today called a "final cut"). See also Íris Ellenberger's more expansive *Íslandskvikmyndir 1916–1966: Ímyndir, sjálfsmynd og vald*, which, as her title suggests, extends their history into the mid-sixties (Reykjavík: Sagnfræðistofnun Háskóla Íslands, 2007).
11. Quoted in Erlendur Sveinsson, "Landsýn-heimssýn: Kynningarmáttur kvikmyndarinnar á fjórða áratugnum," in *Heimur kvikmyndanna*, ed. Guðni Elísson (Reykjavík: Forlagið, 1999), 853.
12. Sabine Hake has defined the *kulturfilm* as "a form of documentary committed to idealized representations of nature, country, and native people." *German National Cinema* (London: Routledge, 2002), 22. See also Kracauer, *From Caligari to Hitler*, 141–43. Burkert made at least four German shorts about Iceland, *Fishing in Iceland* (1935, *Schiffahrt und Fischfang auf Island*), *A Summer in Iceland* (1935, *Sommer auf Island*), *Icelandic Summer* (1935, *Islandssommer*), and *Frightening Earth* (1935, *Unheimliche Erde*).
13. Erlendur Sveinsson, "Árin tólf fyrir daga Sjónvarps og Kvikmyndasjóðs," in *Heimur kvikmyndanna*, ed. Guðni Elísson (Reykjavík: Forlagið, 1999), 868–69.
14. Gunnar Tómas Kristófersson, "Meistari rammans: Um kvikmyndagerð Kjartans Ó. Bjarnasonar," *Skírnir* 197, no. 1 (Spring 2023): 44–45. In other words, Kristófersson is suggesting that this activity stemmed directly from the 1930s institutionalization of Icelandic cinema that was simply temporarily halted during World War II.
15. It is worth nothing that Guðmundsson did make another Iceland-film that was simply titled *Iceland* (1947, *Ísland*) which was something of a color-remake of *Iceland in Living Pictures*.
16. One consequence of this is that the original ninety-minute version of the film is lost, although a slightly longer one exists with some added scenes but without sound. The most widely seen version since is a German one prepared in 1957, which salvaged what it could of the badly damaged original Icelandic film print, that was also reproduced in Icelandic and English. For more detail on the different versions and the extensive distribution of the film, see Gunnar Tómas Kristófersson, "Fyrir listina að lifa af: Um gerð og útgáfur kvikmyndar Óskars Gíslasonar *Björgunarafrekið við Látrabjarg*," *TMM* 84, no. 1 (2023): 82–91.
17. Sveinsson, "Frekar bogna en brotna," 55.
18. Although Ævar Kvaran is credited as the director of *The Last Farm in the Valley*, Gíslason is the film's director in the conventional understanding of film direction, despite "only" being credited as a producer and a cinematographer. Kvaran, a veteran of the stage, was brought in to help with the acting since Gíslason began his career as a photographer and documentary filmmaker, having little experience directing actors. The same work division is found in his other two features, and Gíslason relies on the assistance of other stage directors in his shorter fiction. In all cases I credit Gíslason for directing the films, except for *Covetousness* (1952, *Ágirnd*), which

although shot by Gíslason was directed by Svala Hannesdóttir. It is stylistically of a different sort altogether, as its expressionistic stage setting is supported by playful camera work, canted angles, and rapid editing.
19. Raymond Williams, *The Country and the City* (New York: Oxford University Press, 1973), 1. Iceland also falls within the parameters of Williams's general summary of the opposition between country and city: "On the country has gathered the idea of a natural way of life: of peace, innocence, and simple virtue. On the city has gathered the idea of an achieved centre: of learning, communication, light. Powerful hostile associations have also developed: on the city as a place of noise, worldliness and ambition; on the country as a place of backwardness, ignorance, limitation." Williams, *The Country and the City*, 1. In mid-twentieth-century Iceland, the country continued to be perceived as virtuous, while the city was accordingly approached with more hostility.
20. Like his documentary *Reykjavík of Our Days*, *The Reykjavík Adventure of the Bakka-Brothers* and *New Role* were shot on location in Reykjavík, functioning as valuable historical documents of the city during the mid-century.
21. On Edda-film see Arnaldur Indriðason, "Stofnun og saga kvikmyndafyrirtækisins Edda-film," in *Heimur kvikmyndanna*, ed. Guðni Elísson (Reykjavík: Forlagið, 1999), 886–93.
22. The original Icelandic title *79 from the station* (*79 af stöðinni*) refers to Ragnar rather than Gógó as 79 is his call number at the taxi-station.
23. Indriði G. Þorsteinsson, *Tímar í lífi þjóðar* (Reykjavík: Vaka-Helgafell, 2004), 311.

Chapter 3

1. Friedrich List, *The National System of Political Economy*, trans. Sampson S. Lloyd (London: Longman, Green, 1885), 175–76. Quoted by Eric Hobsbawm, *Nations and Nationalism since 1780: Programme, Myth, Reality* (Cambridge: Cambridge University Press, 1990), 30–31.
2. The surviving saga manuscripts date back to the early fourteenth to the sixteenth centuries, although evidence suggests that the majority of them were composed in the thirteenth century, and that they relied on even older oral traditions. Vésteinn Ólason, *Samræður við söguöld: Frásagnarlist Íslendingasagna og fortíðarmynd* (Reykjavík: Heimskringla, 1998), 17–20. They are typically divided into six subgroups, including sagas of Icelanders that deal with the settlers of Iceland (spanning approximately the time period 850 to 1050) and come closest to describing the daily lives of ordinary people; kings' sagas that focus on Norwegian kings and offer historical outlines of major events; legendary sagas that center on fictional/legendary heroes; and finally, contemporary sagas, that focus on then current events in Iceland, especially the thirteenth-century Civil War. Like the romanticists, Icelandic filmmakers have also singled out the sagas of the Icelanders in their work. But there has also been occasional discussion of approaching the contemporary sagas, and certainly kings' sagas are relevant to *The White Viking* (Hrafn Gunnlaugsson, 1991, *Hvíti víkingurinn*). Many excellent introductions to the heritage are available, including Margaret Clunies Ross, *The Old Norse-Icelandic Saga* (Cambridge: Cambridge University Press, 2010), and Ármann Jakobsson's *Icelandic Literature of the Vikings: An Introduction*, trans. Andrew. E. McGillivray (Reykjavík: Veröld, 2013).
3. *Njal's Saga*, trans. Robert Cook, in *The Complete Sagas of Icelanders*, vol. 3, ed. Viðar Hreinsson (Reykjavík: Leifur Eiríksson, 1997), 86. I refer to the saga titles as translated in *The Complete Sagas of Icelanders*. For a more detailed discussion of "Gunnarshólmi," see Jón Karl Helgason, "The Mystery of Vínarterta: In Search of Icelandic Ethnic Identity," *Scandinavian-Canadian Studies* 17 (2006–2007): 38–42.
4. Jónas Hallgrímsson, "Gunnar's Holm," in *Bard of Iceland: Jónas Hallgrímsson, Poet and Scientist*, trans. Dick Ringler (Madison: University of Wisconsin Press, 2002), 136–38.
5. Gísli Sigurðsson, "Icelandic National Identity: From Romanticism to Tourism," in *Making Europe in Nordic Context*, ed. Pertti J. Anttonen (Turku: NIF, 1996), 43–44.
6. Robert Scholes and Robert Kellogg, *The Nature of Narrative* (Oxford: Oxford University Press, 1966), 43.
7. Benedict Anderson, *Imagined Communities: Reflections on the Origin and Spread of Nationalism* (London: Verso, 1991), 22–36. See also Franco Moretti, *Atlas of the European Novel 1800–1900* (London: Verso, 1999), 11–73.
8. Timothy Brennan, "The National Longing for Form," in *Nation and Narration*, ed. Homi K. Bhabha (London: Routledge, 1990), 49.

9. Ástráður Eysteinsson and Eysteinn Þorvaldsson, "Modern Literature," in *Iceland: The Republic*, ed. Jóhannes Nordal and Valdimar Kristinsson (Reykjavík: Central Bank of Iceland, 1996), 265–66.
10. *The Islander: A Biography of Halldór Laxness*, trans. Philip Roughton (London: MacLehose Press, 2008), 1.
11. This is literally spelled out in the title of Hallgrímur Helgason's novel about Laxness, *The Author of Iceland (Höfundur Íslands)*. In analyzing Helgason's literary struggle with Laxness, Alda Björk Valdimarsdóttir reverts to Harold Bloom's theory of anxiety of influence, which describes how writers respond to and grapple with the artistic reputation of their predecessors. *Rithöfundur Íslands* (Reykjavík: Bókmenntafræðistofnun Háskóla Íslands, 2008), 147–52. As we will see, the notion of an anxiety of influence is equally apt in describing the relationship between Icelandic filmmakers and the national literary heritage. Internationally, Helgason is best known for his novel *101 Reykjavík* (see chapter eight).
12. Pascale Casanova, *The World Republic of Letters*, trans. M. B. DeBevoise (Cambridge, MA: Harvard University Press, 2004), 82–83.
13. Casanova, *The World Republic of Letters*, 240. A salient example of this phenomenon is found in the English-language foreword to *The Complete Sagas of the Icelanders* written by then president Ólafur Ragnar Grímsson: "[The sagas] created a rich heritage which was treasured by the small island nation in the far north. The vision which they fostered has this century brought Iceland independence within the community of nations. The sagas are a unique literary phenomenon and invite comparison with the masterpieces of classical Greece and Rome. Their authors were firmly rooted in the Nordic and Germanic heritage, but also sought material from contemporary European culture. They charted the fate of individuals, heroic deeds and tragedies. In the sagas we find classical human wisdom and breadth of mind which are relevant to all people at all times." *The Complete Sagas of Icelanders*, vol. 1, ed. Viðar Hreinsson (Reykjavík: Leifur Eiríksson, 1997), vii. Grímsson's text reflects the conventional strategy of establishing a national literature globally by arguing for its universal value and comparing it to canonical classics. However, the fact that Icelandic literature is not referenced once in Casanova's voluminous study suggests that long-standing attempts of establishing the heritage at the center of the international literary space have not been fully successful. Perhaps this can be partly explained by Casanova's French background, as Icelandic literature has been more prominent in the Anglophone and Germanic world.
14. Casanova, *The World Republic of Letters*, 104.
15. Casanova, *The World Republic of Letters*, 226.
16. Casanova, *The World Republic of Letters*, 327. However, Casanova may distinguish too strongly between a national tradition of the novel and the tradition of international modernism. Modernist fiction remains in many respects national, and thus the difference is arguably one of degree rather than kind. Furthermore, the explicit national focus of Laxness's fiction has not hindered it from being widely translated, while the Icelandic modernists have found little international success.
17. For a comprehensive English-language overview of Icelandic neo-romanticism, including but not limited to the Varangians, see Guðni Elísson, "From Realism to Neoromanticism," trans. Gunnþórunn Guðmundsdóttir, in *A History of Icelandic Literature*, ed. Daisy Neijmann (Lincoln: University of Nebraska Press, 2006), 327–56.
18. The concept of the transnational does not fully apply here, as this literature reflected a regional relationship involving two nations (and in fact only one nation-state). I would also hesitate to describe colonial, postcolonial, or diasporic literature as transnational because despite often involving two nations, such literature generally deals quite specifically with a single nation-state or a particular national relationship. But this also begets the question of how to define the relationship between Iceland and Denmark, including whether it is a colonial one. In a comparative study of Iceland and Greenland, Sumarliði R. Ísleifsson concludes that "Greenland can without a doubt be defined as a colony while Iceland was closer to a marginal territory in the Danish state." *Í fjarska norðursins: Ísland og Grænland, viðhorfssaga í þúsund ár* (Reykjavík: Sögufélag, 2020), 29. Certainly, Icelanders were never subjected to imperial racism or brutality, and there is no comparing the Danish treatment of Icelanders and its non-European colonies.
19. Casanova, *The World Republic of Letters*, 257.
20. Instead of the published title of the English translation *Eyvind of the Hills*, I refer to the title by which the film is known in English, which is closer to the literal meaning of the original Danish

title. Furthermore, character names are given as they appear in the Icelandic version so as to be consistent with other names. The same goes for *Hadda Padda* and *The Story of the Borg Family*.
21. Jóhann Sigurjónsson, *Eyvind of the Hills*, trans. Henninge Krohn Schanche (New York: American Scandinavian Foundation, 1916), 36.
22. Bengt Forslund, *Victor Sjöström: His Life and Work*, trans. Peter Cowie (New York: New York Zoetrope, 1988), 68. Forslund quotes Sigurjónsson from the original program leaflet of *Berg-Ejvind och hans hustru*
23. Louis Delluc, "Cinema: *The Outlaw and His Wife*," in *French Film Theory and Criticism: A History/Anthology 1907–1939*, vol. 1, ed. Richard Abel (Princeton, NJ: Princeton University Press, 1988), 188. Original quote from "Cinéma: Les Proscrits," *Paris-Midi*, November 10, 1919), 2.
24. The Royal Theatre in Copenhagen originally accepted the play on artistic merit and without any obligation to stage it, as it considered the challenges of staging the fourth act insurmountable. Guðmundur Kamban, "Introduction," *Hadda Padda: A Drama in Four Acts* (New York: Alfred A. Knopf, 1917), viii.
25. Kamban, *Hadda Padda*, 79.
26. I will be referring to the completed novel as *The Story of the Borg Family*, although the English translation I cite uses the title of the third volume. Gunnarsson also wrote a fourth volume, but like the film, he concluded the novel in later publications with the third volume.
27. Gunnar Gunnarsson, *Guest the One-Eyed*, trans. W. W. Forster (New York: Alfred A. Knopf, 1922), 32–33.
28. Gunnarsson, *Guest the One-Eyed*, 62. Ormar's stay in Copenhagen is also an allegorical rendering of the position of Gunnarsson and the other Varangians—deeply committed to Iceland but having to practice their craft in Denmark.
29. Gunnar Gunnarsson, *Borgarættin: Saga* (Reykjavík: Útgáfufélagið Landnáma, 1944), 261. I have provided a translation of the Icelandic text, as the connection between land and character is made more explicit there. In the published English version, the description is as follows: "His whole appearance [...] presented an almost unreal effect, harmonizing to a striking degree with the surroundings. He seemed to be in his element in this waste tract." Gunnarsson, *Guest the One-Eyed*, 190.
30. Gunnarsson, *Guest the One-Eyed*, 44.
31. Helga Kress, "Guðmundur Kamban og verk hans: Í tilefni heildarútgáfu Almenna bókafélagsins," *Skírnir* 144 (1970): 166.
32. Gunnarsson, *Guest the One-Eyed*, 112.
33. Gunnarsson, *Guest the One-Eyed*, 121.
34. This has begun to change in recent years, particularly in the booming field of crime fiction, in which many novels are written with an eventual translation and foreign readership in mind.
35. Although clearly a Danish film production, *The Story of the Borg Family* is often approached as if it were an Icelandic one. The most recent example of this appropriation involves an author who is very much aware of the film's origins. To celebrate the film's centenary, Erlendur Sveinsson wrote a lengthy essay under the title "A Life Story of a Film: or How *The Story of the Borg Family* Became Iceland's National Film." See "Lífssaga kvikmyndar: eða hvernig *Saga Borgarættarinnar* varð þjóðkvikmynd Íslands," *TMM* 81, no. 1 (2020), https://tmm.forlagid.is/lifssaga-kvikmyndar/.
36. Jón Yngvi Jóhannsson, "'Jøklens Storm svalede den kulturtrætte Denmarks Pande': Um fyrstu viðtökur dansk-íslenskra bókmennta í Danmörku," *Skírnir* 175, no. 1 (2001): 40–41. Jóhannsson also offers a survey of the reception of the neo-romantic literature in Denmark.
37. Jóhannsson, "'Jøklens Storm svalede den kulturtrætte Denmarks Pande,'" 40–41.
38. These are usually referred to as film scripts; however, they were actually treatments; Laxness never wrote a full script.
39. Among others, Laxness reached out to western star Bill Cody, who was of Icelandic descent, as well as Victor Sjöström (now Seastrom).
40. Guðmundsson, *The Islander*, 144.
41. Guðmundsson, *The Islander*, 391.
42. Halldór Kiljan Laxness, "Some Outlines of a Motion Picture from Icelandic Coast-Life," *TMM* 65, no. 4 (2004): 11.
43. Laxness, "Some Outlines of a Motion Picture from Icelandic Coast-Life," 18.
44. Guðmundsson, *The Islander*, 141, 27. Although the writers are not named in the English translation, Guðmundsson specifies these three as recipients of Laxness's praise in the original text. *Halldór Laxness: Ævisaga* (Reykjavík: JPV útgáfa, 2004), 237.
45. Trans. F. H. Lyon (New York: Houghton Mifflin, 1936).

46. In many ways, the novels are better suited to television series, similar to those produced by the BBC (British Broadcasting Corporation) of classic works by Jane Austen and Charles Dickens. Although there has been increased partnership between television channels and film production companies in recent years, the financial resources of Icelandic television are even more meager than those of its film industry. Perhaps for that reason, the only two elaborate Laxness adaptations made for television were European co-productions directed by the German Rolf Hädrich: *The Fish Can Sing* (1972, *Brekkukotsannáll*) and *Paradise Reclaimed* (1980, *Paradísarheimt*). But almost half a century has passed without any additional television adaptations.
47. Interview by author, Reykjavík, September 2004.
48. See, for example, GAR, "Sturlungaöldin kostar hálfan annan milljarð," *DV*, January 6, 2004, 9.
49. Apparently, Dreyer had secured funding from Denmark, Sweden, and Norway, but needed the Icelandic state to ensure a quarter of the budget in case the films would lose money; the project seems to have faltered when no such support was forthcoming. Ásgeir Guðmundsson, "Ísland í lifandi myndum: Áform um kvikmyndatöku á Íslandi á 3. og 4. áratug 20. aldar," *TMM* 62, no. 4 (2001), 48–49.
50. On Rósinkranz's script and Edda-film's aspiration of adapting *Njal's Saga*, see Jón Karl Helgason, *Höfundur Njálu: Þræðir úr vestrænni bókmenntasögu* (Reykjavík: Heimskringla, 2001), 149–61. Helgason also discusses film scripts based on the sagas that were written by Henrik Thorlacius in the 1940s. However, they were published as independent works and there is little indication that they were even meant to be filmed. Accordingly, they seem to have functioned as fantasies of what the sagas might have look like if filmed. Helgason, *Höfundur Njálu*, 156–58.
51. Although Edda-film had little say in the project, the company agreed to participate in the film since it was being shot in Iceland. Abstract and formalistic, the end result was almost the exact opposite of what the firm had had in mind with the adaptation of *Njal's Saga*. *The Red Mantle* was also poorly received on its initial release in Iceland, and continues to be an object of ridicule. Birgir Thor Møller, for example, describes it as being "pretentious [and] inadvertently comic." "In and Out of Reykjavík: Framing Iceland in the Global Daze," in *Transnational Cinema in a Global North: Nordic Cinema in Transition*, ed. Andrew Nestingen and Trevor G. Elkington (Detroit: Wayne State University Press, 2005), 310. To the contrary, *The Red Mantle* is among the most aesthetically innovative feature films shot in Iceland, and its creative handling of Icelandic landscape remains unparalleled. Considering local expectations around the saga heritage and the Viking era, it is easy to understand the resistance with which the film was met by Icelandic spectators. Importantly, rather than an adaptation of the Icelandic literary heritage, it was based on the seventh book of Saxo Grammaticus's *The History of the Danes* (*Gesta Danorum*), and it displayed no interest in realistically depicting the Viking world, which, like the Icelandic landscape, functioned primarily as a backdrop to a remarkable exercise in form. The polished look, scant dialogue, handsome and clean-shaven Vikings, and vivid homoeroticism broke with all traditional representations of the heritage. The local objections to the innovative and ethereal Viking world presented in *The Red Mantle* are indicative of a narrow horizon of expectation, and they help explain the creative difficulties faced by filmmakers interested in tackling the heritage—or, perhaps more to the point, the lack of such filmmakers.
52. GAR, "Sturlungaöldin kostar hálfan annan milljarð," 9.
53. Grétarsson Jakob Bjarnar, "Sjö milljarða bíómynd tekin á Íslandi," *Fréttablaðið*, October 5, 2008, 26.
54. To this day, the Icelandic language continues to be held in high regard despite (or perhaps because of) the influx of English, which in the latter half of the twentieth century has replaced Danish as the key lingual "threat" to Icelandic. To "defend" the language, a special committee creates new Icelandic words to ward off foreign adoptions, regulations restrict the use of foreign personal names, writers receive generous financial support, and each year on November 16 (the birthday of the acclaimed nineteenth-century poet Jónas Hallgrímsson) the language itself is celebrated. This underlying anxiety comes from the belief that without the Icelandic language, the nation itself might wither away under the homogenizing power of globalization.

Chapter 4

1. The poem in question is the most celebrated of all the medieval Eddaic poems and describes the Norse cosmos from birth to Ragnarök. Herzog is, of course, not the only one to have noticed the volcanic imagery of Ragnarök in the poem, and the case has been made that it actually reflects the disastrous consequence of gigantic sixth-century eruptions located outside of Europe. See

Neil Price, *Children of Ash and Elm: A History of the Vikings* (New York: Basic Books, 2020), 75–78. Nor is volcanic imagery limited to Norse mythology, as even the Christian conception of Hell makes ample use of it. See, for example, Haraldur Sigurðsson, *Melting the Earth: The History of Ideas on Volcanic Eruptions* (Oxford: Oxford University Press, 1999), 71–79.

2. Volcano eruptions can be measured in various ways (length of time, lava production, ash distribution, explosive power, property damage, loss of lives, etc.), and there exists no single method to assess and arrange them by size (the widely used volcanic explosivity index emphasizes material mass, height, and duration). I single out these four volcanoes because of the direct impact they have had in Iceland, and the role they played in local and global media. For readers interested in more thorough geological and historical overviews of volcanoes in Iceland, see Ari Trausti Guðmundsson, *Living Earth: Outline of the Geology of Iceland* (Reykjavík: Forlagið, 2013). For a more culturally and historically focused overview that is not limited to Iceland, see Sigurðsson, *Melting the Earth*.

3. See, for example, Anne Billson, "Volcano Films—Ranked!" *The Guardian*, July 21, 2022, accessed September 12, 2023, https://www.theguardian.com/film/2022/jul/21/volcano-films-ranked, and Gaia Kriscak, "The 10 Best Movies about Volcanoes and Eruptions, Ranked," *WhatNerd*, June 4, 2023, accessed September 12, 2023, https://whatnerd.com/best-movies-about-volcanoes-ranked/.

4. Siegfried Kracauer, *Theory of Film: The Redemption of Physical Reality* (Princeton, NJ: Princeton University Press, 1997), 27–40.

5. Jean Epstein, "The Cinema Seen from Etna," trans. Stuart Liebman, in *Jean Epstein: Critical Essays and New Translations*, ed. Sarah Keller and Jason N. Paul (Amsterdam: Amsterdam University Press, 2012), 288.

6. Elena Past, *Italian Ecocinema beyond the Human* (Bloomington: Indiana University Press, 2019), 155. I might add that "language" is a bit misleading, at least in my own discussion, where what is important are the impressions (feelings or meanings) that cannot be put into words and must remain visual (and sonic). Language, then, should be understood as a specifically cinematic one. As I was completing this volume, Jessica Mulvogue published her essay "Cinema as Volcano," and like Past's book, it is relevant for anyone with interest in the topic. Mulvogue takes the relationship between the two a bit further than I have done here, and am perhaps willing to do, in arguing that volcanoes are a medium like cinema and there exists something that she calls "volcanic thinking": "A volcanic cinema is a cinema of the elements; it is an audio-visual vortex that invites the spectator to 'think like a volcano,' taking us to the limits of thought, where concept, matter, light, darkness, living, non-living, inside and outside overlap, inform, touch and entangle." "Cinema as Volcano: Thinking Cinema through the Volcano with Malena Szlam, Werner Herzog and Jean Epstein," *Studies in World Cinema* 3 (2023): 100. Thus Mulvogue's argument shares much with my own ideas about the volcano film, and it adds weight to both of our arguments that, with the exception of Herzog, we are dealing with different filmmakers but still arrive at similar conclusions about volcano films.

7. Even though the other two films have no voice-overs, both directors almost certainly intended to explain the imagery themselves during projection. Bjarnason, in particular, typically finished his films without sound because he provided lectures during their exhibition. On Bjarnason's working methods, see Gunnar Tómas Kristófersson, "Meistari rammans: Um kvikmyndagerð Kjartans Ó. Bjarnasonar," *Skírnir* 197, no. 1 (Spring 2023): 48–52. As a result, it is impossible to know how they would have presented the images during projection, but apart from voice-overs the films are also lacking other explanatory material like maps and graphs.

8. My wording here may risk confusion considering Bill Nichols's influential division of film documentary into six modes. What I have in mind is something much broader and distinguishes the documentary mode from narrative and experimental filmmaking. At mid-century that would, in Nichol's terminology, lie closest to the expository mode, while Knudsen's later volcano films also dip into the poetic mode. The latter is close to what I have in mind when describing scenes that go against the grain of the period's conventional documentaries and lie instead closer to experimental cinema. This is supported by Nichol's definition of the poetic mode as one that "emphasizes visual associations, tonal or rhythmic qualities, descriptive passages, and formal organization. This mode bears a close proximity to experimental, personal, and avant-garde filmmaking." *Introduction to Documentary*, 3rd ed. (Bloomington: Indiana University Press, 2017), 22.

9. I typically limit myself to directors and rarely refer to other creative contributors in the book's discussions of authorship. I make an exception regarding voice-over narration in this chapter because Knudsen's two main narrators wrote their own texts and were experts in their respective

NOTES   239

fields. The celebrated volcanologist Sigurður Þórarinsson narrates the Icelandic versions of the volcano films, while the archaeologist Eldjárn, later elected president in 1968, narrates most of the non-volcanic films.

10. This contrasts with, for example, *Man of Aran* (1934) where Robert Flaherty staged a shark hunt even though the practice was long extinct. *Hornstrandir*, on the other hand, explains that shark hunting used to be practiced in the past, but makes it clear that the inhabitants of the time fish only for cod, as shown in the film.

11. Knudsen at times recycled some of his earlier footage. For example, *Sketches* includes a few brief shots of Þórðarson that were originally found in the film devoted to the writer.

12. As previously noted, Þórarinsson narrated his own texts in Knudsen's volcano films, but in many cases, I draw upon the original English language voice-over provided by Boucher. His style is familiar from many British documentaries of the period; it is assured, informative, and controlled. Many of Knudsen's films—especially the volcano films—traveled widely, were screened at festivals where they occasionally won prizes, and were later distributed on video for educational purposes. *Birth of an Island* was available in six different language editions, while the most popular film, *Fire on Heimaey*, was available in at least thirteen. "Íslenskar kvikmynda og videoútgáfur dreifðar erlendis," *Tíminn*, September 21, 1983, 20.

13. This moment of experimental cinema traces its lineage back to pre-narrative film, or what Tom Gunning has described as a "cinema of attractions." See "The Cinema of Attractions: Early Film, Its Spectator and the Avant-Garde," in *Early Cinema: Space, Frame, Narrative*, ed. Thomas Elsaesser (London: British Film Institute), 56–62.

14. Herzog leaves out, though, some very relevant information. We are informed that the shots originate from footage the Kraffts filmed in Hawaii, but Herzog does not tell us if they or he edited the sequence. These questions around editing apply to the entirety of Herzog's film, as well as *Fire of Love*, and neither film provides us with any information about the Kraffts' completed films (not even in the credits). Judging by Maurice Krafft's *Inside Hawaiian Volcanoes* (1989), he was a more conventional filmmaker than suggested by Herzog's documentary. His volcano footage is dazzling, but unlike Herzog's tribute to him, *Inside Hawaiian Volcanoes* is weighed down by endless graphs, maps, and scientific explanation. Not a single volcano montage trusts the images to speak for themselves. A more thorough study of the Kraffts' filmmaking practices and goals is clearly needed, but it remains outside the scope of this volume.

15. This little-known documentary short was the first Icelandic film shown at the Cannes film festival. See Ásgrímur Sverrisson and Gunnþóra Halldórsdóttir, "Sagan af fyrstu íslensku kvikmyndinni í Cannes og höfundi hennar," *Klapptré*, September 6, 2023, accessed September 10, 2023, https://klapptre.is/2023/09/06/sagan-af-fyrstu-islensku-kvikmyndinni-i-cannes-og-hofundi-hennar/.

16. While the original film was made for the airline *Loftleiðir* (that later merged with *Flugfélag Íslands* to form *Flugleiðir/Icelandair*), the latter version is much more promotional, tracing the history of the airline in the years after the rescue and including footage of its new Reykjavík hotel. Both versions, and *The Highlands of Iceland*, were clearly intended for foreign audiences, as even the Icelandic voice-over version of the original film has English titles and credit sequences. For a broader overview of the more explicitly commercial film material made for *Loftleiðir* and *Flugfélag Íslands*, see Íris Ellenberger, *Íslandskvikmyndir 1916–1966: Ímyndir, sjálfsmynd og vald* (Reykjavík: Sagnfræðistofnun Háskóla Íslands, 2007), 86–95.

17. Vilhjálmur Knudsen has described how the documentary exhibition market in Iceland, already small, disappeared altogether: "With the arrival of television in 1966 the market disappeared. No one could be bothered to go see documentaries anymore." Elín Pálmadóttir, "Geymir ómetanleg menningarverðmæti," *Morgunblaðið*, February 14, 1993, 16B.

18. For example, photographer Ragnar Th. Sigurðsson, interviewed in the documentary *Fire and Iceland*, has collaborated with geographer Ari Trausti Guðmundsson on numerous volcano books, many of which are available in English and other languages. It is also worth acknowledging that another "volcano theater," *The Cinema of Fire, Ice and Northern Lights*, was established by the harbor in Reykjavík in 2013, showing the work of filmmaker Valdimar Leifsson. Both have been made obsolete by the *FlyOver Iceland* simulator ride, which combines the thrills of a roller coaster with an immersive tourist film of Iceland. Here we truly have returned to the beginnings of cinema as a spectacular amusement-park ride. See, for example, Lauren Rabinovitz's discussion of the role played by Hale's Tours and early cinema at amusement parks. *For the Love of Pleasure: Women, Movies, and Culture in Turn-of-the-Century Chicago* (New Brunswick, NJ: Rutgers University Press, 1998), 145–57.

19. These mountains are not particularly tall—the aptly named *Litli Hrútur* (literally "small ram," to distinguish it from the slightly taller *Stóri Hrútur*) is only approximately a thousand feet in height (312 m) and thus more akin to a hill in size than a mountain.
20. Having lain dormant for eight centuries, eruptions are expected to continue in the region for the foreseeable future.
21. The same could be said about Icelandic literature, but Sigríður Hagalín Björnsdóttir's *The Fires*, which imagines the threat facing Reykjavík from a major eruption, is a recent exception. *The Fires*, trans. Larissa Kyzer (Seattle: Amazon Crossing, 2023). The Icelandic original *Eldarnir* was published in 2020, or just before the first volcanic activity in the *Reykjanes* region for 800 years.
22. We might include here the climax of *The Northman* (Robert Eggers, 2021), where two naked Vikings duel in the midst of the fallout from a *Hekla* eruption. The film is not Icelandic, but it does employ Icelandic talent in front of and behind the camera.
23. Kracauer, *Theory of Film*, 52–53.

Chapter 5

1. The third film of 1980s was Andrés Indriðason's *The Fishing Trip* (*Veiðiferðin*); although similarly local in scope, it was more of a children/family-fare film. Although such films never become central to Icelandic cinemas, they have been made periodically.
2. See, for example, Helgi Snær Sigurðsson, "Nær helmingur þjóðarinnnar í bíó," *Morgunblaðið*, September 9, 2008, 40.

Chapter 6

1. Raymond Williams, *The Country and the City* (New York: Oxford University Press, 1973), 2.
2. Ástráður Eysteinsson and Eysteinn Þorvaldsson, "Modern Literature," in *Iceland: The Republic*, ed. Jóhannes Nordal and Valdimar Kristinsson (Reykjavík: Central Bank of Iceland, 1996), 283. For extensive overview of modern Icelandic literature in English, in addition to Eysteinsson and Þorvaldsson's essay, see *A History of Icelandic Literature*, ed. Daisy Neijmann (Lincoln: University of Nebraska Press, 2006).
3. Andrew Higson, *Waving the Flag: Constructing a National Cinema in Britain* (Oxford: Oxford University Press, 2003), 26–27.
4. John Tucker, "*Land og synir*: An Interview with Ágúst Guðmundsson," *Scandinavian-Canadian Studies* 19 (2010): 48.
5. Indriði G. Þorsteinsson, *Land og synir* in *Tímar í lífi þjóðar* (Reykjavík: Vaka-Helgafell, 2004), 24.
6. Andrew Higson, *English Heritage, English Cinema: Costume Drama since 1980* (Oxford: Oxford University Press, 2003), 16–25.
7. Árni Þórarinsson, *Krummi: Hrafns Saga Gunnlaugssonar* (Reykjavík: Fróði, 1994), 163.
8. Guðmundsson, "*Land og synir*," 48–49. My italics.
9. Interviews by author, Reykjavík, September 2004.
10. In compiling these numbers, I have set aside children's films, which throughout have been primarily set in the city. In this they seem to follow the pattern of Icelandic literature which saw children's books make their home in the city earlier than other novels. See Eysteinsson and Þorvaldsson, "Modern Literature," 283. Also, I have used a rather broad definition of the countryside by having it include villages and towns, while Reykjavík alone fulfills the city criteria. However, Icelandic films are only rarely set in villages and towns, or only three films in each period.
11. For Hollywood's emphasis on synergy during the 1980s, see Stephen Prince, *A New Pot of Gold: Hollywood under the Electronic Rainbow, 1980–1989* (Berkeley: University of California Press, 2000), 132–41.

Chapter 7

1. Huldar Breiðfjörð, *Múrinn í Kína* (Reykjavík: Bjartur, 2004). It is worth noting that Breiðfjörð has written an essay on the Icelandic road movie and its indebtedness to its Hollywood counterpart. See "Skrítna Ísland: Um íslenskar vegamyndir," in *Heimur kvikmyndanna*, ed. Guðni Elísson (Reykjavík: Forlagið and art.is, 1999), 962–68.
2. Already in *Dear Icelanders*, Breiðfjörð is playing with the English spelling of Iceland, which to a certain extent works as a metaphor for American influence on Iceland. The second chapter of the book is, in fact, titled "Æsland" and begins: "It has been said that Iceland entered modernity chewing American gum. It may therefore not be entirely a coincidence that on the world map

Iceland looks a little like a blotch of chewing gum. The mapmaker may have spit it out just before finishing the job." *Góðir Íslendingar: Ferðasaga* (Reykjavík: Bjartur, 1998), 7.
3. See also a discussion of the same theme in *Noi the Albino* (Dagur Kári, 2003, *Nói albínói*). Björn Norðfjörð, *Dagur Kari's Noi the Albino* (Seattle: University of Washington Press, 2010), 127.
4. Skarphéðinn Guðmundsson, "Örlítið rafman býr til sól," *Morgunblaðið*, May 16, 2001, 56.
5. Skarphéðinn Guðmundsson, "Fálkasalinn Friðrik," *Morgunblaðið*, June 1, 2002, 70.
6. "Áratugur íslensku kvikmyndarinnar," *Morgunblaðið*, December 13, 1989, 2–4C.
7. However, this was not the first time the question was raised whether Icelandic cinema could manage by the home market alone. Already in the midst of its early success, Guðlaugur Bergmundsson asked in 1983: "Can the home market support the Icelandic film-industry in the future?" See "Faith Moves Mountains: The Position of the Icelandic Film-Industry Today," *Icelandic Films 1980–1983* (Reykjavík: The Icelandic Film Fund, 1983), 14. However, the answer to Bergmundsson's question was only becoming fully clear toward the end of the decade.
8. Anne Jäckel, *European Film Industries* (London: British Film Institute, 2003), 78 and 86. In 1993, MEDIA introduced the SCALE (Small Countries improve their Audiovisual Level in Europe) initiative, and its 1999 budget increase was partly justified as supporting countries with limited productivity and geographical and linguistic restrictions. For a general overview of MEDIA and Eurimages, see Jäckel, 68–90.
9. According to Friðriksson, *White Whales* and its unparalleled travels through the international film festival circuit very much paved the way for the success of *Children of Nature*. Einar Kárason, *Með sigg á sálinni: Saga Friðriks Þór Friðrikssonar* (Reykjavík: Mál og menning, 2019), 179–80. Among other things, Friðriksson's biography gives a most candid insight into how this world of film festivals and co-productions functions behind the scenes.
10. Jäckel, *European Film Industries*, 28.
11. Pétur H. Blöndal, "Bíóbarn," *Morgunblaðið*, July 24, 1994, 4B.
12. Wenders filmed Ray's final days in *Lightning over Water* (1980), but Ray had earlier played a supporting role in Wenders's *The American Friend* (1977, *Der Amerikanische Freund*). To give just one example of the *Cahiers* critics' admiration of Ray, Jean-Luc Godard wrote: "There was theatre (Griffith), poetry (Murnau), painting (Rossellini), dance (Eisenstein), music (Renoir). Henceforth there is cinema. And the cinema is Nicholas Ray." See "Beyond the Stars," in *Cahiers du Cinéma: The 1950s, Neo-Realism, Hollywood, New Wave*, ed. Jim Hillier (Cambridge, MA: Harvard University Press, 1985), 118.
13. Þórunn Þórsdóttir, "*Djöflaeyjan* verðlaunuð í Rúðuborg: Friðrik braut verðlaunastyttuna í mótmælaskyni." *Morgunblaðið*, March 25, 1997, 26.
14. Personal interview, conducted in September 2004.
15. Erlendur Sveinsson, "Kvikmyndir á Íslandi í 75 ár," in *Kvikmyndir á Íslandi*, ed. Erlendur Sveinsson (Reykjavík: Kvikmyndasafn Íslands, 1981), 25.
16. Erlendur Sveinsson, "Stökkbreytingin," *Morgunblaðið*, September 17, 1995, 12.
17. Sveinsson, "Stökkbreytingin," 12.
18. It is worth emphasizing that the above is by no means intended as a critique of Oddsson and Pálssons's exemplary work. It is the reception of *Tears of Stone* that I find intriguing, of which Erlendsson's review is but one example, in celebrating what was in many ways a typical European production (rather than a specifically Icelandic film) as an Icelandic masterpiece. Conversely, *Cold Fever*'s foreignness was much more obvious and less well received in Iceland.
19. Indeed, Mads Larsen has compared and contrasted the film with other Nordic and North American slacker texts. See "Sealing New Truths: Film Adaptation as Cultural Capstone for *101 Reykjavik*," *Journal of Scandinavian Cinema* 10, no. 1 (2020): 25–44.
20. Regarding the use of music, an even more revealing comparison is found in measuring the documentary *Pop in Reykjavík* (Ágúst Jakobsson, 1998) with the film evoked by its title. Friðrik Þór Friðriksson's *Rock in Reykjavík* studied a particular scene characterized by often little-known bands, and was addressed to a local audience only. *Pop in Reykjavík*, on the other hand, includes a guide directing a foreign audience through the Reykjavík scene. The bands represented all have aspirations of making it abroad, while much more popular bands singing in Icelandic are not represented. Finally, the live footage is from a specially arranged stadium concert, thus taking place at a much larger venue than these bands would have been performing at otherwise. *Pop in Reykjavík* is ultimately about marketing Icelandic bands abroad, while *Rock in Reykjavík* was a documentation of a specific cultural locale.
21. The novels account to some extent for the considerable local emphasis of *Devil's Island* and *Angels of the Universe*, as compared to some of Friðriksson's earlier work in the 1990s, and the novelists also co-wrote the scripts with the director. *Angels of the Universe* relies particularly

on Guðmundsson's playfulness with the Icelandic language and various specific local cultural references. It is worth noting that Friðriksson knew both authors well, and they had plans for film adaptations even before the novels were published. See Kárason, *Með sigg á sálinni*, 223, and 249. Both novels have been translated into English. Einar Kárason, *Devil's Island*, trans. David MacDuff and Magnus Magnusson (Edinburgh: Canongate, 2000), and Einar Már Guðmundsson, *Angels of the Universe*, trans. Bernard Scudder (London: Mare's Nest, 1995).
22. It is worth noting here that *Niceland* was a project developed by the production company Zik Zak Filmworks, and the first film Friðriksson directed without also scripting and producing. According to its credits, *Niceland* is a co-production between Zik Zak, Bavaria Film International, Film & Music Entertainment, Nimbus Film, and Tradewind Pictures, and supported by Euroimages, Film Forderung Hamburg, Filmstiftung NRW, Icelandic Film Centre, Nordic Film and TV Fund, The Danish Film Institute, Invicta Capital Limited, Sveriges Television AB, TV2 Danmark, Canal+, and Glasgow Film Office. This list is suggestive of the complexities of the transnational financing of not only Icelandic cinema in particular but also a considerable bulk of today's world cinema.
23. By 2005, approximately 50,000 European spectators (other than Icelandic) had seen either *Angels of the Universe* or *Devil's Island* in theaters, while only 10,000 saw *Falcons*. For comparison, 350,000 spectators saw *101 Reykjavík* and 190,000 *Noi the Albino* in Europe. See *European Audiovisual Observatory*, accessed in June 2005, https://lumiere.obs.coe.int/. By July 2023, these numbers had increased considerably, but the ratio between them remained constant: the numbers for the Friðriksson films have approximately doubled, *Noi the Albino* has reached 330,000 while *101 Reykjavík* was up to 420,000. *Niceland* conversely does not even reach 5,000 tickets sold, including Iceland. See *European Audiovisual Observatory*, accessed July 8, 2023, https://lumiere.obs.coe.int/movie/23507#. Attendance records from other market zones are not included, but *101 Reykjavík* and *Noi the Albino* were released in the United States and were made available on home video (DVD), while *Devil's Island* was the last of Friðriksson's to be released on home video in the United States.
24. Friðriksson himself, in discussing *Cold Fever*, has pointed out a certain resistance to films with considerable non-Icelandic dialogue: "Films in English always have a difficulty in Iceland. [...] I believe Icelanders only want Icelandic films in Icelandic." Guðni Elísson and Björn Þór Vilhjálmsson, "Með snjóbolta í báðum," *Morgunblaðið*, December 8, 2000, C5. He also mentions as examples *Tears of Stone* and *101 Reykjavík*. It is worth noting that all three did much better than *Falcons* and *Niceland*, which premiered after this interview took place. The subsequent history of Icelandic cinema bears this out as well, and the role of English decreases somewhat after these box-office failures.

Chapter 8

1. See Vigdís Grímsdóttir, *Kaldaljós* (Reykjavík: Iðunn, 1987).
2. Personal interview, conducted in September 2004.
3. Bergljót Soffía Kristjánsdóttir, "'Hann er kominn.'—'Hann er farinn.': Um *Útlagann* og *Gísla sögu Súrssonar*," *Ritið* 1 (2001): 29.
4. For an overview and critique of fidelity criticism, see Brian McFarlane's *Novel to Film: An Introduction to the Theory of Adaptation* (Oxford: Oxford University Press, 1996). McFarlane's book remains one of the most insightful works in the large and heterogeneous field of adaptation studies, but it does not address the issue of transnationalization, and its case studies are limited to English texts.
5. *The Poetic Edda*, trans. Carolyne Larrington (Oxford: Oxford University Press, 1996), 23.
6. Árni Þórarinsson, *Krummi: Hrafns Saga Gunnlaugssonar* (Reykjavík: Fróði, 1994), 170.
7. The different handling of the saga heritage by Gunnlaugsson and Guðmundsson is similar to their different perspectives on the countryside in *Land and Sons* and *Father's Estate* (see chapter six). Guðmundsson elevates both; Gunnlaugsson debunks both.
8. Bjørn Sørenssen, "Hrafn Gunnlaugsson—The Viking Who Came in from the Cold?" in *Transnational Cinema in a Global North: Nordic Cinema in Transition*, ed. Andrew Nestingen and Trevor G. Elkington (Detroit: Wayne State University Press, 2005), 344.
9. Sørenssen, "Hrafn Gunnlaugsson," 345.
10. Sørenssen, "Hrafn Gunnlaugsson," 346.
11. See Þórarinsson, *Krummi*, 174.
12. For a detailed analysis of *In the Shadow of the Raven* in the context of the romance *Tristan and Isolde*, see Jane Chance and Jessica Weinstein, "National Identity and Conversion through

Medieval Romance: The Case of Hrafn Gunnlaugsson's Film *Í skugga hrafnsins*," *Scandinavian Studies* 75 (Fall 2003): 417–38.
13. Interview by author, Reykjavík, September 2004.
14. See "Er málið málið?," *Morgunblaðið*, February 1, 2000, 63.
15. Of the thirty films made in the period, at least twelve (40%) could be classified as comedies.
16. Notably, many of Baltasar Kormákur's adaptations draw at least indirectly from foreign works, especially *White Night Wedding* (2008, *Brúðguminn*) that is loosely based upon Chekov's *Ivanov*. Conversely, the French director Yves Angelo adapted Steinunn Sigurðardóttir's novel *Stolen Life* (*Tímaþjófurinn*) in *Voleur de vie* (1998), which is for all purposes a French film.
17. Personal interview, conducted in September 2004.
18. Hallgrímur Helgason, *101 Reykjavík* (Reykjavík: Mál og menning, 1996), 239, 27, and 63.
19. Hallgrímur Helgason, *101 Reykjavik*, trans. Brian FitzGibbon (London: Faber and Faber, 2002), 56.
20. Helgason, *101 Reykjavik*, 346.
21. It is worth noting in this context that Guðnason and Vilhjálmsdóttir played Hamlet and Ophelia in Kormákur's production of *Hamlet* at the National Theatre in 1997.
22. Helgason, *101 Reykjavik*, 169 and 171.
23. It is therefore not an easily translated novel, and a comparison between the original and the English translation shows the translator running into almost insurmountable obstacles time and time again. An Icelandic television commentator of wildlife television programs becomes David Attenborough (English translation, 269; original Icelandic, 278) while the Newspaper *DV* becomes simply an evening paper (English translation, 274; original Icelandic, 283). And in some of the more difficult local cases the translator has simply skipped them altogether, like Hlynur quoting the film *The Icelandic Shock Station* (Þórhildur Þorleifsdóttir, 1986, *Stella í orlofi*) (original Icelandic, 371).
24. See an extended discussion of *101 Reykjavík*'s transnational production, narrative, and address in chapter six.
25. See Ólafur Haukur Símonarson, *Hafið: Leikrit* (Reykjavík: Skrudda, 2003). Like most theaters, Icelandic theaters have little to gain from a global address as their audience is a domestic one, and in this the theater has much more in common with the explicit national medium of the novel than cinema.
26. See Einar Már Guðmundsson, *Angels of the Universe*, trans. Bernard Scudder (London: Mare's Nest, 1995).
27. Guðni Elísson, "Farandskuggar á tjaldi: Kvikmyndun *Engla alheimsins*," in *Ritið* 1 (2001): 90.
28. Elísson, "Farandskuggar á tjaldi," 91–92.
29. Kristín Marja Baldursdóttir, *Mávahlátur* (Reykjavík: Mál og menning, 2001), 7.
30. Baldursdóttir, *Mávahlátur*, 182–83.

Chapter 9

1. Karl Th. Birgisson "Menningarbylting Sjálfstæðisflokksins," *Stundin*, May 21, 2017, accessed August 18, 2019, https://stundin.is/frett/menningarbylting-sjalfstaedisflokksins/.

Chapter 10

1. For a broad survey of Nordic noir, drawing on interviews with both authors and translators, see Barry Forshaw's *Death in a Cold Climate* (London: Palgrave Macmillan, 2012), while more analytical essays can be found in Stacy Gillis and Gunnþórunn Guðmundsdóttir, *Noir in the North: Genre, Politics and Place* (London: Bloomsbury, 2020).
2. See "Homicide Rate in Europe in 2020, by Country," *Statista*, accessed July 8, 2023, https://www.statista.com/statistics/1268504/homicide-rate-europe-country/.
3. I have exaggerated a bit here, as popular—especially English-speaking—authors like Alistair Maclean and Stephen King were also translated and published, but typically in hardback, and they were marginal rather than central to the industry. If Icelandic authors dealt with crime, it was almost without exception in a non-generic fashion, like Thor Vilhjálmsson's Nordic Council Literary Prize recipient *Justice Undone* (*Grámosinn Glóir*). Also, a paperback tradition did precede the introduction of crime paperbacks, but it constituted a separate publishing and retailing realm (and rarely dealt with crime) and was mostly limited to gas stations and such where book series were sold next to true crime and semi-pornographic magazines.

4. Although Scandinavian crime fiction is currently the most popular as regards Icelandic translations, best-selling American and British crime novelists are also quite popular. Nor should one underestimate the influence of British crime series long popular on local television channels, as Indriðason acknowledges with his forensics expert Ragnar, who is "a particular devotee of British detective series on television." Arnaldur Indriðason, *Tainted Blood*, trans. Bernard Scudder (London: Vintage, 2006), 210.
5. A notable early exception is the work of director Jón Tryggvason and scriptwriter Sveinbjörn Baldvinsson, including *Foxtrot* (Jón Tryggvason, 1988) and *No Trace* (Hilmar Oddsson, 1998, *Sporlaust*).
6. The Icelandic title of the novel is *Mýrin* or "The Mire," but it was first published in English under the title *Tainted Blood*. After the film's release, that title was replaced with the film's English title, *Jar City*. I have kept faith with *Tainted Blood* for the novel to better distinguish it from the film. In 2014 the fourteenth, and apparently last, novel of the series was published in Iceland, and most of them have been translated into English. I have quoted from the English translation by Bernard Scudder.
7. Indriðason, *Tainted Blood*, 37.
8. Indriðason, *Tainted Blood*, 8.
9. Indriðason, *Tainted Blood*, 188.
10. Indriðason, *Tainted Blood*, 306.
11. Indriðason, *Tainted Blood*, 317.
12. Indriðason, *Tainted Blood*, 270.
13. Indriðason, *Tainted Blood*, 305.
14. Andrew Nestingen, *Crime and Fantasy in Scandinavia: Fiction, Film, and Social Change* (Seattle: University of Washington Press, 2008), 53.
15. Nestingen, *Crime and Fantasy in Scandinavia*, 73–75.
16. Tzvetan Todorov, *The Poetics of Prose*, trans. Richard Howard (Ithaca, NY: Cornell University Press, 1977), 42–52.
17. It may be worth noting that in *The Silence of the Grave* (*Grafarþögn*), the series' next installment after *Tainted Blood*, Indriðason makes use of a similar structure to that found in *Jar City* with the narrative moving back and forth in time. Trans. Bernard Scudder (London: Picador, 2007).
18. Brian McFarlane, *Novel to Film: An Introduction to the Theory of Adaptation* (Oxford: Oxford University Press, 1996), 8–9.
19. Roland Barthes, "Introduction to the Structural Analysis of Narrative," in *Image-Music-Text*, trans. Stephen Heath (New York: Hill and Wang, 1977), 79–124.
20. McFarlane, *Novel to Film*, 14.
21. McFarlane, *Novel to Film*, 14.
22. Kristín Árnadóttir, "Hverra manna er Erlendur?: Sögur Arnaldar Indriðasonar um Erlend Sveinsson og tengsl þeirra við sænsku raunsæissakamálasöguna," *TMM* 64, no. 1 (2003): 53 and 55.
23. Seymour Chatman, *Story and Discourse: Narrative Structure in Fiction and Film* (Ithaca, NY, and London: Cornell University Press, 1978), 31. Emphasis in original. Similarly, regarding remakes, Constantine Verevis has pointed out that a remake has both a syntactic component that concerns the narrative structure, and a semantic one that involves its building blocks or iconography. *Film Remakes* (New York: Palgrave MacMillan, 2005), 84.
24. Steve Neale, *Genre and Hollywood* (London and New York: Routledge, 2000), 46.
25. Thomas Leitch, "Twice-Told Tales: Disavowal and the Rhetoric of the Remake," in *Dead Ringers: The Remake in Theory and Practice*, ed. Jennifer Forrest and Leonard R. Koos (Albany: State University of New York, 2002), 45–50.
26. Robert Eberwein, "Remakes and Cultural Studies," in *Play It Again, Sam: Retakes on Remakes*, ed. Andrew Horton and Stuart Y. McDougal (Berkeley and Los Angeles and London: University of California Press, 1998), 28–30.
27. It also has affinities with kinds 9 and 10 that involve changing the race of a main character and retaining the star in the remake, respectively. Such changes occur in the *Contraband* remake regarding a secondary character and a supporting actor.
28. A few years ago, the idea of Icelandic films being remade in Hollywood would have seemed farfetched. Now, in addition to *Contraband*, David Gordon Green has directed an American version of the road movie *Either Way* (Hafsteinn Þór Sigurðsson, 2011, *Á annan veg*) titled *Prince Avalanche* (2013), and in Australia *Rams* was remade by Jeremy Sims under its original

name in 2020. Conversely, *The Texas Chain Saw Massacre* (Tobe Hooper, 1974) was remade in Iceland as the *Reykjavik Whale Watching Massacre* (Júlíus Kemp, 2009).
29. Lucy Mazdon, *Encore Hollywood: Remaking French Cinema* (London: BFI Publishing, 2008), 67 and 69. Emphasis in original.
30. On the film adaptation of *I Remember You*, see Sigrún Margrét Guðmundsdóttir, "Mother's Tomb: The Haunted House in Óskar Þór Axelsson's *I Remember You*," *Journal of Scandinavian Cinema* 11 (March 2021): 49–58.
31. Julie Sanders, *Adaptation and Appropriation* (New York and London: Routledge, 2006), 18.
32. Robert Stam, "Beyond Fidelity: The Dialogics of Adaptation," in *Film Adaptation*, ed. James Naremore (New Brunswick, NJ: Rutgers University Press, 2000), 65–66.
33. Gérard Genette, *Palimpsests: Literature in the Second Degree* (Lincoln: University of Nebraska Press, 1997), 1–7.
34. Much of my information on the production methods of Zik Zak in general, and *Black's Game* in particular, stem from my interview with Ottó Geir Borg, head of development at Zik Zak and a script consultant on the film. Interview by author, Reykjavík, December 2012.
35. Stefán Máni, *Svartur á leik* (Reykjavík: JPV útgáfa, 2012), 333 and 427.
36. In her review, *Variety* critic Leslie Felperin, for example, wrote that the film was "a little too indebted to a slew of like-minded gangster movies, from 'GoodFellas' to exec producer Nicolas Winding Refn's own original 'Pusher' pic." "Review: Black's Game," *Variety*, accessed April 14, 2013, http://variety.com/2012/film/reviews/black-s-game-1117947055/.
37. It could be argued, though, that such close intertextual ties constitute an explicit citation rather than an unacknowledged metatextuality. Certainly, director Axelsson has freely admitted to being influenced by *Trainspotting*, along with other films like *City of God* (Fernando Meirelles, 2002, *Cidade de Deus*) and *Run Lola Run* (Tom Tykwer, 1998, *Lola rennt*). Connie Wilson, "'Black's Game' Details the Rise of the Drug Trade in Iceland at 48th Chicago Film Festival," Yahoo!, accessed April 14, 2013, http://voices.yahoo.com/blacks-game-details-rise-drug-trade-in-11832303.html. However, *Trainspotting* is the quintessential metatext, its intertextuality strengthened by the similarities between the respective novels.
38. An important exception to this is the music that is all Icelandic in the film, very much unlike the music—with heavy metal bands Metallica and AC/DC prominent—listened to by the novel's characters.
39. Kristín Loftsdóttir, Katla Kjartansdóttir, and Katrín Anna Lund, "Trapped in Clichés: Masculinity, Films and Tourism in Iceland," *Gender, Place & Culture* 24, no. 9 (2017): 1226.
40. Loftsdóttir et al., "Trapped in Clichés," 1226.
41. Loftstóttir, Kjartansdóttir, and Lund mention neither of these films, but they group *Trapped* together with *The Sea* (Baltasar Kormákur, 2002, *Hafið*), *Undercurrent* (Árni Ólafur Ásgeirsson, 2010, *Brim*), and *The Deep* (Baltasar Kormákur, 2012, *Djúpið*), two of which are also directed by Kormákur, as prioritizing "Icelandic masculinity as existing in context of harsh Icelandic nature." Loftsdóttir et al., "Trapped in Clichés," 1232. Interestingly, the three films singled out all deal in one way or another with the ocean, and none have Icelandic cinema's conventional summer nature imagery. So perhaps male figures are tied not only to winter but also to the ocean; but I would still claim that overall, women have carried the burden—such that it is—of representing nature in Icelandic cinema. Certainly, the title of *Children of Nature* may refer to both main characters, but it is clearly the female protagonist Stella that has the stronger ties to nature. It is she who insists they leave the city for the countryside, and it is Stella whom we see walk in the tall grass, and later die on the sandy beach, becoming one with her environment. Another relevant connection is popular singer Björk's star persona that is often presented in terms of Icelandic exoticism and nature. The music video of the song "Jóga" (Michel Gondry, 1997) is a particularly pertinent example in this context, as it not only depicts the landscapes of Iceland as a living phenomenon, but makes them one with her as she sings about "emotional landscapes."

Chapter 11

1. Bertrand Westphal, *Geocriticism: Real and Fictional Spaces*, trans. Robert T. Tally, Jr. (New York: Palgrave Macmillan, 2011), 112.
2. Westphal, *Geocriticism*, 121.
3. See, e.g., Toby Miller, Nitin Govil, John McMurria, Ting Wang, and Richard Maxwell, *Global Hollywood*, 2nd ed. (London: BFI, 2008).

4. Karen Oslund, *Iceland Imagined: Nature, Culture, and Storytelling in the North Atlantic* (Seattle: University of Washington Press, 2011), 9. For a historical overview of Iceland's image abroad, including a "Conclusion" in English, see Sumarliði R. Ísleifsson, *Í fjarska norðursins: Ísland og Grænland, viðhorfssaga í þúsund ár* (Reykjavík: Sögufélag, 2020), 305–11.
5. Not as well known as the long-standing whaling controversy—which is far from limited to Iceland—the genetic one regards the access of medical records given to the biopharmaceutical company Decode Genetics. See discussion of *Jar City* in chapter ten.
6. For example, at the turn of the century Iceland had the world's largest film audience (1999), most internet users (2002), and sixth most mobile phones (2002), calculated per capita. Conversely, it did not rate on lists of earthquake and volcano casualties as there were none in the period 1975–2000, although it did top the per capita list of casualties due to avalanches and landslides. Daniel Dorling, Mark Newman, and Anna Barford, *The Atlas of the Real World: Mapping the Way We Live*, 2nd ed. (New York: Thames & Hudson, 2010), 272, 263, 261, 324–25 and 329.
7. Oslund, *Iceland Imagined*, 169.
8. Jules Verne, *Journey to the Centre of the Earth*, trans. William Butcher (Oxford: Oxford University Press, 1998 [1864]), 213.
9. A section of the book where the protagonists study a map of Iceland exemplifies the often-didactic nature of the text: "'See this island of volcanoes,' said the professor, 'and notice that they all bear the name of "jökull." This means "glacier" in Icelandic and, at that northerly latitude, most of the eruptions reach the light of day through the layers of ice. Hence the name "jökull" applied to all the fire producing peaks of the island.'" Verne, *Journey to the Centre of the Earth*, 28. Although the account is not fully accurate; for example, Mount *Hekla* (mentioned in the novel), at that time Iceland's best-known volcano, is not a glacier, while *Snæfellsjökull* (like *Eyjafjallajökull*) is indeed a glacier. On the national cultural relevance of *Snæfellsjökull*, from the medieval *Saga of Bárður Snæfellsás* to the film *101 Reykjavík*, see Ástráður Eysteinsson, "Snæfellsjökull in the Distance: Glacial/Cultural Reflections," in *The Cultural Reconstruction of Places*, ed. Ástráður Eysteinsson (Reykjavík: University of Iceland Press, 2006), 61–70.
10. Verne, *Journey to the Centre of the Earth*, 48–50.
11. Verne, *Journey to the Centre of the Earth*, 202.
12. Verne, *Journey to the Centre of the Earth*, 81.
13. Although a number of Icelandic musicians, including singer Björk and band *Sigur Rós*, have gained worldwide popularity, they have by and large fallen within the exotic nature representation. Their music has been seen to stem organically from its Icelandic origin, and the performers themselves as some sort of sub-species of mankind, if not elves altogether. The ties between nature and music are emphasized in concerts, music videos, and documentaries, including Björk's music video of "Jóga" (Michel Gondry, 1997) in which the landscape comes alive in rhythm with the music, the *Sigur Rós* concert tour documentary *Heima* (Dean DeBlois, 2007) that draws parallels between the band's music and Icelandic nature, and the more expansive documentary *Screaming Masterpiece* (Ari Alexander Ergis Magnússon, 2005, *Gargandi snilld*), which ties the contemporary music scene to Iceland's nature and its Nordic cultural heritage. For an English-language anthology of Icelandic music, see *Sounds Icelandic: Essays on Icelandic Music in the 20th and 21st Centuries*, ed. Nicola Dibben, Thorbjorg Daphne Hall, Arni Heimir Ingolfsson, and Tony Mitchell (Sheffield: Equinox, 2019).
14. Numerous books on the crisis have been published in English, including Eiríkur Bergman's overview, *Iceland and the International Financial Crisis: Boom, Bust and Recovery* (London: Palgrave Macmillan, 2014), and the wide-ranging anthology *Iceland's Financial Crisis: The Politics of Blame, Protest, and Reconstruction*, ed. Valur Ingimundarson, Philippe Urfalino, and Irma Erlingsdóttir (London: Routledge, 2018).
15. Einar Hansen Tómasson, interview by author, Reykjavík, December 3, 2012.
16. Tómasson, interview by author, 2012.
17. *Film in Iceland* (Reykjavík: Promote Iceland, 2012), 2.
18. To give the reader unfamiliar with the geography of Iceland some idea about the locations of its most popular film sites, it may be worth nothing that the island is 103,000 square kilometers and the capital Reykjavík is located in its southwest corner. Its steep fjords are primarily located in the northwest (called Westfjords) and the east (called Eastfjords). Tall mountains and glaciers can be found all over the uninhabited highlands of the interior, although most glacial shooting is done in the southern part of *Vatnajökull* Glacier, especially of such outlet glaciers as *Svínafellsjökull*. Nearby one also finds the glacial lagoon *Jökulsárlón* and the many black sands that characterize the southern coast of Iceland. The Southwest is the greenest and flattest part

of the country, and while lavascapes and rock formations can be found all over, the striking Þingvellir, close to the capital, has been especially popular. Waterfalls are similarly plentiful in all regions, but *Skógarfoss* in the south and *Dettifoss* in the northeast are favorites of runaway productions.
19. Tómasson, interview by author, 2012.
20. *Film in Iceland*, 2. Directors and other creative personnel who have worked in Iceland emphasize this variety in a similar manner. Simon West, director of *Lara Croft: Tomb Raider*, states in "Digging into Tomb Raider" (2001), a "making-of" documentary on the DVD: "[Iceland] gives me a lot of variation on location. There are lakes with icebergs, different sorts of mountains, rolling hills. So I can get a lot of different environments." And Emily Cheung, associate producer on *Oblivion*, observes in "Promise of a New World: The Making of *Oblivion*" (2013): "As soon as you arrive here you understand quite easily why it is being shot for all these different sci-fi locations because there are just so many wonderful different geothermal spots everywhere. You are just driving down the road and you come across a beautiful waterfall, or a geyser or a hot spring and the colors are just amazing. It's like being in another world." Similarly, in "Shooting in Iceland: Miller's Planet/Mann's Planet" (2015), director Christopher Nolan describe his reason for filming *Interstellar* (2014) there: "It's one of the few places in the world where you can get two or three very, very different extreme looks within the space of a couple of miles. And so we went there initially looking for the ice planet. And then we started looking for the water planet because we noticed on the map something that we'd seen years before which was these great deltas where the water goes across the black volcanic material into the sea."
21. *Film in Iceland*, 10.
22. Malcolm Andrews, *Landscape and Western Art* (Oxford: Oxford University Press, 1999), 129.
23. For example, Nilo Otero, first assistant director on *Interstellar*, states: "[For] a science fiction picture like this, you have to go to places that really stamp a kind of reality on the script." Similarly, its star Matthew McConaughey echoes: "Imagination is fun, but when you can get the reality, it's a bonus" ("Shooting in Iceland: Miller's Planet/Mann's Planet," 2015).
24. Andrews, *Landscape and Western Art*, 129.
25. Yi-Fu Tuan, *Space and Place: The Perspective of Experience* (Minneapolis: University of Minnesota Press, 1977), 73.
26. It is worth noting here what may be obvious already to many readers: that this overseas trend, and especially *The Games of Thrones* series, is in many ways inspired by Peter Jackson's *The Lord of the Rings* trilogy (2001–2003) whose fantastical Middle-earth was filmed in his home country of New Zealand. The geology and landscape of the two countries is quite similar, and it has been said (by Icelanders no doubt) that considering the influence of the Old Norse literature heritage upon J. R. R. Tolkien, it would have been more appropriate to film it in Iceland.
27. Following her work with WikiLeaks, Jónsdóttir become part of the incredibly successful political arm of the Pirates party movement. In a historical first, she along with two other members of the party won seats in the national Parliament in 2013, a success much later followed only by the Czech Republic and Luxembourg. However, their success in Iceland remains quite unparalleled, as they won 14.5% of the vote in 2016, and they remain an important part of the current political scene, with 8.6% of the vote in the 2021 election. WikiLeaks has continued to play a crucial role in Iceland; the release of the *Panama Papers* in 2016 led to the resignation of Prime Minister Sigmundur Davíð Gunnlaugsson, while the exposure of the *Fishrot Files* (*Samherjaskjölin*) in 2019 revealed the involvement of Iceland's largest fishing company *Samherji* in briberies intended to secure fishing quotas in Namibia.
28. This is hardly surprising, though, considering it was an Icelandic-US co-production with Friðrik Þór Friðriksson's Icelandic Film Corporation playing a key role.
29. There is also some attempt at incorporating Icelandic folklore and other cultural specificities into the plot of *Eurovision Song Contest: The Story of Fire Saga* (David Dobkin, 2020), as its main characters, singing couple Lars Erickssong (Will Ferrell) and Sigrit Ericksdóttir (Rachel Adams), come from the town of *Húsavík* (mispronounced throughout the film) in the northeast of Iceland. But it is rather half-hearted, and surely any non-cosmopolitan small town in Europe could have played the role of *Húsavík* in the film.
30. Interestingly, Reykjavík was not initially among the series' intended locations, but after Lana and Lilly Wachowski did some minor shooting for their film *Jupiter Ascending* (2015) in Iceland, they redrew their map. Einar Hansen Tómasson, interview by author, Reykjavík, August 27, 2020. It is as good an example as any of the domino effect that even a small runaway production can have for future projects. Similarly, director Nolan explains why he returned to Iceland for

Interstellar in "Shooting in Iceland: Miller's Planet/Mann's Planet" thus: "We went to Iceland because, having shot sections of *Batman Begins*, the stuff set in the Himalayas, we knew the terrain really well. We knew it offered us different looks that we hadn't been able to use in that film."
31. Interview by author, 2020.
32. Norway would have been a more obvious choice than Iceland, as it is so central to the series, but the country has been rather late to join the competition for runaway productions. This has changed in recent years, but interestingly, the Icelandic production company True North has played a leading role in that shift, including work for *Downsizing* (Alexander Payne, 2017), *Mission: Impossible—Fallout* (Christopher McQuarrie, 2018), *No Time to Die* (Cary Joji Fukunaga, 2021)a, and *Dune* (Denis Villeneuve, 2021). In fact, the company is now offering film production services for the entire North Atlantic rather than Iceland specifically and has offices and/or partners in Norway, Faroe Islands, Greenland, and even the Canary Islands/Spain.
33. Tómasson, interview by author, 2020.
34. Pétur Blöndal, "Bíólandið," *Morgunblaðið*, November 25, 2012.
35. Grétarsson Jakob Bjarnar, "Brosið stirðnar á andlitum bíófólks," *Vísir*, September 15, 2022, https://www.visir.is/g/20222311764d/brosid-stirdnar-a-andlitum-biofolks. See also numerous reports and editorials on the film website *Klapptré*, some of which include a belated return to the original national cultural argument, pointing out the limited cultural "value" for Iceland in representing Alaska in an American crime show. Ásgrímur Sverrisson, "Þegar stjórnvöld sigruðu menninguna," *Klapptré*, September 18, 2022, accessed September 19, 2022, https://klapptre.is/2022/09/18/thegar-stjornvold-sigrudu-menninguna/.

Chapter 12

1. For an overview of women directors throughout Icelandic film history, see Guðrún Elsa Bragadóttir, "Out in the Cold? Women Filmmakers in Iceland," in *Women in the International Film Industry: Policy, Practice and Power*, ed. Susan Liddy (London: Palgrave Macmillan, 2020), 179–95. The essay also includes extensive statistical analysis, with Bragadóttir concluding that "women [have directed] roughly one out of [every] ten" Icelandic features, 186.
2. *Academy Awards Acceptance Speech Database*, accessed August 5, 2023, https://aaspeechesdb.oscars.org/link/092-14/.
3. Bragadóttir has proposed that the extreme lack of women filmmakers during the early teens stems from the overall unequal gendered response to the financial collapse of 2008. See "Out in the Cold?" 187.
4. Birna Anna Björnsdóttir, Oddný Sturludóttir, and Silja Hauksdóttir, *Dís* (Reykjavík: Forlagið, 2002).
5. For the problematic integration of gender and tourism, see Heiða Jóhannsdóttir, "Under the Tourist Gaze: Reykjavík as the City That Never Sleeps," in *The Cultural Reconstruction of Places*, ed. Ástráður Eysteinsson (Reykjavík: Háskólaútgáfan, 2006), 111–21.
6. The novel *Dís* drew equally on a plethora of references to Western pop culture and local specificities. As with the novel *101 Reykjavík*, the purpose was not to address foreign readers, but to present realistically Reykjavík's youth as well versed in English slang, pop music, and Hollywood films. At the turn of the century, Reykjavík Icelanders and foreigners interact in English, and conversely, Icelandic youths travel, study, and live abroad. In *Dís* the golden plover no longer introduces the arrival of spring, but the "L.A. boy" who returns home for the summer after a winter-stay in California. Björnsdóttir et al., *Dís*, 5.
7. See, e.g., the documentary *At the Edge of the World* (Bergsteinn Björgúlfsson and Ari Alexander Ergis Magnússon, 2007, *Syndir feðranna*).
8. It is difficult for most filmmakers to finance and produce their first feature film, but during the period 1987–2017 it appeared almost impossible for women to do so. Indeed, the realization that filmmaking was an inherently gendered activity came early to Uggadóttir, when she was a twelve-year-old elementary student preparing for a class party and the girls put together a play while the boys shot a film. Being an acute film fan, she felt both surprise and jealousy that they were able to do this; as a result, she garnered access to a camera soon afterward and began to shoot her own material. Many years later, she took her first film-production courses in Iceland and discovered that they were almost solely taught by men, and as she started to search for her first job in the field she soon realized the expectation was to hire men first and foremost. Ísold Uggadóttir, interview by author, Reykjavík, September 1, 2020.
9. Uggadóttir herself states that with *Committed* style preceded plot, and that she was inspired by both the Dardenne brothers and Andrea Arnold in making the film. Interview by author.

10. This relates to the dilemma I discuss in chapter eleven, where foreign runaway productions provide well-paid jobs for the local film industry, but can also affect and even undermine conventional local productions.
11. Interview with author. Originally Uggadóttir wanted to shoot the film during winter, but as production was delayed she insisted on fall rather than summer.
12. The allegory outlined here need not be evident to all viewers, partly as it draws upon some local specificities. I first saw the film at the International Film Festival in Minneapolis, where it was followed by an unusually heated Q&A session. While some in the audience saw the film as critical of Gísella, others were dismayed by the representation of the lodgers and found their representation problematic. It may not be the sole explanation, but I wonder if it has something to do with the fact that the more explicit allegorical indicators—the blue/white color palette, the falcon, the concluding song—may be less obvious to a non-Icelandic audience.
13. Laura Mulvey, "Visual Pleasure and Narrative Cinema," *Feminist Film Theory*, ed. Sue Thornham (Edinburgh: Edinburgh University Press, 1999), 59–60. First published in *Screen* 16, no. 3 (1975): 6–18.
14. Claire Johnston, "Women's Cinema as Counter-Cinema," in *Feminist Film Theory*, ed. Sue Thornham (Edinburgh: Edinburgh University Press, 1999), 39. First published in *Notes on Women's Cinema*, ed. Claire Johnson (London: Society for Education in Film and Television, 1973), 24–31.
15. Alison Butler, *Women's Cinema: The Contested Screen* (London: Wallflower Press, 2002), 21–22.
16. Butler, *Women's Cinema*, 22. We see this argument supported by many studies of female authorship. For example, Kate Ince analyzes the manifestation of female subjectivity in the works of her chosen directors, including Agnes Varda, Claire Denis, and Andrea Arnold, and in ways that distinguish their films from male subjectivity. *The Body and the Screen: Female Subjectivities in Contemporary Women's Cinema* (London: Bloomsbury, 2017).

Chapter 13

1. For population statistics, see "Inhabitants," *Statistics Iceland*, accessed November 11, 2022, https://statice.is/statistics/population/inhabitants/.
2. "Natural Views: Animals, Contingency and Death in Carlos Reygadas's *Japón* and Lisandro Alonso's *Los Muertos*," in *Slow Cinema*, ed. Tiago de Luca and Nuno Barradas Jorge (Edinburgh: Edinburgh University Press, 2016), 219. My italics.
3. Jonathan Burt, *Animals in Film* (London: Reaktion Books, 2004), 11–12. My italics.
4. "Human and Non-Human Agency in Icelandic Film: *Of Horses and Men*," in *Shared Lives of Humans and Animals: Animal Agency in the Global North*, ed. Tuomas Räsänen and Taina Syrjämaa (London: Routledge, 2017), 27.
5. Compare this to the famous scene in Robert Bresson's *Au Hazard Balthazar* (1966), where we see caged circus animals in point-of-view shots from the perspective of the donkey Balthazar. It is a rare moment in the film that otherwise avoids anthropomorphizing the donkey, but Erlingsson has clearly purposefully avoided such shots altogether.
6. Burt, *Animals in Film*, 38–39.
7. Notably, the film not only begins the end credits with the staple "no animals were harmed" message—actually it only says "horses"—but also informs us that the "entire cast and crew are horse owners and horse lovers."
8. Both directors continued working on similar themes in their next films, but left behind the role played by animals. Erlingsson's *Woman at War* (2018, *Kona fer í stríð*) was another international hit for the director, winning a second Nordic Council Film Prize. Its heroine Halla lives in downtown Reykjavík, but the camera follows her out into nature numerous times as she tries to sabotage environmentally harmful aluminum production in Iceland. So nature certainly continues to play an important role in the film, but it is in the macro sense of big industry and climate change, whose global character is further enforced with a plotline that includes Halla adopting a Ukrainian orphan. However, the micro-level attention to nature on the level of the individual is mostly lost, and animals play little or no role in this environmental drama. Similarly, Hákonarsson's follow-up to *Rams* takes place in a comparable farming community and its title *The County* (2019, *Héraðið*) refers directly to it, but it is no longer focused on animals. In a certain sense it is a much more perplexing departure than *A Woman at War*; *The County* returns to the politics of the 1980 seminal *Father's Estate* but for what purpose is not entirely clear. If the co-op monopoly at the heart of the film is intended to represent contemporary commerce in Iceland, rams or other animals play no role in it.

9. Burt, *Animals in Film*, 177.
10. Burt, *Animals in Film*, 177.
11. Burt, *Animals in Film*, 177.

Epilogue

1. I am not suggesting, though, that it provides a reliable road map that other small nations can follow to develop their own cinemas. Every nation finds itself in a very unique and specific situation depending on its domestic population, economy, culture, religion, social organization, tradition, and heritage, while also being shaped by its geographic location, international relations, and, more specifically, relationship with Hollywood and other centers of film production in the world. In other words, what works for Icelandic national cinema need not work for all. Nonetheless, it would seem as if diversity in terms of financing, production, and distribution would strengthen most, if not all, smaller national cinemas.
2. Both novels have been translated by Philip Houghton and the latter under the title of the original novel rather than the shortened English film title. Jón Kalman Stefánsson, *Summer Light, and Then Comes the Night* (New York: HarperVia, 2022) and Bergsveinn Birgisson, *Reply to a Letter from Helga* (Seattle, WA: Amazon Crossing, 2013).
3. Björn Norðfjörð, *Dagur Kari's Nói the Albino* (Seattle: University of Washington Press, 2010), 120.
4. I discuss the Friðriksson tradition in more detail in my essay "The Emergence of a Tradition in Icelandic Cinema: From *Children of Nature* to *Volcano*," in *A Companion to Nordic Cinema*, ed. Mette Hjort and Ursula Lindquist (New York: Wiley-Blackwell, 2016), 529–46. In this context it is also worth noting the opening credits of the much earlier film *Private Lives* (Þráinn Bertelsson, 1995, *Einkalíf*), a film about filmmaking, which make extensive use of clips from *Iceland in Living Pictures* (Loftur Guðmundsson, 1925, *Ísland í lifandi myndum*).
5. Such a number would have been impossible prior to the digital era, as there is no way A24 would have struck so many prints of the film.
6. It should be noted that when the current banknotes were first introduced, another national hero, the politician Jón Sigurðsson, graced the most valuable banknote, but Hallgrímsson was selected for the latest addition. In the meantime, his birthdate of November 16th was selected for an annual celebration of the Icelandic language.
7. Benjamin Bigelow has also proposed that *Lamb* draws upon Halldór Laxness's most celebrated novel, *Independent People* (*Sjálfstætt fólk*). See "(Un)settling the Land: Colonial and Environmental Violence in Nordic Horror Cinema," in *Transnational Horror, Folklore, and Cultural Politics*, ed. Cüneyt Çakırlar (Liverpool: Liverpool University Press, 2025).
8. Whether to understand this as another reference to Icelandic film history or simply a borrowing of an interesting technique hardly matters, as either way the filmmakers have looked toward Icelandic film history in developing their own film, if also foreign horror traditions like the subjective *Halloween* (John Carpenter, 1978)–style point-of-view opening.
9. Martin Lefebvre, "Between Setting and Landscape in the Cinema," in *Landscape and Film*, ed. Martin Lefebvre (New York: Routledge, 2006), 29.

Bibliography

Anderson, Benedict. *Imagined Communities: Reflections on the Origin and Spread of Nationalism*. London: Verso, 1991.
Andrews, Malcolm. *Landscape and Western Art*. Oxford: Oxford University Press, 1999.
Árnadóttir, Kristín. "Hverra manna er Erlendur?: Sögur Arnaldar Indriðasonar um Erlend Sveinsson og tengsl þeirra við sænsku raunsæissakamálasöguna," *TMM* 64, no. 1 (2003): 50–56.
Baldursdóttir, Kristín Marja. *Mávahlátur*. Reykjavík: Mál og menning, 2001.
Barthes, Roland. "Introduction to the Structural Analysis of Narrative." Translated by Stephen Heath, 79–124. In Barthes, *Image-Music-Text*. New York: Hill and Wang, 1977.
Bazin, André. "The Ontology of the Photographic Image." In *What Is Cinema?* vol. 1, edited by Hugh Gray. Berkeley: University of California Press, 1967.
Benjamin, Walter. "Little History of Photography." Translated by Edmund Jephcott and Kingsley Shorter. In *Walter Benjamin, Selected Writings*, vol. 2, edited by Michael W. Jennings, Howard Eiland, and Cary Smith, 507–30. Cambridge, MA: Harvard University Press, 1999.
Benjamin, Walter. "The Work of Art in the Age of Mechanical Reproduction." Translated by Harry Zohn. In *Illuminations: Essays and Reflections*, edited by Hannah Arendt, 217–51. New York: Schocken Books, 1968.
Bergman, Eiríkur. *Iceland and the International Financial Crisis: Boom, Bust and Recovery*. London: Palgrave Macmillan, 2014.
Bergmundsson, Guðlaugur. "Faith Moves Mountains: The Position of the Icelandic Film-Industry Today." In *Icelandic Films 1980–1983*. Reykjavík: The Icelandic Film Fund, 1983.
Bernharðsson, Eggert Þór. "Landnám lifandi mynda: Af kvikmyndum á Íslandi til 1930." In *Heimur kvikmyndanna*, edited by Guðni Elísson, 803–31. Reykjavík: Forlagið, 1999.
Bigelow, Benjamin. "(Un)settling the Land: Colonial and Environmental Violence in Nordic Horror Cinema." In *Transnational Horror, Folklore, and Cultural Politics*, edited by Cüneyt Çakırlar. Liverpool: Liverpool University Press, 2025.
Billson, Anne. "Volcano Films—Ranked!" *The Guardian*, July 21, 2022. Accessed September 12, 2023, https://www.theguardian.com/film/2022/jul/21/volcano-films-ranked.
Birgisson, Bergsveinn. *Reply to a Letter from Helga*. Translated by Philip Houghton. Seattle, WA: Amazon Crossing, 2013.
Birgisson, Karl Th. "Menningarbylting Sjálfstæðisflokksins." *Stundin*, May 21, 2017. Accessed August 18, 2019, https://stundin.is/frett/menningarbylting-sjalfstaedisflokksins/.
Björnsdóttir, Birna, Anna Oddný Sturludóttir, and Silja Hauksdóttir. *Dís*. Reykjavík: Forlagið, 2002.
Björnsdóttir, Sigríður Hagalín. *The Fires*. Translated by Larissa Kyzer. Seattle, WA: Amazon Crossing, 2023.
Blom, Ivo. "The First Cameraman in Iceland: Travel Film and Travel Literature." In *Picture Perfect*, edited by Laraine Porter and Bryony Dixon, 68–81. Exeter: University of Exeter Press, 2007.
Blöndal, Pétur. "Bíóbarn." *Morgunblaðið*, July 24, 1994.
Blöndal, Pétur. "Bíólandið." *Morgunblaðið*, November 25, 2012.
Borg, Ottó Geir. Interview by author. Reykjavík, December 2012.

Bragadóttir, Guðrún Elsa. "Out in the Cold? Women Filmmakers in Iceland." In *Women in the International Film Industry: Policy, Practice and Power*, edited by Susan Liddy, 179–95. London: Palgrave Macmillan, 2020.
Breiðfjörð, Huldar. "Skrítna Ísland: Um íslenskar vegamyndir." In *Heimur kvikmyndanna*, edited by Guðni Elísson, 962–68. Reykjavík: Forlagið and art.is, 1999.
Breiðfjörð, Huldar. *Góðir Íslendingar: Ferðasaga*. Reykjavík: Bjartur, 1998.
Breiðfjörð, Huldar. *Múrinn í Kína*. Reykjavík: Bjartur, 2004.
Brennan, Timothy "The National Longing for Form." In *Nation and Narration*, edited by Homi K. Bhabha, 44–70. London: Routledge, 1990.
Burt, Jonathan. *Animals in Film*. London: Reaktion Books, 2004.
Butler, Alison. *Women's Cinema: The Contested Screen*. London: Wallflower Press, 2002.
Casanova, Pascale. *The World Republic of Letters*. Translated by M. B. DeBevoise. Cambridge, MA: Harvard University Press, 2004.
Chance, Jane, and Jessica Weinstein. "National Identity and Conversion through Medieval Romance: The Case of Hrafn Gunnlaugsson's Film *Í skugga hrafnsins*." *Scandinavian Studies* 75 (Fall 2003): 417–38.
Chatman, Seymour. *Story and Discourse: Narrative Structure in Fiction and Film*. Ithaca, NY, and London: Cornell University Press, 1978.
Conolly, Jez, and Caroline Whelan, eds. *World Film Locations: Reykjavík*. Bristol: Intellect, 2012.
Crofts, Stephen. "Concepts of National Cinema." In *The Oxford Guide to Film Studies*, edited by John Hill and Pamela Church Gibson, 385–94. Oxford: University of Oxford Press, 1998.
Crofts, Stephen. "Reconceptualizing National Cinema/s." *Quarterly Review of Film or Video* II, no. 3 (1993): 49–67.
De Luca, Tiago. "Natural Views: Animals, Contingency and Death in Carlos Reygadas's *Japón* and Lisandro Alonso's *Los Muertos*." In *Slow Cinema*, edited by Tiago de Luca and Nuno Barradas Jorge, 219–30. Edinburgh: Edinburgh University Press, 2016.
Delluc, Louis. "Cinema: The Outlaw and His Wife." In *French Film Theory and Criticism: A History/Anthology 1907–1939*, vol. 1, edited by Richard Abel, 188. Princeton, NJ: Princeton University Press, 1988.
Dibben, Nicola, Thorbjorg Daphne Hall, Arni Heimir Ingolfsson, and Tony Mitchell, eds. *Sounds Icelandic: Essays on Icelandic Music in the 20th and 21st Centuries*. Sheffield, UK: Equinox, 2019.
Dorling, Daniel, Mark Newman, and Anna Barford. *The Atlas of the Real World: Mapping the Way We Live*, 2nd ed. New York: Thames & Hudson, 2010.
Eberwein, Robert. "Remakes and Cultural Studies." In *Play It Again, Sam: Retakes on Remakes*, edited by Andrew Horton and Stuart Y. McDougal, 15–33. Berkeley and Los Angeles and London: University of California Press, 1998.
Elísson, Guðni. "Farandskuggar á tjaldi: Kvikmyndun *Engla alheimsins*." *Ritið* 1, no. 1 (2001): 77–97.
Elísson, Guðni. "From Realism to Neoromanticism." Translated by Gunnþórunn Guðmundsdóttir. In *A History of Icelandic Literature*, edited by Daisy Neijmann, 327–56. Lincoln: University of Nebraska Press, 2006.
Elísson, Guðni, and Björn Þór Vilhjálmsson. "Með snjóbolta í báðum." *Morgunblaðið*, December 8, 2000.
Ellenberger, Íris. *Íslandskvikmyndir 1916–1966: Ímyndir, sjálfsmynd og vald*. Reykjavík: Sagnfræðistofnun Háskóla Íslands, 2007.
Epstein, Jean. "The Cinema Seen from Etna." Translated by Stuart Liebman. In *Jean Epstein: Critical Essays and New Translations*, edited by Sarah Keller and Jason N. Paul, 287–92. Amsterdam: Amsterdam University Press, 2012.
"Er málið málið?" *Morgunblaðið*. February 1, 2000.
European Audiovisual Observatory. Accessed July 8, 2023, https://lumiere.obs.coe.int/movie/23507#.
European Audiovisual Observatory. Accessed June 2005, https://lumiere.obs.coe.int/.

Eysteinsson, Ástráður. "Snæfellsjökull in the Distance: Glacial/Cultural Reflections." In *The Cultural Reconstruction of Places*, edited by Ástráður Eysteinsson, 61–70. Reykjavík: University of Iceland Press, 2006.

Eysteinsson, Ástráður, and Eysteinn Þorvaldsson. "Modern Literature." In *Iceland: The Republic*, edited by Jóhannes Nordal and Valdimar Kristinsson, 264–86. Reykjavík: Central Bank of Iceland, 1996.

"Feature Films." Icelandic Film Centre. Accessed October 14, 2023, https://www.icelandicfilms.info/films-list/gm/genre/movie.

Felperin, Leslie. "Review: Black's Game." *Variety*, February 10, 2012. Accessed April 14, 2013, http://variety.com/2012/film/reviews/black-s-game-1117947055/.

Film in Iceland. Reykjavík: Promote Iceland, 2012.

Forshaw, Barry. *Death in a Cold Climate*. London: Palgrave Macmillan, 2012.

Forslund, Bengt. *Victor Sjöström: His Life and Work*. Translated by Peter Cowie. New York: New York Zoetrope, 1988.

GAR. "Sturlungaöldin kostar hálfan annan milljarð." *DV*. January 6, 2004.

Genette, Gérard. *Palimpsests: Literature in the Second Degree*. Lincoln: University of Nebraska Press, 1997.

Gillis, Stacy, and Gunnþórunn Guðmundsdóttir, eds. *Noir in the North: Genre, Politics and Place*. London: Bloomsbury, 2020.

Godard, Jean-Luc. "Beyond the Stars." In *Cahiers du Cinéma: The 1950s, Neo-Realism, Hollywood, New Wave*, edited by Jim Hillier, 118–19. Cambridge, MA: Harvard University Press, 1985.

Grétarsson, Jakob Bjarnar. "Brosið stirðnar á andlitum bíófólks." *Vísir*, September 15, 2022, https://www.visir.is/g/20222311764d/brosid-stirdnar-a-andlitum-biofolks.

Grétarsson, Jakob Bjarnar. "Sjö milljarða bíómynd tekin á Íslandi." *Fréttablaðið*, October 5, 2008.

Grímsdóttir, Vigdís. *Kaldaljós*. Reykjavík: Iðunn, 1987.

Grímsson, Ólafur Ragnar. "Foreword." *The Complete Sagas of Icelanders*, vol. 1, edited by Viðar Hreinsson, vii–viii. Reykjavík: Leifur Eiríksson, 1997.

Guðmundsdóttir, Sigrún Margrét. "Mother's Tomb: The Haunted House in Óskar Þór Axelsson's *I Remember You*." *Journal of Scandinavian Cinema* 11, no. 1 (2021): 49–58.

Guðmundsson, Ágúst. Interview by author. Reykjavík, September 2004.

Guðmundsson, Ari Trausti. *Living Earth: Outline of the Geology of Iceland*. Reykjavík: Forlagið, 2013.

Guðmundsson, Ásgeir. "Ísland í lifandi myndum: Áform um kvikmyndatöku á Íslandi á 3. og 4. áratug 20. Aldar." *TMM* 62, no. 4 (2001): 48–59.

Guðmundsson, Einar. *Angels of the Universe*. Translated by Bernard Scudder. London: Mare's Nest, 1995.

Guðmundsson, Halldór. *Halldór Laxness: Ævisaga*. Reykjavík: JPV útgáfa, 2004.

Guðmundsson, Halldór. *The Islander: A Biography of Halldór Laxness*. Translated by Philip Roughton. London: MacLehose Press, 2008.

Guðmundsson, Skarphéðinn. "Fálkasalinn Friðrik." *Morgunblaðið*, June 1, 2002.

Guðmundsson, Skarphéðinn. "Örlítið rafman býr til sól." *Morgunblaðið*, May 16, 2001.

Guðnadóttir, Hildur. *Academy Awards Acceptance Speech Database*. Accessed August 5, 2023, https://aaspeechesdb.oscars.org/link/092-14/.

Gunnarsson, Gunnar. *Borgarættin: Saga*. Reykjavík: Útgáfufélagið Landnáma, 1944.

Gunnarsson, Gunnar. *Guest the One-Eyed*. Translated by W. W. Forster. New York: Alfred A. Knopf, 1922.

Gunning, Tom. "The Cinema of Attractions: Early Film, Its Spectator and the Avant-Garde." In *Early Cinema: Space, Frame, Narrative*, edited by Thomas Elsaesser, 56–62. London: British Film Institute, 1990.

Gunnlaugsson, Hrafn. Interview by author. Reykjavík, September 2004.

Hake, Sabine. *German National Cinema*. London: Routledge, 2002.

Halldórsdóttir, Guðný. Interview by author. Reykjavík, September 2004.
Hallgrímsson, Jónas. "Gunnar's Holm." Translated by Dick Ringler. In *Bard of Iceland: Jónas Hallgrímsson, Poet and Scientist*, 136–38. Madison: University of Wisconsin Press, 2002.
Helgason, Hallgrímur. *101 Reykjavík*. Reykjavík: Mál og menning, 1996.
Helgason, Hallgrímur. *101 Reykjavik*. Translated by Brian FitzGibbon. London: Faber and Faber, 2002.
Helgason, Jón Karl. "The Mystery of Vínarterta: In Search of Icelandic Ethnic Identity." *Scandinavian-Canadian Studies* 17 (2006–2007): 36–52.
Helgason, Jón Karl. *Höfundur Njálu: Þræðir úr vestrænni bókmenntasögu*. Reykjavík: Heimskringla, 2001.
Higson, Andrew. "The Concept of National Cinema." *Screen* 30, no. 4 (1989): 36–46.
Higson, Andrew. *English Heritage, English Cinema: Costume Drama since 1980*. Oxford: Oxford University Press, 2003.
Higson, Andrew. *Waving the Flag: Constructing a National Cinema in Britain*. Oxford: Oxford University Press, 2003.
Hill, John. "The Issue of National Cinema and British Film Production." In *New Questions of British Cinema*, edited by Duncan Petrie, 10–21. London: British Film Institute, 1993.
Hjort, Mette, and Duncan Petrie, eds. *The Cinema of Small Nations*. Edinburgh: Edinburgh University Press, 2007.
Hjort, Mette, and Duncan Petrie. "Introduction." In *The Cinema of Small Nations*, edited by Mette Hjort and Duncan Petrie, 1–19. Edinburgh: Edinburgh University Press, 2007.
Hobsbawm, Eric. *Nations and Nationalism since 1780: Programme, Myth, Reality*. Cambridge: Cambridge University Press, 1990.
Hockenhull, Stella. "Human and Non-Human Agency in Icelandic Film: *Of Horses and Men*." In *Shared Lives of Humans and Animals: Animal Agency in the Global North*, edited by Tuomas Räsänen and Taina Syrjämaa, 24–36. London: Routledge, 2017.
"Homicide Rate in Europe in 2020, by Country." *Statista*. Accessed July 8, 2023, https://www.statista.com/statistics/1268504/homicide-rate-europe-country/.
Ince, Kate. *The Body and the Screen: Female Subjectivities in Contemporary Women's Cinema*. Bloomsbury: London, 2017.
Indriðason, Arnaldur. "Áratugur íslensku kvikmyndarinnar." *Morgunblaðið*, December 13, 1989.
Indriðason, Arnaldur. *The Silence of the Grave*. Translated by Bernard Scudder. London: Picador, 2007.
Indriðason, Arnaldur. "Stofnun og saga kvikmyndafyrirtækisins Edda-film." In *Heimur kvikmyndanna*, edited by Guðni Elísson, 886–93. Reykjavík: Forlagið, 1999.
Indriðason, Arnaldur. *Tainted Blood*. Translated by Bernard Scudder. London: Vintage, 2006.
"Inhabitants." *Statistics Iceland*. Accessed November 11, 2022, https://statice.is/statistics/population/inhabitants/.
Ingimundarson, Valur, Philippe Urfalino, and Irma Erlingsdóttir, eds. *Iceland's Financial Crisis: The Politics of Blame, Protest, and Reconstruction*. London: Routledge, 2018.
Ísleifsson, Sumarliði R. *Í fjarska norðursins: Ísland og Grænland, viðhorfssaga í þúsund ár*. Reykjavík: Sögufélag, 2020.
"Íslenskar kvikmynda og videoútgáfur dreifðar erlendis." *Tíminn*, September 21, 1983.
Jäckel, Anne. *European Film Industries*. London: British Film Institute, 2003.
Jakobsson, Ármann. *Icelandic Literature of the Vikings: An Introduction*. Translated by Andrew E. McGillivray. Reykjavík: Veröld, 2013.
Jóhannsdóttir, Heiða. "Under the Tourist Gaze: Reykjavík as the City That Never Sleeps." In *The Cultural Reconstruction of Places*, edited by Ástráður Eysteinsson, 111–21. Reykjavík: Háskólaútgáfan, 2006.
Jóhannsson, Jón Yngvi. "'Jøklens Storm svalede den kulturtrætte Denmarks Pande': Um fyrstu viðtökur dansk-íslenskra bókmennta í Danmörku." *Skírnir* 175, no. 1 (2001): 33–66.

Johnston, Claire. "Women's Cinema as Counter-Cinema." In *Feminist Film Theory*, edited by Sue Thornham, 31–40. Edinburgh: Edinburgh University Press, 1999. First published in *Notes on Women's Cinema*, edited by Claire Johnson, 24–31. London: Society for Education in Film and Television, 1973.

Kamban, Guðmundur. *Hadda Padda: A Drama in Four Acts*. Translated by Sadie Luise Peller. New York: Alfred A. Knopf, 1917.

Kárason, Einar. *Devil's Island*. Translated by David MacDuff and Magnus Magnusson. Edinburgh: Canongate, 2000.

Kárason, Einar. *Með sigg á sálinni: Saga Friðriks Þórs Friðrikssonar*. Reykjavík: Mál og menning, 2019.

Kracauer, Siegfried. *From Caligari to Hitler: A Psychological History of the German Film*. Princeton, NJ: Princeton University Press, 1947.

Kracauer, Siegfried. *History: The Last Things before the Last*. Princeton, NJ: Markus Wieners, 1995.

Kracauer, Siegfried. *Theory of Film: The Redemption of Physical Reality*. Princeton, NJ: Princeton University Press, 1997.

Kress, Helga. "Guðmundur Kamban og verk hans: Í tilefni heildarútgáfu Almenna bókafélagsins," *Skírnir* 144 (1970): 164–84.

Kriscak, Gaia. "The 10 Best Movies about Volcanoes and Eruptions, Ranked." *WhatNerd*, June 4, 2023. Accessed September 12, 2023, https://whatnerd.com/best-movies-about-volcanoes-ranked/.

Kristjánsdóttir, Bergljót Soffía. "'Hann er kominn.'—'Hann er farinn.': Um *Útlagann* og *Gísla sögu Súrssonar*." *Ritið* 1, no. 1 (2001): 23–40.

Kristófersson, Gunnar Tómas. "Fyrir listina að lifa af: Um gerð og útgáfur kvikmyndar Óskars Gíslasonar *Björgunarafrekið við Látrabjarg*." *TMM* 84, no. 1 (2023): 82–91.

Kristófersson, Gunnar Tómas. "Meistari rammans: Um kvikmyndagerð Kjartans Ó. Bjarnasonar," *Skírnir* 197, no. 1 (Spring 2023): 43–44.

Kristófersson, Gunnar Tómas. "Ódauðleg dansspor: Ruth Hanson og dansmyndin." *Saga* 54, no. 2 (2021): 7–17.

Kristófersson, Gunnar Tómas. "Upphaf kvikmyndaaldar á Íslandi." *Ritið* 19, no. 2 (2019): 43–68.

Larsen, Mads. "Sealing New Truths: Film Adaptation as Cultural Capstone for 101 Reykjavik." *Journal of Scandinavian Cinema* 10, no. 1 (2020): 25–44.

Laxness, Halldór Kiljan. *Salka Valka: A Novel of Iceland*. Translated by F. H. Lyon. New York: Houghton Mifflin, 1936.

Laxness, Halldór Kiljan. "Some Outlines of a Motion Picture from Icelandic Coast-Life." *TMM* 65, no. 4 (2004): 11–18.

Lefebvre, Martin. "Between Setting and Landscape in the Cinema." In *Landscape and Film*, edited by Martin Lefebvre, 19–59. New York: Routledge, 2006.

Leitch, Thomas. "Twice-Told Tales: Disavowal and the Rhetoric of the Remake." In *Dead Ringers: The Remake in Theory and Practice*, edited by Jennifer Forrest and Leonard R. Koos, 37–62. Albany: State University of New York Press, 2002.

List, Friedrich. *The National System of Political Economy*. Translated by Sampson S. Lloyd. London: Longman, Green, 1885.

Loftsdóttir, Kristín, Katla Kjartansdóttir, and Katrín Anna Lund. "Trapped in Clichés: Masculinity, Films and Tourism in Iceland." *Gender, Place & Culture* 24, no. 9 (2017): 1225–42.

Máni, Stefán. *Svartur á leik*. Reykjavík: JPV útgáfa, 2012.

Mazdon, Lucy. *Encore Hollywood: Remaking French Cinema*. London: BFI, 2008.

McFarlane, Brian. *Novel to Film: An Introduction to the Theory of Adaptation*. Oxford: Oxford University Press, 1996.

Miller, Toby, Nitin Govil, John McMurria, Ting Wang, and Richard Maxwell. *Global Hollywood*, 2nd ed. London: BFI, 2008.

Møller, Birgir Thor. "In and Out of Reykjavík: Framing Iceland in the Global Daze." In *Transnational Cinema in a Global North: Nordic Cinema in Transition*, edited by Andrew Nestingen and Trevor G. Elkington, 307–40. Detroit: Wayne State University Press, 2005.

Moretti, Franco. *Atlas of the European Novel 1800–1900*. London: Verso, 1999.

Mulvey, Laura. "Visual Pleasure and Narrative Cinema." In *Feminist Film Theory*, edited by Sue Thornham, 58–69. Edinburgh: Edinburgh University Press, 1999. First published in *Screen* 16, no. 3 (1975): 6–18.

Mulvogue, Jessica. "Cinema as Volcano: Thinking Cinema through the Volcano with Malena Szlam, Werner Herzog and Jean Epstein." *Studies in World Cinema* 3 (2023): 83–103.

Neale, Steve. *Genre and Hollywood*. London and New York: Routledge, 2000.

Nestingen, Andrew. *Crime and Fantasy in Scandinavia: Fiction, Film, and Social Change*. Seattle: University of Washington Press, 2008.

Nichols, Bill. *Introduction to Documentary*, 3rd ed. Bloomington: Indiana University Press, 2017.

Njal's Saga. Translated by Robert Cook. *The Complete Sagas of Icelanders*, vol. 3, edited by Viðar Hreinsson, 1–220. Reykjavík: Leifur Eiríksson, 1997.

Norðfjörð, Björn. "Adapting a Literary Nation to Film: National Identity, Neoromanticism and the Anxiety of Influence." *Scandinavian Canadian Studies* 19, no. 1 (2010): 12–40.

Norðfjörð, Björn. "Crime Up North." In *Nordic Genre Film*, edited by Pietari Kääpä and Tommy Gustafsson, 61–75. Edinburgh: University of Edinburgh Press, 2015.

Norðfjörð, Björn. *Dagur Kari's Nói the Albino*. Seattle: University of Washington Press, 2010.

Norðfjörð, Björn. "The Emergence of a Tradition in Icelandic Cinema: From *Children of Nature* to *Volcano*." In *A Companion to Nordic Cinema*, edited by Mette Hjort and Ursula Lindquist, 529–46. New York: Wiley-Blackwell, 2016.

Norðfjörð, Björn. "Hollywood Does Iceland: Authenticity, Genericity and the Picturesque." In *Films on Ice*, edited by Anna Westerstahl Stenport and Scott MacKenzie, 176–86. Edinburgh: University of Edinburgh Press, 2014.

Norðfjörð, Björn. "Iceland." In *The Cinema of Small Nations*, edited by Mette Hjort and Duncan Petrie, 43–59. Edinburgh: Edinburgh University Press, 2007.

Norðfjörð, Björn. "Iceland in Living Pictures: A Meeting Place of Cinema and Nation." *Studia Humanistyczne* 10, no. 1 (2011): 169–183.

Norðfjörð, Björn. "Icelandic Cinema." In *Oxford Bibliographies in Cinema and Media Studies*, edited by Krin Gabbard. New York: Oxford University Press, 2023.

Norðfjörð, Björn. "The Transnational Remake: Crossing Borders with *Contraband*." *Journal of Scandinavian Cinema* 4, no. 2 (2014): 93–97.

Norðfjörð, Björn. "'A Typical Icelandic Murder?' The 'Criminal' Adaptation of *Jar City*." *Journal of Scandinavian Cinema* 1, no. 1 (2011): 37–49.

"Number of National Feature Films Produced: Countries Compared." *NationMaster*. Accessed October 14, 2023, https://www.nationmaster.com/country-info/stats/Media/Cinema/Number-of-national-feature-films-produced#2010.

Ólason, Vésteinn. *Samræður við söguöld: Frásagnarlist Íslendingasagna og fortíðarmynd*. Reykjavík: Heimskringla, 1998.

Oslund, Karen. *Iceland Imagined: Nature, Culture, and Storytelling in the North Atlantic*. Seattle: University of Washington Press, 2011.

Pálmadóttir, Elín. "Geymir ómetanleg menningarverðmæti." *Morgunblaðið*, February 14, 1993.

Past, Elena. *Italian Ecocinema beyond the Human*. Bloomington: Indiana University Press, 2019.

Petersen, Peter. "Ævisaga kvikmyndahúsaeigandans P. Petersen." Translated by Gunnar Tómas Kristófersson. Unpublished (original date 1932).

Petrie, Duncan. "The New Scottish Cinema." In *Cinema & Nation*, edited by Mette Hjort and Scott MacKenzie, 153–69. London: Routledge, 2000.

The Poetic Edda. Translated by Carolyne Larrington. Oxford: Oxford University Press, 1996.

Price, Neil. *Children of Ash and Elm: A History of the Vikings.* New York: Basic Books, 2020.
Prince, Stephen. *A New Pot of Gold: Hollywood under the Electronic Rainbow, 1980–1989.* Berkeley: University of California Press, 2000.
Rabinovitz, Lauren. *For the Love of Pleasure: Women, Movies, and Culture in Turn-of-the-Century Chicago.* New Brunswick, NJ: Rutgers University Press, 1998.
Ross, Margaret Clunies. *The Old Norse-Icelandic Saga.* Cambridge: Cambridge University Press, 2010.
Sanders, Julie. *Adaptation and Appropriation.* New York and London: Routledge, 2006.
Scholes, Robert, and Robert Kellogg. *The Nature of Narrative.* Oxford: Oxford University Press, 1966.
Sigurðsson, Gísli. "Icelandic National Identity: From Romanticism to Tourism." In *Making Europe in Nordic Context*, edited by Pertti J. Anttonen, 41–75. Turku: NIF, 1996.
Sigurðsson, Haraldur. *Melting the Earth: The History of Ideas on Volcanic Eruptions.* Oxford: Oxford University Press, 1999.
Sigurðsson, Helgi Snær. "Nær helmingur þjóðarinnnar í bíó." *Morgunblaðið*, September 9, 2008.
Sigurjónsson, Jóhann. *Eyvind of the Hills.* Translated by Henninge Krohn Schanche. New York: American Scandinavian Foundation, 1916.
Símonarson, Ólafur Haukur. *Hafið: Leikrit.* Reykjavík: Skrudda, 2003.
Sørenssen, Bjørn. "Hrafn Gunnlaugsson—The Viking Who Came in from the Cold?" In *Transnational Cinema in a Global North: Nordic Cinema in Transition*, edited by Andrew Nestingen and Trevor G. Elkington, 341–56. Detroit: Wayne State University Press, 2005.
Stam, Robert. "Beyond Fidelity: The Dialogics of Adaptation." In *Film Adaptation*, edited by James Naremore, 54–76. New Brunswick, NJ: Rutgers University Press, 2000.
Stefánsson, Jón Kalman. *Summer Light, and Then Comes the Night.* Translated by Philip Houghton. New York: HarperVia, 2022.
Sveinsson, Erlendur. "Árin tólf fyrir daga Sjónvarps og Kvikmyndasjóðs." In *Heimur kvikmyndanna*, edited by Guðni Elísson, 868–73. Reykjavík: Forlagið, 1999.
Sveinsson, Erlendur. "Frekar bogna en brotna: Um frumkvöðul í íslenskri kvikmyndagerð." In *Enginn getur lifað án Lofts: Loftur Guðmundsson konunglegur hirðljósmyndari og kvikmyndagerðarmaður í Reykjavík*, edited by Inga Lára Baldvinsdóttir, 19–62. Reykjavík: Þjóðminjasafn Íslands, 2002.
Sveinsson, Erlendur. "Kvikmyndir á Íslandi í 75 ár." In *Kvikmyndir á Íslandi*, edited by Erlendur Sveinsson, 25–32. Reykjavík: Kvikmyndasafn Íslands, 1981.
Sveinsson, Erlendur. "Landsýn-heimssýn: Kynningarmáttur kvikmyndarinnar á fjórða áratugnum." In *Heimur kvikmyndanna*, edited by Guðni Elísson, 852–58. Reykjavík: Forlagið, 1999.
Sveinsson, Erlendur. "Lífssaga kvikmyndar: Eða hvernig *Saga Borgarættarinnar* varð þjóðkvikmynd Íslands." *TMM* 81, no. 1 (2020): 28–58, https://tmm.forlagid.is/lifssaga-kvikmyndar/.
Sveinsson, Erlendur. "Stökkbreytingin." *Morgunblaðið*. September 17, 1995.
Sverrisson, Ásgrímur. "Þegar stjórnvöld sigruðu menninguna." *Klapptré*, September 18, 2022. Accessed September 19, 2022, https://klapptre.is/2022/09/18/thegar-stjornvold-sigrudu-menninguna/.
Sverrisson, Ásgrímur, and Gunnþóra Halldórsdóttir. "Sagan af fyrstu íslensku kvikmyndinni í Cannes og höfundi hennar," *Klapptré*, September 6, 2023. Accessed September 10, 2023, https://klapptre.is/2023/09/06/sagan-af-fyrstu-islensku-kvikmyndinni-i-cannes-og-hofundi-hennar/.
Þórarinsson, Árni. *Krummi: Hrafns Saga Gunnlaugssonar.* Reykjavík: Fróði, 1994.
Þorgeirsson, Halldór. Interview by author. Reykjavík, September 2004.
Þórisson, Snorri. Interview by author. Reykjavík, September 2004.
Þórsdóttir, Þórunn. "*Djöflaeyjan* verðlaunuð í Rúðuborg: Friðrik braut verðlaunastyttuna í mótmælaskyni." *Morgunblaðið*, March 25, 1997.

Þorsteinsson, Indriði G. *Tímar í lífi þjóðar*. Reykjavík: Vaka-Helgafell, 2004.
Todorov, Tzvetan. *The Poetics of Prose*. Translated by Richard Howard. Ithaca, NY: Cornell University Press, 1977.
Tómasson, Einar Hansen. Interview by author. Reykjavík, December 3, 2012.
Tómasson, Einar Hansen. Interview by author. Reykjavík, August 27, 2020.
Tuan, Yi-Fu. *Space and Place: The Perspective of Experience*. Minneapolis: University of Minnesota Press, 1977.
Tucker, John. "*Land og synir*: An Interview with Ágúst Guðmundsson." *Scandinavian-Canadian Studies* 19 (2010): 42–54.
Uggadóttir, Ísold. Interview by author. Reykjavík, September 1, 2020.
UNESCO. "A Survey on National Cinematography." Accessed April 7, 2005, http://www.unesco.org/culture/industries/cinema/html_eng/prod.html.
Valdimarsdóttir, Alda. *Rithöfundur Íslands*. Reykjavík: Bókmenntafræðistofnun Háskóla Íslands, 2008.
Verevis, Constantine. *Film Remakes*. New York: Palgrave MacMillan, 2005.
Verne, Jules. *Journey to the Centre of the Earth*. Translated by William Butcher. Oxford: Oxford University Press, 1998.
Westphal, Bertrand. *Geocriticism: Real and Fictional Spaces*. Translated by Robert T. Tally, Jr. New York: Palgrave Macmillan, 2011.
Williams, Raymond. *The Country and the City*. New York: Oxford University Press, 1973.

Index

For the benefit of digital users, indexed terms that span two pages (e.g., 52–53) may, on occasion, appear on only one of those pages.

Figures are indicated by an italic *f* following the page number.

2 Guns (2012), 127–28, 146
3D, 162
101 Reykjavík (2000), 41, 68–69, 87, 103–6, 118–20, 122–23, 124, 134–35, 178–80
400 Blows, The (1959), 94–95

Abbababb! (2022), 214, 217–18
Abril, Victoria, 103
action film, 143–44, 176–77, 218
actualities, 7–8, 13–14
Aðalsteins, Elfar, 215–16
adaptation. *See* film adaptation
Adrift (2018), 127–28
Adventures of Jon and Gvendur, The (1923), 10, 21–22
Against the Ice (2022), 219
Agnes (1995), 68–69, 197–98
Agnes Joy (2019), 178, 180–81, 192–93
Ágústsson, Bogi, 171–72
Ahead of Time (2004,), 124–25
Akranes, 86, 105–6, 180
Akureyri, 64, 197
Albarn, Damon, 104
Alistair, Maclean, 243n.3
Alma (2021), 216–18
Almodóvar, Pedro, 103
And Breathe Normally (2018), 128–29, 178, 186–88, 187*f*, 190–93, 194
Andersen, Hans Christian, 228
Anderson, Benedict, 31
Andree, Ingrid, 103*f*
Andrews, Malcolm, 165–66
Angelo, Yves, 243n.16
Angels of the Universe (2000), 74–75, 106, 107, 120, 122–23, 124
animals, 197–212, 223–24
animation, 127–28, 173–74
Anspach, Sólveig, 176
Arctic (2018), 169
Arctic, 68–69, 70, 158, 164–70

Arenson, Eli, 224
Árnadóttir, Kristín, 141–42
Arnalds, Ólafur, 177
Around the World in 80 Days (1956), 161–62
art cinema, 1–2, 4–5, 74, 90–91, 101–3, 104–5, 106–7, 116–17, 125, 129, 151, 197, 198–99, 213–14, 216–18
As in Heaven (1992), 74, 83, 99–100
Ash (2013), 67
Askja, 51–52, 67–68
Assange, Julian, 171–72
Astropia (2007), 126
At the Edge of the World (2007), 248n.7
Atom Station (1984), 45, 48, 72, 83–84, 98–99, 109–10
Atomic Blonde (2017), 176–77
Au Hazard Balthazar (1966), 249n.5
auteur, 94, 96, 101, 103, 106–7, 113–14, 149, 199
avant-garde cinema, 60–62, 61*f*
awards,
    Academy Award, 93, 176–77
    BAFTA, 176–77
    Emmy, 176–77
    Golden Globe, 176–77
    Grammy, 176–77
    Nordic Council Film Prize, 129, 200, 221–22, 224, 249n.8
    Nordic Council Literary Prize, 243n.3
    Un Certain Regard, 129, 202
Axel, Gabriel, 10–11
Axelsson, Óskar, 127–29, 147, 148–49, 151, 218–19
Axelsson, Ragnar, 70

Back Soon (2008), 176
Baldursdóttir, Kristín Marja, 121–22
Baldvinsson, Sveinbjörn, 244n.5
Bale, Christian, 168*f*
Balling, Erik, 10–11, 24, 25
Balog, James, 69–70

Barthes, Roland, 140
Batman Begins (2005), 167
Bazin, André, 232n.2
Beast, The (1987), 74, 101
Beautiful Beings (2022), 216–17
Behind Schedule (1993), 74, 86–87, 104
Benediktsson, Einar Örn, 104
Benjamin, Walter, 15–16
Bennent, Heinz, 101–2, 103*f*
Bergsson, Guðbergur, 181–82
Bertelsson, Þráinn, 83
Between Mountain and Shore (1948), 10, 21, 24–25
Big Rescue, The (2009), 126
Bigelow, Benjamin, 250n.7
Birgisson, Bergsveinn, 215–16
Birta (2021), 214
Birth of an Island (1965), 59–63, 61*f*, 65–66
Bjarnason, Kjartan Ó., 9–10, 52–53, 54–55
Björk, 99, 245n.41, 246n.13
Björnsdóttir, Birna Anna, 178–79
Björnsson, Björn Br., 48
Black Angels (2008), 133–34
Black's Game (2012), 127–28, 147–51, 153, 155
Blómkvist, Stella, 133
Bloom, Harold, 235n.11
Blue Lagoon, 96–97, 171–72
Boone, Pat, 161*f*
Borgarfjörður eystri, 211
Boucher, Alan, 59–60
box office, 3–4, 17, 21–22, 46–47, 48, 72–73, 74–75, 83, 91, 106, 107, 120, 124–25, 129, 131, 134–35, 139, 147, 213–14, 215–16, 218, 221–22
Boy and a Girl, A, 31
Bragadóttir, Guðrún Elsa, 248n.1, 248n.3
Bragason, Ragnar, 124, 125, 193–94
Breathless (1960), 145–46
Breathless (1983), 145–46
Breiðfjörð, Huldar, 88
Brennan, Timothy, 31
Bridge, The (2011–2018), 131, 151, 152–53
Broström, Gunnel, 45
Brynolfsson, Reine, 100–1, 115
Bullet Train (2022), 176–77
Burkert, Paul, 19
Burning-Njal's Saga (1981), 89
Burt, Jonathan, 198–99, 201–2, 204–5, 209, 212
Butler, Alison, 195–96

Cahiers du Cinema, 94
Carradine, Keith, 106–7
Casanova, Pascale, 32–33
Case: Ritual of Abduction (2015), 151
Celebration, The (1998), 176
Chaplin, Charlie, 20–21, 98–99
Chasing Ice (2012), 69–70
Chatman, Seymour, 143–44
Chernobyl (2019), 176–77
Cheung, Emily, 247n.20
Child of Nature, 43
Children (2006), 125, 193–94
Children of Nature (1991), 57, 74, 90–91, 92–94, 99–100, 106, 153–55, 192–93, 220–21
children's films, 126, 127–28, 213–14, 217–18, 240n.1, 240n.10
Circle, The (1985), 89
City State (2011/2014), 127–28, 147, 149–51, 155
city symphony, 19–20
Clean (2010), 185–86
Cliff, The (2009), 133–34
Cliff: Depth of Darkness, The (2014), 151
climate change, 69–70
Clooney, George, 168–69
Codex Regius, 50
Cold Fever (1995), 41, 68–69, 95–97, 99–100, 105, 106–8, 188, 197–98
Cold Light (2004), 68–69, 101, 109, 119–20, 153–55
Cold Trail (2006), 68–69, 126, 133–34, 155
colonialism, 224–25, 226–28, 235n.18
comedy, 20–21, 23–24, 67–68, 72–73, 82–84, 85, 116–17, 125–26, 193–94, 213–14, 217–18
Committed (2008), 185–86
computer-generated imagery (CGI), 165–67, 168–69
Contraband (2010), 127–28, 142–46, 155, 176–77
Cop Secret (2021), 218
Copenhagen, 29–30, 33–35, 36–37, 43
Country between the Sands, The (1964), 57
Country Wedding (2008), 176
countryside, 22–23, 24–27, 76–83, 94–95, 97–98, 99–100, 181–84, 197–98, 204, 205, 216
County, The (2019), 249n.8
Covetousness (1952), 10, 233–34n.18
COVID-19, 173
Cowboys of the North, The, (1984), 89–90, 96–97
co-productions, 24, 27, 48, 73–74, 89, 91–92, 104, 115, 224–25
crime fiction, 131, 132–33, 134–42, 148–49
crime films, 126, 127–28, 131, 133–46, 147–51, 218

INDEX 261

crime television series, 126, 127–28, 131, 133–34, 151–55
Crofts, Stephen, 2–3
Cruise, Tom, 126–27
currency, 164, 173

Damon, Matt, 163–64
Dance, The (1998), 117
Dancer in the Dark (2000), 99, 177
Dark Horse (2005), 125
Days of Destruction (1973), 63
Days of Sunshine in Iceland (1950), 9
de Luca, Tiago, 198–99, 205
Dead Snow 2: Red vs. Dead (2014), 169
Dear Icelanders, 88
deCODE Genetics, 138–39, 246n.5
Deep, The (2012), 68–69, 127–28, 245n.41
Delluc, Louis, 36
Deposit, The (2019), 128–29, 178, 189–94, 191f, 196, 217–18
Dettifoss, 64–65, 156, 246–47n.18
Devil's Island (1996), 74–75, 97–99, 98f, 106, 107
Die Another Day (2002), 126–27, 169–70
Dís (2004), 176, 178–80
Displaced One, The, (1951), 23
distribution. *See* exhibition
diversity, 72–73, 184–88, 194
documentary, 8–12, 14–20, 53, 54–66, 67–70, 72–73, 89–90, 126, 213–14
Dosa, Sara, 49–50, 63–64
Dot Dot Comma Dash (1981), 48, 72, 83–84, 109–10
Douglas, Róbert I., 124
Downsizing (2017), 248n.32
Dream Hunters (1996), 74–75
Dreamland (2009), 126
Dreyer, Carl Theodor, 47–48
Driving Mum (2022), 216–17, 221
Dune (2021), 248n.32

early cinema, 7–8, 13–20
Eberwein, Robert, 144–45, 153
Echo (2019), 192–93
ecocinema, 54
Edda-film, 10–11, 24, 45, 47–48
Egil's Saga, 46–47
Einarsson, Jakob Þór, 114f
Either Way (2011), 129, 220–21
Ekmanner, Agneta, 100–1
Eldjárn, Kristján, 56–58
Elísson, Guðni, 120
Ellenberger, Íris, 232n.6, 233n.10

End of Summer (2014), 70
environment, 11, 35, 40, 43–44, 54, 56–59, 62, 70, 126, 156–57, 163–64, 165–66, 205–8, 225–28, 249n.8
Epstein, Jean, 53–54
Erlingsson, Benedikt, 128–29
Erlingsson, Gísli Snær, 74, 86–87
Eruption on Mount Fimmvörðuháls (2010), 67
Eskifjörður (1924), 15
Eternal Sunshine of the Spotless Mind (2004), 176
ethnicity, 128–29, 180, 191–92, 194
Eurimages, 73–74, 91–92, 95, 219–20
Eurovision Song Contest: The Story of Fire Saga (2020), 219, 247n.29
Every Colour of the Sea Is Cold (2005), 133–34
exhibition, 2–3, 7–8, 9, 14, 73, 82, 86–87, 91, 134–35, 174
    international, 23–24, 48, 93, 96–97, 106, 107–8, 213–14
exoticism, 1, 19, 35, 50, 95, 103–4, 129–30, 164, 165–67, 169–70, 188, 206–8, 226–28
experimental cinema, 59–62, 70, 89
Eyfjörð, Guðrún Ýr, 50
Eyjafjallajökull, 66–67, 126, 164
Eyjafjörður, 222
Eyjólfsdóttir, Edda Björg, 123f
Eyjólfsson, Gunnar, 24–25, 26f

Falcons (2002), 43–44, 106–7
Family Reunion (2006), 184–85
fantasy film, 67–68, 126, 168–69, 222–23
Fate of the Furious, The (2017), 166–67
Father's Estate (1980), 72, 76–83, 90, 99, 114, 197–98, 249n.8
femme fatale, 141–42
Ferch, Heino, 121
Fernander, David, 7–8
festivals, 74, 90–91, 129, 213–14
    Cannes, 90–91, 129, 239n.15
    Patreksfjörður (Skjaldborg), 126
    Reykjavík, 90–91
    Rouen, 99
    Sundance, 184–85
    Tribeca, 129
Fiasco (2000), 124
fidelity criticism, 140
Fifth Estate, The (2013), 171–72
film adaptation,
    of contemporary novels, 74–75, 97, 104, 118, 178–80, 214–16
    of crime fiction, 134–42, 147–51, 218–19

film adaptation (*cont.*)
    of Icelandic sagas, 46–48, 72, 89, 109–16, 123
    of *Journey to the Centre of the Earth*, 160–62
    of neo-romanticist works, 33–43
    of prestige literary works, 72, 77–79, 82–83, 109–10, 117
    transnational, 75, 116–23
    of works by Halldór Laxness, 45–46, 100–1, 123
financial crisis (2008–2011), 126, 152–53, 162–64, 171–72
Fire and Iceland (2022), 50, 67
Fire in Hekla (1949/1972), 54–56, 56*f*
Fire of Love (2022), 49–50, 51, 52, 63–64
Fire on Heimaey (1974), 62–63, 67–68
Fire Within: A Requiem for Katia and Maurice Krafft, The (2022), 63–64
Firemen Practice in Reykjavík (1906), 7–8, 13–14*f*, 15–16, 229
Fires, The, 240n.21
Fischer, Bobby, 162–63, 171–72
Fish Can Sing, The (1972), 237n.46
Fishing Trip, The (1980), 240n.1
Fistful of Dollars, A (1964), 113–14
FitzPatrick, James A., 19
Flags of Our Fathers (2006), 169
Flaherty, Robert, 239n.10
Flat Charleston (1927), 232n.7
Flatey Enigma, The (2018), 151
Flying to Greenland (1966), 11
folklore, 22–24, 67–68, 101, 172
Fortitude (2015–2018), 169
Foxtrot (1987), 99–100, 244n.5
Friðriksson, Friðrik Þór, 27–28, 72–73, 74–75, 89–100, 106–8, 116–17, 120, 124–25, 128–29, 192–93, 220–21
Frost (2012), 68–69, 127–28

Game of Thrones (2011–2019), 168–69, 173–74
gangster film, 148, 151
Ganz, Bruno, 92–93, 93*f*
Garden, The (2020), 193–94
Geldingardalir Valley, 66–68
gender, 128–29, 140–42, 153–55, 176–96, 217–18
Genette, Gérard, 147–48
genre cinema, 1–2, 68–69, 125, 126–28, 133, 196, 213–14, 217–19
geology, 1, 17
Girl Gogo, The (1962), 10–11, 24–28, 26*f*, 48, 77, 98–99, 220–21
Gíslason, Óskar, 9–10, 19–20, 22–24, 219–20
Gisli Sursson's Saga, 46–47, 72, 109–13

Glacial Adventure (1953), 64–65
Glacial Land: A World of Changes (2016), 70
glaciers, 9–10, 64–65, 69–70, 165
Glinska, Agnieszka, 224
Godard, Jean-Luc, 145–46
Godland (2022), 67–68, 129, 216–17, 224–29, 227*f*
Good Heart, The (2009), 125
Great Latrabjarg Sea-Rescue, The (1949), 9–10, 19–20
Great Weaver of Kashmir, The, 44–45
Green, David Gordon, 129
Grímsdóttir, Vigdís, 109
Grímsson, Ólafur Ragnar, 235n.13
Grímsvötn, 51–52
Grindavík, 66–67
Guðmundsson, Ágúst, 46–47, 72, 76–83, 109–10, 111, 117, 121–22, 124–25, 128–29
Guðmundsson, Einar Már, 92, 106, 120
Guðmundsson, Guðmundur Arnar, 128–29, 216–17
Guðmundsson, Halldór, 32
Guðmundsson, Loftur, 8, 9–10, 16–17, 19–22, 57, 219–20
Guðnadóttir, Hildur, 176–77
Guðnason, Hilmir Snær, 222*f*
Guðnason, Sveinn, 15
"Gunnar's Holm," 30, 32–33
Gunnarsdóttir, Elma Lísa, 191*f*
Gunnarsson, Gunnar, 8, 34, 37–44, 57–58
Gunnarsson, Þröstur Leó, 103*f*, 144*f*, 221
Gunning, Tom, 239n.13
Gunnlaugsson, Hrafn, 72, 75, 76–83, 112–16, 117, 124–25
Gunnlaugsson, Sigmundur Davíð, 247n.27

Hadda Padda (1924), 8, 36–37, 38*f*, 43–44, 122, 153–55
Hädrich, Rolf, 237n.46
Hagalín, Sigríður, 92–93
Hákonarson, Grímur, 128–29
Halldór Kiljan Laxness (1962), 58–59, 59*f*
Halldórsdóttir, Guðný, 45, 72–73, 74, 100–1, 117–18, 124–25, 176
Halldórsson, Gísli, 92–93, 93*f*, 95–96
Halldórsson, Hannes Þór, 218
Hallgrímsson, Jónas, 30, 32–34
Halloween (1978), 250n.8
Hallseth, Rasmus, 7–8
Hamlet, 119
Hannesdóttir, Svala, 10, 233–34n.18
hard-boiled fiction, 133, 148, 151
Haukdóttir, Silja, 176, 178–81

INDEX

HBO, 174, 219
Heartstone (2016), 128–29, 197–98, 199, 209–12, 216–17
Heima (2007), 246n.13
Heimaey, 51, 63–64, 65–66
Heinesen, William, 117
Hekla (1947), 52, 53
Helgafell, 59–60
Helgason, Hallgrímur, 104, 118–19, 235n.11
heritage film, 77, 78
Herzog, Werner, 50, 59–60, 63–64
Higher Force (2008), 126, 133–34
Highlands of Iceland, The (1954), 64–65
Higson, Andrew, 2–3, 4, 77, 78
Hill, John, 4
Hilmarsson, Hilmar Örn, 92, 96
History of the Danes, The, 237n.51
Hjörleifsdóttir, Ása Helga, 128–29, 181–82, 205
Hockenhull, Stella, 200–1
Hollywood, 1–2, 4–5, 43–45, 68–69, 94, 126–28, 133, 134, 142, 144–46, 150–52, 156–57, 164–75, 176–77, 213–14, 217–20
Honour of the House (1999), 45, 100–1, 117–18, 122–23
Hornstrandir, 56–57
Hornstrandir (1956), 56–57
horror film, 67–68, 126, 127–29, 213–14, 218, 221–23
horses, 76–77, 80, 182–83, 200–2, 201*f*, 204, 211, 223, 228
Hrafnsdóttir, Tinna, 217–18
Hraundrangi, 222, 222*f*
Hurt Locker, The (2008), 177
Hvannalindir, 202–3
Hveravellir, 35

I Hunt Men (2008), 133–34
I Remember You (2017), 127–28
I Remember You, 133, 147
Iceland in Living Pictures (1925), 8, 16–17, 18*f*, 250n.4
Iceland: Island of Sagas (1954), 47–48
"Iceland: The Land of the Vikings" (1932), 19
Iceland's Bell, 32, 45
Iceland-film, 8, 17–20, 54–55, 65–66, 226–28
Icelandic Dream, The (2000), 124
Icelandic Film Corporation, 92, 95–96, 99, 124–25
Icelandic Film Fund, 10–12, 71, 73–74, 95, 126, 127, 174, 213–14, 219–20
Icelandic sagas, 30–32, 46–48, 109–10, 113–14
Icelandic Shock Station, The (1986), 72–73, 124–25, 176, 243n.23

Idziak, Slawomir, 101–2
immigration, 180, 189–94
"In Denmark I Was Born," 228
In the Shadow of the Raven (1988), 46–47, 72, 113–16
In the Shoes of the Dragon (2002), 126
Ince, Kate, 249n.16
Independent People, 45–46, 250n.7
Indriðason, Arnaldur, 91, 131, 132–33, 134–42, 218–19
Ingaló (1992), 74–75
Ingólfsson, Viktor Arnar, 133
Inhale (2010), 146
Inside Hawaiian Volcanoes (1989), 239n.14
Inside Job (2010), 163–64
Insomnia (1997), 139
Inter Nos (1982), 82–83
Interstellar (2014), 168–69, 247n.20, 247n.23
intertextuality, 147–55
Into the Inferno (2016), 50, 59–60
Ísafjörður, 15, 16
Ísleifsson, Sumarliði R., 235n.18
It Hatched (2021), 218
Italian neo-realism, 24

Jäckel, Anne, 91–92, 94
Jackson, Peter, 247n.26
Jakobsdóttir, Elsa María, 217–18
Jar City (2006), 125, 134–42, 137*f*, 149–50, 151, 153, 155
Jarmusch, Jim, 96
Jhabvala, Ruth Prawer, 46
"Jóga" (1997), 245n.41, 246n.13
Jóhannesdóttir, Kristín, 72–73, 74, 99–100, 176, 216–18
Jóhannesson, Ólafur, 127–28, 147
Jóhannsson, Jóhann, 70, 177
Jóhannsson, Jón Yngvi, 42–43
Jóhannsson, Magnús Blöndal, 59–62
Jóhannsson, Magnús, 9–10, 64–65, 69–70
Jóhannsson, Valdimar, 228
John Wick (2014), 176–77
Johnston, Claire, 194–96
Joker, The (2019), 176–77
Jökulsárlón, 165, 166–67, 169–70
Jónasson, Jóhannes Bjarni (Jóhannes úr Kötlum), 191
Jónasson, Jón Atli, 128–29
Jónasson, Óskar, 83–84
Jónasson, Ragnar, 131, 133
Jónsdóttir, Auður, 189, 217–18
Jónsdóttir, Birgitta, 171–72
Jónsdóttir, Rannveig, 217–18

Jonsson, Bo, 112
Jónsson, Þór Ómar, 128–29
Jónsson, Þorsteinn, 45, 48, 83
Jósepsson, Ævar Örn, 133
Journey to the Center of the Earth, 158–60
Journey to the Center of the Earth (1959), 160–62, 161*f*
Journey to the Center of the Earth (2008), 162, 169–70
Judge Dredd (1995), 168–69
Júlíusson, Karl, 177
Jupiter Ascending (2015), 247–48n.30
Justice League (2017), 168–69
Justice Undone, 243n.3

Kadorian, Samuel, 9–10
Källberg, Per, 100–1
Kamban, Guðmundur, 8, 19, 34, 36–37, 38*f*, 42–44
Kárahnjúkar, 163–64
Kárason, Einar, 47, 97
Kári, Dagur, 125, 129, 220–21, 224
Karlsson, Steingrímur, 96
Katla (2021), 67–68, 155, 219
Keflavík, 66–67, 186–88
Keflavík Naval Air Station, 24, 64–65, 97, 98–99, 187–88
Kellogg, Robert, 31
Kemp, Júlíus, 83–84
Kettler, Ernst, 63
Kieślowski, Krzysztof, 101–2
Kill Bill (2003/2004), 176–77
Killing, The (2007–2012), 131, 151, 152–53
King, Stephen, 243n.3
King Lear, 119–20, 125
King of Kings, The (1961)
King's Road (2010), 176
Kinks, The, 104
Kjartansdóttir, Ásthildur, 128–29, 189–94
Kjartansdóttir, Katla, 153–55
Kjartansson, Sigurjón, 86
Kjeld, Kristbjörg, 26*f*, 220–21
Klapptré, 248n.35
Knudsen, Ósvaldur, 9–10, 19–20, 54–66, 67–68, 70, 219–20
Knudsen, Vilhjálmur, 65–66
Kormákur, Baltasar, 48, 98*f*, 118–20, 124–25, 134–35, 138–41, 142, 144–45, 144*f*, 146–47, 173–74, 176–77, 179–80, 243n.16, 245n.41
Kracauer, Siegfried, 16–17, 18*f*, 53–54, 69–70
Krafft, Katia, 49–50, 63–64
Krafft, Maurice, 49–50, 63–64

Krafla, 51
Krause, Peter Joachim, 121
Kress, Helga, 40
Kristinsson, Ari, 92, 96
Kristjánsdóttir, Bergljót Soffía, 111–12
Kristófersson, Gunnar Tómas, 9, 19
kulturfilm, 19
Kurosawa, Akira, 113–15
Kvaran, Ævar, 233–34n.18

Lalli Johns (2001), 126
Lamb (2021), 216–17, 221–24, 222*f*
Land and Sons (1980), 27, 48, 72, 76–83, 78*f*, 90, 99, 109–10, 197–98, 221–24
"Land of My Father," 191
Land Out of the Ocean (1973), 62–63
landscape, 30–31, 56–57, 58–59, 68–69, 81, 92–93, 136–37, 151–52, 153–55, 154*f*, 156–57, 160, 164–72, 183, 183*f*, 188, 206–8, 225–26, 227*f*, 228, 246n.13
language, 29, 30, 104, 132–33, 166–67, 180, 190, 224, 226–28
  Danish, 33–43, 95, 224, 226–29
  English, 86–87, 96, 107, 118–19, 224
  foreign, 41
  German, 101–2
Lara Croft: Tomb Raider (2001), 166–67, 247n.20
Larsen, Thomas Bo, 155
Larson, Stieg, 131, 132–33
Last and First Men (2020), 70
Last Days of the Arctic (2011), 70
Last Farm, The (2004), 220–21
Last Farm in the Valley (1950), 10, 22–23
Last Fishing Trip, The (2020), 214
Last Stop (2002), 126
Látrabjarg, 19–20
Laxness, Halldór, 10–11, 31–33, 58–59, 59*f*, 98–99, 100–1, 109–10, 117, 118–19, 131
Lefebvre, Martin, 225–26
Legends of Valhalla: Thor (2011), 127–28
Leifs, Jón, 101–3
Leitch, Thomas, 144–45, 153
Lemarquis, Tómas, 221
Leone, Sergio, 113–15
Let Me Fall (2018), 127–28, 178
Letter from Helga, The (2022), 214–16
liberalism, 190–92
Life in a Fishbowl (2014), 127–28
Life-Trilogy (1983–1985), 72–73
Lind, Alfred, 7–8, 14, 15, 229
List, Friedrich, 29
literature, 29, 30–33

contemporary, 41, 76–79
crime, 131, 132–34, 148
medieval, 30
national, 32–33
neo-romanticism, 29–30, 33–44
novel, 31–32
romanticism, 32–33
Varangians, the, 33–43, 226–28, 229
Little Trip to Heaven, A (2005), 125, 133–34
Living with Violent Earth (1989), 65
Loftsdóttir, Kristín, 153–55
Long, Ásgeir, 63
Lord of the Rings, The (2001–2003), 247n.26
Lund, Katrín Anna, 153–55
Luther: The Fallen Sun (2023), 219
Lyngdal, Bára, 123*f*
Lyngdal, Reynir, 128–29

Magnus (1989), 83
Magnúsdóttir, Nanna Kristín, 217–18
Magnússon, Jón, 117
Mamma Gógó (2010), 27–28, 128–29, 220–21
Man and Factory (1967), 11
Man of Aran (1934), 239n.10
Máni, Stefán, 133
Mankell, Henning, 131, 132–33
Marker, Chris, 63–64
Mason, James, 161*f*
Mattson, Arne, 10–11, 45, 58–59
Mazdon, Lucy, 145–46
Mbabazi, Enid, 191*f*
McConaughey, Matthew, 247n.23
McFarlane, Brian, 140
MEDIA, 91–92
medium concept, 138–39
Men's Choir, The (1992), 74, 100–1
Message to Sandra, 109–10
Message to Sandra (1983), 176
Midnight Sky, The (2020), 168–69, 219
Mission: Impossible—Fallout (2018), 248n.32
Møll, Henrik, 121
Money Monster (2016), 171–72
Montagne infidèle, La (1923), 53–54
Morricone, Ennio, 114
Morthens, Bubbi, 126
Mother (1926), 95
Mount *Eldfell*, 51
Mount *Fagradalsfjall*, 50, 66–67
Mount *Hekla*, 7, 9–10, 51–52, 53, 54, 64–65, 246n.9
Mount *Katla*, 51–52, 67–68
Mount *Litli Hrútur*, 66–67
Mount *Unzen*, 49

Movie Days (1994), 74, 94–95, 99
Mr. Bjarnfredarson (2009), 125, 193–94
Mulvey, Laura, 194–96
Mulvogue, Jessica, 238n.6
Murder at the End of the World, A (2023), 219
Murder Story (1977), 11–12, 27
music, 59–62, 74–75, 86–87, 89–90, 104, 114, 176–77, 180–81, 190–91, 246n.13
Mýrdalsjökull, 67–68
Mystery Train (1989), 96

Nagase, Masatoshi, 95–96, 106–7
narratology, 140, 143–44, 147–48
national cinema, 1, 4–5, 71, 127, 174–75, 195–96, 213–14, 219–20, 221, 229, 232–33n.6
versus national film industry, 4, 124–25, 126–27, 164–65, 173–75
in terms of scale, 2–4
National Cooperative, 81
National Fishing Agency, 9, 19
national identity, 29–33, 88, 107, 132–33, 146, 153–55, 157–58, 204
nationalism, 22–23, 27, 76, 79
nation-state, 2–3, 29, 158, 197–98
nature, 25–26, 26*f*, 35–39, 41–42, 42*f*, 43–45, 50, 54–66, 68–69, 92–93, 96, 102–3, 106–7, 122, 153–55, 157, 158–60, 163–65, 171–72, 175, 198–99, 204–12, 225–26, 227*f*
Neeson, Liam, 168*f*
neoliberalism, 127, 134, 141–42
Nestingen, Andrew, 138–39
Netflix, 155, 219
New Role (1954), 23–24
Niceland (2004), 88, 107–8, 124–25
Nichols, Bill, 238n.8
Njal's Saga, 30, 46–48, 89
Njalssaga (2003), 48
No Such Thing (2001), 99, 172
No Time to Die (2021), 248n.32
No Trace (1998), 244n.5
Noah (2014), 126–27, 168–69, 173
Nöggerath, Franz Anton, 7
Noi the Albino (2003), 1, 68–69, 125, 153–55, 221
Nolan, Christopher, 247n.20, 247–48n.30
Norðfjörð, Óttar, 133
Nordic Film and Television Fund, 73–74, 95, 219–20
Nordic noir, 131, 132–33, 151–52
Nordin, Sven, 119–20
Northman, The (2022), 173, 240n.22
Nykvist, Sven, 10–11, 45

Oath, The (2016), 127–28, 147
Oblivion (2013), 126–27, 168–69, 173, 247n.20
Occupation, The (1967), 11–12
Oddsson, Hilmar, 74, 100–3, 109, 116–17, 216–17
Oddsson, Reynir, 11–12
Of Horses and Men (2013), 129, 197–98, 199–202, 201f, 204, 223
Olafsdóttir, Ruth, 103f
Ólafsson, Ólafur Darri, 143
On Top (1982), 72–73, 124–25, 221
Once Upon a Time in Hollywood (2019), 176–77
Once Upon a Time in the West (1968), 113–14
Operation Napoleon (2023), 68–69, 218–19
Orientalism, 157–58
Óskarsdóttir, Valdís, 176, 177
Óskarsson, Atli, 177
Oslund, Karen, 157–58
Otero, Nilo, 247n.23
Outlaw, The (1981), 46–47, 72, 110–13
Outlaw and His Wife, The (1917), 8, 34–39, 43–44
Öxnadalur, 222, 222f

Pabolettoni, Manrico, 176
Pálmason, Hlynur, 128–29, 224, 229
Pálsdóttir, Kristín, 72–73, 176
Pálsson, Sigurður Sverrir, 72–73, 101–2
Paradise Reclaimed (1980), 237n.46
Parents (2007), 125, 193–94
Past, Elena, 54
Pawn Sacrifice (2015), 171–72
Pegasus, 124–25
Perfect Strangers (2016), 67–68, 214
Petersen, Peter, 7–8, 14–15, 229
Petrie, Duncan, 4
Phillip, Hans-Erik, 114
Picturesque, 157, 165–70, 175
Plan B (2000), 124
Ploey (2018), 127–28
police procedural, 131, 133, 135, 141–42, 151–53
Policeman's Life, A (1985), 83
Pop in Reykjavík (1998), 241n.20
Press (2008), 133–34
primitivism, 35, 40, 42–44, 46–47
Prince Avalanche (2013), 129
Prisoners (2017), 151
Private Lives (1995), 250n.4
Prometheus (2012), 156, 160, 163–64
"Prophecy of the Seeress, The," 50, 59–60

Quake (2021), 217–18
queer identity, 128–29, 210, 211–12, 218

racism, 184–85, 194, 235n.18

Ragnarsdóttir, Guðrún, 128–29, 182–84
Rainbow's End (1983), 176, 192–93, 195, 216
Rams (2015), 129, 197–98, 199, 202–4, 203f
Rangárvallasýsla (1948), 52
Rapace, Noomi, 224
Ray, Nicholas, 94
Red Mantle, The (1967), 10–11
Redux (2022), 218
Refn, Nicolas Winding, 149
reimbursement program, 164, 173, 174, 219–20
remakes, 67–68, 129, 142–46, 147–48, 152–53
Remote Control (1992), 74–75, 83 87, 85f, 100, 104, 105–6, 124, 134, 218
Revelation for Hannes, A (2003), 124–25
Revolution Reykjavík (2011), 185–86
Reyðarfjörður, 169
Reykjanes, 66–67, 136–37, 137f, 169
Reykjavík, 13–16, 19–20, 23–24, 25–26, 26f, 76, 83–87, 85f, 94–95, 103–4, 105–6, 118–19, 136–37, 159, 162–63, 165, 171–72, 197–98, 213, 216–18
Reykjavík 1955 (1955), 57
Reykjavík Adventure of the Bakka-Brothers, The, (1951), 23–24
Reykjavík of Our Days (1947/1948), 9, 20
Reykjavík Rotterdam (2008), 126, 134, 142–46, 144f, 151, 155
Reykjavík Whale Watching Massacre (2009), 126
Rift (2017), 127–29
Riva, Emmanuelle, 216
Rock in Reykjavík (1982), 89–90, 241n.20
Rocky (1976), 216
Rogue One: A Star Wars Story (2016), 168–69
Ronaldsdóttir, Elísabet, 176–77
Rósinkranz, Guðlaugur, 47–48
Róska, 72–73, 176
Róska (2005), 189
Rowing (1972), 11
Rúnarsson, Rúnar, 128–29, 192–93, 220–21, 224
runaway productions, 1–2, 4, 124–25, 126–28, 156–57, 164–75, 213–14, 219–20
Rust (1990), 116
Rvk. Studios, 124–25, 173–74

Saga Film, 124–25
Saga of the People of Laxardal, The, 46–47
Salka Valka, 43–44, 122
Salka Valka (1954), 10–11, 24, 45, 58–59
Sanders, Julie, 147–48
Sanders, Otto, 94
Sans Soleil (1983), 63–64

Scholes, Robert, 31
Screaming Masterpiece (2005), 246n.13
Sea, The (2002), 119–20, 122–23, 125, 134–35, 140–41, 245n.41
Seagull's Laughter, The (2001), 43–44, 121–23, 123*f*, 153–55
Season of the Witch (2011), 151
Secret Life of Walter Mitty, The (2013), 126–27, 170, 173
Seer and the Unseen, The (2019), 49–50
Sense8 (2015–2018), 172
Shining Star (2004), 126
Sicario (2015), 177
Siglufjörður, 16
Sigmarsson, Jóhann, 124
Sigur Rós, 172, 246n.13
Sigurbjörnsson, Jón, 78*f*
Sigurðardóttir, Raffaella Brizuela, 191*f*
Sigurðardóttir, Yrsa, 131, 133
Sigurðsson, Gísli, 30–31
Sigurðsson, Hafsteinn Gunnar, 128–29, 220–21
Sigurðsson, Jón, 31
Sigurgeirsson, Vigfús, 9–10, 52, 53, 54–55
Sigurjónsson, Jóhann, 8, 34–36, 43–44
Sigurjónsson, Sigurður, 78*f*, 203*f*
Silence of the Grave, The, 244n.17
Símonarson, Ólafur Haukur, 119–20
Sims, Jeremy, 129
Simson, Martinus, 15
Sjöström, Victor, 8, 35–36, 236n.39
Sjöwall, Maj, 131, 132–33
Sketches (1965), 57–58
Skógarfoss, 246–47n.18
Skúlason, Helgi, 114*f*
slow cinema, 198–99, 205
Snæfellsjökull Glacier, 100–1, 158–59, 160, 161, 161*f*, 162, 246n.9
Snæfellsnes, 74, 170
Sogið (1954), 56–57
Sóley (1982), 176
Sólheimajökull Glacier, 69–70
Sørenssen, Bjørn, 113–14
Sparrows (2015), 197–98, 199, 209, 212
Spassky, Boris, 162–63, 171–72
special effects, 22, 143–44, 224
Spooks and Spirits (2013), 128–29
Stam, Robert, 147–48
Stardust (2007), 168–69
Stark, Jim, 95–96
Stefánsson, Jón Kalman, 215–16
Stefánsson, Kári, 138–39
Steingrímsson, Páll, 63, 65–66
Stella Blómkvist (2017–2021), 127–28, 151

Stella for Office (2002), 124–25
Stevens, Fisher, 95–96
Stitch n' Bitch (2021), 217–18
Story of the Borg Family, The, 37–41, 109, 229
Story of the Borg Family, The (1920), 8, 42–43, 42*f*
Straumfjörður, 99–100
Stromboli (1950), 52
Sturludóttir, Oddný, 178–79
Sturlunga Saga, 47
Stykkishólmur, 170
Summer Children (2017), 128–29, 178, 181–84, 183*f*, 196
Summer Light, and Then Comes the Night (2022), 214–16
Sundhnúkur, 66–67
Surtsey, 59–60, 62–63, 65–66
Suzuki, Seijun, 95–96
Svarfaðardalur, 222
Sveinbjörnsson, Herbert, 67
Sveinsson, Erlendur, 16, 19, 72–73, 101–2
Sveppi series (2010–2014), 127–28, 214
Svínafellsjökull Glacier, 167, 168*f*, 246–47n.18
Swan, The (2017), 128–29, 178, 181–82, 184, 196, 197–98, 199, 204–9, 207*f*, 212

Tainted Blood, 134–42
Tár (2022), 176–77
Tarantino, Quentin, 176–77
Taylor, Lili, 95–96
Tazief, Haroun, 63–64
Tears of Stone (1995), 74, 101–3, 103*f*
television, 10–11, 94–95, 124–25, 126, 131–34, 151–55, 173–74, 237n.46
Tents in the Woods (1949), 55–56
Theory of Everything, The (2014), 177
Þingvellir, 18*f*, 25–26, 246–47n.18
This Is Iceland (1960), 9
Thor: The Dark World (2013), 126–27, 173
Þjórsárdalur (1967), 56–57
Þórarinsson, Árni, 133
Þórarinsson, Sigurður, 238–39n.9
Þórbergur Þórðarson (1961), 58–59
Þórðarson, Þórbergur, 58–59
Þorgeirson, Þorgeir, 11
Þorgeirsson, Halldór, 100–1
Þórisdóttir, Heba, 176–77
Þórisson, Snorri, 46
Þorleifsdóttir, Þórhildur, 72–73, 176
Thoroddsen, Ásdís, 74–75, 176
Thoroddsen, Jón, 31
Þórsmörk, 52
Þórsson, Bjarni Haukur, 128–29

Þórsson, Marteinn, 128–29
Thorsteinsson, Guðmundur, 41–42, 42f
Þorsteinsson, Indriði, 24, 48, 77–78
Þrastarskógur, 55–56
To Build (1967), 11
Todorov, Tzvetan, 140
Tolkien, J. R. R., 247n.26
Tómasson, Einar Hansen, 164–65, 173–74
Torfadóttir, Ólöf Birna, 217–18
tourism, 7, 9, 17, 66–67, 127, 164, 175
Trainspotting (1996), 149, 153
transnational, 4–5, 17, 93, 139, 152–53, 156–57, 187–88, 214
  adaptation, 109, 116–23
  funding, 95, 107, 121, 219–20
  narrative, 41, 96, 106–7
  production, 95, 107, 120, 121, 151–52, 155, 186, 218–19, 224–25
  proto, 8
  remakes (*see* remakes)
  turn in Icelandic cinema, 89–106
Trapped (2015–2021), 127–28, 131, 147, 151–55, 154f, 219
travel literature, 88, 157–58
Trip to the Moon, A (1902), 7–8
Tristan and Isolde, 115
True Detective: Night Country (2024), 174, 219
True North, 219–20, 248n.32
Tryggvason, Jón, 99–100, 244n.5
Tuan, Yi-Fu, 165–66

Uggadóttir, Ísold, 128–29, 184–88
Under the Glacier, 32–33
Under the Glacier (1989), 45, 72, 100–1, 116, 176
Under the Tree (2017), 129
Undercurrent (2010), 245n.41

Valdimarsdóttir, Alda Björk, 235n.11
Valhalla Murders, The (2019), 151, 155
Valsdóttir, Gríma, 207f
Vatnajökull Glacier, 51–52, 57, 64–65, 246–47n.18
Verevis, Constantine, 244n.23
Verne, Jules, 158–60, 161–62
Very Last Fishing Trip, The (2022), 214
Vestmannaeyjabær, 59–60, 62–63
Vestmannaeyjar, 16, 51, 59–60, 62–63
View to a Kill, A (1985), 126–27, 166–67
Vík, 67–68
Vikings, The (2013–2020), 173
Vilhjálmsdóttir, Margrét, 43–44, 123f

Villi Knudsen's Iceland, 65–66
Vinterberg, Thomas, 129
Virgin Mountain (2015), 129
Volcano (1997), 52
Volcano (2011), 67–68, 220–21
volcano film, 52–56, 59–62, 225–26
Voleur de vie (1998), 243n.16

Wachowski, Lana, 247–48n.30
Wachowski, Lilly, 247–48n.30
Wahlberg, Mark, 127–28
Wahlöö, Per, 131, 132–33
Wall in China, The, 88
Wallpaper (1992), 74–75, 83–84, 86–87, 99–100, 104, 124
Waniewitz, Ronen, 121
Washington, Denzel, 127–28
Wayward Heroes, 32, 46–47, 112
Wenders, Wim, 90–91, 92–93, 94
West, Simon, 247n.20
western film, 113–15, 114f
Westfjords, 56–57, 209, 246–47n.18
Westphal, Bertrand, 156–57
When the Raven Flies (1984), 46–47, 72, 82–83, 112–16, 114f
Where to Invade Next (2015), 186
Whitaker, Forrest, 125
White Night Wedding (2008), 243n.16
White Viking, The (1991), 46–47, 72, 113–16, 234n.2
White Whales (1987), 90–91, 99
White, White Day, A (2019), 129, 151, 224
WikiLeaks, 171–72
Wild Game (2023), 67–68, 214
Williams, Raymond, 23, 76
Wings of Desire (1987), 92–93, 94
Winter Brothers (2018), 129, 224
Winter Trip, A (1952), 64
Witchcraft (1999), 117, 124–25
Woman at War (2018), 129, 178, 249n.8
Women Talking (2022), 176–77
women's cinema, 72–73, 74–75, 128–29, 176–79, 194–96, 217–18
world cinema, 1, 13, 90–91, 122–23, 213–14
World Light, 45
Wrath (2023), 218

Yojimbo (1961), 113–14
YouTube, 67

Zetterström, Tonie, 100–1, 121
Zik Zak Filmworks, 124–25, 148, 242n.22
Zophoníasson, Baldvin, 128–29